INVISIBLE ROMANS

INVISIBLE
ROMANS

ROBERT KNAPP

HARVARD UNIVERSITY PRESS

Cambridge, Massachusetts | 2011

First published in Great Britain in 2011 by Profile Books Ltd,
3A Exmouth House, Pine Street, London EC1R 0JH

First Harvard University Press edition, 2011

Library of Congress Cataloging-in-Publication Data

Knapp, Robert C.
Invisible Romans / Robert Knapp.
p.   cm.
Includes bibliographical references and index.
ISBN 978-0-674-06199-6 (cloth : alk. paper)
1. Rome—History.   2. Rome—Civilization.
3. Rome—Social life and customs.   I. Title.
DG78.K57 2011
937—dc23   2011019978

CONTENTS

SEEING THE INVISIBLE

I SEEK TO UNCOVER and understand what life was like for the great mass of people who lived in Rome and its empire from the time of Augustus at the start of the first millennium to the accession of Constantine three centuries later. 'For the history of Greece and Rome,' the British classical historian Michael Crawford writes in his guide to ancient sources, 'there is a great deal which is simply unknowable.' Evidence is uneven and often difficult to interpret. Scholars energetically debate how far the Roman world can be known. The world of the twenty-first century differs in numberless ways from the world of ancient Rome, not least in our attitudes and assumptions. Given what little evidence of everyday Roman life survives, the ordinary Romans begin to seem irretrievably invisible.

But we need not despair. We can, for example, supplement the evidence from our chosen time period with some careful use of sources before and beyond it. Ancient cultures were more stable than our own. The continuity of agrarian culture and economy in the ancient world makes it likely that people generally behaved in much the same way, not through contact and sharing, but because they had the same struggles for survival. The focus of this book is not merely on the city of Rome but on the whole of the Roman world. One might think the Latin-speaking parts more Roman than those where other languages predominated, but neither sources nor logic suggest this was so. We can find much useful evidence from the mostly Greek-speaking part of the empire, especially from Egypt. As well as containing revealing observations of life in the country, much of it is concerned (as we will be) with urban life; the experience of living in cities and towns, often founded or ruled in Roman patterns, encouraged many common attitudes. This is not to deny the huge variety of cultures in the empire, nor to claim that every person would think and behave in just such a way. But likenesses in attitudes and behavior make it reasonable to use evidence from scattered sources so long as our questions are formulated with care and our answers subject to critical scrutiny.

If we can begin to overcome the difficulties of time and space, we have still to confront the most challenging aspect of the evidence. This is simple and simply put. What survives was generally created by or for the rich and the powerful, and hides the actions and perspectives of any but their own class. As the elite historian Ammianus Marcellinus aptly puts it:

> There are many things which are irrelevant to the underlying themes of history, itself accustomed to deal with the highpoints of affairs. Its role is not to investigate the minor details of unimportant circumstances. If someone wished to do that, he might as well try to count the tiny bodies coursing through space, the atoms, as we call them. (*Roman History* 26.1.1)

The historian can thus write with least difficulty about what the elite Romans cared about, such as politics and war, and the issues they talked about, such as the making and enforcement of law, philosophy, aesthetics, and the inevitability of a social structure that held them at its pinnacle. Many books on these topics appear every year, but the sources, so dear to the heart of Roman historians, do more to obscure than reveal what we're after. Ancient evidence comes in two types: the one intentionally provided and the other incidentally. The first is generally irrelevant to our purpose, but the second can be crucial. An elite author setting out, for example, to write on the Roman wars of expansion, will sometimes include contextual details and bits of information which, when combined with other evidence, begin to create a picture of ordinary people. The experience of ordinary people has no direct voice in the histories the Romans have left us. Yet sometimes it is possible to garner insights into the lives of the invisible people even where none was intended and to amplify these by deploying perspectives and evidence from a variety of other sources.

I have searched for a term to capture the invisible demographic group that is the subject of this book and have chosen to call them 'ordinary people.' This distinguishes them from the elite and leaves their definition open to the wide range of their existence, from fairly wealthy to modestly well-off and downright poor, male and female, slave and free, law-abiding and outlaw. These ordinary people lived in a world dominated by a tiny, self-perpetuating elite that was limited and defined by wealth, tradition, blood, and power. They belonged to one of the three orders or *ordines* into which they divided themselves. The senatorial order was the most exalted in social and political terms but not always the wealthiest. The equestrian order focused on the acquisition of wealth rather than the power and rank of the senatorial order. The decurial order ran towns and cities across the empire and mirrored the senatorial-equestrian divisions of Rome; these men were generally less wealthy than members of senatorial-equestrian orders, although sometimes local decurials were also equestrians. The three orders amounted to no more than 100,000–200,000 people, less than half a percent of the empire's population of 50–60 million. Among them only the adult males counted; these numbered about 40,000 and so, as the empire at this time was roughly 2.5 million square miles, there was on average one adult member of the male elite for every sixty or so square miles. As the elites were concentrated in Rome, the proportion elsewhere was even lower. Yet these numerically minuscule and widely scattered leaders controlled almost everything. Though they are not the direct concern of the present project, we shall need to bear in mind their impact on the other 99.5 percent.

The chapters that follow divide the invisible people into various groups, some less mutually exclusive than others; there are separate chapters, for example, on ordinary men and soldiers and on ordinary women and prostitutes, though most of the latter were female. The aim will be to get, so far as we can, inside the minds of these different people: what attitudes and outlooks they had, what fears haunted and what hopes inspired them. David Potter, an American classical historian writes, 'There can be no universal definition of history or the historical process that does not allow for the ultimately subjective selection of both evidence and presentation.' In this book, I make choices and value judgments as I weave disparate threads into tapestries of what life for ordinary Romans was all about. Creating a readable and revealing account of the neglected majority in a great empire was an exciting challenge to undertake. I hope the reader will enjoy the fascinating panorama of invisible people made visible at last.

1

IN THE MIDDLE:
ORDINARY MEN

THE ELITE OF THE ROMAN EMPIRE – emperors, senators, equestrians, and the local elite of magistrates, town councilors, and priests – produced almost all the literature and extraordinary material culture which is commonly spoken of as 'Roman.' As a result, treatment of 'Roman' normally means applying the mind world and culture of the elite to a description of the entire Roman population, as when people write and speak of 'Roman civilization' or 'Roman attitudes toward women.' Here I move away from that habit and focus rather on the ordinary men, people below and generally invisible to those high in the social pyramid. By 'ordinary men' I mean every free person below the elite and above the poor day-laborer or peasant. Their outlook, seen through their own eyes, reveals a rich mosaic of attitudes and actions as they live their lives outside the blinkered view of the empire's aristocracies. Although their mind world is the same as the elite's in some basic ways – they were both part of the same overarching culture, after all – outlooks and attitudes in general differ significantly.

The imperial elite stood at the top of the Roman socioeconomic pyramid. To qualify, a person had to be worth over 400,000 sesterces (equestrian) or over 1 million sesterces (senatorial). Among the approximately 50–60 million people in the Roman Empire, there were perhaps 5000 adult men possessing such extreme wealth. Beneath (but mostly far beneath) these were the elite of the local towns of the empire. An average of 100 or 125 adult males in each of the 250 or 300 towns of the empire that rose above the level of village would produce another 30,000 to 35,000 very wealthy persons. Because of the steep socioeconomic gradation of the Roman world, these elite together probably held 80 percent or more of the total wealth. The Romans themselves recognized this break in socioeconomic situation between elite and nonelite by calling the super-wealthy *honestiores* ('more honorable ones') and all the rest of the free persons *humiliores* ('lesser beings'). This 'all the rest' was 99.5 percent of the population.

Below these super-wealthy were a fair number of persons who had many fewer resources in comparison to the very rich, but resources sufficient, at the lower end, to be fairly certain of their daily bread and, on the upper end, to enjoy a lifestyle that allowed enough leisure to pursue some social, political, and cultural interests. These were the more modest landowners, the merchants and artisans, successful soldiers, and those financed by these groups and by the elites (professional teachers, doctors, architects, and so on). These men and their families numbered perhaps 25 percent of the total population. Besides a certain stability in resources, another commonality unites these ordinary people. They all value labor whether they are merchants or artisans or wealthy peasants; they share that important socioeconomic fact, which binds together their outlooks even though the actual wealth-level and occupation of individuals varies greatly. It is these people I am concerned with here. The challenge is to capture their mind world.

Social attitudes

Marks of hierarchy and place were everywhere. For example, the 10,000-denarii donation of Manius Megonius Leo, a citizen of the Italian town of Petelia (modern Strongoli), for a foundation was to be invested and the income distributed hierarchically: 450+ denarii income per year was spent on the anniversary of his birth. Three hundred denarii funded a banquet, but only for the local elite, the decurions; after costs of the banquet, anything left of the 300 was distributed in cash to the decurions present. In addition, 150 denarii were designated for a banquet for the Augustales, the elite priestly group of wealthy freedmen, with the remainder after costs divided among the Augustales present. Finally, each male citizen and his wife were given a single denarius, equivalent to a working man's good daily wage; no banquet was provided (*ILS* 6468). This sort of graded gifting made the social hierarchy very visible, much as the graded seating in the amphitheaters did. Living in an unremittingly stratified world, the middling sort absorbed one of the basic attitudes of such a life: deal with equals as equals, take advantage of those below you when possible, defer to those above you always. An individual's mental state focused his abilities on avoiding infliction of injury on himself, either physical or mental, and on inflicting injury on others – in Roman terms, defending his honor and standing by lessening the honor and standing of others, while at the same time protecting his own from diminution at the hands of those thought inferior. Subordination to a lesser being, or assimilation to a group below his station (e.g. slaves), in the mind or action of a superior, was a horrible thing. The mind world was simpler with regard to those obviously superior (elite) and obviously inferior (slaves) than with the common man's peers. In the latter group there were huge differences of status and power, but no clear markers of 'legitimate' subordination or superiority. It was in this world that slights to honor, hostilities, and rivalries worked themselves out in the liveliest manner.

Hierarchical thinking places specific expectations and stereotypes in the minds of each group. The ordinary men were no exception. Scholars identify five of the most common prejudices: against freedmen, against the poor, against slaves, against merchants, and against work. It is worth examining each through the eyes of ordinary people.

Free birth was the default preferred condition; it had no legal liabilities and had none of the constraints imposed by slavery and manumitted status. The vast majority of the free population at any given time would be freeborn, as the legal status of the manumitted disappeared with the manumitted generation. It is clear that the elite held strong prejudices against freedmen who pretended to usurp their social or economic capital. While it is generally assumed that the elite prejudice against freedmen would have been held in all segments of freeborn society, there is little evidence for this; a full discussion appears in the chapter on freedmen. Certainly, however, the prejudice against the poor was real. The graffito on a wall in Pompeii says it all:

> I hate poor people. If anyone wants something for nothing he is a fool. He should pay for it. (*CIL* 4.9839b)

Likewise, the Epistle of James in the New Testament indicates clearly this prejudice, although the author's purpose is to argue against it within the context of the Christian community:

> My brothers, as believers in our glorious Lord Jesus Christ, don't show favoritism. Suppose a man comes into your meeting wearing a gold ring and fine clothes, and a poor man in shabby clothes also comes in. If you show special attention to the man wearing fine clothes and say, 'Here's a good seat for you,' but say to the poor man, 'You stand there' or 'Sit on the floor by my feet,' have you not discriminated among yourselves and become judges with evil thoughts? (James 2:1–4)

A great prejudice also existed between the ordinary man and the enslaved population. Here we can turn to Paul. In his addresses to groups of Christians, he constantly emphasizes by negation the fundamental distinction between free and slave in society; his repetitiousness is evidence that old prejudices died hard – his addressees clearly struggled with his advice to treat their slaves with less prejudice, and often failed. Another illustration of the chasm between free and slave comes from *The Golden Ass*: Lucius' transformation into an ass and back again can easily be read as an allegorical journey from freedom to slavery to freedom; all of his adventures show that the condition of being a slave is bad, that slaves are subhuman.

Another prejudice must be disposed of: ill feeling against merchants. The general view of the elite was that merchants were lying thieves. Did ordinary people share this view? Paul's letter to the Philippians uses language that is extensively mercantile – verbs of accounting and exchange are common, and they are used to convey Paul's ideas about the Christian community. Not only does this indicate Paul's own background as a man of commerce, but also that the audience was operating in this exchange and business environment, and felt positive about it. Lydia the purple merchant was active in the same milieu; again, there is no negative connotation. Businessmen themselves took great pride in their accomplishments, as did this long-distance merchant:

If it is no trouble, passerby, hold up and read this [epitaph]. I often coursed over the great sea with swift-sailed craft and reached many lands. This is the end which once upon a time the Fates spun for me at my birth. Here I have laid down all my cares and labors. Here I do not fear the stars, nor the clouds, nor the savage sea, nor do I fear that expenses will outrun my profits. (*CIL* 9.60, Brindisi, Italy)

And beside the long-distance traders there were local, short-range businessmen who dealt either in locally produced goods on a small scale, or bought wholesale and resold at the local level. Epigraphy attests to these merchants seeing themselves as the mirror image of the cheating, dishonest dealers of elite lore. Lucius Nerusius Mithres, a merchant from a small town, noted:

I sold goods which the people could use, my honesty was always praised everywhere, life was good ... I always paid my taxes, I was straightforward in everything, as fair as I was able to everyone I dealt with. I helped as much as I could those seeking my aid. Among my friends I was highly thought of ... (*CIL* 9.4796, Vescovio, Italy)

Praecilius, an *argentarius* in Cirta, and so a member of the highly suspect banker class of merchant, notes that he always had the trust of his customers and was always truthful and good:

Here I am silent, describing my life in verse. I enjoyed a bright reputation, and the height of prosperity. Praecilius by name, a native of Cirta, I was a skillful banker. My honesty was wonderful, and I always adhered to truth; I was courteous to all men, and whose distress did I not succor? I was always gay, and hospitable to my dear friends; a great change came over my life after the death of the virtuous Valeria. As long as I could, I enjoyed the sweets of holy matrimony; I celebrated a hundred happy birthdays in virtue and happiness; but the last day has arrived, as the spirit leaves my exhausted limbs. Alive I earned the titles which you read, as Fortune willed it. She never deserted me. Follow me in like manner; here I await you! Come. (*CIL* 8.7156, Constantine, Algeria/Malahide)

Naturally, merchants saw no problem in seeking gain, and thanked the gods for it:

> Dedicated three days before the first of June in the consulship of Dexter (for the second time) and Fuscus. Sacred to Mercury, Mighty Profit Giver and Profit Preserver. Gaius Gemellius Valerianus, son of Gaius, of the Oufentina district, Member of the Four Man Board with Police Authority, Judicial Prefect, with Cilonia Secunda his wife and Valeria and Valeriana Secunda, his children. He set this up in fulfill-ment of a vow and dedicated it in a spot authorized by the municipal authorities. (*CIL* 5.6596 = *ILS* 3199, Fontanetto da Po, Italy)

Thus, merchants had a good opinion of themselves. Of course it is easy to suppose that relations in specific instances could become strained, but the evidence from Artemidorus and elsewhere is conso-nant with the positive impression Paul's experiences give of ordinary men associating normally with such fellows. Likewise, businessmen in Apuleius' *Golden Ass* and in Petronius' *Satyricon* are treated as normal people; they are not stigmatized.

In a similar vein, there is no indication among ordinary folk of the disdain for craftsmen felt by elites such as Cicero, who states that 'All craftsmen are engaged in base trades' (*On Duties* 1.42.15). Rather, the father of the literary Lucian is exemplary of how middling men looked at trades. Lucian's father wanted his son educated to a certain degree, but his long-range goal was to apprentice him to one of his wife's broth-ers so he could learn a trade. Lucian rebelled against this, but that fact does not take away from the reality that his father believed a career as an artisan would be good for everyone. There was no shame felt by Lucian's family about the artisan life and in fact even Lucian was tempted until, in a further dream, Education convinced him that the elite view of the trades – that they are vulgar – was correct, and per-suaded him to pursue a career through learning and rhetoric.

A further note of pride tempered with sadness comes from the epitaph of Vireius Vitalis Maximus. He had adopted Vireius Vitalis, 'a lad of incomparable promise in the craftsman's calling,' had raised him up in the profession, and hoped that the boy would carry on his trade, supporting him in his old age. In both Artemidorus' *Interpretation of Dreams* and the *Carmen Astrologicum*, various artisanal activities are mentioned, as well as business situations; there is no hint that people so engaged were looked down upon.

Thus the ordinary man's world was open to craftsmen and merchants without prejudice. Many epitaphs mention the profession or work of the deceased. Work is part of the self-identity of the dedicatee, for almost all epitaphs (98 percent) are made either by the deceased himself or by family – almost none are made by fellows in the profession or work, or by patrons. The elite, of course, do not mention work, as for them it is not something to be proud of; however, all others – free, freed, and slave – do mention it prominently. Here is clear evidence that one of the marks of the ordinary man's mind world (and of all below the elite, for that matter) is the value of work. This is one of the most striking differences between the elite and the common man's perspective. Indeed, the elite prejudice that looks down on labor and business helps to explain ordinary man's invisibility. We must firmly lay aside any idea that work was not valued in the Roman world; the elite's devaluation of labor does not extend to the vast majority of Roman-Greek society.

Although the hierarchical nature of society required that prejudices be important, the moral world of ordinary men was much more complex than a collection of stereotypes. It is worthwhile constructing a picture of that world, although, naturally, any single moral outlook was not necessarily reflected in the daily life of an individual. I can summarize briefly the main points of a man's moral world.

Marriage is a good thing; monogamy is the norm. Loyalty in marriage is important. Wives are to be faithful, available and alluring; husbands chaste. Men reject the philosophic view that sex is a distraction done for procreation and without enjoyment. Chastity is valued, but does not extend to the point that male homosexual relationships and occasional male infidelity are unacceptable. Visiting prostitutes is a neutral activity, as is discussed elsewhere. Divorce is possible and acceptable. Lying, cheating, and stealing are in principle bad. Honesty in dealings within kinship groups and with socioeconomic equals or superiors is expected; however, business with others exists in an ambiguous state which allows 'sharp dealing' and deceit for personal gain. Fair and just treatment of all is good, although 'fair' is based on a distributive concept of justice. Acquisitiveness is a positive virtue; excessive acquisitiveness,

1. A happy marriage. Conjugal couple cuddling in bed, their faithful dog at their feet.

i.e. avarice, and taking possessions that are not rightfully yours, is bad. For the more philosophically inclined, self-sufficiency is a moral commonplace.

Self-confidence is a positive virtue, while arrogance and boasting, i.e. self-confidence outstripping appropriate expression according to socio-economic status, is a bad thing; humility is a commonplace (the opposite of excessive pride). A strong sense of self-worth is good. A person has the obligation to protect his standing (honor); almost any action is justified by this. But at the same time there is a sentiment for self-restraint, which is a common topos in popular philosophy. Drunkenness, for example, is frowned upon. Murder is bad. Minding one's own business is yet another common topos; gossip and being a busybody are bad. Taking care of those in need within your family, e.g. widows, is good. Looking to the welfare of those more distant from you is not good. Beyond immediate family, friends are highly valued. Indeed, friendship is another constant topos of popular philosophy and culture.

Seeking control in an uncertain world

While this range of moral vision seems unexceptional and served to guide a man through normal life experiences, when any uncertainty disrupted the smooth flow of life – and it must have done so almost constantly – men turned to the supernatural: superstition, magic, and religion. The ordinary person found many willing to allay his concerns. The priests in the temples, the purveyors of charms and potions on the streets and in small kiosks, the professional magicians ready to supply incantations for any need, the dream interpreters eager for the opportunity to reveal all based on one's latest somnolent imaginings, the booksellers with tomes of useful information: all were at the ready in even the smallest town.

Superstition in general guided life. Amulets have been found in great number; bracelets, necklaces, and rings were all thought to be effective charms against the unknown. Charms were commonly used against all manner of ills. Pliny the Elder writes:

> Certainly spells exist against hail, against a wide range of diseases, and to treat burns – some even of proven effectiveness … and arrows pulled from a body, provided they have not touched the ground, are powerful aphrodisiacs if placed under a lover's bed. (*Natural History* 28.6.34)

Marcellus Empiricus gives an example of a charm against disease:

> To be recited sober, touching the relevant part of the body with three fingers: thumb, middle finger, and ring finger; the other two are stretched out. 'Go away, no matter whether you originated today or earlier: this disease, this illness, this pain, this swelling, this redness, this goiter, these tonsils, this abscess, this tumor, these glands and the little glands I call forth, I lead forth, I speak forth, through this spell, from these limbs and bones.' (*On Medicaments* 15.11/Luck)

Spells came in handy too if you had a wager on a chariot race and wanted to insure your victory, as this lead tablet from Africa shows:

> I conjure you, daemon, whoever you may be, to torture and kill,

from this hour, this day, this moment, the horses of the Green and the White teams; kill and smash the charioteers Clarus, Felix, Primulus, Romanus; do not leave a breath in them. I conjure you by him who has delivered you, at the time, the god of the sea and the air: *Io, Iasdao … aeia.*/Luck

Or if you sought revenge:

Lady Demeter, I appeal to you as one who has suffered wrongs. Hear me, goddess, and render justice, so that you bring the most terrible and painful things on those who think such things about us and who rejoice together against us and bring suffering on me and my wife, Epiktesis, and despise us. Oh Queen, lend an ear to those of us who suffer and punish those who look happily on such as us. (Amorgos, Greece/Gager, no. 75)

Or punishment for a personal wrong:

Whoever stole the property of Varenus, whether woman or man, let him pay with his own blood. From the money which he will pay back, one half is donated to Mercury and Virtus. (Kevendon, Essex/Gager, no. 97)

Or even to steal another man's wife:

Let burning heat consume the sexual parts of Allous, her vulvas, her members, until she leaves the household of Apollonios. Lay Allous low with fever, with sickness unceasing, starvation – Allous – and madness! Remove Allous from Apollonios her husband; give Allous insolence, hatred, obnoxiousness, until she departs the household of Apollonios. Now. Quickly. (Oxyrhynchus, Egypt/Gager, no. 35)

And, of course, love was a constant motivation for magical incantations:

Let Matrona, to whom Tagene gave birth, whose 'stuff' you have, including hairs of her head, love Theodoros, to whom Techosis gave birth … Do not ignore me, whoever you are, but awaken yourself for me and go off to Matrona, so that she may freely give me everything that is hers … so that Matrona love Theodoros for all the time of her life. I invoke you in the name of Abrasax. (Oxyrhynchus, Egypt/ Gager, no. 29)

Amateur incantations were common for everyday occurrences. Some amulets were inscribed with the magical word *Abraxus*, which has been passed down to the present day as 'abracadabra'; in Christian times, ritual formulae could also be turned to magical purposes, for example the intonation of *hoc est corpus* ('this is the body'); this gives the modern term 'hocus pocus.' But for serious matters, professionals male and female were at hand to offer aid. Of course witches such as Circe in the *Odyssey* and Medea in Euripides had a long literary pedigree, but their real-life counterparts were thick on the ground. Egypt was the land and source of magicians par excellence. Magical papyri represent the textbooks for training, with the critical piece of information left out so that the professionals couldn't be entirely supplanted by a self-taught person. Kits for magical performance survive from antiquity, including one that seems to be a sort of roulette wheel used for divining the future. A professional could also come equipped with drugs such as incense to create an atmosphere, as well as with tools such as wands to 'direct' the magical power wielded.

Jesus of Nazareth had many of the attributes of a magician – the ability to cure illness and to control nature, for example. When the devil tries to tempt him to use this power for personal gain and influence, Jesus refuses, but other magicians had no such scruples. In Apuleius' novel *The Golden Ass*, Pamphile uses her magic for her own purposes; other magicians were more commercial, however. Paul was seized and hauled before the local authorities because his 'cure' of a slave soothsayer deprived her owners of income (Acts 16:16–19). Another magician competed with Paul for the attention of Sergius Paulus, the proconsul in Cyprus, and lost (Acts 13:6–12). Simon Magus ('the magician') was one such person who made a living purveying magic:

But there was a man named Simon who had previously practiced magic in the city and amazed the nation of Samaria saying that he himself was somebody great. They all gave heed to him, from the least to the greatest, saying, 'This man is that power of God which is called Great.' And they gave heed to him, because for a long time he had amazed them with his magic. [Simon, impressed with the magical power of the apostle Philip, is baptized.] ... Now when Simon saw that the Spirit was given through the laying on of the apostles' hands, he offered them money, saying, 'Give me also this power, that any one on whom I lay my hands may receive the Holy Spirit.' But Peter said to him, 'Your silver perish with you, because you thought you could obtain the gift of God with money! ... I see that you are in the gall of bitterness and in the bond of iniquity.' (Acts 8:9–24)

Simon, a good magician who could see when he was out-magici-aned, was terrified and asked Peter, his recognized superior magician, 'that nothing of what you have said may come upon me.'

Another episode in Acts involving Paul further illustrates the situation. Paul went to Ephesus and immediately became an attraction as his powers to perform miracles, i.e. to have magical powers, became apparent to the populace. Articles such as a handkerchief and clothing that had merely touched him cured disease and drove out evil spirits. Other Jewish would-be miracle workers attempted to duplicate his success by invoking the name of Jesus, as Paul did. Seven sons of a Jewish head priest tried this. But an evil spirit they were exorcizing said to them, 'I acknowledge Jesus, and Paul who preaches him, but who are YOU?' And the possessed man bloodily thrashed the sons on the spot. This clear proof of the power of Jesus' name brought many converts (Acts 19:11–20), because the efficacy of a sorcerer was judged by his success rate. Paul was successful, and many ordinary men were convinced of his supernatural power; the 'Seven sons of Sceva' were not successful, and so were discredited. Many other magicians recognized Paul's power and even burned their valuable magical guidebooks since he had proved his power greater. All these episodes in Acts serve to show how pervasive the belief in the power of the supernatural was, and in the numerous people around who claimed to be purveyors of that power.

Religion provided another avenue for addressing concerns. A broad range of religious activity was on offer. There were the reflexive actions, the traditional, hardly conscious daily rites like pouring some drops of offering to the household gods before a meal. There was festival religiosity when, in the midst of this or that god's holy day, banqueting or entertainments or just raucous behavior were in order, part and parcel of the worship of the deity or deities in question. This type of religiosity was centered on the major local or civic divinities. On festival days the local gods were feted, as were the people; more elaborate sacrifices were offered, and entertainments were often sponsored in honor of the god or goddess. It was a time to affirm the community.

Then there was utilitarian religiosity, the use of a priest or prophet or diviner to help solve an immediate problem. In fact, people who claimed to be able to foretell the future were always available in a town. The elite Cicero notes that 'wherever you go, it follows you, whether you listen to a prophet or an omen, whether you sacrifice a victim or catch sight of a bird of warning, whether you interview an oriental soothsayer or an Italian diviner, whether you see lightning or hear thunder' (*On Divination* 1.48). These diviners were available because there was a deep need to make sense of the world and to somehow reconcile the incongruence of the personal world and the external world's assaults upon it. And everyone agreed that the future was established and therefore knowable, that prophecy and augury and other means of reaching out to that future were real and efficacious. Dream interpretation was a favorite recourse, with professionals such as Artemidorus ready both to offer their services and to write a book about interpretations. Men like Dorotheus wrote books about astrology. And self-help tools like Ouija boards were readily available, an inexpensive way to discern the future.

In his world, the ordinary man rarely dwelled on the intricacies of religious thought. Everyone agreed that there were supernatural powers in the world. Since the divine agencies were in control, all agreed that these powers could be accessed by prayer and sacrifice and incantation and magic. If an agreement could be made and carried out, a reciprocal action in favor of the worshipper could be expected. What one did and what brought results were what mattered. Carrying out the correct action in the correct way was the key to securing divine aid; there was no creed or moral code to adhere to in order to gain the god's favor. For this reason there were no arguments about dogma in the bars and streets; the proof of a divinity's power lay in his or her ability to produce results in real time. It is illustrative of this that the many confrontations with magic in the New Testament literature all revolve around whose magic is most efficacious, never about the philosophy or theology of the practitioner.

Major disruptions occurred not over theology, but when the power of a favored divinity was questioned or insulted. This is well illustrated by another of Paul's experiences in Ephesus. The temple of Artemis was known widely and was a popular votive destination. A silversmith named Demetrius and his fellow workers made a good deal of money creating and selling silver images of the goddess. This craftsman took action to protect his trade: he incited his fellows by pointing out that Paul was convincing many to turn from polytheism; the danger, he said, was not only that Artemis herself was being discredited, but also that their trade in votives would dry up. With a shout of 'Great is Artemis of the Ephesians,' the gang radicalized the city against Paul. A mob laid hold of him, dragged him to the theater, and tried to have him punished (Acts 19:23–34). The accusation was that Paul had blasphemed against the goddess. 'Great is Artemis of the Ephesians!' was not a theological issue for them; it was a simple affirmation by the people that their goddess not only existed, but was powerful. Anyone threatening that reality was an enemy. Although among the elite the idea of a relationship between moral behavior and the favor of the gods gained some ground through, for example, Stoic thought, there is little indication that such thinking penetrated to those who remained tied to their basically satisfying and satisfactory religious beliefs. These were based upon efficacious supernatural powers who could, with the proper approach, be enlisted in solving the practical problems of the day such as illness, frustration in love, and vengeance against one's enemies and rivals. To attack the existence of, as here, a goddess, undercut a central tool ordinary people used to address their everyday problems.

In all these attempts to access the power of the supernatural in order to deal with the uncertainties in their lives, men were not terribly concerned when their efforts did not work. The prevailing attitude was that if an incantation or a religious offering did not do the trick, then something had gone wrong with the process, not with the basic functioning of the magico-religious world – the wrong spell-prayer had been cast, or it has been cast carelessly, or had used the wrong accoutrements. There is no indication of a lessening of reliance on religion and magic throughout our period or, indeed, in all of antiquity.

Worries

As ordinary men ordered their lives through popular morality and bringing the supernatural to bear, their personal concerns could throw life into turmoil at any moment. Ordinary men lived in a world full of actual and potential changes in fortune. These might be for good or for evil; the natural reaction to living in a world full of uncontrollable physical and social threats to survival, not to say to happiness, was worry and (if possible) action. Given the differentials in power, the heavily hierarchized social structure, and the vagaries of weather, disease, and natural disaster, people turned to supra-rational means to predict and so deal with the future. Although mentions of elites are fairly common since they, too, utilized dream interpreters and astrologers to help deal with their life issues, both the *Carmen Astrologicum* and Artemidorus' *Interpretation of Dreams* clearly reflect the mind of ordinary men and women.

Because of their usefulness as resources for dealing with life's issues, these handbooks offer a valuable insight into what was worrying men in their daily lives. The overarching theme (not surprisingly) of both the *Carmen* and Artemidorus' treatment of dreams is changes in fortune. The advice, interpretations, and prognostications reveal core issues for success or failure in life, encompassing such concerns as death, disease, financial challenges, marriage and family, and risks of journeys. They also focus on the violence of everyday life, stressful interpersonal interactions, and dealings with the law. The emphasis is on down-to-earth problems; there is a significant lack of concern for what might be called 'large' calamities. There is only one reference in Artemidorus to 'approach of enemies, barren land, and famine' (*Dreams* 2.9). While history focuses on wars and rumors of wars, disasters, and political maneuverings of the elite, ordinary men had little or no thought for such things. They were preoccupied rather with their immediate situations.

Magical papyri also offer a window. Death, while the commonest topic in Artemidorus' dream interpretations book, does not receive much mention in these; magic apparently cannot ward off the Grim Reaper except indirectly, by curing disease. Likewise family relations, a topic that figures largely in Artemidorus, is largely missing from the incantations of the papyri, although it does occasionally appear. Otherwise, the topics of the *Carmen* and Artemidorus' interpretations frequently track the same concerns shown in the magical papyri: disease and financial success, success in disputes at law, and standing in the eyes of others. Together, the three sources leave a very clear impression of the day-to-day concerns of ordinary people.

Although bad things happening to people far outnumber good things, good fortune is mentioned at times. The *Carmen* speaks of a good fate as 'wealth and praise' for men, 'wealthy, rich, powerful in business affairs, great in prosperity, seizing eminence and fortune and increasing them' and 'fortune, eminence, commendation, praise, and a good livelihood.' Although these might seem to fit the high end of ordinary 'good fortune' more than the experience of most, *mutatis mutandis* we can suppose that for ordinary persons as well, sufficient wealth, success in business, and good standing among his neighbors, friends, and associates would constitute 'good fortune.' Elsewhere the *Carmen* also mentions a beautiful and faithful wife, good friends, and victory over one's enemies as good fortune for men, and good health and a fine reputation as good fortune for women. These are the things that everyone would hope to come to pass in his life, but prediction literature dwelled much, much more on the possibilities of these not happening in one aspect or another. This is quite natural, for people who seek advice are mostly worried people; as Artemidorus says, 'People with no cares have no need of a seer' (*Dreams* 3.20).

Death is the single commonest concern. In the *Carmen* there is a long list of possible deaths, almost all bad; it is mentioned in other contexts repeatedly. In Artemidorus, death, grief, and mourning are the most cited events by far. This could be one's own death, or the death of a person close to you, family member or friend. The pervasive presence of death is striking in its dominance of worries. The 'normality' of death as we might view it statistically – very many children dead by age ten; half the population dead by twenty; a life expectancy of under fifty – clearly was of no consolation to people. Rather, the reality held them, and they worried about it constantly. Like all the concerns I will discuss, we should not think that ordinary men moped about in perpetual fear of the angel of death, but since death was so real, so unpredictable, and so disruptive to the living, it is no surprise that they thought about it a lot.

Disease was also constantly on men's minds. Despite or because of the state of herbal and medical remedies in their world, disease that could easily debilitate or kill was an ever-present threat to well-being. As with references to death, Artemidorus is full of examples of illness; and, of course, death and disease are often joined:

> The inability to leave or discover a way out of one's own abode or home in which he dreams himself to be indicates obstacles causing delay for those having in mind to be away from home, hindrances for those planning to accomplish something, serious disease for one who is sick, and death to one with a lingering disease. (*Dreams* 2.2)

In the *Carmen*, disease is frequently present as a fate as well. For example:

> If Saturn is in quartile of Mars while Saturn is in the tenth sign, he will have little medical treatment, he will be weak in his body, unceasing in diseases because of fevers, he will be shaking ... (*Carmen* 2.15)

Or:

> If Saturn and Mars are in the same sign and the Moon is between them, then this native will be a leper, and scabies and itching will seize him. (*Carmen* 4.1)

By definition an ordinary man had enough to live on, but his concern was whether more resources would come his way, enhancing his life, or fewer, endangering his ability to manage. And, of course, the range of financial situations was great. Artemidorus mentions all sorts, from the laborer, sailor, artisan, and service provider (e.g. innkeeper) to what would seem to be long-distance merchants and wholesalers. Whatever their financial position, however, major worries preoccupied them.

Financial success heads the list. Artemidorus can say 'a great treasure indicates distress and anxieties' (*Dreams* 2.59) and 'a rich man must spend his money lavishly, and be the object of plots and envy' (*Dreams* 4.17), but this perhaps only reflects either a little bit of popular philosophizing, or the myth of the unhappy rich, ever popular among ordinary men of all ages. By far the most references in Artemidorus are concerned with increased financial success. That success was often precarious.

Men had scant opportunity to make a great leap in economic condition. But hard-working persons could be successful, although just how many managed this is impossible to know. Artemidorus tells the tale of the child of a farmer who became a shipmaster and, indeed, 'was extremely successful' (*Dreams* 5.74). A similar story is told by the peasant of Maktar (Tunisia) who rose from poverty to local office:

> I was born into a poor family. My father had no possessions or house of his own. Since the day of my birth, I have always worked my land; neither my land nor I have ever rested. When the harvest season of the year came around and grain was ripe, I was the first to cut my stalks. When the gangs of harvesters who hire themselves out around Cirta, the capital of the Numidians, or in the fertile plain of Jupiter, appeared in the country, then I was the first to reap my field. Then, leaving my country, I harvested for other men for twelve years under a burning sun. For eleven years, I commanded a gang of harvesters and harvested grain in the fields of the Numidians. By my work, having made do with little, I at last became the owner of a house and a rural estate. Today I don't lack for anything. I have even risen to honors: I have been enrolled among the magistrates of my city, and my colleagues have elected me, me who began life as a poor peasant, Censor. I have seen my children and grandchildren come into the world and grow up around me. I have lived blamelessly, deservedly honored by all. (*CIL* 8.11824 = *ILS* 7457)

Although this man's success is spectacular, it was by no means unique. Artemidorus gives an interpretation of a dream that one has a large head:

> To dream that you have a large head is a good thing for a rich man who has not yet held high office, as well as for a poor man, an athlete, a moneylender, a banker, and the collector of monetary subscriptions. For a rich man, it portends a leadership role in which there is need of a crown for him, or a priestly fillet, or a diadem. For the others, it means successful business and additional monetary gain. So the increase in the size of the head points to these things. (*Dreams* 1.71)

Success came to some, but worries came to all. First, there is debt. Debt is a focus of the *Carmen* and there are many references in Artemidorus to debt and debtors; this indicates widespread use of loans. For example, usurers who hold a mortgage on a man's ship appear in dreams given in Artemidorus, as does an artisan who because of debt has to leave his workshop and city. Land was used as collateral for loans to pay taxes or raise capital, and men worried that default would mean its loss. The specter of failed business ventures is a fairly common dream motif; one example involves a perfume maker who 'lost his store'; this is said matter-of-factly by Artemidorus. Then there is unemployment, another common economic evil mentioned repeatedly; this does not seem to involve day-laborers, who might be expected to be unemployed much of the time, but rather tradesmen and artisans, whose work might be supposed, in normal situations, to be steadier. We know from other preindustrial societies that underemployment is endemic; these fears of unemployment mean that there were many men out of work or with tenuous or part-time work among ordinary Romans, and they feared the prospect. Although one might be a fine artisan or even a shipowner, this was no guarantee that work would be available. So the potential for unemployment was constantly on men's minds.

And in business there was always the possibility of a falling-out with business partners and associates. The *Carmen* focuses on these worries, as well as on concerns about dealing with local officials, especially the market supervisors who had the power to harass a businessman. Artemidorus notes:

And even if a man conducts his business well and goes so far as to take on unprofitable expenditures, he is still always censured by the market supervisor. For it is impossible to be a supervisor without constantly doing this. (*Dreams* 2.30)

Petty harassments were a fact of life and could go beyond this to outright corruption, as in the *Satyricon* 15 episode in which local officials attempt to seize stolen property, scare off its owners with the threat of prosecution, then sell the articles for their own profit.

The only thing that takes up more space in the *Carmen* than business and travel is family matters of various sorts. Men had intense concerns about marriage and about children and relatives. Dorotheus goes into great elaboration about what the charts have to say on prospects and the future of marriages. What kind of a husband will he be? What kind of a wife? What status differences will be involved? That is, will the man marry 'low,' for example to a slave or a prostitute, or will he marry well? Will a relative be married? Will the person charted marry multiple times? What is little mentioned is romantic love. On the contrary, when women are involved, strong emphasis is put on sexual control. In the magical papyri an overwhelming number of charms and incantations deal with securing the (apparently unwilling) sexual subservience of a woman to a man. In only one case is it explicitly a husband-and-wife issue; the impression in all others is that either an undefined relationship exists, or an adulterous one. Thus sexual drive was very much on the minds of ordinary men. Given the fact that in the magical papyri there are so many charms, incantations designed to compel a woman's affections, it is somewhat surprising that sexual attraction does not seem to be on the worry list for men seeking astrological and dream-interpretation advice. Success in love (whatever that might mean in a variety of contexts) is missing from the *Carmen*. In Artemidorus, some dreams do interpret a man or a woman's love life – 'If a young man or woman is wounded in the breast by someone s/he knows, it indicates love' (*Dreams* 1.41) – but this is quite rare. There is reference to wifely love, to mistresses, to whores and debauchery, but there is no preoccupation with what we would think of as the emotion of love per se. It seems that thinking about 'romantic love' is a luxury men cannot afford – their concerns are much more concrete. If 'love' is a part of a man's life, so be it – but it is not a concern of the first order. He is much more concerned with the realia of 'love,' for example if he will get access to a woman he loves, or, on a more personal level, if he will be impotent ('joy will not come to him in the acts of Aphrodite') or 'oversexed': excess in sexual intercourse is predicted for both men and women in the case of one natal horoscope.

The possibility of a happy marriage is there, but overshadowed by many fates of poor outcome, and there is much worry about quarrelsome marriage, emphasized by the frequency with which epitaphs of happily married couples state that they 'lived without quarrels,' perhaps sometimes protesting overmuch and at the very least validating that lack of

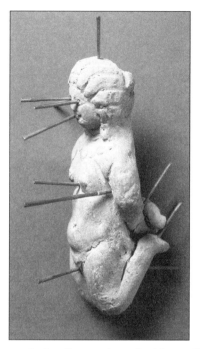

2. Domination of women. A clay figure pierced with needles. The accompanying spell, written on a lead tablet, shows the magical intent of a man to control a woman sexually.

quarrelsomeness was something to be sought in a marriage. Good and bad outcomes to marriage have a whole section of Artemidorus' book to themselves. The necessities of a good marriage are 'agreement and love,' but it is entirely possible that one partner will dominate the other like his or her master a slave; only occasionally is a purely good outcome mentioned, as for example in Artemidorus when he gives wifely excellences as attractiveness, faithfulness, being a good housekeeper, and showing obedience to her husband (*Dreams* 2.32).

Misfortunes for the wife and children weigh significantly upon the mind. Within marriage two concerns are uppermost. First of all, will the marriage be stable or unstable? There seems to be a good deal of worry over both female and male debauchery and sexual misconduct, especially in the *Carmen*, but also in Artemidorus, where licentious wives are mentioned a number of times. A focus on the extramarital relations of both partners comes into many horoscopes. There is explicit and frequent concern that the husband will be a philanderer (this was clearly not accepted as a 'given'). A good wife should be faithful, but the concern for loose, debauched woman is preeminent. Artemidorus notes that the husband 'exercises control and authority over [his wife's] body'; 'controls and governs' his wife. So when she goes astray, this is a direct catastrophe for the husband's reputation and standing. The horoscopes and dream interpretations paint a picture resembling the disloyal, sexually loose women mentioned so frequently and in such detail in Apuleius' novel. Whatever the reality, the ordinary man evidently worried a lot about the faithfulness of his wife (and she about her husband's).

There is also worry about sexual relations in marriage or, rather, women's actions as a sexual partner. If a woman is 'desirous of intercourse' then this 'indicates debauchery and wickedness' according to the *Carmen*. It follows that a good woman does not 'perform the act of Aphrodite in an unnatural way.' Oral sex on one's wife is not acceptable, nor is fellatio by the wife. Presumably the worry here is that sex with a wife should not be confused with a casual sexual encounter with a slave or prostitute. Another bad marriage outcome to worry about is that the woman is a lesbian. Artemidorus is more generous in his thinking than the *Carmen*. Although the wife should be submissive – thus 'the one having sex according to Aphrodite's norms completely controls the body of his compliant and willing sexual partner' (*Dreams* 1.79) – she is entitled to enjoy the act too: 'To have intercourse with one's willing and submissive wife – one not reluctant regarding sex – this is a good thing for both.' (It is, however, entirely possible that the wife only yield 'with some resistance' – and this is not interpreted as good (1.78)). In intercourse with one's wife, the face-to-face position is called 'natural' (1.79); other positions include from the rear and while standing ('men use this position only when they have neither bed nor mattress'); while the woman is kneeling or while prostrate; and with the woman on top. All positions except the 'natural' one are 'taught in their wantonness, licentiousness, and drunken follies …' The woman's perspective is not considered important, although as noted above, Artemidorus does admit that she might enjoy the act. The desire, therefore, is for a marriage in which both partners are faithful, and the wife remains demure and passive – does not 'play the whore' – in their sexual life together.

Another worry was about marriages ending badly – even in murder, as in a wife poisoning her husband. More mundane bad endings are frequently mentioned, either divorce or desertion. There are many astrological scenarios concerning a woman leaving her husband's house; this would seem to mean that it was a common fear. Likewise, Artemidorus frequently mentions divorce, indicating that it was a common occurrence. Presumably this worry was linked to the dowry, which the woman would take away with her; a dowry is assumed as normal.

The sum of a successful marriage seems to be children. There is much worry about sterility, the number of children, and whether they will be 'good children,' as expressed in many charts cast. There is a preference for males ('male children [seen in a dream] are good; female are good for nothing' (*Dreams* 4.10)), but there is never reference to infanticide, abortion, or contraception. Indeed, one of the great miseries and misfortunes of life is to have few children or to be childless.

Those children are under the complete control of their fathers. The relationship can be good or bad, but the expectation is that it will be good, with the parents providing what is necessary for upbringing, and for an inheritance for the children. Intergenerational relations are often stressed as parents worry about children wasting parental property and resources and in general not turning out well. There is concern for the number of children, and that they get along well; there is a particular concern that brothers get along. Here again quarreling raises its ugly head, as children are apt to get into disputes with one another, with an outcome unfortunate for the family. Beyond the nuclear family, which seems to be the assumed unit in all the evidence, and into the extended family, quarreling is again mentioned. It does seem as if a lot of arguing went on in an ordinary man's family.

I have noted the role of sex in marriage, but it is also necessary to look more generally at ordinary men's sexual activity. The sexual life of a male included sex with a wife for procreation; however, its other aspects are harder to gauge. The elite sources, especially Ovid, Martial, and Juvenal but also historians, rhetoricians, and literary figures of almost all sorts, contain material relating to male sexual activity. Even if complicated in the details, the overriding elite male ethos valuing domination and being ashamed of subjection meant that all sex, whether homosexual or heterosexual, was evaluated as specific circumstances of control and submission. So a particular sexual act was acceptable or not depending not so much on the physiology of the act itself, but on who was involved and the part played by an individual in it. People considered the actors (male? female?), their status (slave? free?), their matrimonial status (unmarried? married?), the economic circumstances (paid? gratis?), the biological intent (for procreation?), and most importantly the dominant/submissive element just noted. A given sexual act was judged according to where it was positioned on the matrix of these considerations, which created the 'rules of the game'; obviously, the situation was very complicated.

Within the basic model of sex and marriage, a wide range of other sexual activity was open, provided the rules of the game were adhered to. Most specifically, we do not find a 'type' of person or 'identity' that can be called 'homosexual' or 'heterosexual.' In fact, there is no Latin word for 'homosexual' – or for 'heterosexual' for that matter. It is essential rather to think in terms of specific acts and situations within an elite culture that never questions the centrality of male domination as the pattern of behavior and self-identity for the male.

The question is, can this fluid ethos apply to ordinary men? These men also conceptualized sexual acts as domination or submission. Sling projectiles give a wonderfully vivid proof of the equation of sexual violence and masculinity. Soldiers readying these lead, acorn-shaped objects for hurling inscribed them with a message for the enemy. Some just had thoughts like 'Take that!' But many others use colorful sexual language to make the message of domination clear. This *glans* (the Latin word for 'penis' is the same as for 'sling projectile') from the war against Octavian, later Augustus, bears witness: 'I seek Octavian's ass' (*CIL* 11.6721.7) is one of the daintier thoughts; all related to sexual penetration as emblematic of domination. This view of masculine domination as sexual metaphor comes straight from ordinary men.

The magical papyri confirm this picture of aggressive male sexuality. Many of the charms and incantations are designed to subject women to men, sometimes in the grossest terms:

> Let the myrrh smoke on coals and recite the spell. 'You are Zmyrna [i.e. myrrh], the bitter and effective one … Everyone calls you Zmyrna, but I call you Eater and Burner of the Heart … I am sending

you to X, daughter of Y, to serve me against her and bring her to me. If she is sitting, she may not sit; if she is talking to someone, she may not talk; if she is approaching someone, she may not approach; … if she is eating, she may not eat; if she is kissing someone, she may not kiss … She may think only of me, desire me only, love me only, and fulfill my every wish … Enter her through her soul and remain in her heart and burn her entrails, her breast, her liver, her breath, her bones, her marrow, until she comes to me to love me and fulfill my every wish. I urge you, Zmyrna … to make sure that you carry out my orders. Just as I am burning you and you are potent, just so you must burn her brain, the woman I love, burn it completely and rip out her entrails and shed her blood, drop by drop, until she comes to me.' (*PGM* 1:121–4/Luck)

The violent imagery fits the aggressive, dominant male. And the action in the plays of Plautus, Apuleius' *Golden Ass*, and Petronius' *Satyricon* all features males who are concerned about domination. These works also picture a world in which homosexual acts occur together with heterosexual, and in which the elite matrix of acceptable behavior seems to apply.

Set alongside this clear concept of domination as the litmus test of masculinity and the resulting openness to acts of sexual domination, whether over males or females, is an equally clear concept that the collection of acts we might call nonstraightforward male-on-female intercourse is, as a group, considered unacceptable, not to say perverse or even deviant. Artemidorus is very specific about the view of sex that informs his dream interpretations; I assume that unless that view was widespread among ordinary people, this would not have been the case. As previously noted, his view is that there is one 'natural' sexual position:

Basic Nature teaches men that the 'body-to-body' sexual position is the only natural one; all the other positions men are taught in their wantonness, licentiousness, and drunken follies. [After noting that animals all have their own 'natural' sexual habits, he continues.] And so it is appropriate that men hold the proper sexual position to be the 'face-to-face' one; the others are invented as suitable to lewdness and drunken excess. (*Dreams* 1.79)

So Artemidorus states that 'If the sun disappears this is a bad sign for all except for those endeavoring to escape notice and performing abominable acts (*Dreams* 1.36). But what exactly might those be? In his long series of interpretations based on dreams he mentions just about every possible sexual encounter and activity. He lists three general types: (1) intercourse that is natural, legal, and customary. This includes sex with one's wife, with prostitutes, with 'unknown women,' with one's own slaves, male or female, or with a female who is familiar and 'on intimate terms'; (2) intercourse that is illegal: intercourse with a young (five- to ten-year-old) boy or girl; with one's own son or daughter or sibling; with one's mother; with a 'friend' (presumably, a free grown-up person); and (3) intercourse that is 'unnatural.' Here he includes pretty odd things, such as 'having sexual intercourse with himself,' 'kissing his own penis,' necrophilia, and bestiality – but not, importantly, homosexual acts.

Artemidorus is ambivalent about a clear dominant/submissive model. On the one hand, he confirms the supposition that to be possessed in a sexual act is bad; the only exception is a dream of possession by a rich man, for you will then 'receive' riches (*Dreams* 1.78). On the other, even in dominating positions some acts are reprehensible, such as having fellatio performed by a wife or mistress, or a friend, or a relative, or a child. While Artemidorus also condemns the person performing the act, the passive partner, it is noteworthy that in either position a dream bodes ill.

Artemidorus, then, nuances the elite categorization of sexual acts. Moreover, to him, there is a norm: face-to-face sex between a male and a female. Other acts are mentioned, specifically fellatio and various sexual positions. The former seems at least with wives and free persons to be reprehensible, and he implicitly criticizes the 'non-normal' sexual positions. One comes away with the distinct sense that he is fully aware of the sexual habits of his contemporaries, but has a clear idea of what is 'good' and what is 'bad' about them. In his work there is an affirmation of marital sex, but unlike the elite viewpoint there also seems to be a rejection of homosexual activity, whether male or female.

The *Carmen* adds to our knowledge of how the ordinary man viewed homosexual acts. In the chapter 'Knowledge of Sodomy,' which completes his larger section on marriage, Dorotheus clearly has in mind not just individual acts, but people who habitually prefer same-sex acts to heterosexual ones. In one astrological casting the person 'will not love women, but his pleasure will be in boys'; in another 'he will be covetous of males.' There is analogous casting: 'it indicates she will be desirous of women,' just as for a male 'he will be desirous of males.' In a third instance: 'if a woman then she will be a Lesbian … if a male, then they will not do to women as they ought to do' (*Carmen* 2.7). So the *Carmen* adds to our understanding by making it clear that some men (and some women) acted out a long-term preference, not just more or less isolated homosexual acts.

As a final window on sexuality, the attitude of Paul needs to be mentioned. In a tirade against polytheists, he writes:

> For although they knew God, they neither glorified him as God nor gave thanks to him, but their thinking became futile and their foolish hearts were darkened. Although they claimed to be wise, they became fools and exchanged the glory of the immortal God for images made to look like mortal man and birds and animals and reptiles. Therefore God gave them over in the sinful desires of their hearts to sexual impurity for the degrading of their bodies with one another. They exchanged the truth of God for a lie, and worshiped and served created things rather than the Creator – who is forever praised. Amen. Because of this, God gave them over to shameful lusts. Even their women exchanged natural relations for unnatural ones. In the same way the men also abandoned natural relations with women and were inflamed with lust for one another. Men committed indecent acts with other men, and received in themselves the due penalty for their perversion. (Romans 1:21–7)

He goes on to catalogue all their other horrible moral shortcomings, but what is important to note is that he paints polytheists as open to homosexual acts (to put it kindly). Now this no more means that all Romano-Greeks practiced homosexual acts than that they were all malicious, deceitful, arrogant, heartless, and so on – other epithets he piles upon them in this same passage. But it surely means that such acts were an accepted part of polytheist culture. The fact that Paul makes a point of being opposed to these acts indicates that his hearers were as well, or, at least, were able to be persuaded that they should be. Such an argument does not come out of the blue; Paul's correspondents and hearers either were or could easily be made to be disposed against homosexual acts. Given the evidence of Artemidorus and the *Carmen*, I would argue that for a wide swath of ordinary men such a disposition would come naturally because such acts and, therefore, their practitioners were looked down upon.

The picture of ordinary men's outlook on sex is not, therefore, consistent. Evidently in the culture there were men who took a detached view of sexual acts, not connecting them to a greater social picture but only to individual situations, much as the elite did. The graffiti from Pompeii, scribbled by a self-selected group of aggressive males, fit this picture. But then there were also those who felt that restrained sex for procreation within marriage was the appropriate model, recognizing various degrees of deviation (perhaps excusing sex with slaves, for example) but not rejecting the core value. This aspect comes out much more strongly in the material I have just given. It is a complex picture, and should be accepted as such, but in general it seems that ordinary men were more committed to marriage, and more inclined to be critical of homosexual acts, than their elite leaders.

We would expect a concern for marriage and sex among ordinary men. On the other hand, journeys receive a rather unexpected emphasis in the astrological and dream literature. This emphasis tells us two things. First, we see that journeys were not out of the ordinary. We can think immediately of travel for pleasure, such as going to a festival near or far; for business; and as an enforced undertaking. In Apuleius we see all three types of movement, and especially the latter two are strongly witnessed in the prediction literature. Likewise in the New Testament material we see people moving about the empire whether on business or as part of religious activity. But travel was dangerous for any number of reasons, including bad weather, bandits and pirates, accidents, and dishonest officials. So it is only natural that men would worry about travel either in the future, or while actually engaged in it. Long-term emigration is also on their minds; we know from the many inscriptions noting a person as an *alienus* (a nonresident) that such movement was in practice fairly common. They also worry about loved ones who are abroad, for example a son, and whether they will return safely. And enforced travel added another dimension, for a person might be exiled

– although this can hardly have been a worry for an ordinary man – or otherwise forced to leave his home to escape debt, or because he was a criminal transported as punishment, or because some natural disaster made a move imperative. The best outcome of travel was economic gain, but the risks in shipping, the primary source of long-distance profit, were immense, as was the investment (and so often debt) required to engage in it. Travel was therefore a major source of worry for men.

As if there wasn't already enough to be concerned about, men had to pay attention to the authorities, to avoid a run-in if at all possible. The *Carmen* has a long passage on being cast into chains, and Artemidorus has many references to dreams that pertain to the fate of criminals and prisoners: becoming condemned, being put in bonds or in prison, anticipating torture and beatings, or execution (crucifixion, beheading). Those in authority generally liked to throw their weight around, and it was best not to get in the way. Likewise, as they controlled the legal system, it was best to prevent entanglement.

The law, crime, and violence of everyday life

According to the elite literature, Roman law was fundamental to the reality that was Roman culture. Scholars through the ages have repeated this, even as they have noted the differential treatment within the law of various segments of the population. But the ordinary person had other, hostile thoughts when the legal system came to mind. This simple statement by Paul indicates much:

> Suppose one of you wants to bring a charge against another believer. Should you take it to the ungodly to be judged? Why not take it to God's people? Don't you know that God's people will judge the world? And if you are going to judge the world, aren't you able to judge small cases? Don't you know that we will judge angels? Then we should be able to judge the things of this life even more! (1 Corinthians 6:1–2)

Paul urges disputes be settled within the community; people should not take cases to public law courts. This advice indicates a fundamental mistrust of the civil courts to treat Paul's people fairly. Although Paul's situation might be seen to be unique because of the religious element, in fact there is much other evidence that ordinary men did not use and even avoided the legal system fairly systematically. This is hardly surprising: The Roman legal system was created by and managed in order to favor the elite. While it is clear that some cases of ordinary men were heard and acted upon – there are rescripts in the *Digest* that are addressed to humble folk – a builder (4.65.2), a flat-tenant (4.65.3) – the structural hindrances were significant.

But the official hindrances were just the tip of the iceberg. In a world where personal connections and wealth provided access to everything worth having, a person was at an increasing disadvantage if he was positioned lower on the socioeconomic scale. It was a parlous situation: Legal action was expensive and all the things that could make legal action work – the help of the powerful (*clientela*), the aid of equals (*amicitia*), the expectation of reciprocal help (*officium*) – were as likely to work against a person as to work in his favor. The Epistle of James (2:6) takes note of this reality: 'Is it not the rich who are exploiting you? Are they not the ones who are dragging you into court?' Surely the mental habit that created official hindrances operated well beyond those strictures and produced a situation in which, in effect, a person of lower status had great difficulty bringing a case against one of higher status, and virtually no chance of winning such a case once put unless, through the patronage of a powerful person, the case had become de facto one between social equals. Apuleius has a scathing indictment of the whole legal system as he mocks 'justice':

> You dregs of humanity – or should I say courtroom beasts – or better still, togate vultures – why do you wonder if nowadays all judges hand down their decisions for a price … (*The Golden Ass* 10.33)

Petronius also plays upon the obvious injustice of the legal system in an episode. His two leading characters, Encolpius and Ascyltos, lost a cloak with gold coins sewed into the seams. They spied this very cloak on the shoulders of a poor market seller and discussed how to get it back. Encolpius was in favor of taking the current owner to court to claim the garment; Ascyltos, however, objected, 'fearing the law.'

'Who knows us in this place? Who will believe what we say? Certainly it seems preferable to me to just buy the cloak, even though it is ours by right. It is better to get it back at a small cost rather than get involved in a lawsuit of very uncertain outcome. What good are laws, when money alone rules, and when a poor man can never prevail? A judgment at law is nothing more than a public sale, and the aristocrat who sits on the jury casts his vote according to who pays him.' (*Satyricon* 13–14)

Artemidorus, in a similar vein, notes that seeing courts of law, judges, lawyers, and teachers of law in a dream 'troubles, unhappiness, bothersome expenses, and that secret things will be revealed'(*Dreams* 2.29); and that a judge is someone who does whatever he wishes without being accountable to anyone (4.66). The *Carmen* is just as harsh. Negatives that could queer a decision include injustice by judge; bribes; force; and favoritism (*Carmen* 5.33). In such a corrupted environment, the ordinary man would have lacked both money and influence in sufficient quantity to go up against anyone of significant standing. Thus the legal system was always risky. So in the *Carmen* there is extensive consideration of the resolution of quarrels and, most especially, of the outcomes of legal proceedings. In these situations other avenues of dispute resolution were on the mind. The most popular was the mediation of a dispute within a family, or a peer group such as an association. Paul recommended this to his comrades in Corinth. The basic situation is clear, however: Ordinary men sought to avoid actions at law. In the vast majority of cases, they looked to the legal system only when there was a really important matter transcending local affairs, or when there was enough standing, connection, and resources to hope for success. *Jurisconsultus abesto* (lawyer, be gone!), indeed.

Theft was a constant problem in a society with so much un- and under-employment, not to say out-and-out poverty. There was no regular police force patrolling the streets; and although in towns there was often a nightwatchman out after dark, and he could make arrests, this was not much of a deterrent. The *Carmen* has a number of references to things being stolen, and dedicates a chapter to 'If you want to know the matter of a theft that has been committed or something that has been lost, whether he will possess it again or not.' Under this heading, various castings indicate that:

These goods will be recovered quickly without pain or trouble … these goods of his which were lost will be found after a long time and with trouble and that the thieves will have moved the goods from the first place in which they put it when they stole it to another place … that it will be found after a time and trouble … that it will be more proper that this be found … that those goods which were stolen or lost will be found … that it will not be found … that the thing which was stolen or lost will disappear so that he will not possess it … that he will soon possess the thing which was lost or stolen … that he will not possess the thing which was stolen or lost and it will not be necessary for its owner to search for it since he would toil without accomplishing anything … that he will not possess the thing which was stolen or lost except with slowness and trouble or a quarrel and insult and fighting. (*Carmen* 5.35)

Artemidorus even has an interpretation directed at a criminal. If such a person dreams of stars falling from the heavens, 'this would only be propitious to those plotting some great crime' (*Dreams* 2.36). Other dreams indicate that someone will be defrauded, temples will be robbed, and thieves will attack a man on a journey; seeing a hawk or wolf in a dream means a bandit or robber.

Stolen goods were difficult to recover. There were no formal investigative police available, although officials did have the capacity to act if they wished. For example, when Lucius in *The Golden Ass* is accused of robbing his host and fleeing, the magistrates do follow this up, torturing Lucius' slave and sending their attendants to Corinth to look for him. But most often a person had to seek the item and the thief himself. Enlisting the help of a god was one way. Another was to check the stars; the *Carmen* gives many castings that indicate where one should look for stolen or lost goods, such as:

… in the dung of sheep or the shelters of animals … in the forges of blacksmiths … in or near a sea or in a spring or a stream or a valley or a river or a canal or a place in which there is water … (*Carmen* 5.35)

Items of all kinds were stolen: fine, expensive cloth; clothing; jewels and perfume; implements of construction and farming; metalwork;

ceramics; religious idols; books and business ledgers; as well as common, everyday 'coarse and rough' possessions. Stolen goods were easily fenced, with no questions asked. According to the details of the *Carmen*, both male and female slaves were frequently used, but wealthy, well-connected men also handled stolen goods.

Like the items themselves, thieves were many and various. They could be acquaintances from outside the house, total strangers, or someone familiar to the family, a thief who 'has entered for conversation and there is friendship between him and the people of the house and their trust is in this man, but then he steals' (*Carmen* 5.35). They could be young, middle aged, or old. Once again, slaves were a common possibility. Their approaches and methods were varied. They might be 'thieves of opportunity' – in a house for another reason, for example, then seeing something tempting, steal it; they might use trickery and guile; they might dig through a wall, or break a lock, or get copies of keys, or sneak in through a skylight.

If you search for the culprit, it helps to know what he looks like. Fortunately, if you did not get a look at him, the stars could provide a description, depending on the dominant planet in the charts:

> Jupiter: white, fat, great in his eyes, the whites of his eyes will be smaller than what is necessary for it to be because of the measure of that eye; and their beards will be rounded and curly, their personality will be gentle and good; Saturn: repulsive in his face, black in his color, his gaze toward the ground, broken and small eyes, slim, twisted in his gaze, of pallid color, a lot of body hair and bushy eyebrows, a liar and sickly; Mars: red in color, reddish hair, sharp vision, fat cheeked, a gay fellow, a master of jokes; Venus: handsome, a full head of hair, fat, black eyes, pale skin, gentle and courteous; Mercury: slim, emaciated, pale, confused in thinking. (*Carmen* 5.35)

All of this information clearly indicates that theft was a serious concern. When you add theft by slave property running away, perhaps the most consistently valuable and certainly most moveable possession, there is almost as much treatment in the *Carmen* of this topic as there is for marriage and the family. And in literature, thieves and theft are everywhere. Allusions to them are sprinkled throughout the New

Testament: Death comes 'like a thief in the night' (Thessalonians 5:2); 'lay up treasures in heaven where moth and dust do not corrupt, nor thieves break in and steal' (Matthew 6:20); 'But understand this: If the owner of the house had known at what hour the thief was coming, he would not have let his house be broken into' (Luke 12:39); 'the thief comes only to steal and kill and destroy' (John 10:10); 'the day of the Lord will come like a thief' (2 Peter 3:10). Then there are the frequent violent assaults on persons and property in Apuleius' *Golden Ass*. And worries over theft became even greater because the authorities took ineffectual action at best. They were concerned with 'keeping the peace' and could form a posse to attack bandits, as happens in *The Golden Ass*, but unless a heinous crime was committed against the elite, or citizens took the initiative, inaction was the order of the day. In fact, both as individuals and as groups, men were left to their own devices in dealing with theft, as the *Carmen* clearly indicates by dwelling on what suspects might look like, where stolen goods might be found, who might be the thieves, and so on. This situation in turn meant that men took measures to guard their possessions and were constantly nervous about the possibility of theft.

Thieves once caught might be turned over to legal process, but they were also susceptible to mob violence, i.e. lynching. This is what happens in *The Golden Ass* when a posse from Hypata catches robbers and promptly kills them with swords or by hurling them over a cliff. If slaves were caught, they were tortured for evidence. Any persons convicted suffered punishments that to the modern mind are extremely cruel. But that was the point, to deter others by fear of ghastly punishments like severed hands, lashings, condemnation to the mines or gladiatorial farces, beheadings, hanging, death at the claws and jaws of wild beasts, and crucifixion. Such punishments were part and parcel of a larger aspect of the ordinary man's world, its pervasively violent nature. Recent emphasis has been placed on our horror at the gladiatorial games and public spectacles which included reenactments of myths featuring the death of one of the participants. It is much more important to acknowledge that for the ordinary man violence was embedded in every aspect of his life to the point where it was, quite simply, normal. He might mistreat his (and sometimes another's) slave by beatings, sexual assault, mental abuse; his children were entirely under his authority and could be physically punished at will. His wife likewise had little recourse against the violence of her husband. Outside the home, fights were a normal way to resolve personal differences as his honor-shame culture endorsed violent forms of self-assertion in the face of insult real or imagined. Although in general he was 'unarmed' in the sense that he, especially if poorer, often did not have offensive equipment like swords ready at hand, other items such as stones, sticks, hunting spears, implements, paving stones, and the like were weapons at his disposal, and he used them, and they could be used on him. The dreams given in Artemidorus make it clear that personal enemies could seek to do harm and one must always be on guard against betrayals:

> [If you see in a dream] dogs that belong to another fawning, this indicates wicked men and women lying in wait to trick you. (*Dreams* 2.11)

Quarrels led to fighting even in, or perhaps especially in, committed communities such as early Christian groups:

> What causes fights and quarrels among you? Don't they come from your desires that battle within you? You want something but don't get it. You kill and covet, but you cannot have what you want. You quarrel and fight. (James 4.1)

Attacks could be of various sorts, but they included physical assaults resulting in injuries or even death. And then, of course, there was always the danger of assault by bandits, especially on the road:

> A man was going down from Jerusalem to Jericho, when he fell into the hands of robbers. They stripped him of his clothes, beat him and went away, leaving him half dead. (Luke 10.30)

Vigilante self-help was the rule. When robbers attack a citizen's house in *The Golden Ass*, they are twice beaten off by those in the house and their neighbors. At other times citizens take the initiative and seize a suspect, turning him over to the authorities. If a dispute were taken before magistrates, official violence such as flogging could be sought, but self-help in interpersonal disputes was the first recourse for most people, with or without subsequent involvement by officials.

On a larger scale, if people had a dispute with the authorities, or felt that, for example, the wealthy were withholding grain during a famine, the natural recourse was to riot, either in an attempt to intimidate or actually to kill alleged perpetrators or to destroy their property. In *The Golden Ass* there is an episode in which townsmen in a mob drag Lucius before the town magistrates and he only escapes when it turns out that he is the victim in a 'festival of laughter.' Paul was not so lucky on a number of occasions. In fact his case is a good example of how men acted when a social irritant appeared. In Ephesus Paul preached and taught in the synagogues, but, as we have seen, the silversmith artisans of the town thought their livelihood was being threatened, and they took action, seizing Paul and his companion and taking them to the theater where the people and magistrates were assembled. At this point the magistrate tried to quiet the crowd and move the process out of the hands of the mob, but in the end the mob had won: Paul left Ephesus immediately (Acts 19:35–41). And well he might, for at Philippi earlier he had had a similar experience with a mob, with a worse outcome. There he had cured a prophetic slave girl, much to the anger and economic loss of her owners. They seized Paul and his companion, Silas, and dragged them into the marketplace to face the authorities, who complied with the mob's wishes:

> The crowd joined in the attack against Paul and Silas, and the magistrates ordered them to be stripped and beaten. After they had been severely flogged, they were thrown into prison, and the jailer was commanded to guard them carefully. Upon receiving such orders, he put them in the inner cell and fastened their feet in the stocks. (Acts 16:22–4)

Anyone who seemed disruptive could be set upon, and a small number of locals could raise a mob, as in Ephesus with the silversmiths and at Philippi with a wealthy pair of brothers. A local ordinary man had less fear of this, although such things could happen, as when the father of a younger son accused the elder son of murder and tried to incite the crowd to forego a trial and stone the accused (*The Golden Ass* 10.6–12). Most often, though, the ordinary man was in the mob, for those set upon were most usually either outsiders or members of the elite. Apuleius gives us an example of vigilantes in his tale of the priests of the Syrian goddess. They had been traveling through towns performing their rites and offering prophecies for sale. In one town they stole a golden goblet from the temple of the Great Mother goddess. This discovered, the townsmen set out to retrieve their stolen goods:

> And then suddenly a band of armed horsemen came up from behind us at a gallop. Only with difficulty did they rein in their steeds' mad dash. The men seized the lead priest and his companions, too. Shouting that they were foully sacrilegious, they proceeded to beat them up with their fists. Then they tied them all up and again and again demanded in the strongest language that they produce the golden chalice, the evidence of their wicked theft ... One of the men stretched his hand over my back and rummaged around in the very bosom of the goddess whom I carried until in the sight of all he brought forth the chalice ... The villagers then escorted the priests back to town, immediately chained them, and threw them into the local lock-up. (*The Golden Ass* 9.9–10)

Men were also involved in riots over food shortages, a common occurrence, in demonstrations against local magistrates during theater, racing, and gladiatorial contests, among local factions over just about anything, and as part of inter-town rivalries, the most famous of the latter being the riot in AD 59 after a gladiatorial contest between citizens of the neighboring towns of Pompeii and Nuceria, which I discuss in more detail later. When a riot really got out of control, especially in a large city like Rome or Alexandria or Antioch, the troops were called out. The important point is that ordinary men were constantly ready to express their anger in violent ways in a wide range of circumstances. While it is misleading to think of mob violence or riots as a daily event in their lives, the possibility was always there, and there was no hesitancy to join in the action.

In general, magical papyri offer reinforcement that the concerns I have outlined are the focus of ordinary people. Thus from dream interpretations, astrological charts, prayers, and incantations we can summarize that the commons desired a good life full of health, with enough resources to live decently, friends, good reputation, and a supportive family life with children. In dealings beyond the family, these people sought standing in the community, protection from enemies, victory over rivals whether they be in business, the law courts, or in love, and glory or good repute in their social circle. Their greatest fears involved life-changing circumstances, most especially ill health, robbery, death, poverty, or even slavery.

Life in the community

Out in their world, ordinary men led active social lives. Religious ceremonies and celebrations were important. The overtly social context of the festival of Isis as described in Apuleius' *Golden Ass* has townspeople in large numbers participating as individuals in the festival. Apuleius focuses on the sacred participants, but the intense activity of the general population at dawn before the main procession even begins, for example, and the ladening of Isis' ship with baskets of offerings by those participants alongside the uninitiated, illustrates the community-wide nature of such a celebration, and the enthusiasm for the rites at the temple all show the wide level of participation; after an exhilarating day, people return to their homes (11.8–18).

Likewise, days with public entertainment were social foci. Crowds assembled even before a display. There were preliminary entertainments such as pantomimes, and street vendors and performers were everywhere. And the main event focused the community and created a social bond. While sometimes this event was something bloody like a gladiatorial contest, often it was a theatrical or circus-like performance. The Pyrrhic Dance, pantomime, and popular drama described by Apuleius as preliminaries to the execution to follow are good examples of such popular displays (*The Golden Ass* 10.29–34).

Executions themselves provided yet another opportunity for assembling in public. In the case of Apuleius' account, this event is the coupling of an ass and a convicted woman, a comico-serious play on the normal punishment of being thrown to wild beasts. But any display would serve the same purpose of social integration. Typically, there would be a public feast the evening before the execution; a grand opportunity to gather, mingle, and get free food.

On the everyday level, associations played a very important role in social life outside the family. They typically had a common bond (household, profession, focus of interest), a geographical place of meeting, a religious purpose (at least nominally), obligations for burial of members, and a convivial aspect. The membership in associations was expansive. Household groups were common, and these might include not only freeborn members of the household but also slaves and freed slaves; women were also members. Associations based upon a religious focus could also be open to all – male, female, free, freed, and slaves. There were in addition professional associations whose focus was a production category – construction workers, for example. Finally, there were associations based only on geographical or ethnic commonality; these were open to free and freed, and sometimes to women.

Ordinary men as well as slaves and freedmen were the mainstay of associations. The elite had little or no need for such associations, except perhaps for participation in some religious ones. But although they did not participate as a rule in the regular meetings, associations often had wealthy patrons. These would be the local elite. Thus in addition to a 'horizontal' social function, associations also provided a 'vertical' means of adjusting to the severely hierarchical nature of society by linking these little groups to the power and influence only the elite held.

The social nature of associations could lead to trouble from the elite's point of view. The Roman government was always suspicious of clubs; for example, clubs in Pompeii evidently became caught up in the 'fandom' of gladiatorial games and had to be banned in the aftermath of riots centered on the games (Tacitus, *Annals* 14.17). The emperor Trajan emphasized the position of authority, stating that associations always turned 'political': 'Whatever title we give them, and whatever our object in giving it, men who are banded together for a common end will all the same become a political association before long' (Pliny, *Letters* 10.34). There is much modern discussion of the categories of associations, 'legitimate' and 'illegitimate,' what were 'authorized' and what were 'disapproved' by the State. Here it is important to emphasize that despite governmental suspicion and worse, the associations clearly continued widely and formed an important part of the social life of ordinary people.

Another valued social venue was the baths. Communal bathing – not swimming in a pool, but actual attempts to achieve cleanliness – is not a usual part of a modern's life. For the Roman population in towns and cities it was a fundamental part of daily existence. The famous and luxurious baths of Rome and large provincial cities are well known; much smaller facilities proliferated both in those cities and in smaller towns across the empire. While the elite could and did frequent these public places, they also had private bathing facilities of their own, or belonging to their friends, and so an alternative existed. Not so for the ordinary man. In the public baths he could find a combination of fitness gym, massage parlor, spa experience, and social rendezvous. In *The Golden Ass,* one of the first things Lucius does after he settles in with his host at Hypata and has seen that his horse is taken care of is to go to the local baths. A number of episodes in Petronius' *Satyricon* use the baths as a backdrop. Soldiers always had a bathing facility as part of their permanent camps; wealthy citizens bestowed baths on their fellow citizens in much-appreciated acts of generosity. As the forum was the focus and symbol of economic and legal life, the baths were the focus of communal social life. Here you found food and drink, friends and foes, political intrigue, neighborhood gossip, business tips, sex, and much, much else.

> Tiberius Claudius Secundus lived 52 years … Wine, sex, and the baths ruin our bodies but wine, sex, and the baths make our life good! Merope, freedwoman of Caesar, set this up to her dear mate, for herself, and for their descendants. (*CIL* 6.15258, Rome)

There were worries to accompany the good times. Assignations might not be successful. Adultery might occur at your expense. Your clothes might be stolen while you bathed, leaving you seething and cursing the thief. In Rome, this was such a problem that the Prefect of the City Guard was put in charge of doing something about it. He had:

… authority to make an investigation of attendants at the baths who look after bathers' clothing for a fee, if they act dishonestly in taking care of clothes. (*Digest* 1.15.3.5)

You might worry about your women going to the baths, for bad things could happen, as this formal complaint from Egypt documents:

From Hippalos son of Archis, public farmer from the village of

Euhemeria of the Themistos division. On the 6th Tybi, while my wife Aplounous and her mother Thermis were bathing, Eudaimonis daughter of Protarchos, and Etthytais daughter of Pees, and Deios son of Ammonios, and Heraklous attacked them, and gave my wife Aplounous and her mother in the village bath-house many blows all over her body so that she is laid up in bed, and in the fray she lost a gold earring weighing three quarters, a bracelet of unstamped metal weighing 16 drachmas, a bronze bowl worth 12 drachmas; and Thermis her mother lost a gold earring weighing two and a half quarters, and … (Rowlandson, no. 254)

But the fellowship of the baths was an indispensable, positive part of the social life of ordinary men.

As we picture this social venue, crowded as it was with men (women usually had separate hours), we unthinkingly set beside it the shiny marble of the Baths of Caracalla in Rome or the splendor of Cluny in Paris and imagine this as a sign of grand Roman civilization. There was an element of this, of course; who would not have been impressed with the grandest of these establishments? But this should not blind us to the reality that for the ordinary and elite alike the baths offered not only social interaction but a dangerous lack of hygiene shocking even to contemplate. We do not know how often the water was changed, but there is no indication that this happened frequently. There was no 'prewash'; rather, the lathering with oil and then scraping off of the same as a cleansing action prior to bathing just meant that the removed material was swept by some bath maintenance person into the pool. Although latrines were sometimes available, apparently some folks just used the pool:

The most dangerous and dreaded thing of all would be to defecate in the temple of a god or in the marketplace or in a public street or bath. For this portends the wrath of the gods and great disgrace and severe loss. In addition often the person who dreams becomes the object of hatred, and his hidden things are revealed. (*Dreams* 2.26)

In short, whatever dirt, grime, bodily fluids, expulsions, and germs people brought with them to the baths, the water quickly shared with other bathers. Especially in the warm bathing room the bacterial count must have been astronomical. Although this entire combination surely spread contagious diseases, there is no indication that anyone realized any danger at all. In fact, a standard recommendation by doctors was to 'take the baths,' so diseased persons were actually encouraged (as we know now) to spread their afflictions to others, all the while acquiring new illness from the waters meant to cure them. Although on occasion even emperors shared the public baths with ordinary people, one at least probably stayed away. Marcus Aurelius caught the ugliness of the bathing process when he wrote:

> What does bathing look like to you? Oil, nasty refuse, sludgy water, everything disgusting. (*Meditations* 8.24)

The scene at the baths was also loud and chaotic. Artemidorus notes that dreaming of singing in the baths is bad luck; dreaming of baths themselves some thought was bad luck too, because all the raucous noise indicated turmoil in life. The elite Seneca eloquently complains of this as he imagines trying to work in an apartment above a public bath:

> Behold! On every side all kinds of uproar sound. I live above a public bathing establishment. Imagine now for yourself all the wide range of noises that are enough to make me sorry my ears can hear at all. One time I hear body-builders exercising, pumping their arms, holding heavy lead weights, sweating it out – or pretending to; I hear grunts and groans at the lift, whenever they stop holding their breath, I hear wheezes and sharp breathing. Then I have to endure some lazy fellow, happy with his cheap oil rub-down; I hear the noise of hands smacking his shoulders, the varying sounds as now the flat, now the cupped hand slaps away. Yet more – if the ball player adds to the bedlam by starting to count his score at the top of his lungs, it's all over! Add to this the vulgar people shouting at each other, the thief caught in the act, and that fellow who just loves to hear his singing resonate through the bathhouse – along with other singers, too, who at least have decent voices. And still more! Those fellows who cannonball into the pool, hitting the water with an horrendously loud splash! Besides, just think about those slaves who pluck armpits going about

advertising themselves with their continuous, squeaky, shrill shouts – they never stop, unless actually plucking an armpit – and making someone *else* scream instead. And amid all this are the mixed and confused shouts of the many vendors – the cake seller, the sausage hawker, the confectioner, and food purveyors, all pushing their wares with distinctive cries. [Meanwhile, outside the apartment, I mark] carriages rattling by, clangs from a neighboring workshop, a nearby saw-sharpening service at work, and to top it all off, a pipe and flute seller who can't sing, so he just shouts everything out. (*Letters* 56.1, 2)

Trying to put this reality out of our heads, I return to the main point: the baths were social gathering places for ordinary men and, indeed, for their families as well. Children could and did frequent at least some baths with their parents. An epitaph from Rome tells a sad story:

Daphnus and Chryseis, freedpersons of Laco, set this gravestone up to their dear Fortunatus. He lived 8 years. He perished in the pool at the Baths of Mars. (*CIL* 6.16740)

And it is probably echoed in another, made, sadly, by the stone carver himself:

I, most unlucky father, carved this for my boy who, poor soul, perished in the pool. He lived 3 years and 6 months. (*CIL* 9.6318, Chieti, Italy)

Although this was not the norm by any means, women even sometimes bathed with the men. Pompeius Catussa set up a touching epitaph:

To the Gods of the Underworld and the everlasting memory of Blandinia Martiola, a most pure girl who lived 18 years, 9 months, and 5 days. Pompeius Catussa, a Sequanian citizen, a plasterer, set this monument up to an incomparable wife, most kind to me, who lived with me 5 years, 6 months and 18 days without any base reproach, and to himself while still alive. You who read this, go to the Baths of Apollo to bathe, a thing which I did with my wife. How I wish I could do it still! (*CIL* 13.1983 = *ILS* 8158, Lyon, France)

Leaving home or an association meeting or the baths, the ordinary man went out into the street expecting to enter a busy, noisy world. Much of his life was spent outside, as was the life of everyone else in society. He found what he needed, especially food, in the stalls or spread out on mats which were set up not only in the few open spaces, but along any street; these complemented the relatively few actual shops where goods were sold. Weaving in and out of the crowds, beggars accosted him, street musicians played or sang for handouts, teachers tried to keep the attention of their pupils amid the loud hum, street philosophers, sooth-sayers, magicians, and assorted accosters plied their trade.

> And we often see how even in the midst of a very great turmoil and throng the individual is not hampered in carrying on his own occupation; but, on the contrary, the man who is playing the flute or teaching a pupil to play it devotes himself to that, often holding school in the very street, and the crowd does not distract him at all, or the din made by the passers-by; and the dancer likewise, or dancing master, is engrossed in his work, being utterly heedless of those who are fighting and selling and doing other things; and so also with the harper and the painter. But here is the most extreme case of all: The elementary teachers sit in the streets with their pupils and nothing hinders them in this great throng from teaching and learning. And I remember once seeing, while walking through the Hippodrome, many people on one spot and each doing something different: one playing the flute, another dancing, another doing a juggler's trick, another reading a poem aloud, another singing, and another telling some story or myth; and yet not a single one of them prevented anyone else from attending to his own business and doing the work that he had in hand. (Dio Chrysostom, *Discourses* 20.9–10/Cohoon)

The society of the street was crucial. Even if one had a business, and certainly if, as was very widely the case, a person was underemployed and had lots of time on his hands on a regular basis, visits to the local tavern were a daily affair. One vignette must suffice. Wall paintings from the Tavern of the Seven Sages in Ostia illustrate the humor of the men in such places. The tavern was an unexceptional 'local'; there were no pretensions to architectural or other grandeur. The Seven Sages were favorites of the elite; they were often illustrated with busts, quotations, and so on in house decoration. But the paintings in the tavern have the Seven Sages of antiquity uttering scatological advice; the humans who are painted relieving themselves mimic this in earthy pictorial language. Education was one of the marks of the elite, along with birth and wealth. Although education was accessible to the ordinary man – and the sayings of the Seven Sages had permeated to the level of popular philosophy – nevertheless, ridicule of 'highfalutin' education clearly struck a chord. On the vault of the tavern, expensive wines are illustrated. Obviously, ostentatious wealth is the target of the humor. Although 'birth' is not singled out for ridicule, it went hand in glove with the other two marks of the elite. I am reminded of the fable of the Battle of the Mice and the Weasels; illustrations of this fable were a favorite decoration of taverns, as Phaedrus tell us. In it, weasels and mice were constantly at war, with the weasels always winning. The mice decided that what they needed was an elite leadership, so they chose the strongest, wisest, bravest, and those of noblest blood to take over and train the mouse army. Once the new elite had done its best in reorganizing and training their army, the mice declared war on the weasels. The mouse generals bound their heads with straw to stand out from the common herd. Immediately as it began, the battle turned against the mice, who broke rank and fled en masse for the protection of their underground homes. Unfortunately, the large straw 'plumes' of the leaders kept those mice from disappearing into mouseholes – they were to a mouse caught and eaten by the weasels (Babrius 31, Phaedrus 4.6). This fable's content, surely known to the viewers, mocked the arrogance, not to say stupidity and uselessness, of those of high birth.

Life in the bars and taverns was lively. There was food as well as drink, and women were often available. Dice games broke out there or on the street; conversations with neighbors and strangers about local events and politics and gossip entered the general hubbub. This personal interaction kept a man connected with his community and up to date (whether with good or bad information) on situations and events that might affect him.

The street also provided the venue for learning and making use of what was learned. With books being mostly an expensive luxury of the wealthy, literature of all levels was purveyed orally. Poets on corners and in parks recited to anyone who would listen. All of this provided men with opportunities for entertainment ranging from the crazy on the corner to discussion of serious politics, at least in the first centuries of the empire when many towns elected their magistrates. While the local elite controlled these offices and the local council made up of ex-magistrates, their actions affected ordinary people. Besides day-to-day interactions, these men and especially the aediles were responsible for public benefactions such as bread distribution, and putting on public entertainments such as gladiatorial shows and theatrical productions. So for both economic and social reasons, people were invested. However, just as in Rome itself the popular voting assemblies ceased to have real power during the empire, so, too, in towns the local assemblies lost out to an increasingly powerful entrenched ruling class.

Despite this long-term trend, in the moment many ordinary men were involved in political campaigning and voting. The many electoral graffiti from Pompeii vividly demonstrate the political life of men, both their seriousness and their sense of humor about it:

I ask that you make Gaius Julius Polybius Aedile. He supplies good bread! (*CIL* 4.429 = *ILS* 6412e)

(Vote for) Marcus Casellius Marcellus, a good Aedile who puts on terrific games. (*CIL* 4.999)

Proculus, make Sabinus Aedile and he will make you one too. (*CIL* 4.635 = *ILS* 6436)

Other notices show a bit of humor:

The pickpockets want Vatia as Aedile (*CIL* 4.576 = *ILS* 6418f)

I beg you to elect Marcus Cerrinius Vatia Aedile. The late drinkers all ask it! Florus and Fructus wrote this. (*CIL* 4.581 = *ILS* 6418d)

The dice gamblers urge for Gnaeus Helvius Sabinus. (*CIL* 4.3485)

Economic groups supported candidates:

The united fruit mongers with Helvius Vestalis urge you to make Marcus Holconius Priscus duumvir with judiciary powers. (*CIL* 4.202 = *ILS* 6411a)

The millers ask you to vote for Gnaeus Helvius Sabinus for Aedile; the people who live nearby want this too! (*CIL* 4.7273)

As did religious groups:

All the worshippers of Isis urge you to vote for Gnaeus Helvius Sabinus for Aedile. (*CIL* 4.787 = *ILS* 6420b)

Geographically related persons banded together:

His neighbors urge you to vote for Marcus Lucretius Fronto as Aedile. (*CIL* 4.6625)

I urge you, O neighbors, to elect Lucius Statius Receptus Chief Magistrate with Judicial Powers, a man worthy of your votes. Aemilius Celer wrote this, your neighbor. Whoever hatefully destroys this, a pox on you! (*CIL* 4.3775 = *ILS* 6409)

The people living around the Forum ask that you vote for … (*CIL* 4.783)

Even women, although they could not vote, put in their word:

Elect Gnaeus Helvius Sabinus Aedile. Junia asks this. (*CIL* 4.1168)

It is hard to tell how many graffiti represent actual popular sentiment, because large numbers seem to be professionally written; since elections were yearly, graffiti needed to be put up regularly, and clearly there were hired electoral gangs set to work for each new campaign. But still it is fair to say that at the very least men were aware of the elections and talked about them in baths and bars; many probably participated both in the electioneering and in the actual voting, which itself was a festive occasion, with food and drink handed out. As time went on, this political activity probably waned, but although varying from place to place throughout the empire, it was an important thing for men to think about, especially since the elected officials could influence their daily lives. While political activity lasted, the street was an important venue for discussion and advertisement.

Conclusion

The ordinary lives of ordinary men in Rome and its empire were filled with family, business, socializing, and cares and concerns common to much of humanity. The poet Horace, son of a freedman father, captures this:

> His name is Volteius Mena, an auctioneer, quite poor, free from scandal, hardworking when that's called for, easy going when it's not, knows both how to make money and how to spend it, taking pleasure in his inconsequential club-mates, his own humble home, and the games in the Campus Martius after concluding his business. (*Letters* 1.7.55–9)

In many ways, life for ordinary men was different in degree or kind from the lives of the elite. The two could not help interacting and they did, engaging in business and legal issues and voicing their concerns through violence if necessary. But their world and their attitudes reflected the reality of their own existence in close relationship to freedmen, slaves, and ordinary women. They forged their way, following their own moral compasses, fearing and hoping, and putting their trust in superstition, magic, and religion to help make sense of and control their challenging world.

2

LIVES OF THEIR OWN: ORDINARY WOMEN

ROMANO-GRECIAN WOMEN LIVED IN A WORLD dominated by a very clear male view of them and their place, a view formulated by the elite for themselves, but shared widely by ordinary men as well. However it worked itself out in real life, the ideal is well expressed by John Chrysostom, who in describing the division of male and female focus in the community reflects thinking throughout classical antiquity:

A woman's whole role is to care for children, for her husband, and for her home ... For human activity is divided into two spheres, one pertaining to life outside the home, and one to life within it; as we might say, 'public,' and 'private.' God assigned a role to each sex; women have the care of the home, men of public affairs, business, legal and military activities – indeed, all life outside the home. For a woman cannot let loose a spear, or shoot an arrow; rather she can do the spinning, weave fabric, take on all the other domestic tasks – and do them splendidly. She is not able to speak in the town council, but can speak her piece regarding household matters. In fact, she often has a better grasp of the needs of the home than the husband does. Although she can't perform public duties, it is a beautiful thing to raise up fine children, who are the light of our lives. She is able to discipline female slaves who need it, and to keep the entire household on the right track. She removes all concerns and frees her

husband from all worries as she takes care of the larder, wool spinning, cooking and clothing needs, and all the other tasks unsuitable
for husbands. In fact, she can do these better than a husband could,
even if he tried to take over these tasks. (*The Kind of Women Who
Ought to be Taken as Wives*, 4)

Within this ideal, the Romano-Grecian world inserted the affirmation of the physical and mental inferiority of women into every possible interstice of life. Few males would have disagreed with Plautus
when he wrote in his play *The Bacchae* (41), *Miserius nihil est quam mulier*
('Nothing is more miserable than a woman'). So deep was the feeling
that only men were worthy that it could generate a scene such as that
in the noncanonical Gospel of Thomas, where Mary the mother of Jesus
must become a man in order to succeed:

Simon Peter says to them: 'Let Mary go away from us, for women
are not worthy of The Life. To this Jesus replies: Behold, I myself
shall fill her with the Spirit and so make her male, in order that she
shall also become a Living Spirit like you males. For every female
who becomes male shall enter the Kingdom of Heaven.' (Thomas
114)

In Artemidorus, there is often misogyny, such as the male being
associated with the right, female with the left (*Dreams* 1.21); or dreams
of changing from male to female being bad (*Dreams* 1.50). In general,
the dream interpretations and astrological charts are steadfastly male-
oriented and referenced. Men pervasively assumed that women were
weak and needed protection from financial or physical manipulation.
They were thought to be physically weak; to be disabled by child-bear-
ing; to be inexperienced (which of course they were, in 'men' things);
dependent on male relatives or guardians for actions regarding property, law, etc.; gossipy, emotionally unstable, fickle, vulnerable, and
libidinous.

Nonetheless, within this male analysis, women's actions and attitudes are also praised. The exchange between Aurelia and her husband
Aurelius is one of the most touching in Latin epigraphy. The husband
speaks:

I am Lucius Aurelius Hermia, freedman of Lucius, a butcher working on the Viminal Hill. This woman, Aurelia Philematio, freedwoman of Lucius, who went before me in death, my one and only wife, chaste of body, faithfully loving a faithful husband, lived equal in devotion with no selfishness taking her from her duty.

There is an image of Aurelia looking lovingly at Aurelius. Aurelia answers:

This is Aurelia Philematio, freedwoman of Lucius. I alive was called Aurelia Philematio, chaste, modest, ignorant of the foul ways of the crowd, faithful to my husband. He was my fellow freedman, the same now torn from me – alas! He was in truth and indeed like and more than a father to me. He took me on his lap a mere 7 years old – now after 40 years I am dead. He flourished in all his doings among men on account of my faithful and firm devotion. (*CIL* 1.01221 = *CIL* 6.9499 = *ILS* 7472, Rome)

Aurelia Philematio exemplifies an ideal woman when she is praised for her modesty, excellence, moral uprightness, and loyalty; she expresses these ideals herself, but since her husband outlived her and set up the gravestone we can assume the sentiments are his, although she may well have shared them. In Richmond Lattimore's collection of Greek and Roman epitaphs, women are most often typified as beautiful, lovable (dear, sweet, lacking in quarrelsomeness), fertile, chaste, and keeping the house well. The core values of women in epitaphs are thus loyalty, chastity, and hard work. And certainly they must know their place; they are not to be uppity in the presence of men. Rather they should 'learn in silence with all submissiveness. I permit no woman to teach or to have authority over men; she is to keep silent' (1 Timothy 2:11).

A woman was a means to an end, and she probably thought of herself in this way. The end was a family unit that would provide heirs and thus a way to pass on property. Although there were ancillary possibilities for activity (in commerce, for example), any woman who would have and could have chosen one of these as her primary goal in life was a *rara avis* indeed. As I move into the world of women it is well to recall that their outlooks as expressed in their own words – their individual subjectivity – is lacking in almost all of our literary and archaeological sources. Epitaphs (if we allow ourselves to believe that some are actually composed by women themselves) and papyrological material are the main exceptions. But even in these I do not find opposition to the male views or alternatives to the male positioning of women in society and culture. Although our modern sensitivities find this situation somewhat unsettling, the response should not be speculation about secret desires and aspirations to liberation which lie forever hidden from us, but rather consideration that there were no such secret desires or aspirations at all. So far as we know or, on comparative evidence, can even readily imagine, there were no alternative lifestyles and aspirations either offered or considered – no inkling that Romano-Grecian women ever conceived of a world different from the one they were born into, ever had a thought-basis from which to consider alternative arrangements. The prudent way to proceed is to assume that women accepted their what to us might seem oppressed condition and sought to live it out in the most satisfying way possible, sometimes pushing the limits, most often living within them, sometimes rebelling against them, but never overthrowing them. Within this conceptual framework we can construct a useful and realistic picture of ordinary women and their mind worlds.

It is true that women did not participate in the classic elements of public life. They did not have legal standing; they could not vote and were excluded de facto from advanced education. But on the other hand, as we look at women living according to the elite and male model, but in their own realities, we will see women functioning well in a much wider world than the elite picture presents. Their letters from Egypt show women in charge and women with strong minds. They do not show women as shrinking violets or left to house management, cooped up in a women's quarter. Indeed it is regrettable that these letters actually tell little of many things such as 'secret' thoughts might reveal. Their often elliptical nature gives the sense that the authors do not want others who might read the letter to know what exactly is being talked about. There is little of the 'sharing' that goes on in the letters of Cicero, for example. But the general impression is one of women in charge of their lives in a positive, proactive way.

Women appear outside the house on a routine basis. They shop. They run errands. They participate in public religious ceremonies. They also make their presence known in the fairly frequent public disturbances. Philo in railing against just such activity testifies to women taking part in street riots:

> If any woman, hearing that her husband is being assaulted, being out of her affection for him carried away by love for her husband, should yield to the feelings which overpower her and rush forth to aid him, still let her not be so audacious as to behave like a man, outrunning the nature of a woman; but even while aiding him let her continue a woman. For it would be a very terrible thing if a woman, being desirous to deliver her husband from an insult, should expose herself to insult, by exhibiting human life as full of shamelessness and liable to great reproaches for her incurable boldness; for shall a woman utter abuse in the marketplace and give vent to unlawful language? … But as it is now, some women are advanced to such a pitch of shamelessness as not only, though they are women, to give vent to intemperate language and abuse among a crowd of men, but even to strike men and insult them, with hands practiced rather in works of the loom and spinning than in blows and assaults, like competitors in the *pancratium* or wrestlers. And other things, indeed, may be tolerable, and what any one might easily bear, but that is a shocking thing if a woman were to proceed to such a degree of boldness as to seize hold of the genitals of one of the men quarreling. For let not such a woman be let go on the ground that she appears to have done this action in order to assist her own husband; but let her be impeached and suffer the punishment due to her excessive audacity, so that if she should ever be inclined to commit the same offence again she may not have an opportunity of doing so; and other women, also, who might be inclined to be precipitate, may be taught by fear to be moderate and to restrain themselves. (Philo, *Special Laws* 172–5/Yonge)

Of course there was a wide variety of public experience according to local customs. Some women were more stay-at-home than others, and customs in such things as dress varied as well, for we know that in some places women went out veiled (Petronius, *Satyricon* 14, 16) and in others even complete body covering was the norm. In all things women needed to be careful not to cross the boundaries of 'decency'; for example, although women attended religious gatherings with their husbands, Paul instructs them not to speak, but rather to wait until they get home to ask them about things (1 Corinthians 14:33–5). But in the end in households with few or no slaves, and these households were many, it was simply impractical to sequester women away from the world. They would have needed to be out in the market buying and perhaps even selling, and taking care of household needs. Even in her own home she was not sealed off. The writer of the letter of Timothy states that preachers get 'into households and capture weak women. Burdened with sins and swayed by various impulses, she will listen to anybody and can never arrive at a knowledge of the truth' (2 Timothy 3:3–7). Evidently, a woman's life exposed her to a fairly broad spectrum of experiences.

Fundamentally, the vast majority of women were committed to making a household and family successful. The oft-repeated ideal of spinning wool and keeping a good house corresponds to the norm in pre-industrial societies in general. Although there were some other options available, every girl was taught from the youngest age that marriage was the future to be expected and desired, along with children. When a woman internalized this teaching, she gained a certain steadiness in her life, and if she stuck to it would find reassuring guidance, examples, and precedents in dealing with any problems she encountered. As she matured from a young bride to mother to 'elder matron', gaining in age and experience, things valued in the culture, her influence within the household gradually increased. Throughout her life, however, legal and customary standards did mark her off from the world that males knew. As previously noted, she had no legal standing and so a guardian was needed except in unusual circumstances if she was to engage in public transactions such as making a will, a sales contract, or other legal obligation, as in the case of Aurelia Ammonaion from Oxyrhynchus:

> [request] To Gaius Valerius Firmus, Prefect of Egypt, from Aurelia Ammonaion. I ask you, my lord, to give me as guardian Aurelius Ploutammon in accordance with the *lex Iulia et Titia* and the Decree of the Senate. Dated in the consulship of our lords Philippus Augustus for the second time and Philippus Caesar. (AD 247)

[response] In order that ... may not be absent, I appoint Ploutammon as guardian in accordance with the *lex Iulia et Titia*. I have read this. (Rowlandson, no. 140)

Escape from this legal disability came with three children (four if a freedwoman). An educated woman, Aurelia Thaisous, petitions for this right:

... [Laws long ago have been made], most eminent Prefect, which empower women who possess the right of three children to be mistresses of themselves and act without a guardian in whatever business they transact, especially those who know how to write [in actuality, a legal irrelevancy]. Accordingly, as I too enjoy the happy honor of being blessed with children and as I am a literate woman able to write with a high degree of ease, it is with abundant security that I appeal to your highness by this my application with the object of being enabled to accomplish without hindrance whatever business I henceforth transact, and I beg you to keep it without prejudice to my rights in your eminence's office, in order that I may obtain your support and acknowledge my unfailing gratitude. Farewell. I, Aurelia Thaisous also called Lolliane, have sent this presentation. Year 10, Epheiph 21.

[response] Your application shall be kept in the [office, i.e. 'on file']. (Rowlandson, no. 142)

But the combination of child mortality, ignorance of legal rights, and a heavy male hand must often have discouraged thinking in these terms.

Marriage and sex

Even at the lower end of the stratum I am calling 'ordinary,' the culturally embedded desire to have children in order to continue a family and the need of a helpmate to enhance survival chances pushed men and women to marriage. This relationship is illustrated by a dream interpreted by Artemidorus: 'If a man changes into a woman it is fortunate for a poor man ... for he will have someone to take care of him, as a woman does. ...' (*Dreams* 1.50). That women shared the desire for marriage with men can be seen from one of the questions posed in the *Predictions of Astrampsychos*: 'Am I going to marry and is it profitable for me?' (Rowlandson, no. 247). Women sought to know what sort of husband they would have. *Carmen* 2.3–4 lists through various nativities the sort of husband(s) a woman might end up with: no marriage at all; a series of husbands; an old man; 'her grandfather or paternal uncle or maternal uncle or one of those possessing relationship to her'; an overbearing man; a stranger soldier; a man well known in his town; a philanderer. Although marriage was the goal, married life itself might hold 'disgrace, debauchery, and destruction,' and divorce might be sought owing to alcoholism or deceit and quarreling. But such possibilities would not have curbed the desire to marry in the first place.

Some might even pursue an unwilling man and marry him:

A man dreamed he was being pursued by a woman whom he had known for a long time; she was trying to wrap him up in a cloak – the one called a paenula in Latin – ripped down the middle seam. Finally, very unwillingly he was overcome. This woman, being in love with the man, married him against his will. After a few years she divorced him – all foreseen by the rent cloak. (Artemidorus, *Dreams* 5.29)

And she might use magic to reach her goal:

(I bind) Aritokudes and the women who will be seen with him. May he not marry any other woman or young maiden [than me]. (Gager, no. 23)

I invoke you, who shook the entire world, who breaks the back of mountains and casts them up out of the water, who causes the whole earth to tremble and then renews all its inhabitants. I invoke you, who make signs in the heaven, on earth and on sea, to bring Urbanus, to whom Urbana gave birth, and unite him as husband with Domitiana, to whom Candida gave birth, loving her, sleepless with desire for her, begging for her, and asking that she return to his house and become his wife ... (Gager, no. 36)

In order for marriage to be legal for a Roman citizen it had to have four elements: both partners needed to be free, without legal restrictions that prevented marriage, to be of the age of puberty, and to have the consent of relevant parties (i.e. the man, the woman, and their parents). There was no requirement to seek authoritative permission or to register a marriage with any official or even to have any religious ceremony or communal celebration (although both usually occurred).

An essential part of every marriage was the dowry; for ordinary people the amounts were often absolutely small, but presumably appreciable within their local economy. For example, Jane Rowlandson offers a number of Egyptian documents: no. 252 gives a dowry for what appears to be an 'apparently humble village family' wedding valued (in clothing and jewelry) at 200 drachma; no. 127 has a contract with about the same value of dowry in jewelry and dress; no. 128 amounts to 200 drachma, and a 'house and lot' are to be sold to raise this amount when the wife demands its return; no. 129 has something over 240 drachma in clothing, jewelry, and 120 drachma in cash; no. 132 seems to be just 72 drachma in (informal) dowry. Compare the dowry of an elite (no. 141), which amounts to half a talent of gold in goods, jewelry worth 1500 drachma, clothing valued at 5000 drachma, and 4 talents and 2000 drachma in cash.

As a dowry had to be returned in the case of divorce, it provided some little leverage over the husband, who often needed these resources and/or hoped to inherit them. Thus a woman was understandably possessive of these dowries. She might go into a rage over misuse by her husband: 'the bride's dowry is damaged, and she will be furious with him like the burning of fire because of women, and the marriage will be with this thing' (*Carmen* 2.1). And a wife was not slow to demand (or just take back) a dowry in divorce disputes. In Plautus' play *Aulularia*, Megadorus goes on and on about how wives with dowries control and order about their husbands, and he praises the idea of no dowries in order to keep women in their place (*Pot of Gold* 475ff.).

Although a dowry might provide some leverage in a marriage relationship, a woman was almost always under some male's authority. Before marriage it was her father's; after marriage, it is not clear whose authority the wife was normally under, husband's or father's, but the usual living arrangement was for the wife to move in with the husband.

3. Affection in marriage. Aurelius Hermia and his wife Aurelia Philematio describe a beautiful marriage relationship on her tombstone: 'This is Aurelia Philematio, freedwoman of Lucius. I alive was called Aurelia Philematio, chaste, modest, ignorant of the foul ways of the crowd, faithful to my husband. He was my fellow freedman, the same now torn from me – alas! He was in truth and indeed like and more than a father to me. He took me on his lap a mere 7 years old – now after 40 years I am dead. He flourished in all his doings among men on account of my faithful and firm devotion.' (*CIL* 1.01221 = *CIL* 6.9499 = *ILS* 7472, Rome)

Would she have worried about competing authorities? Artemidorus gives the interpretation of the following dream: 'A man dreamed that his sister was dragged away from her husband by her father and given to another in marriage' (*Dreams* 5.43). If this were not possible in real life, the dream would have no meaning to the interpreter. But how common was this? Rowlandson, no. 138, gives a case of a father claiming under Egyptian law the right to take back his daughter, now married, against her will. The Roman authorities reject this as too harsh, however – and note that as they are under Egyptian (i.e. Greek) law, not Roman, *patria potestas* (the absolute power of a father under Roman law) is not recognized. In the petition, the wife claims to have presented documents 'all proving that women who have attained maturity are mistresses of their own persons, and can remain with their husbands or not as they choose;

and … are they not subject to their fathers …' One of the prefects being appealed to ruled, 'The decisive question is with whom the married woman wishes to live.' It would seem that tradition was on the side of women de facto lying under the control of their husbands, not of their fathers, and that once married, the husband's home became practically irrevocably her own.

Although love could be a part of a marriage, romantic love was not an essential and perhaps usually not any part of that relationship. Romantic love was looked upon with suspicion, masking true nature, as in the fable of the 'weasel as bride':

> A weasel fell madly in love with a handsome man. Aphrodite, mother of all desires, granted her wish to be changed into the form of a woman so beautiful that it would be impossible for him not to love her. The instant the man of her choice saw her, he was consumed by a violent passion and desired to take her for his wife. The wedding feast was well underway when a mouse scooted by. The bride jumped from her luxurious couch and began to chase after it. The wedding feast ended in an uproar. Love had played out his jest well. But he left, beaten by basic Nature. (Babrius 32)

Gnomic utterances also disparage romantic love as misleading. It is hard to know whether the passionate graffiti of Pompeii represent romantic love or masculine conquest; for example 'Vibius Restitutus lay here alone and yearned for his Urbana' (*CIL* 4.2146) – but, if the same Restitutus, it wasn't only Urbana he longed for: 'Restitutus often deceived many girls' (*CIL* 4.5251). Whatever young swains wrote on walls, marriage was too important to be left to romantic whims; family continuity and property were at stake, even in poor families, and certainly among ordinary folk.

Although the basic expectation for women in proverbs and elsewhere in popular literature is to be the focus of family – and they are denied any role outside that unit (for example they are ridiculed as being un-soldierlike) – marriage itself could involve a whole gamut of experiences for both husband and wife. The ideal was a life without conflict, one in which there was never a quarrel; this is attested on many, many tombstones, such as:

> This is the gravestone Gaius Aonius Vitalis set up for Atilia Maxi-
> mina, she of purest spirit, an incomparable wife, who lived with
> me without any quarrels for 18 years, 2 months, and 9 days, having
> lived 46 years, leading a life of honor and good name, my everlasting
> solace. Farewell. (*CIL* 5.3496 = *ILS* 8457, Verona, Italy)

Or this:

> Pompullius Antiochus, her husband, set up this gravestone to Cae-
> cilia Festiva, his dearest, sweet wife, hard-working and well-deserv-
> ing, who lived with me 21 years without a contrary word. (*CIL* 9.3215
> = *ILS* 8433, Corfinio, Italy)

A marriage contract from Egypt indicates monogamy on both sides, respect, sharing of responsibilities, and so on. Ideally, then, there was respect, if not love, mutual cooperation, as well as fidelity on both sides of the marriage. But, in fact, strifeless marriage was often not on the cards: Artemidorus notes that a man dreaming of marriage 'portends upheavals and scandals. For marriage cannot be conducted without disorder' (*Dreams* 2.65). The *Carmen* makes this clear too, as Dorotheus' nativities predict such things as a man marrying an agreeable wife, happiness for the father of a child, or, conversely, 'disaster and disgrace because of women and anxiety and grief because of them.' Or perhaps the wife will turn out to be a whore, or a sign 'indicates the badness of the marriage from men and women so that his life will revolve in grief and misery because of women …' (*Carmen* 2.1).

Despite the overtly male-dominated nature of marriage, women were active partners and certainly not pushed into the background. The wife's basic duty was to maintain the house, including foodstuffs and clothing, and raise the children. This expectation carries over into Christianity. Around AD 200, St. Clement notes that a woman 'is destined for pregnancy and housekeeping' (*Miscellanies* (*Stromata*) 4.8.58.2–60.1 – Rowlandson, no. 51). But a wife had many expectations beyond or intertwined with home management and child-rearing. Most of all, she was expected to uphold certain standards. In Plautus' *Amphitryon* he has Alcmena say:

As for me, I don't think of my 'dowry' the way it is commonly conceived. I think of it as modesty, a sense of shame and controlled desires, fear of the gods, love of parents, harmony with relatives, compliance with your wishes, ever ready to do good to others, ever useful in praiseworthy deeds.

SOSIA: Good God! If she is speaks truly, she is a paradigm of the very best. (*Amphitryon* 839–43)

There is exaggeration for comedic effect, but the portrait is essentially the same as the one we see on epitaphs of excellent women. Chastity was particularly praised. An inscription from Rome speaks for numerous evocations of the high value placed on a wife's moral uprightness:

Titus Flavius Flavianus set up this monument to Papinia Felicitas who lived 25 years, 5 months, and 25 days. She was a wife most virtuous and chaste, incomparable among women. (*CIL* 6.23773 = *ILS* 8441, Rome)

Or this from North Africa:

Postumia Matronilla was an incomparable wife, a good mother, a devoted grandmother, chaste, devout, hard working, frugal, efficient, watchful, responsive, life-long partner to one man only, whose bed alone she ever shared, a matron full of industry and good faith, who lived 53 years, 5 months, and 3 days. (*CIL* 8.11294 = *ILS* 8444, Zaatli, Jabal az,Tunisia)

Household management is exemplified by Papinia's inscription as well, with her efficiency and frugality praised along with other virtues; her loving care within the family always had to be foremost in a good wife's mind. Although presumably some ordinary men adorned their women as advertisements of their wealth, as the elite did, modesty usually included dressing in an appropriate manner. Women were urged to 'adorn themselves modestly and sensibly in seemly apparel, not with braided hair or gold or pearls or costly attire …' (1 Timothy 2:9; see also 1 Peter 3:3–4). And last but certainly not least, a wife was to maintain good relations with her husband. Beyond the banal 'we never had a quarrel' of the ideal conjugal pair, the picture of a wife's place was clearly one of submission to her husband. Artemidorus says that wives are bad when they 'bark or bite' (*Dreams* 2.11), i.e. talk back to their husband/master. 'Likewise [i.e. like the slaves relating to their masters] you wives, be submissive to your husbands …' advises the male author of 1 Peter 3:1. However, the husband was not to take advantage of this submission, but rather was to be considerate of his wife; he urges men to 'live considerately with your wives, bestowing honor on the woman as the weaker sex …' (1 Peter 3:7).

Not only is she to uphold standards, she is to teach younger women and children to do so. Older women are to teach younger the proper way to behave, namely to love their husbands, children, be sensible, chaste, domestic, kind, and submissive to their husbands – see Titus 2:4.

The traditional elite view was that Roman marriage was a cold relationship arranged by adults for their children, its purpose and heart being procreation and the protection of family resources and influence; within this the wife 'lay back and thought of Rome,' while the man exercised his sexual virility not just on her, but also on concubines, whores, and slave girls. This view never quite fit with the expressions of a warm, sustaining family life found in funeral inscriptions and elsewhere outside the elite's literary constructs – or even, in some instances, within those constructs. But still, even though there is no direct access to the Roman marital bed, it is possible to say with a fair degree of confidence that in social and religious conventions alike the purpose of sex in marriage was less enjoyment than procreation.

Nevertheless, sex is certainly a normal part of a woman's life in marriage. It reflected the dominant/submissive cultural pattern of that institution, but within that habit was the possibility, even the necessity, that a wife would be a good sexual partner. If the literary version of a wedding song composed by the elite poet Catullus captures the actual, normal essence of advice for the bride, her submissive sexual role is clear: 'Bride make sure that you do not deny what your husband asks for, or he will go elsewhere to seek it' (*Poems* 61.147.49). Artemidorus confirms this attitude for ordinary people:

> To have intercourse with one's willing and submissive wife – one not

reluctant regarding sex – this is a good thing in the judgment of all. For the wife represents for the one who dreams the craft or profession from which he derives pleasure, or over which he rules, as also he controls his wife. For the dream portends profit from such things, as men on the one hand take pleasure in the acts of Aphrodite, and, on the other, take pleasure in making a profit. But if a wife is reluctant or does not offer herself, this is a sign of the opposite. (*Dreams* 1.78)

It is easy to imagine 'old wives' advising young brides to do what the husband wants, 'men will be men' – an acknowledgment of the psychological element of sex in marriage along with the procreative aspect. The raw explicitness of assumedly chaste females' exposure to male sexuality, whether in rituals such as the Lupercalia or the genitalia greeting them as they shared the male baths in the ritual of the Virile Fortune (Ovid, *Fasti* 133–56), was a reminder that the male was the master and creator, the female the receptacle; submissive she must be.

Overt allusions to sex were found all around. In Pompeii, for example, the notice 'here lies happiness' (*hic habitat felicitas*) is written above and below the symbol of male sexual and protective power, the phallus (*CIL* 4.1454). But men were more or less free to express their sexual drives with slaves and prostitutes; women were not. So 'respectable' women's sexual pleasure was restricted to marriage. And enjoy sex she certainly could – and, indeed, *must* if conception was to take place. Medical writers from Hippocrates to Galen to Soranus linked female orgasm, or at the very least a positive attitude toward intercourse, to conception. So within the fundamental function of a married woman – procreation – enjoying sex was not only permitted, but hoped for.

The range of enjoyment naturally varied from 'doing one's duty gladly' to reveling in sexual excess. Paul's attitudes at 1 Corinthians 7:2–6 exemplify a wife's experience of sex as a 'duty':

The husband should fulfill his marital duty to his wife, and likewise the wife to her husband. The wife's body does not belong to her alone but also to her husband. In the same way, the husband's body does not belong to him alone but also to his wife. Do not deprive each other except by mutual consent … (compare 1 Thessalonians 4:3–6)

Galen endorsed this sort of restrained although at least potentially still enjoyable connubial sex when he praised Christians' 'restraint in cohabitation,' and again among the elite Seneca praised the under-ardent wife. If the elite Lucretius is to be believed, the less passionate rear-entry position was preferred for conjugal intercourse:

And how the pleasing pleasure is taken is also of very great impor-tance, for wives are thought to conceive more often through inter-course after the manner of wild and domesticated animals, because thus with breasts down and genitals raised, the male seed can reach where it needs to go. (*On the Nature of Things* 4.1263–7)

The 'missionary position' was too apt to lead to useless, excessive passion, and to *coitus interruptus* as a way to avoid pregnancy:

Sexually stimulating movements are of absolutely no use to wives. For a woman keeps herself from conceiving – even fights against it – if she enthusiastically encourages a man's penetration by the movement of her hips and makes him ejaculate onto her writhing bosom. For she turns the furrow from the plowshare and keeps the seed from falling where it should. (*On the Nature of Things* 4.1268–73)

Toward the other end of the spectrum of conjugal sex, Publilius Syrus has a saying worth repeating: 'A compliant wife turns a man against whores' (Maxim 492). Considering the sexual skill of at least some pros-titutes, this might have set the bar fairly high for some couples.

While wives could enjoy 'natural' sex, in general 'deviant' behav-ior (any sexual activity beyond procreative) was frowned upon in the conjugal bed. Phaedrus in one of his fables notes: 'Then using the same material, Prometheus made a woman's tongue from the substance of her private parts. This is what produces the shared connection to obscene acts of both' (*Fables* 4.15). But some married couples clearly engaged in oral sex: Firmicius in one of his astrological castings notes that a sign indicates a husband and wife 'practice impure intercourse,' probably referring to oral sex (*Mathesis* 6.31.38–9). And Artemidorus is clearly aware of the full range of sexual activity, as he writes of married couples in dreams performing the whole array of standard and deviant sexual positions and acts, although his interpretations always rely on the basic principle that domination is good, subordination is bad.

The extent that lesbianism entered the life of ordinary women is impossible to gauge, but certainly such experiences existed. As Pseudo-Lucian writes:

> Come now, epoch of the future, legislator of strange pleasures, devise fresh paths for male lusts, but bestow the same privilege upon women, and let them have intercourse with each other just as men do. Let them strap to themselves cunningly contrived instruments of lechery, those mysterious monstrosities devoid of seed, and let woman lie with woman as does a man. Let wanton lesbianism – that word seldom heard, which I feel ashamed even to utter – freely parade itself, and let our women's chambers emulate Philaenis, disgracing themselves with Sapphic amours. (*Affairs of the Heart* 28/ MacLeod)

Artemidorus provides evidence that lesbianism was practiced by the general population, as the possibility of a woman possessing another woman appears in his work:

> If a woman penetrates another woman, she will share her own secrets with the one being penetrated. But if she does not know the one penetrated, she will attempt frivolous undertakings. If a woman is penetrated by another woman, she will be divorced from her husband or widowed. Nevertheless, she will learn the secrets of the one doing the fucking. (*Dreams* 1.80)

Such matter-of-fact notation of lesbianism is balanced by others who held that female same-sex relationships were to be avoided, as for example Paul, who criticized polytheistic women as 'exchanging natural relations for unnatural ones' (Romans 1:26).

Women in the household

Beyond the basics of the sexual life in marriage, a woman had many sources of joy and pleasure. As I have already pointed out, because of intense and effective acculturation, and the lack of alternate acceptable patterns of behavior, a woman would not have questioned her role; this acceptance led to a large measure of emotional security and, once she had established her worth and so position by bearing children, she encountered few fundamental problems her upbringing had not prepared her to deal with effectively. Traumas of childlessness, of barrenness, of childhood mortality must have come aplenty. But the psychological support system was ready to deal with these 'expectable' reversals, and a woman was seldom alone.

The most essential activity of marriage was the concentration of the parents on children. It is so fundamental that for the early Christians motherhood was woman's special gift, her path to eternal life: 'Woman will be saved through bearing children, if she continues in faith and love and holiness, with modesty' (1 Timothy 2:15). Although as in any society there would be aberrant behavior, in the normal course of things, a mother loved her children. A letter from Egypt is eloquent in its care and concern and worry:

> Isidora to Hermias her lord brother, very many greetings. Do everything you can to put everything off and come tomorrow; the child is sick. He has become thin, and for 6 days he hasn't eaten. Come here lest he die while you're not here. Be aware that if he dies in your absence, watch out lest Hephaistion find that I've hung myself … (*PSI* 3.177, Oxyrhynchus, second and third centuries AD/Bagnall & Cribiore)

Hard reality could impinge, however. The exposure of children is one of the most difficult things for moderns to come to terms with in the ancient world. Although it was opposed by Jews and Christians, the habit was ingrained and widespread throughout society. Still, it is hard to imagine the calculus of a family including the intentional abandonment, perhaps to death, of their own infant. These decisions perhaps affected women more than men. And certainly the result punished girls more than boys. A famous letter from Egypt testifies to this reality:

> Hilarion to his sister Alis, very many greetings. Also to my lady Berous and Apollonarion. Know that we are even now in Alexandria.

Do not worry. If they actually set out, I am going to remain in Alexandria. I ask you and beg you, take care of our little one, and as soon as we get our pay, I intend to send it up country to you. If, among the many things that are possible, you do bear a child and if it is a male, let it be, but if it is a female, cast it out. You have told Aphrodiaias, 'Do not forget me'; but how can I forget you? I ask you, then, not to worry. Year 20, Pauni 23. (Rowlandson, no. 230)

So here is combined a clear love of a child ('take care of our little one') and a steely determination to get rid of the next, if it be a girl ('if it is a female, cast it out'). Although there were contraceptives and miscarriage-inducing treatments available for 'family planning,' the surest way to keep the wanted child and get rid of the unwanted one was abandonment. So exposure continued to be a useful option throughout antiquity, however agonizing a particular decision might have been for a particular woman. Even if a child was raised, a desperate family situation could lead to selling the female into prostitution to get money for food and clothing, another wrenching decision.

Turning to a happier aspect of a woman's life, she would have had many opportunities for socializing outside the home and family. There is every indication that she maintained a strong interconnectivity with other women. She would visit relatives and friends; there were family events to plan and go to; going to market fell to her since most ordinary people would not have had a slave to do this, or other daily chores outside the home such as retrieving water from the local fountain and gossiping along the way. And, of course, there were religious ceremonies to attend to, not only within the household, but beyond it at the neighborhood cult centers and larger sanctuaries nearby – perhaps even a pilgrimage to a fairly distant site now and again. These many religious occasions of all sorts 'got women out of the house' and provided sometimes solemn, sometimes raucous opportunities for celebration. This socializing was stigmatized by males as an opportunity for at best frivolous gossiping and at worst malicious slandering; they often assumed that heavy drinking went along with it. Early Christian literature is particularly fond of pointing out and criticizing these alleged weaknesses. While the author of Titus tells older men to be sensible and serious and temperate, he tells older women not to be slanderers

and addicted to wine; by this he emphasizes these two 'womanly' fail-
ings: gossip and boozing (Titus 2:3). Those women who are seeking
leadership as deacons must be 'serious, no slanderers, but temperate,
faithful in all things' – temperateness has been mentioned among male
qualifications too (1 Timothy 3.2), but slander is not insinuated as ema-
nating from males (1 Timothy 3.2–4). And widows are singled out as
particularly susceptible to the social weaknesses of sex, gossip, med-
dling, and heavy drinking: 'But refuse to enroll younger widows; for
when they grow wanton against Christ they desire to marry, and so
they incur condemnation for having violated their first pledge. Besides
that, they learn to be idlers, gadding about from house to house, and not
only idlers but gossips and busybodies, saying what they should not'
(1 Timothy 5:13). This conception of female irresponsibility is part and
parcel of the downgraded opinion of women in general that pervades
the male culture. But with the hostility and suspicion set aside, one finds
a picture of women networking to maintain contact with one another,
exchange information, and create an environment in which important
decisions regarding themselves and their families can be made.

While men worried about the social habits of their women, the
women themselves had a more serious list of concerns. Their primary
worry was about health – their own and that of their loved ones – and
the welfare of various family members. The letters of women written
on papyrus focus on these two issues in addition to concerns about
business operations, an emphasis that points once again to the active
role women played outside the home as well as within it. It is no surprise that women dwelled on health issues, especially their own. The
frequent mention of female death in epigraphy and letters points to
how common death in childbirth must have been; historically, this has
always been a primary cause of female mortality. It must have been on
a woman's mind constantly as the cultural expectation to bear children
played itself out.

Dreams were interpreted to help the pregnant woman with her
worries. Artemidorus notes how common stillborn births were:

> If a pregnant woman has a dream that she is giving birth to a fish,
> when born the child will only live a short time, for every fish dies
> when it is taken from its natural environment. (*Dreams* 2.18)

Parental support and assistance were also crucial:

Mother NN to Ptollis, Nikandros, Lysimachos, Tryphaina, greetings. If you are well, it would be as I pray to the gods to see you well. I received the letter from you in which you inform me that you have given birth. I prayed to the gods daily on your behalf. Now that you have escaped [from danger], I shall pass my time in the greatest joy. I have sent you a flask full of oil and … mina of dried figs. Please empty the flask and send it back to me safely because I need it here. Don't hesitate to name the little one Kleopatra, so that your little daughter … (*P. Münch.* 3.57/Bagnall & Cribiore)

As children grew, worries over their health and safety and education were normal and frequent. The letter from Isidora to her brother quoted above is eloquent. The following letter expresses the concerns of a grandmother for her daughter and grandchildren – as well as a complaint about nonsupport!

Eudaimonis to her daughter, Aline, greetings. Above all, I pray that you may give birth in good time, and that I shall receive news of a baby boy. You sailed away on the 29th and on the next day I finished drawing down [?the wool] … Your sister Souerous gave birth. Teeus wrote me a letter thanking you so that I know, my lady, that my instructions will be valid, for she had left all her family to come with you. The little one sends you her greetings and is persevering with her studies. Rest assured that I shall not pay studious attention to God until I get my son back safe. Why did you send me 20 drachmae in my difficult situation? I already have the vision of being naked when winter starts. Farewell. (*P. Brem.* 63/Bagnall & Cribiore)

A further worry attested by letters is concern about widowhood, with its implications of powerlessness. If the widow was young, she had possibilities, as the author of the letter to Timothy attests: 'So I counsel younger widows to marry, to have children, to manage their homes …' (1 Timothy 5:14). But to judge by the evidence from Egypt, most widows were older and few remarried – perhaps the risk of childbearing was too great, perhaps men looked to younger women and despised widows; when in the tale of Cupid and Psyche embedded in Apuleius' *Golden Ass* Venus berates Cupid for disrespecting her, she says he is treating her with the contempt reserved for widows (5.30). Whatever the specific reasons, nonremarriage seems to have been a widespread phenomenon. A widow's powerlessness was widely acknowledged, and her position often precarious; life as a widow was not in general something to look forward to. But although widows were universally seen as disadvantaged, in need of help and protection, and easily taken advantage of, some widows at least managed well in their new condition. Artemidorus gives the following dream interpretation: '… the second woman will lose her husband and will manage her household alone, being, in fact, both wife and husband at the same time.' This indicates that in widowhood some women carried on just fine without a man in the house.

There was also worry for the safety of loved ones who were traveling:

Eutychis to Amertrion her mother, many greetings. Before everything I pray to God to find you well. I want you to know that I came to the Tyrannion on the 30th of Tybi, and I could not find any way to come to you, because the camel drivers refused to go to the Oxyrhynchite. Not only that, but I went up to Antinooupolis for a boat and did not find any. So now I consider bringing my loads to Antinooupolis and staying there until I find a boat and sail down … Greet for me all in the house and all our friends; I'll be coming to you soon. I pray for your health. (*P. Oxy.* 14.1773/Bagnall & Cribiore)

Indeed, these letters reveal that women traveled to an astonishing extent, whether to visit family (especially to help in child birthing), to do business, or to attend to land owned abroad. They thought nothing of setting out on the road (or river, as the case might be). Elsewhere, other, equally mobile women appear, such as Prisca/Priscilla (Acts 18:1–3); she and her husband were from Pontus, had lived in Rome, and were in Corinth when Paul stayed in their home. But travel always occasioned worry, and it is no surprise that a large number of dreams interpreted by Artemidorus involve possibilities for good and not-so-good things happening while on a journey.

Egyptian households were in large measure made up of extended and multiple families; I take this pattern as normal across my geographical area because they closely resemble in general what is expected of a preindustrial culture and, specifically, what has been found throughout the Mediterranean in premodern times. In Egyptian documents we find about 60 percent of households living as extended and multiple families, with 35 percent as conjugal (nuclear) families, and only 5 percent of people living as solitaries with no family. In this environment, with a large number of people usually sharing often constrained living conditions, it is little wonder that the papyri are full of family drama. Children were especially prone to inspiring concern and worry. In this fragmentary letter, for example, a mother writes to her own mother about a daughter who is causing her grief:

Heliodora to my mother, many greetings. I am strongly embittered toward you because you did not even deem me worthy of receiving news through a letter of yours. From the time when I went away from you, many troubles have been inflicted upon me by my daughter. See how much she provoked to anger the landlord and his neighbors and then was vexed at him. She stripped me of everything and got hold of my gold jewels and my earrings and gave me a [worn] tunic so that … Invoke the god for me so that he would pity me. Do everything to send my brother to me. I am going to Senepta with Hermous. Do not send me …: what I have is enough for me. Salute all my brothers and the people who love you. I pray for your health. (*SB* 16.12326/Bagnall & Cribiore)

Intra-family tensions abound; intergenerational issues frequently come to the fore. Here a mother lectures her son on how his wife, her daughter-in-law, is to blame for problems, and how she twists him around her little finger:

To Kopres [from his mother], greeting. I know your quick temper, but your wife inflames you when she says every hour that I do not give you anything. When you came up, I gave you small coins because I received some grain; but this month I could not find [anything] to give you. I am keeping nothing back from you because I trust you in everything. Your wife says in fact, 'She does not trust you' …

Nobody can love you, for she shapes you according to her advantage … (*SB* 3.6264/Bagnall & Cribiore)

A wife was expected to tolerate faults of a husband that moderns might think quite serious (e.g. alcohol abuse, gambling, or womanizing). This despite the fact that 'objectively' such behavior could easily threaten the property and well-being of the family's children. A good wife simply ignored a husband's dalliances with slaves and prostitutes; his use of them might even be beneficial if she disliked him or wished to have fewer children. She was only concerned when there was true adultery or open concubinage, which threatened her position and that of her children. But a husband's neglect often went beyond sexual straying. Violence and abuse were very common. The abusive relationships in family and marriage swirling around the life of Monica, St. Augustine's mother, give a good picture of this. Her life as given in the *Confessions* presents wife abuse as pervasive in her town of Thagaste – her own experience with her husband, Patricius, is replicated over and over again in the households of other women in the town, most of whom show bruises from their encounters with their husbands. Augustine's family is a member of the local elite (his father, Patricius, is a town councilor), so Monica's experience is not that of an ordinary woman. But there is no reason to suppose that male attitudes toward wife abuse in marriage would be any different among nonelites and the poor. Note the threats of violence and strong language of Petronius at *Satyricon* 74–5 concerning Trimalchio and wife:

Then for the first time (but not the last) our good times were thrown into confusion. For now when a cute lad had entered along with other servants, Trimalchio grabbed him and began to give him long kisses. And so Fortunata [Trimalchio's wife], in order to emphasize her rights at law, began to swear at Trimalchio, calling him a filthy fellow and a disgrace who couldn't control his lusts. The final insult she hurled was, 'You dog!' Trimalchio was offended by the insults and hurled a cup at Fortunata's face. She screamed as though she'd lost an eye and put her trembling hands to her face. Scintilla was alarmed as well. She pulled her terrified friend to her bosom to protect her.

This shows Trimalchio's essential vulgarity despite his wealth – thus Petronius, at least, thought that the subelite behaved like this. In *The Golden Ass*, too, a husband angered at being cuckolded would have done violence to his wife if a friend had not convinced the wife to go away until the husband's anger had cooled – a tactic that would have met with Monica's approval, while the beating itself falls within the acceptable, as Artemidorus' interpretation of a dream shows: 'To strike someone is auspicious, so long as you have authority over them – except in the case of a wife; for if she is struck, it means she is committing adultery' (*Dreams* 2.48).

A letter on papyrus is eloquent about an abusive husband:

To Protarchos. From Tryphaine, daughter of Dioskourides. Asklepiades, to whom I am married, persuaded my parents, although I, Tryphaine, was unwilling, to give me to him as my caretaker, and … [Asklepiades] entered into the marriage, [?receiving] also on my behalf a down payment on my dowry consisting of clothing worth 40 drachmas and 20 drachmas of coined silver. But my accuser, Asklepiades, since he kept going off throughout the marriage for no reason, squandered the aforementioned goods, abused me and insulted me, and, laying his hands on me, he used me as if I were his bought slave … (Rowlandson, no. 257)

Abuse is even recorded on a couple of gravestones. One Iulia Maiana is described as having been slain in a domestic argument:

Julia Maianae, a highly honorable woman, was murdered at the hands of a most cruel husband. She lived married to that man for 28 years and they had two children, a boy, 19, and a girl, 18 years old. O Faithfulness personified! O Duty itself! Julius Maior, her brother, set this up to a sister so sweet, along with Ingenuinius Januarius her son. (*CIL* 13.2182 = *ILS* 8512, Lyon, France)

And as can been seen from the following example, a family set up a monument to a sixteen-year-old wife who, it says, had been murdered, hurled into the Tiber by Orfeus, her husband:

Restutus Picenesis and Prima Restuta made this gravestone for Prima Florentia, their dear, dear daughter, who was thrown into the Tiber river by her husband, Orfeus. The man named December set this up to one who lived only 16 years. (*IPOstie-A*, 210 = *ISIS* 321)

Women had to fear violence in other aspects of their lives, too. A letter from Egypt tells of an employer who beat an employee's wife:

When I was calculating accounts with Bentetis, son of Bentetis, a shepherd of Oxyrhynchus in the same division, and when he wanted not to pay me, but to cheat me, he behaved in an insulting manner to me and to my wife Tanouris, daughter of Heronas, in the aforesaid Areos Kome. In addition, he also pelted my wife unsparingly with hard blows on every part of her body he could, although she was pregnant, so that she gave birth to a dead fetus, and she herself lies in her bed and is in danger of her life. (Rowlandson, no. 229)

And women also could be in danger from fellow citizens:

From Hippalos son of Archis, public farmer from the village of Euhemeria of the Themistos division. On the 6th Tybi, while my wife Aplounous and her mother Thermis were bathing, Eudaimonis daughter of Protarchos, and Etthytais daughter of Pees, and Deios son of Ammonios, and Heraklous attacked them, and gave my wife Aplounous and her mother in the village bath-house many blows all over her body so that she is laid up in bed, and in the fray she lost a gold earring weighing three quarters, a bracelet of unstamped metal weighing 16 drachmas, a bronze bowl worth 12 drachmas; and Thermis her mother lost a gold earring weighing two and a half quarters, and … [text becomes fragmentary] (Rowlandson, no. 254)

A wife used the weapons of reason and self-controlled restraint in the face of a husband's tantrums and abuse. Monica, St. Augustine's mother, presents another way of dealing with abusive husbands: manipulating them. The language of slavery is often used to describe the relationship of husband and wife, and in a hostile relationship the strategies of a slave in avoiding beatings would serve a wife well. As slaves were wise to be obsequious, so wives: 'The upright wife runs her home by paying attention to her husband's wishes,' says Publilius Syrus (Maxim 108). They were advised to practice *blanditiae* from an early age, wheedling, and like means as a way to deal with the men in their lives.

As a last resort there was the possibility of divorce. Sometimes this was motivated by bad circumstances of a marriage, such as infidelity or abuse, but sometimes by what was apparently mutual consent, as this letter from Egypt shows:

> To Promachos from Zois, the daughter of Heraclides, along with her legal guardian, her brother Irenaeus son of Heraclides, and also from Antipater son of Zeus: Zois and Antipater agree that they are separated from each other with the agreed upon marriage arrangements null and void … Zois has received from Antipater by his own hand from their common household that which he held in dowry, namely clothing worth 120 drachmas and a pair of gold earrings. As of this moment the marriage contract is completely invalid … and from this time on it will be legal for Zois to marry any man and for Antipater to marry any woman, with both free from any threat of legal action. (*BGU* 4.1103)

Finally, in responding to a crisis in a marriage, or simply to the whims of fortune, women were perfectly capable of taking things into their own hands, leaving a husband, and taking up with someone else, whatever the 'legal' situation:

> To Claudius Alexandros, centurion, from NN son of Panetbeous, public farmer from the village of Theadelphia. The wife with whom I was living [and by whom] I have begotten a child, becoming dissatisfied about her marriage with me, [seized] an opportune absence of mine, and left my house … Months ago, without a so-called [?divorce], taking away her own goods and many of mine, among which were a large white unfulled cloak and an Oxyrhynchite pillow, and a striped *dilassion* [a garment], materials for two *chitons*, and other farmers' working implements. And although I have many times sent to her seeking to recover my things, she has not responded or returned them, and yet I am supplying to her the cost of support for our child.

Besides, having now learned that one Neilos son of Syros from the same village had lawlessly taken her and married her, I submit [this petition] and request that she and Neilos may be summoned before you in order for me to be able to obtain legal redress and get back my things and be helped. Farewell. (Rowlandson, no. 137)

Women in the economy

The most striking thing about the economic role of Roman women of all classes and incomes is that they kept the household functioning. Their duties ranged from mundane chores to sometimes complicated commercial dealings. Hierocles, a second-century AD philosopher, seems to describe a peasant household. The women do wool work, cook, make bread, light fires, draw water, make beds, and carry out some things around the house that require physical strength: grinding corn, kneading dough, cutting wood, getting wood, moving large containers around, and shaking out bedcovers. Women also help out in the fields and with harvesting when they are needed. This picture is very congruent with that given of a similar life in Galilee. The attested jobs done there include baking bread and selling it in the market; keeping a shop; helping with agricultural work, especially during the harvest; selling produce from the home, as well as delivering it to the market for sale; and being wet nurses. The Mishnah lists a woman's work in the home as (in order): grinding corn, baking, and laundering; preparing meals and nursing children; making her husband's bed; and working wool; but notice that tasks that must have been done (e.g. sweeping out, cleaning up, keeping lamps and fires, purchasing supplies in the market, and doing the household accounts) are not mentioned here. For each slave brought into the house, one of these listed tasks might be deleted, in order, although Gamaliel felt that wool working should be done no matter what, to avoid idleness.

The oft-quoted epitaph of Claudia echoes this sentiment; she kept the house and worked at wool:

Visitor, I have a little something to say to you; stop and give it a read. This is a common tomb for an uncommon woman. Her parents gave her the name, Claudia. She loved her husband with all her heart. She brought forth two children. One she left above the earth, the other below. Her conversation was lovely, her gait was graceful. She managed the household. She wove in wool. I have spoken. Go on your way. (*CIL* 6.15346 = *ILS* 8403, Rome)

Weaving was so much seen as a quintessential wifely thing that 'A woman dreamed that she finished her weaving. She died the next day. Since she no longer had work, she no longer had reason to live' (Artemidorus, *Dreams* 4.40). Food preparation was also central, as was childbearing and care. The need for many children to offset high infant mortality meant that women were completely socialized into their role as child-producers from their typical age of menarche, fourteen, until fertility tapered off by thirty and ended in their mid forties.

Despite the fact that work such as this in the home was central to the vast majority of women's lives, females in their attested roles as home managers never appear in images on grave reliefs, which is curious, since the fact of fine household management – working in wool, and other roles – is often mentioned in words in grave epitaphs. For example, Amymone, who died in Rome, is praised by her husband as most good and most beautiful, as a wool spinner, as dutiful, modest, pious, faithful, frugal, chaste, and a stay-at-home – but her image on the gravestone does not illustrate actual duties (*CIL* 6.11602 = *ILS* 8402). For some reason there was a hesitancy to show women engaged in the jobs that were so highly valued in the culture in general.

The importance of wool weaving extended beyond the household. In addition to providing material from which to make clothing, a woman could produce a surplus that could be sold. This 'cottage work' was crucial to the survival of poor households, as Apuleius' story illustrates:

This indigent fellow, pressed down by desperate poverty, managed to stay alive by doing construction work for a few asses a day. He had a wife who was just as poor, but infamous for her insatiable lust. [the wife's lover visits her while the husband is out; the husband returns unexpectedly; the wife brazenly challenges him] … 'Just look at you, acting like you have nothing to do, ambling about with your hands in your pockets, not going to work like you usually do to help us get by and put some bread on the table. And here I am, wretch that I be, working my fingers to the bone day and night spinning wool so that at least we can have a lamp to light our miserable hovel.' (*The Golden Ass* 9.5)

But ordinary women wove as well. John Chrysostom notes that a woman should make cloth at home, but if she didn't she could buy other women's cloth; these women sold it themselves, vending it in the markets (*Against Those Men Cohabiting with Virgins* 9, PG 47.507). And also from Egypt there are many contracts and documents illustrating the participation of women in weaving both as a cottage industry and within a manufacturing environment. Women could even own and run whole weaving establishments (Rowlandson, no. 205). Women doing piecework at the loom to earn a meager wage had a very long history – one can even point to a Homeric simile: '… and as some honest, hard-working woman weighs wool in her balance and sees that the scales be true, for she would gain some pitiful earnings for her little ones' (*Iliad* 12.433–5). In Egypt, a whole family including mother and wife sought such employment:

Apollophanes and Demetrios, brothers, craftsmen in all the skills of weaving women's clothing, to Zenon, greetings. If you please and you happen to have the need, we are ready to provide what you need. For hearing of the reputation of the city and that you, its leading man, are a good and just person, we have decided to come to Philadelphia to you, we ourselves and our mother and wife. And in order that we might be employed, bring us in, if you please … (Rowlandson, no. 201)

So besides cottage labor, women worked outside the home. How many did so is impossible to say, but the notices of their work are common enough. Susan Treggiari's study of occupations shows that men were attested in six times as many occupations as women; it is telling, in addition, that a woman's gravestone mentions an occupation only one time in a hundred. In Artemidorus' dream book and the astro-logical handbooks, women's occupations are also mentioned much less frequently than men's, although such jobs as actress, midwife, nurse,

4. Women at work. A merchant aids a customer purchasing slippers at the felt products shop of Verecundus. She is probably his wife, aiding in the business.

priestess, cleaning lady, and prostitute are noted. It is not hard to say why this is. Work was not seen as an integral part of a woman's identity, so it did not feature so much in advice on such things as marriage, family, and children. Treggiari notes, 'Women appear to be concentrated in "service" jobs (catering, prostitution); dealing, particularly in foodstuffs; serving in shops; in certain crafts, particularly the production of cloth and clothes; "fiddly" jobs such as working in gold-leaf or hairdressing; certain luxury trades such as perfumery. This is a fair reflection of at least part of reality.' As previously noted, she estimates that only 1 percent of the epitaphs of women mention an occupation; this small number is actually consonant with the evidence from preindustrial Brazil where, in the middle of the nineteenth century, notorial registry records show that only about 3 percent of women listed some occupation outside the home.

Natalie Kampen's investigations of images of women working concludes that contrary to the realistic portrayal of males in occupations, women are always presented in a mythologized or allegorized context,

5. Women at work in a shop. Two women assist customers purchasing fruits and vegetables.

i.e. not as actual artisans. As Treggiari notes, inscriptions show that they existed as artisans, and texts corroborate that women performed 'production jobs' – for example, a woman's letter from Egypt states that she 'works with her hands' (Rowlandson, no. 130) – it is simply that they are not portrayed in this way in primary imagery. There are also no images of women working in the fields or running a large business. Kampen suggests that this was because doing a job was not appropriate to the mythology of womanhood as the homebody/manager, and even speculates that such work outside the home lowered a woman's status. If this is so, then it is evidence that the homebody image of women extended down into the artisan class.

An interesting discrepancy is that women are shown realistically as vendors. Why? Kampen speculates that the unequivocally outside-the-home nature of vending (compared with, for example, cloth merchandizing, which might be confused with work done at home) meant that men and women could be represented by the same sort of iconography. But the relatively modest amount of imagery as well as the few mentions on inscriptions are probably due to the supplementary nature of this sort of work – that is to say, to judge by comparative material from other preindustrial cultures, a woman's work outside the home was not normally carried out in the role of the primary wage-earner, although special situations, such as the death of the husband, could change that picture in individual cases.

6. Cooperating at work. A wife keeps the books, the husband slices the meat. A butcher shop in Rome.

The census returns from Egypt corroborate this; of all the declarations, not a single female gives an occupation. Surely this does not mean that women did not work, for there is much evidence that they did; but only that it was not thought of as a separate act worthy of recording. The apprenticeship contracts from Egypt were also mostly for boys; although slave boys and slave girls do appear, there are no freeborn women who can be identified as such. Probably, therefore, such girls were not intentionally targeted by families as potential workers; rather, (wealthier) families maintained the ideal of daughters-future-wives being based only at home, while other (poorer) families assumed that girls would upon marriage help out in the husband's work however and whenever possible, but without formal training. Indeed, Treggiari also points out that when a woman is mentioned on an inscription she is usually paired with a man, presumably her husband in most cases; she interpreted this to mean that they worked together. An inscription from North Africa is eloquent about how important the wife 'helpmate' could be to a man's business:

Urbanilla, my wife, lies here, a woman of complete modesty. At Rome, she was my companion and associate in business dealings, sustained by her frugality. With everything going well, she returned with me to my homeland. Ah! Carthage ripped my wretched companion from me. There is no hope of living without such a wife. She managed my household and she gave me good advice. Taken from the light, pitiable she quiet lies enclosed in marble. I, Lucius, your husband covered you in marble here. Fate's chance gave this woman to me on the day we were born. (*CIL* 8.152, Sommet el Amra, Tunisia)

A partnership such as this is also represented by the merchant couple Aquila and Priscilla, dealers in tents at Rome and Corinth in Acts 18:1. Evidence from Egypt shows that women were not only helpmates, but actual owners of enterprises. The letters and documents on papyrus show ordinary (as well as elite) women engaged in owning and dealing in agricultural land (Rowlandson, no. 180), in wage work (Rowland-son, no. 130), in business ownership and in lending (Rowlandson, nos. 182–4, 190), in leasing camels and purchasing (Rowlandson, nos. 186–7, 192) – in fact, in many of the aspects of business that were associated with males. The second-century AD dossier of Tasoucharion shows a woman deeply involved in the details of business transactions. There is no indication of her station, but the modest items of business would point to an ordinary woman. Artemidorus' dream book notes women in business as well: a woman 'who has something for sale' and who will 'sign a contract' for it is noted (2.66); and a woman signing a contract for sale is mentioned in passing, as if this was usual (4.30).

Lest it is still thought that Egypt represents a peculiarity, graffiti from Pompeii once again collaborate that evidence and remind us that Egyptian material deserves to be widely applied. A woman named Faustilla is a moneylender, as she takes jewelry as a pawn for a loan:

July 15th. Earring left with Faustilla as collateral. For a loan of two denarii [= 32 asses] she took as interest one bronze as from the sum of 30 [?32] [asses]. (*CIL* 4.8203)

This or a different Faustilla also took a loan, apparently in a bar, for this was scribbled on the wall:

November. From Faustilla, 8 asses in interest for 15 denarii. (*CIL* 4. 4528)

Other activities seem more expectable for females. Midwifery by definition is a female domain. Doctors male and female might be available, but for the ordinary person the midwife would be the expert to call in for childbirth. There are many contracts for wet nurses from Egypt. Most of the contracts are for hire to nurse foundlings; there are few notices of hiring for free persons' children – but when these are the clients, the wet nurses are paid more (Rowlandson, no. 231). Domestic help is mostly female, too, when it is not provided by slaves. The habit of trading the services of a woman, often a daughter, for a monetary loan is well attested in Egypt, although it is not clear how widespread this was in the empire as a whole.

On the public stage, women were active in 'male' businesses, as we have seen, but traditionally they were restricted to certain less reputable occupations. Literally on the stage, some women were engaged in performances and other entertainment. The contract from Egypt for a dancer and castanet players illustrates this:

Sosos son of Sosos, Syracusan of the *epigone,* has hired himself to Olympias ... from Attika [?Athenian], dancer, acting with Zopyros, son of Marikkos [?], Galatian of the *epigone,* as her guardian, to work with her as a flute-player for 12 months from the month of Hyperberetaios of the 16th year for a wage of 45 bronze drachmas per month. And Sosos has received in advance from Olympias 50 bronze drachmas. He shall not fail to appear at any festival or any other engagement at which Olympias is present and he shall not provide service for anyone else without the authority of Olympias. The keeper of the contract is Olympichos, son of Herodotos, Kleopatreus ... (Rowlandson, no. 215)

Such employment, like innkeeping and working as a bar girl, easily transmuted into the main occupation of women outside the household, prostitution. I discuss this in a later chapter.

Some women specialized in fortune-telling, other forms of advice (the 'wise woman'), and magic. The elite Pliny the Elder attributes to the common people – our ordinary folk – a firm belief in the power of women and their herbs and potions; he thought that knowledge of charms and magical herbs was the singular specialty of women (*Natural*

History 25.5.10). Magic was often resorted to in problem solving, and lovers frequently went to 'old hags' to talk about their love issues (see Philostratus' *Life of Apollonius* 7.39, for example). But their expertise extended far beyond advice to the lovelorn, as Philostratus again illustrates when he has the religious figure Apollonius of Tyana speaking to an Egyptian critic:

> … there are certain old women who go about with sieves in their hands to shepherds, sometimes to cow-herds, pretending to heal their flocks, when they are sick, by divination, as they call it, and they claim to be called wise women, yea wiser than those who are unfeignedly prophets. (*Life of Apollonius* 6.11, also 3.43/Conybeare)

Lucius, the protagonist of *The Golden Ass*, runs afoul of just such an expert sorceress, although she is in fact a member of the local elite, not an ordinary woman. Interestingly, the sorceress is often portrayed as a procuress as well – a conjunction of two independent female professions. The connection is the assumed use of philters by prostitutes to gain and keep customers.

Although presumably wise women and prostitutes did not join associations, there is evidence that other women working outside the home did. This environment would have given them good opportunities to mix with other women, and with men. They were probably allowed into trade guilds only rarely, but certainly they were members of funerary associations and sometimes they were officers. One all-female group is even attested to, the 'gathering of women' found at Lanuvium in Italy (*CIL* 14.2120); this was probably a household burial or cult association though, with restricted membership. Beyond these, there is much evidence for women (along with men, i.e. mixed groups) in religious associations. There was egalitarianism among the regular members, while they were stratified vertically by officers and, at the top, founders or patrons. So rich and poor, masters and slaves, men and women, free and freed could be together; an example is the membership of the religious association worshiping Zeus at Philadelphia, which included men and women, freeborn and slaves. Before males came to dominate the early Christian communities, women could hold roles as teachers and other leaders; for example, the woman Jezebel was an influential prophetess and teacher, allegedly of immorality, in the church at Thyatira (Revelations 2:19–23). These women leaders were probably just continuing the accepted roles that women had in preexisting non-Christian associations in their communities.

Outside the town, we find women actively engaged in agriculture. In Egypt, by the Roman period, about a third of landowners were women, owning between 16 and 25 percent of the land. Clearly the fact that almost all women needed a guardian to conduct business and make legal contracts did not slow them down in terms of carrying out economic activity. Here a woman purchases land for her daughter:

> To Aelius Aprodisios, strategos, from Ptolemais daughter of Agenor son of Philiskos from Oxyrhynchus city, mother of Claudia Areia, through the scribe Hermes. I wish to purchase for my daughter, Claudia Areia and however she styles herself, from the properties put up for sale near the epoikion [settlement] of Artapatou in the middle toparchy [district], from the allotment of Simias, 16 arouras [10+ acres] of katoikic [private] land … and ownership shall remain with Claudia Areia and her descendants and those acting for her. (Rowlandson, no. 171)

These women not only owned land, but actively oversaw the agricultural arrangements and work:

> Thais sends greetings to her own Tigrios. I wrote to Apolinarios to come to do the measuring in Petne. Apolinarios will tell you how the deposits and public duties stand; what name they are in, he will tell you himself. If you come, take out six artabas of vegetable-seed and seal them in sacks so that they are ready, and if you can, go up to search out the ass. Sarapodora and Sabinos greet you. Do not sell the young pigs without me. Farewell. (Rowlandson, no. 173)

As landowners, they actually go themselves and collect rents (Rowlandson, no. 172). Others hired male agents, who sometimes defrauded them, 'despising [the woman's] lack of business sense' (Rowlandson, no. 177). And poorer women actually worked for wages in agriculture:

> I, Thenetkoueis daughter of Heron, Persian woman, with as guard-
> ian my kinsman Leontas son of Hippalos, agree that I have received
> from Lucius [Bellenus Gemellus, the owner of the olive press] the 16
> drachmas of silver as earnest money, and I shall carry in the oil-press
> from the day you bid me, receiving from you, Lucius, wages at the
> same rate as the other carries, and I shall do everything as agreed.
> (Rowlandson, no. 169)

Other documents show women employed as winnowers. So just as
other women worked as weavers in establishments, some rural women
were hired directly to work in the fields.

Women controlling their lives

A woman's legal status clearly demarcated a position of disadvantage
before the law. She was not a person at law and could not except in rare
instances represent herself as a legal entity, being always in the power,
under the legal authority, of a male. However, the legal system could
be worked. A compliant male relative could represent her interests; she
could instruct a legal guardian to make her will; she could represent
herself in court if her own person or property were at issue; she could
even, if she qualified and knew her rights, obtain full legal personhood
by being the mother of, depending on her status, three or four children. Women used these mechanisms in the system to participate fully
in property ownership, making contracts and wills, and other activities. In fact, adult women from all classes except the high elite received
fully a fifth of the judicial decisions recorded from the early second to
the end of the third centuries AD. Women also appealed to the law in
adversity, sometimes using the 'poor little me, a weak woman' ploy to
gain sympathy from the male legal world, which actually believed such
to be true. The best evidence for all this comes from Egypt, but is also
relevant to women's experiences elsewhere in the empire. Nevertheless,
women in all probability did not in general seek solutions to their issues
in the legal system. Like other ordinary people, they used an array of
other approaches, for the legal system was corrupt, clumsy, and dominated by elite males – all reasons to avoid it if possible. Of course, documents do not show this – the documents themselves are the products of

those women who did engage with the system – but indications can be gleaned that show how women managed.

In marriage the possession of a dowry, as well as male relatives available for support, helped to mitigate the husband's domination of a marriage. In most instances, what the husband wished came to be; but in extreme situations divorce was always possible as a way out. The dowry, moreover, served to remind the husband of his economic interest in the relationship; even a dowry that was very small by elite standards could make a big difference for an artisan or small business-man. Children were also a protection. The cultural standard of marriage and family, plus the practical and hubristic desire to have heirs, gave a woman some leverage in the relationship, since her active and passive participation were required. In some situations the partnership of man and wife that was the ideal actually existed; in less ideal situations the realistic importance of the wife as mother, household manager, and help-mate in economic activities was not lost on men, and gave women lever-age. And in other instances a woman's contributions to the family went beyond those of the helpful wife: the ownership of land, the inheritance of significant resources, the connections a wife might bring through her family were all chits that sat waiting to be called in if a husband acted too independently in matters the wife deemed important to her and her family's welfare. And the strong bond of affection and camaraderie which existed in many relationships should not be neglected. Arranged marriages – the norm in the world of ordinary people – were usually far from cold. The assumption that a couple would grow into a relationship was often realized in reality. Cultural expectations, family pressures, and the bond of children all combined to create a situation in which the marriage would work.

When these failed, a woman could resort to pressure of various kinds. As noted, she could bring the weight of relatives to bear; she could remind her husband, perhaps none too subtly, of her economic importance. But she could also resort to charms and spells to control her husband and her situation. Indeed, men often felt that magic was the most dangerous weapon in a wife's armory, a corollary to their feeling that women in general had recourse to magic to get their way in inter-personal relationships – a tacit and unacknowledged admission of the powerlessness of women to confront them in their own 'manly' world.

These magic spells – bought in the local magic shop, written on slips of papyrus, or simply spoken – were indeed a major weapon for women against the perils of their world, whether in personal or physical trials. One could purchase an individualized spell, or have recourse to general resources such as directing Homeric verses toward specific ills. A papyrus records such a use of verses from the *Iliad*, for example, to deal with a woman's menstrual problems:

> … *the wrath of Apollo, the lord who strikes from afar* [*Iliad* 1.75]. This charm, spoken to the blood, heals a bloody flow. If the patient gets well and is ungrateful, take a pan of coals, put [?the amulet on it] and set it over the smoke. Add a root, and also write this verse: … *for this reason he who strikes from afar sent griefs and still will send them* [*Iliad* 1.960].

In such need, women also could have recourse to action magic, as opposed to charms. The healing of a woman with a 'bloody flow' in Matthew 10:20–22 is an example of such recourse to magic, for the woman who suffered sought out Jesus, a person with access to supernatural power, in order to find a cure for her ill.

In marriage, as previously noted, the asymmetrical power relationship of husband and wife could be righted by the wife's use of magic – a thing to be feared and, indeed, in this instance prohibited in the marriage contract:

> Thais, daughter of Tarouthinos, swears … I will not nor shall I prepare love charms against you, whether in your beverages or in your food … (Rowlandson, no. 255)

In another instance, magic solves a family problem. A woman whose son had been possessed by a demon for two years came to Apollonius; she begged him to rid her son of this curse. Apollonius wrote a letter to the demon threatening severe action if he did not quit the boy, and gave it to the woman; presumably the demon, when served with the letter, left the boy for good (Philostratus, *Life of Apollonius* 3.38). And of course women had recourse to that ever popular use of spells, for love, whether to force a male's attentions:

I will bind you, Nilos alias Agathos Daimon, whom Demetria bore, with great evils … you are going to love me, Capitolina, whom Peperous bore, with a divine passion, and you will be for me in everything a follower, as long as I wish, in order that you may do for me what I want and nothing for anyone else; that you may obey only me, Capitolina; that you might forget your parents, your children, and your friends … I, Capitolina, possess the power, and you, Nilos, will give back the favors, when we meet … I shall insert this pledge [into its box] in order that you might carry out all the things written on this slip of papyrus, for this is why I am summoning you, my divinities, by the violence that constrains you and the compulsion. Bring all things to completion for me and leap in and snatch up the mind of Nilos, to whom belong these magic articles, so that he may love me, Capitolina, and that Nilos, whom Demetria bore, may ever be with me at every hour of every day. (Rowlandson, no. 285)

Or another woman's affection:

… demon set on fire the heart, the liver, the spirit of Gorgonia, whom Nilogenia bore, with desire and love for Sophia, whom Isara bore. Compel Gorgonia, whom Nilogenia bore, to be thrown, for Sophia, whom Isara bore, into the bath-house, and you become a bath-woman, burn, inflame, set on fire her soul, her heart, her liver, her spirit, with desire for Sophia, whom Isara bore, drive Gorgonia, whom Nilogenia bore, drive her, torture her body night and day, force her to be an outcast from every place and every house, loving Sophia, whom Isara bore, she, given away like a slave-girl, handing herself and all her possessions over to her … (Rowlandson, no. 286)

Religion also provided weapons a woman could use to control her environment. Her exclusion from the male social world and most specifically from leadership in state and community-wide religious rites was partly compensated for by social interaction gained during religious activities. Festivals were a reason for extended families to get together, and so for women to renew ties and mutual support. They were often direct participants in these festivals, not merely bystanders. The thronging procession in honor of the Egyptian goddess Isis described in the

7. Female entertainers. Female as well as male dancers are shown on this textile from late antique Egypt.

previous chapter gives a taste of the drama and excitement of such participation. And in Heliodorus' novel *An Ethiopian Story* (5.15), we find that during a festival in honor of Hermes, with public sacrifice and a banquet, the women eat together in the temple and then dance a hymn of thanksgiving to Demeter, while the men eat in the temple forecourt and afterward sing and pour libations. Festivals were so common in the Romano-Grecian world that it is easy to forget the many opportunities they gave for women to gather, to celebrate, and to interact.

But beyond peripheral participation in the cults, what is thought of as 'official' religion was largely closed to ordinary women. It was otherwise with regard to cults that could solve a woman's problems. The multiplicity of sanctuaries and votive offerings related to pregnancy and childbirth indicates the active role of women in these rites; healing divinities also got much attention. And although it is hard to say how prominent women were in the nonstate, noncommunity-oriented cults such as Isis and Christianity – expectation, and the reality, would be that men led these, as in other nondomestic religion – the impression is that these appealed because they were more open to participation by women, rather than leaving them to be bystanders. This very openness provided women with more support in their daily concerns. The prominent role of Isis as a strong, protective, family-centered Mother, the woman who featured in the Gospel narratives, and appeals to family ideals so prominent in early Christian literature, for example, resonated as women sought ways to deal with issues in their lives. In sum, although women were not leaders in cultic activity beyond the household, they found a steady source of mutual aid in the social networking that festivals and worship allowed, and solutions for their daily problems in specific cultic rituals and activities.

When challenged on their own turf, women could take the offensive to protect their own interests. Far from the Mediterranean, but in a story that surely reflects the aggressiveness of women there, Philostratus has Apollonius tell of an Ethiopian village ravaged by a satyr:

> … when suddenly they heard loud shouts from the village as the women there screamed and called to each other to take up the chase and capture the thing (*Life of Apollonius* 6.27)

Although this is fiction – unless we want to believe in satyrs – women in real life could act with the same aggressiveness when their interests were at stake. Earlier in this chapter I quoted the evidence from Philo that women in Alexandria were violent participants in riots. In that graphic passage, women were in the street, cursing their foes and assaulting them, too. Women were also present in the theaters, shouting along with their male kin, when those venues were used, as so often, to harangue and punish disturbers of the peace and worse. Their voices were heard.

Conclusion

I have provided much evidence for the active role of ordinary women in their own lives, in the lives of their families, and in life beyond the household, including business contracts, landowning and management, and public socioreligious activities. Within their culture they were not child-producing drones, or mere ornaments. Their activities were woven vividly into every inch of the cultural cloth. This is exactly as should be expected. The elite could and did as much as possible to keep its women as accouterments rather than as partners. But in the world of ordinaries the 'luxury' of closeted, protected women did not exist. All hands were needed to keep the household running smoothly (under good circumstances) and to earn enough to keep the wolf from the door (in more straitened ones). The outspokenness of women, the leverage they had in various ways in their lives with husbands, their economic contributions, their role in the socialization of the next generation: while all these things had to exist within the culture of male domination, the latitude for action and influence was great. It is too much to speak of 'liberation'; Romano-Grecian culture was unliberated by any modern standard. But as in other preindustrial societies, ordinary women pulled a lot of weight, had a lot of influence, and were strong partners with their husbands or other males in making life choices.

3

SUBJECTION AND SURVIVAL: THE POOR

IT IS QUITE REASONABLE TO SUPPOSE that the great mass of people in the Roman world were poor. The poor were free men and women who lived an essentially hand-to-mouth existence, i.e. those who were on the edge of having enough just to live on, who seldom had enough to save, invest, and use to change their situation. Their consuming economic and psychological orientation was just staying alive. Getting ahead remained a possibility, but not a probability and, as I will show, it was not an active concept in their mind world. From the Romano-Grecian world itself, the astrological work *Carmen Astrologicum* has much the same definition of poverty. There it is defined as not having 'bread to fill his belly or clothes in which to clothe himself' and 'not finding his daily bread' (1.22, 1.24). Artemidorus in his *Interpretation of Dreams* locates the poor at the very bottom of society: 'The poor are like the paltry, obscure places into which shit and other refuse is thrown, or anything else of inconsequence' (2.9).

A subsistence way of life is an easily understood measure that encompasses a wide range of situations, from the beggar on the street to the peasant, tenant farmer, and day-laborer. It stops short of what I call ordinary people, those who had some resource cushion, but were not wealthy enough to break into the sociopolitical-economic world of the elite. This upper level of 'the poor' is necessarily fuzzy, however. Although a slightly more successful artisan would be an ordinary person, the poor artisan, barely making a living, would qualify as 'poor,' much like cobbler Micyllus in Lucian's tale of Hades:

> Well, I'll lament, then, since you wish it, Hermes – Alas, my scraps of leather! Alas, my old shoes! Alackaday, my rotten sandals! Unlucky man that never again will I go hungry from morning to night or wander about in winter barefooted and half-naked, with my teeth chattering for cold! (*Downward Journey* 20/Harmon)

To offer a rough quantification, it is likely that a cash income of around 300 denarii per year would keep a reasonably sized family above the subsistence level in all but the larger cities; this would be the equivalent of about a denarius a day throughout the year. Although this was probably about the best standard wage, the lower wage of half a denarius a day was common. In addition, the chronic underemployment and fluctuating demand for labor and products in both urban and rural worlds meant that most people were not regularly employed and not paid the best wages; they lived on the edge much if not all of the time. These are the poor.

It is reasonable to ask if it is justifiable to lump all those living a hand-to-mouth existence together when I examine a mind world. After all, it can well be argued that a poor family farming a meager plot, regularly on the edge of starvation but at least with some access to their own food supply, has a fundamentally different outlook from that of a beggar or day-laborer. However, what they share is the highly conditional state of their lives: they are the least able to control their lot and to deal with an always uncertain future. A similar state of powerlessness and always near, if not real, desperation unites them in their attitudes toward what is important, which strategies work best for survival, and how to view their place in the world. And so in this chapter I focus on all free folk in difficult if not desperate circumstances as a permanent condition.

It is not hard to imagine who these people might be. Peasants on the land are an obvious group. The standard definition of a peasant is someone who works his own land, and there were many such independent farmers during the empire. The *Moretum*, a literary composition in the style of Virgil, captures to a degree the reality of a farmer's life lived in squalor, with very basic food to eat and an income supplemented by meager sales of garden vegetables in the town market. Likewise tenant farmers were common men who, if they ever had owned the land they worked, had lost it through debt to a landlord who now allowed them to stay in return for a fee or percentage of the land's produce each year. The parable of the tenants illustrates not only their situation, but the possibility they might cause trouble for the landlord:

> There was a landowner who planted a vineyard. He put a wall around it, dug a winepress in it, and built a watchtower. Then he rented the vineyard to some farmers and went away on a journey. When the harvest time approached, he sent his servants to the tenants to collect his fruit. The tenants seized his servants; they beat one, killed another, and stoned a third. Then he sent other servants to them, more than the first time, and the tenants treated them the same way. Last of all, he sent his son to them. 'They will respect my son,' he said. But when the tenants saw the son, they said to each other, 'This is the heir. Come, let's kill him and take his inheritance.' So they took him and threw him out of the vineyard and killed him. Jesus asked: Therefore, when the owner of the vineyard comes, what will he do to those tenants? 'He will bring those wretches to a wretched end,' they replied, 'and he will rent the vineyard to other tenants, who will give him his share of the crop at harvest time.' (Matthew 21:33–41)

The good tenant, therefore, works the landowner's land and pays what is owed on time. But he does not own the land, and the parable illustrates the tension that existed between the renter and the owner, including the possibility of eviction.

In rural areas, nonslave agricultural laborers also abounded, men without land but with muscle and skill to rent out as needed during the year. The New Testament parable of the workers in the vineyard captures the lot of these men:

> For the kingdom of heaven is like a landowner who went out early in the morning to hire men to work in his vineyard. He agreed to pay them a denarius for the day and sent them into his vineyard. About the third hour he went out and saw others standing in the

marketplace doing nothing. He told them, 'You also go and work in my vineyard, and I will pay you whatever is right.' So they went. He went out again about the sixth hour and the ninth hour and did the same thing. About the eleventh hour he went out and found still others standing around. He asked them, 'Why have you been standing here all day long doing nothing?' 'Because no one has hired us,' they answered. He said to them, 'You also go and work in my vineyard.' When evening came, the owner of the vineyard said to his foreman, 'Call the workers and pay them their wages, beginning with the last ones hired and going on to the first.' (Matthew 20:1–8)

And Timon in Lucian's tale makes even less for his labors. Timon, a once-rich man, has lost everything and so his position in society. To avoid the loss of face this entails:

… therefore my wrongs have driven me to this outlying farm, where, dressed in skins, I till the soil as a hired laborer at four obols [that is, half a denarius] a day, philosophizing with the solitude and with my pick. (*The Misanthrope* 6/Harmon)

Such men waited all day for work, sometimes in vain; certainly, those seeking work almost always outnumbered those hired, so on any given day a man could easily go home with no income to show for it.

As for the poor in towns, the elite poet Martial points his epigrams at a number of examples. Beggars, of course, abounded; they begged in hoarse voices for the bread that would be thrown to dogs (*Epigrams* 10.5.5). He refers to 'beggar's bridge', apparently a hangout, as were any covered spaces, such as beneath an aqueduct (*Epigrams* 12.32.25). He describes the life of a homeless person: shut out of the archway where he holed up, the winter makes him miserable; the dogs set upon him; birds try to take what he has – the image is of one the dead and unburied (*Epigrams* 12.32.25). The New Testament has a number of examples of beggars at town gates – apparently a favorite spot – and elsewhere. Others sought work as it might occasionally present itself – being a porter, messenger, day-laborer in construction, or whatever proved available. Lucian, for example, notes that typical jobs of the poor included selling salt fish, cobbling sandals, and begging at crossroads.

Although in some larger towns a public dole might to some extent alleviate the situation of the poor, such a dole would have reached only a small fraction of the poor population of the empire as a whole and can be ignored as a factor in the elaboration of the poor's mind world. In fact it is important to ignore much of what has been written about the poor based upon our sources for the city of Rome. Rome and its population was an aberration in the empire both for its size and for its political importance as the immediate milieu of the governing class. As tempting as it is to equate the Roman plebs with the urban poor when writing about the poor of the empire, the temptation must be resisted and material from Rome used very judiciously to be sure that only elements representative of the wider empire's poor are used as evidence.

While the general outline is clear enough, the state of the sources means that it is impossible to write a detailed account of how the poor lived and how they viewed their world in Roman times. Their treatment in death embodies their perceived worth in life: their remains were cremated and placed in unmarked urns, or their carcasses were thrown into mass graves; in Italy, on the Isola Sacra between Ostia and Rome, and in North Africa such interments have been discovered, while Horace speaks of an area of the Esquiline Hill as the place where 'a fellow slave would arrange to have his companions' dead bodies, heaved out of their miserable cells, carried to burial in cheap caskets' (*Satires* 1.8.8–13). In life as in death the poor are silent, or virtually so – as they mostly are even in modern times.

A scholar's list of the few sources found to provide material on the poor's own outlooks illustrates the difficulty: proverbs, fables, folksongs, oral history, legends, jokes, language, ritual, and religion. But of these, Roman social historians have only proverbs and fables, and bits and snippets of jokes and religion. Proverbs exist in many forms and contexts. Fables, an elaborated form of proverbs, exist in the collection of Aesop's tales and others. Of course there were folksongs, as there are many passing references such as this one by the elite Dio Chrysostom:

> My case is like that of men who in moving or shifting a heavy load beguile their labor by softly chanting or singing a tune – mere toilers that they are and not bards or poets of song.' (*Discourses* 1.9/Cohoon)

8. The dead poor. Paupers would be unceremoniously buried in potters' fields on the outskirts of towns, but the poor might still be able to afford humble burials such as those found at Isola Sacra, near Ostia.

But none survives. Legends, language, and ritual exist only in minuscule snatches or in very elite-distorted contexts.

Scholarly work on proverbs and fables is extensive, but only very recently has there been an attempt to relate their content to the actual life of the poor. Ancients were clear that these genres were expressions of what is now called 'popular morality.' Comparative studies also emphasize the validity of using them to see into the mind world of nonelites and, especially, for the most subjected members of society, the poor and slaves. Of course individual examples can be contingent on the context of their application, and ordinary folk and elites, too, valued and used fables in their own lives. In addition, some proverbs and fables are quite opaque. But judiciousness can produce useful results. Grouped patterns of narrative illustrate core values. Teresa Morgan in her *Popular Morality in the Early Roman Empire* shows the way; her careful and comprehensive work reaches similar conclusions to those I have drawn in my own research. I use selected proverbs and fables here as an essential window onto a real mind world of the poor.

There is one joke book from the ancient world, although we know that many others existed; however, even more so than with proverbs and fables, it is hard to pin down referential material specifically applicable to the outlook of the poor. Notices involving religion and philosophical thinking are sprinkled throughout classical literature; these notices have first to be recognized as relating to the perspective of the poor and then applied appropriately in the course of formulating an overall picture. Finally New Testament material, especially the illustrative situations and parables of the Gospels, provides insight into the outlook of the poor. When the evidence from all these sources comes together, a perhaps surprisingly coherent picture of the mind world of the poor emerges which is valid through time and space across the empire.

Demography

There is no quantifiable data from the Romano-Grecian world – or the ancient world in general – that helps much in determining the relative size of the demographic groups in the empire; even the total population is something of a guess, perhaps 50–60 million. Besides, the relative numbers would vary somewhat from place to place and from time to time. Nevertheless, I suppose a certain similarity of basic pattern among preindustrial societies in Europe and the Mediterranean area, and from this I offer a very broad idea of how many poor there were. Based upon studies of early modern Europe, where documentation exists to allow intelligent estimates of the size of various economic groups in society, I propose that about 65 percent of the population, slave and free combined, lived 'on the edge' – i.e. was at risk of death from any disruption of their subsistence existence by natural catastrophe, plague, famine, or other disaster.

To return to the poor themselves: They lived in a socioeconomically disadvantaged and contingent condition, and this determined their mind world. This sweeping statement hides an important everyday reality of the Romano-Grecian world. The condition of the poor differed in detail from place to place. Careful analysis would involve looking at the poor in Britain to study their local traditions and ecology;

or examining poor inhabitants of Egypt in the light of their very different cultural background and economic possibilities. The poor who lived in a world of climate extremes that erratically produced floods or sandstorms or drought might have a different attitude toward fate than those living in a more predictable environment. I do not mean to minimize this variety of human experience. I do want to emphasize, however, the commonality of their life-on-the-edge experience and how that led to sharing outlooks in important ways. For the world of dearth was the only world they knew firsthand. The natural world was an ever-present, if at times only a potential, threat; the social world was organized to oppress them. The poor's outlook saw the world of the empire as one of turbulence and inequality. Uncertainty in the instant was the constant in their lives. Their sociopolitical situation was one of subjection, whether it be to tax collector, state official, landlord, money-lender, or simple want; they were not free agents in any sense. On the other hand, the inevitability of the status quo also provided a constant for their thinking. The fable of 'The Snake's Tail' shows the wisdom of bowing to the natural essence of elite leadership:

> One day a snake's tail decided that the head shouldn't go first and was no longer willing to follow its lead creeping along. 'I ought to run things in my turn,' the tail said. [It tries to lead, but the snake falls into a pit and is very bruised.] … A victim of its presumption, the tail humbly implored the head, saying, 'Save us, please, mistress head. I confess that evil strife has ended badly for us all. I'll obey you, if you'll just put me back as I was before. You will not have to think about those things that happened before – they will never happen again.' (Babrius, *Fables*, 134)

Proverbs seem to view the world as stable, rather than (as often in elite literature) as in decline. The implication is that the order of the universe is static, that social perspectives do not change; they must be the way they are. The 'is' and 'ought to be' of the world are the same. This creates a very constraining, conservative mind world. People have and can make choices, but the range is very limited – they often lack options. A corollary is that there is no indication of social progress over generations in popular thought. Every life is the same life, only with different players. This very stability shows a sense of how much was impossible for most people; proverbs express popular wisdom's attitude that life is very difficult, and that much is done in vain. 'The frailty and destruction of all human life is a pervasive theme,' as Teresa Morgan puts it. The poor must deal with both environmental uncertainty and social certainty. Neither allows much chance of navigating away from the current situation, and both encourage attitudes that will enable survival within it.

Coping

At the heart of the poor's response to their precarious lives lies a system of beliefs and values that, growing out of life's realities, organizes it, drives it, sustains it, and keeps it from changing. This mind world is dominated by responses to their fundamental condition: dealing with the ever-present reality of possibly failing to have enough to survive. It focuses on dealing with the inevitable crises of life and tries to encourage social and moral action that will most aid survival in the immediate situation and social continuity in the long run. There is not a lot of time for thought and contemplation; the focus is on action, not beliefs. The wisdom of the poor is full of what to do and what not to do; abstractions of specific interactional behavior are rare. This does not mean that the poor person is uncreative; it just means that his creative thinking is limited because he has to focus on the first order of business, overcoming challenges of his fellow men and the physical world around him. The poor are very practical as they strive to survive.

A corollary to this perspective is that there is in their thinking little 'interiority' – the attempt to examine oneself and arrive at behavior-dictating conclusions from it. To the mind of the poor, 'know thyself' is not a contemplative admonition, but rather an admonition to active thinking about how to balance competing imperatives (e.g. friendship vs. gain). Philosophy tended to be idealistically oriented; the mind of the poor was fixed in practicality. Thus the outlook of popular morality as evidenced in fables and proverbs is markedly different from that of 'high' philosophical systems of the day. The mind of the poor views wisdom as a way for an individual to survive in a hostile world, not as a source of 'knowledge' or social problem-solving on a supra-individual scale, or any other abstraction. It is difficult if not impossible to find any of the main philosophical concepts of the elite's philosophical schools reflected with much importance in the mind world of the poor. Popular morality cares not a fig for the search for *eudaimonia* (happiness); contemplating the good as the main aim of human life, i.e. virtue for its own sake (Plato), is foreign; the Stoic ideals of *apatheia* and *ataraxia* (detachment) would only mystify; the Cynic obsession with the value of poverty would be completely lost on the irrevocably poor; any conflict between fate and free will is unknown, for they coexist without tension; the whole idea of rejecting norms of social life per Epicureans or Cynics is a luxury outside the experience of the poor. However, high philosophy and the outlook of the poor do share many points of view and many 'heroes'; in popular thinking the most-quoted authorities are (in order) the Seven Sages, Aesop, and Socrates, who account for over half of all cited famous men. Just how and to what extent they came to interact with one another and influence one another is another matter, and hard to determine. On the whole, it is much more likely that high philosophy drew on the well of popular thinking than that ideas of any significance or number percolated down from that philosophy to the poor man on the street. We lack evidence for such 'percolation' and, indeed, it is very hard to think how this could have happened, while the integration of 'folk wisdom' into more elaborated philosophical discourse seems easier to imagine.

Within their practical world the basic values of the poor are complex. Driven by the fundamental, ever-present imperative of the struggle to survive, these values emphasize two opposite 'pulls.' The first is the need to maintain a general environment in which, should everything fall apart, the cooperation of one's fellows can be relied upon to provide emergency aid. In tension with this is the imperative to push the needs of the basic social unit – usually the family – as the most important activity, even if it means acting to the detriment of one's fellows. The first 'pull' is worked out in the universe of positive reciprocity. Obligations of reciprocity, whether they be vertical (most typically, of the patron-client variety), or horizontal, are the key to 'social insurance' for times of trouble. At this macro-level, families develop relationships with other families in order to have their aid in difficult times. In this context, positive behavioral traits include friendship, bravery, harming enemies, hospitality, justice, honesty (including speaking the truth), helpfulness, and generosity to those in need; fables deal with these extensively, often dwelling on ambiguities.

At the micro-level, the members of a family use kinship as the basis for a complicated network of mutual expectations that are met in a social environment where everyone is simply and unexpressedly expected to help in certain ways, without getting any specific reward in return. Interestingly, the poor's mind world does not dwell on these crucial intra-family relationships. To judge by the fables and proverbs, relationships such as husband and wife, the economy of the household, and parent-child issues are not problematized in their thinking, for these things are seldom if ever the topic of popular thinking as it is recorded. These aspects of their existence seem to be so clearly regulated in their minds that conflicts of the sort resolved in fables and proverbs do not occur. Unfortunately, therefore, wisdom literature does not help us to understand the poor in these aspects of their lives.

The second 'pull' is expressed in habits of strife. For the poor, human life is full of failure and negation. In this environment, strife is endemic. The world of fables is one of constant danger and conflict. This, interestingly, has not received nearly the attention in the secondary literature that one would expect, given that all primary research on the poor – in fact, mostly on peasants – stresses the competitive nature of daily life. As social units struggle to maximize their potential for survival, antisocial habits are rampant. Popular literature focuses constantly on how to deal with the negative qualities of arrogance, flattery, untrustworthiness, stubbornness, ill-temper, cowardice (the subject of many proverbs), deceit, slander, greed, boasting, and inappropriate social behavior in general.

Most particularly, among the poor there is competition – for honor and status as well as for material advantages – and its fellow travelers, pride, envy, and revenge. The fable world is full of antisocial behavior. For example, in 'The Roosters and the Partridge,' 'like' (the roosters) are in conflict with each other as well as with 'different' (the partridge):

A certain man who kept roosters came upon a tame partridge for sale, bought it, and took it home to rear along with the roosters. Since, however, the other birds beat and pursued the partridge, it was heavy at heart, concluding that it was looked down upon as being a different kind of bird. But when it shortly observed that the roosters also fought one another, not parting till they had drawn blood, it said to itself: 'Well, I'm no longer going to be upset when I'm beaten by them, for I see that they don't even spare one another.' (*Collectio Augustana*/Hansen)

The destructive nature of greed is told in 'The Dog and His Shadow':

A dog stole a piece of meat from a kitchen. He trotted along the bank of a river. Seeing the shadow of his meat much magnified in the stream, he let go of the piece he had and lunged for the shadow. But he ended up with neither the shadow-meat, nor the real meat he had let go. So he returned, very hungry, back again across the ford by which he had come. (Babrius, *Fables* 79)

As it is in the proverb 'Never thrust your sickle into another's wheat' (Publilius Syrus, Maxim 593). Equally destructive habits such as boasting and envy are also taken to task in the fables. As a final example, a person will directly harm others to protect his own survival, as the fable of 'The Fisherman Striking the Water' illustrates:

A fisherman was fishing in a certain river. He stretched his net tight so as to span the stream from one side to the other, then tied a cord onto a stone and started striking the water with it so that the fish in their reckless flight might happen into his net. One of the persons, who lived in the area, seeing him doing this, upbraided him for muddying the water and so not allowing them to drink clear water. But he replied: 'But if I don't stir up the river like this, I'll have to die of starvation.' (*Collectio Augustana*/Hansen)

These potentially (and, often enough, actually) disruptive modes of behavior are, however, by tacit agreement not allowed to overwhelm the fundamentally cooperative nature of the enterprise. The fables are full of lessons on cooperation. Here are some examples. 'The Horse and the Ass' teaches the value of sharing burdens:

A man had a horse he was in the habit of leading around without any burden, since he laid the entire load onto an aged ass. The ass, being at the end of his rope, went up to the horse and said, 'If you would be so kind as to take a portion of my burden, I'd be able to manage; if not, I'll surely die.' 'Go away,' replied the horse, 'I don't give a damn.' The ass plodded along in silence. Finally, exhausted by toil he fell down dead, just as he had predicted. The master brought the horse over and removing all the load from the dead ass, he put it on the horse's back along with the pack saddle, adding for good measure the hide of the ass that he first flayed. 'What an idiot I was!' said the horse to himself. 'I didn't want to carry a little of the load and necessity has now laid everything on my back.' (Babrius, *Fables* 7)

'The Fire-Bearing Fox' teaches the importance of keeping one's temper:

A man wanted to take a novel type of revenge on a fox who was ravaging his vineyard and garden. He tied a bundle of tow to the animal's tail and setting it aflame, he turned the fox loose. But a god looking down guided the fox to the very field of the man who had harmed the animal. There the fox set fire to all around him. It was harvest season; the fat heads of grain held high hopes. The man ran after the fox, anguishing over the loss of his considerable labor. None of his grain ever saw the threshing floor. (Babrius, *Fables* 11)

'Divide and Conquer' also teaches that the poor must stick together:

Three bulls grazed along always together. A lion lying in wait for an opportunity to seize them realized that he wouldn't be able to take them all at once. Sowing contention among them by sly suggestions and outright lies, he caused them to become enemies of one another. Having divided them against each other, the lion easily took each as prey, one at a time. (Babrius, *Fables* 44)

'No Use Praying for a Robber' shows that unfair actions mean you will not get help when you need it:

A sick raven said to his weeping mother, 'Don't cry, mother. Rather, ask the gods to deliver me from my deadly disease and from my sufferings.' 'My child,' his mother replied, 'which god will want to save you? For which is the god whose altar you have not robbed?' (Babrius, *Fables* 78)

The enforcing mechanisms – most saliently and effectively gossip, ridicule, reproach, oral censure, and, ultimately, ostracism – are social, lacking anything like a police presence, which seldom if ever is visible as a part of the mind world of the poor. These are, of course, imperfect weapons, often directed unfairly (to our way of thinking) and often without appeal – the *opinio communis* of the group being imposed without a formal venue for reply. The roiling effects of this situation are seen in family feuds, in a generalized conviction that self-aggrandizement (within certain limits, of course) is acceptable, and similar selfish acts. As a result, the poor are loath to be too trusting, even of friends, as the proverb attests: 'Treat your friend as if he might become an enemy' (Publilius Syrus, Maxim 401).

An aspect of the mind world of the poor that has always attracted the attention of the not-poor has been the poor's attitude toward work. Throughout ancient literature there runs the accusation that the poor are lazy. However, looking beyond the negative stereotype of the elite, the fact is that the poor value working hard. Fables along these lines are numerous: 'The Ant and the Fly,' 'The Old Bull and the Young Steer,' 'How the Lark Knew When to Leave,' and 'When the Sluggard Went to the Ant' are a few examples. Nevertheless, although the poor work hard, they are *not* interested in working themselves to death. In fact, their outlook makes it senseless to do that. The basic existential fact for the poor is that they are poor, and that there is very little possibility to become un-poor. Their goal is to survive, not to thrive, for their precarious existence has taught that the risks needed to 'move on up' – to thrive instead of merely survive – are not worth the very real chance that striving for more through changed technologies or social arrangements will, in fact, boomerang and destroy them. Hence they are very cautious and wary of venturing beyond the conservative. This risk aversion is well expressed in the fable of 'The Fisherman and the Sprat':

A fisherman who fished all over the sea and lived by the produce of his pole once caught on his horsehair line a little fish of the kind suitable to be fried up. The struggling fishlet begged the fisherman to listen to his plea: 'What profit will I gain you? How much will I sell for? I still could grow a lot bigger. It's only a few days ago that mother brought me forth among the seaweed near this rocky shore. Let me go today; don't kill me to no purpose. Later, after I have grown fat on feeding in the sea, I'll become a grand fish, suitable for the table of the rich, and you will come back here and catch me again.' So the little fish spoke, lamenting as he gasped for life. But he could not persuade the old man, who, while sticking him on his sharp cane stringer, replied, 'It is crazy to let go of the little you have for certain in the hope of gaining what is uncertain in the future.' (Babrius, *Fables* 6)

Modern studies have indicated that as the poor work harder and squeeze more out of whatever resources they have, their family size grows and a new equilibrium between product and needs is established at approximately the same level of living as before – only now for more people. In addition, the poor sense that producing more will just mean that more is taken from them, not that they will have more in the long run. The zero-sum nature of the economy (or, at least, its perceived 'zero-sum-ness') also reinforces this tendency to stop working at a certain point, for the group as a whole will put pressure on the subunits not to work too hard, not to garner more than an appropriate share of available resources, because for one unit to gain, another must lose. These factors channel clearly into Alexander Chanyanov's 'theory of drudgery,' originally developed through the study of Russian peasants in the early twentieth century, but subsequently found to be generally applicable. According to this theory, a poor person will stop working once the judgment is made that more work will not yield sufficient gain to outweigh the irksomeness of the extra work. Seen from without, a poor person may seem to be irrationally lazy when in fact the calculation has been made, in all likelihood subconsciously based on past experience and/or tradition, that more work is not remunerative, so why do it? Thus, the outlook of the poor makes it perfectly acceptable to work until the basic needs are met, and then to knock off. Just the same sort of calculation, over the long haul, leads to the poor not striving mightily to escape their poverty, whether or not this represents an acceptance of the dominant ideology locating them in a subordinate position in society. The 'laziness' of the poor is embedded in their practical view of life's possibilities.

Religion

Human societies have difficulty policing themselves by themselves. There is often recourse to the supernatural as the ultimate enforcer; the rules of the community, supra-communal, emanate from and are enforced by a higher power or powers, which thus in theory at least puts all the players on the same level playing field and at the same time provides a ready reason why some things/persons succeed and others fail. Not surprisingly, the mind world of the poor embraces this human constant. But it does it in a particularly pragmatic, down-to-earth way, because of the proximity of the poor to the contingencies of life.

A basic element in the poor's religious outlook is the 'will of the gods.' This 'will' aspect supports the traditional values and situation of the social group by emphasizing that, in theory at least, the gods set down rules of action and reward behavior such as piety and justice, while punishing their opposites. But observable reality is that the gods do not consistently enforce this 'will' by punishing those who err and rewarding those who comply. Faced with this clash of expectation and reality, the power of Fate/Fortune steps in to fill the need for an explanation. This power exists not only outside human control, but even that of the gods; both are powerless against Fate. In a way, Fate stands outside of the entire natural order of things, the great explainer of why things often do not seem to happen as the rules of the game indicate they should. Fate comes into play both through a resignation to the hand the future might deal and through a conviction that life's good and bad experiences somehow ultimately balance out. The former is illustrated in 'The Force of Destiny' (Babrius, *Fables* 136), in which a father tries to avoid the fated death of his son by locking him away, only to lose him through an accident in his prison. The moral is 'Bear bravely what is given you by Fate and do not try to avoid it by clever devices; you cannot not escape what is bound to be.' The latter is exemplified in a fable from the *Collectio Augustana*:

Some fishermen were drawing a dragnet. Since it was heavy they danced for joy, thinking that they had a great catch. But after they had drawn it to shore and found that the net was full of stones and wood but few fish, they became very heavy-hearted, not so much angry at what had happened as at their having expected the contrary. But one of them, an old fellow, said: 'Friends, let's stop this. Grief, it seems, is the sister of joy, and since we had so much pleasure beforehand, we had to have some grief as well.' (*Collectio Augustana*/Hansen)

A fatalistic vision also permeates much of the proverb literature: 'It is easier to get a favor from Fortune than to keep it' (Publilius Syrus, Maxim 198); 'When Fortune flatters, she does it to betray' (Maxim 197); 'Fortune is not satisfied with inflicting one calamity' (Maxim 213).

A perhaps unexpected result of Fate's role in the world of the poor is its encouragement of self-reliance. Since the gods cannot be counted upon, and Fate is whimsical, the safest bet is on one's own hard work and resourcefulness. The fable of 'Heracles and the Ox-Driver' illustrates this:

An ox-driver was driving his cart home from a village, when the cart pitched down into a deep ditch. The drover, rather than try to pull it out, just sat there, not doing anything except calling on Hercules, the only god he honored and sincerely worshiped. The god appeared to him and spoke: 'Put your hands to the wheels and whip the oxen. Call on the gods only when you are doing something to help yourself, or you will call on them in vain.' (Babrius, *Fables* 20)

Such an outlook feeds into the generally positive attitude toward work (but not too much of it) I have discussed as another aspect of the mind world of the poor.

As I have mentioned, an intrinsic aspect of being poor is being in a subordinate relationship to others, who, among other things, redirect some of the poor's produce toward their own ends. Thus the poor find themselves in a subjected position; the origins of that subjection are often mythologized, sometimes historicized, but the ultimate reality is that it is the way life is, and the poor act within this reality. One would suppose that there was a dark humor about this condition, and perhaps a joke from the *Philogelos*, a Greek book of humor, fits that mold:

Wanting to train his donkey not to eat, a numbskull stopped giving him any food. When the donkey died of starvation, the man said: 'What a loss! Just when he had learned not to eat, he died.' (*Philogelas*/Hansen)

The fundamental fact of subjection means that the poor's production is always to some extent at the mercy of those in power. The fable 'More Fearsome than Ever' catches this reality:

A lion went crazy with anger. A fawn who saw him from the forest cried out, 'Woe is us! What will he not do in a rage – he is already unbearable for us when he is sane!' (Babrius, *Fables* 90)

Lucian captures some of the frustration of the poor in the face of the rich when he has a character in his *Saturnalia* address the titan Cronos and ask him to reinstate the Golden Age, when:

… men themselves were gold and poverty was nowhere near. As for us [poor folk], we could not even be thought of as lead, but something meaner, if such there be; and for most of us food is won with toil; and poverty, want, and helplessness, and 'alas!', and 'how can I get it?', and 'oh, what bad luck!' and such exclamations are plentiful, at least among us poor. We should be less distressed about it, you may be sure, if we did not see the rich living in such bliss, who, though they have such gold, such silver in their safes, though they have all that clothing and own slaves and carriage-horses and tenements and farms, each and all in large numbers, not only have never shared them with us, but never deign even to notice ordinary people. This is what sticks in our throats most of all, Cronos, and we think it an intolerable thing for such a man to lie in his purple clothes and gorge himself on all those good things, belching, receiving his guest's congratulations, and feasting without a break, while I and my sort dream where we can get four obols to be able to sleep after a fill of bread or barley, with cress or thyme or onion as a relish. (Lucian, *Saturnalia* 20–21/Kilburn)

In their subordinate position, the poor still felt self-worth and desired to be treated decently. An episode in the *Satyricon* captures this. Corax has been hired as a porter, a typical day-laborer's job, and roughly asserted his value as a person:

Come on now! Do you think that I am a beast of burden or some ship to carry stone? I hired out to do a man's work, not a horse's. I am no less free than you, even if my father left me a pauper. (*Satyricon* 117)

Yet within the potential of absolute power over the poor, a *modus vivendi* is established that sees the demands of the powerful take as much as possible, while leaving the poor with just enough to survive on. I am, of course, speaking of a relationship in equilibrium: if the powerful demand too much, they can destroy themselves as the poor rise up (a rare occurrence, admittedly), or they can destroy the poor – driving them off, or killing them through starvation. In the latter case the powerful are working against their own self-interest; hence, the equilibrium, even given the very asymmetrical power relationship.

Reciprocity, as in horizontal relationships, is the key leverage that the poor have to deal with this vertical asymmetry. Usually expressed in patron-client structures, the basic ideal is that each side has something the other needs, and so they symbiotically support each other. The poor have respect and income for the powerful; the powerful have resources that can help the poor in times of distress, and are obligated to use them. There is an interesting fable that speaks to this from the perspective of the poor, 'The Lion and the Mouse.' In it, the ability of the powerless to help the powerful is affirmed:

A lion having caught a mouse was going to eat it. But that little domestic thief, seeing his end near, babbled out a plea: 'If you want to fill your stomach with meat, you really should hunt animals with large horns – deer and bulls. But to eat a mouse! This really isn't enough to even taste as it touches the edges of your lips. Spare me, I beg you. Just possibly, as small as I am, I shall some day be able to show you my gratitude.' The lion laughed and let the suppliant live. Later, pursued by youthful hunters, he fell into their nets and found himself tied very tightly so he could be killed. The mouse then stealthily emerged from his hole, cut the strands of rope with his tiny teeth, and set the lion free. By saving the lion in his turn, he repaid him who had let *him* live. (Babrius, *Fables* 107)

The reality was that the powerful held all the cards, as usual. Clients may have cast their case in moral terms – they didn't have much real bargaining power – but the patronage that came in return was hardly reliable. One good strategy often seemed to be to just escape notice and stay out of trouble, as in the fable of 'The Fisherman and the Fish':

A fisherman cast out his net and after a short time drew it back in. His luck was good: It was full of all sorts of delectable fish. But the smaller ones swam to the bottom of the net and escaped through the meshes, while the larger ones were pulled up and lay flopping in the boat. (Babrius, *Fables* 4)

Of course, there was always the possibility of violent conflict between the poor and those with power over them. Aelian gives an example from Hellenistic times of the poor reaching the end of their rope, and rising up:

Theokles and Thrasonides in Korinth and Praxis in Mytilene placed little value in property and instead displayed magnanimity seeing their co-citizens in a state of poverty while they themselves were rich. They also advised others to lighten the burden of poverty for those in need. And, after they did not succeed in convincing others, they themselves remitted the debts owed to them, and thus gained not money but life itself. For those whose debts were not remitted attacked their creditors, and wielding the arms of rage, and proffering the most reasonable claim, that of utter destitution, slew their creditors. (Aelian, *Historical Miscellany* 14.24/Gallant)

The possibility of less radical, but still bothersome resistance is illustrated in the fable 'The Battle of the Bull and the Mouse':

A mouse bit a bull. The bull rushed on the mouse to avenge himself. The mouse forestalled the bull by taking refuge at the back of his hole. The bull found himself reduced to striking the wall with his horns until, worn out, he sank down and went to sleep before the opening. Then the mouse peeped out, emerged, slipped over to him, bit him again, and quickly fled back. The bull jumped up, not knowing what to do. The mouse said to him in his tiny voice, 'The biggest are not always the most powerful. Sometimes the small and humble prevail.' (Babrius, *Fable* 112)

A revolt that could turn the tables on the rich had a certain appeal, as this oracle prophecy from Oxyrhynchus in Egypt testifies:

... upheaval and war ... and the rich will suffer sorely. Their arrogance will be defeated, and their possessions seized and given to others ... (*P. Oxy.* 31.2554)

Revolts of the poor have caught the attention of both the powerful and those sympathetic to the poor. But the usually overwhelming ability of the powerful to direct effective force against the recalcitrant poor explains in large measure why such revolts are few and far between, and why they are never successful in replacing the powerful with a hegemony of the poor. The norm is that a revolt is suppressed with as much blood as necessary, and probably more; or the leadership of the revolt becomes distant from the poor themselves. In either case, things return to the status quo of subjection; this is as true of the Romano-Grecian world as of any other. The memory of failed revolts probably lingered in the culture of the poor, and served as an effective deterrent to further revolt, at least until conditions became again totally intolerable in terms of subsistence and survival.

But there is another possibility: That the poor believed in the status quo – the 'great chain of being' – internalized their position in society as just and right, and played their subjected role willingly. In another time, Charles Dickens captured this underling mentality in his novelette *The Chimes*:

Oh let us love our occupations,
Bless the squire and his relations,
Live upon our daily rations,
And always know our proper stations.

I would call this a consciousness of acceptance – of the alignment of the poor's values with those of the elite. 'How the Kite Lost His Voice' teaches that if you try to become something better than you are, you risk losing everything:

> A kite of old had a different cry than now, a sharper one. Having heard a horse let out a sonorous neigh, he determined to copy it. But in imitating the horse he ended up with neither the powerful voice he wanted, nor the cry he had had before. (Babrius, *Fables* 73)

Every ancient social uprising that I know of had as its aim the twin goals of cancellation of debt and redistribution of land. These are, at heart, conservative goals – an attempt to reestablish the just world of before in which everyone had land and was free from debt-dependence on others. Presumably, the same hierarchical and hegemonic power distribution would continue to exist in this reformed world – the only change would be that everyone would have a fair share of resources. In other words, the complaint is not against the power structure per se, but against its unjust incarnations. Such an attitude implies that the poor accepted an exploitative system.

But the poor could also conceive of a world when the worm had turned. While there is no evidence that there was anything like the ideologies of human worth available from the eighteenth century and seen most explosively in Marxist reconfiguration and aggressive presentation of the rightful expectations and potentialities of the working poor, a world turned upside down could be imagined. Lucian in one of his satires has Micyllus, a poor tanner who has been called to Hades by the Fates, remark:

> But as for me, having nothing at stake in life, neither farm nor tenement nor gold nor gear nor reputation nor statues, of course I was in marching order, and when Atropos did but sign to me I gladly flung away my knife and my leather (I was working on a sandal) and sprang up at once and followed her, barefooted as I was and without even washing off the blacking. In fact, I led the way, with my eyes to the fore, since there was nothing in the rear to turn me about and call me back. And by Heaven I see already that everything is splendid

here with you, for that all should have equal rank and nobody be any better than his neighbor is more than pleasant, to me at least. And I infer that there is no dunning of debtors here and no paying of taxes, and above all no freezing in winter or falling ill or being thrashed by men of greater consequence. All are at peace, and the tables are turned, for we paupers laugh while the rich are distressed and lament. (*Downward Journey* 15/Harmon)

More than revenge, though, the poor sought justice. The poor were convinced that were everyone, most especially the rich, to live within the rules, there would be a stable environment for staying alive, performing their ceremonies, and paying their dues. The fable 'Once in Utopia' captures the normal height of aspiration for the poor – a happy world in which the powerful were somehow compelled to properly exercise their power appropriately:

A lion became the ruler, but he did not have the usual cruel, mean temper. He did not always resort to violence to settle affairs; rather he was just and gentle, rather like a man. As he ruled, so they say, the wild animals gathered in assembly in order there to have their cases heard, and to give and receive legal decisions. Each animal called another to account, the lamb the wolf, the wild goat the leopard, the deer the tiger; each was satisfied. Everyone was at peace. Then the rabbit spoke up: 'This is the day I have long prayed for, the day when even the weak are feared by the strong.' (Babrius, *Fables* 102)

And there are a number of fables that urge the rich to shear, not flay, the poor, such as the tale concerning the widow and her sheep quoted below, and the following:

A groom sold the barley meant for his horse to an innkeeper. After drinking late into the evening, he spent the next day currying the horse. The horse said to him, 'If you really want me to look great, don't sell my food.' (Babrius, *Fables* 83)

But as there was a lack of practical alternatives to the status quo, this must have had the effect of making acceptance of the dominant worldview as the right and just one much easier than we can imagine it today. So there were few local and no empire-wide disturbances by the poor because the poor demanded not the overthrow of the existing order, but rather, if anything, its reform. And that reform never came, just as the poor strongly suspected it would not.

If we think of the definition of justice as giving each person his due, we are on the track of the view of the poor. Thus the powerful can remain powerful, but must allow the poor their 'due' as well – the basic opportunity to live out their lives without the sort of exploitation that endangers their social and alimentary subsistence. Apollonius of Tyana is made by Philostratus to give just such advice to the emperor Vespasian; he tells him that '[you] make better use of your wealth than any ruler before you, if you employ it in offering aid to the poor, while at the same time that you render the possessions of the rich secure' (*Life of Apollonius* 5.36).

The fables are full of lectures on justice. For example, 'Fleece Me, But Don't Flay Me':

> Once a widow kept a sheep in her home. Wishing to clip its wool in as long strands as possible, she sheared it clumsily and trimmed the fleece so close to the skin that she cut into its flesh here and there. The suffering sheep bleated to her, 'Don't abuse me. My blood won't increase the weight of my fleece. Mistress, if you need my flesh, there is a butcher who can kill me efficiently. If you need fleece and not flesh, there is a professional shearer who can shear and yet spare me.' (Babrius, *Fables* 51)

Other fables deal with similar issues: 'Close to the Law but Far from Justice' (human justice often does not touch the poor); 'The Knight and His Horse' (an appeal against arbitrary exploitation); 'A Double Standard of Justice' and 'The Mills of the Gods Grind Slow' (be fair to your fellows as you wish the gods to be fair to you). Proverbs are quite skeptical of judicial systems, although they emphasize justice. The poor are like the swallow, near to the courts, but far from their protection:

> A trilling swallow, a bird that shares the dwelling of men, built in the springtime her nest under the roofline of a law-court building

where old men in charge of the laws held forth. There she became a mother to seven small ones whose wings were not yet covered with purple feathers. A snake gliding from a hole ate them up one and all. The poor mother lamented their untimely deaths. 'Alas,' she said, 'how unfortunate I am! Right here where the laws and judgments of men abide, from that place I must flee – a swallow who has been wronged.' (Babrius, *Fables* 118)

Justice is therefore independent of any human way to achieve it – the enforcement is left to the gods, as in sayings such as 'the divine brings the bad to justice.' Humans have in reality little access to it – certainly no sure access to it. The law is mostly mentioned to emphasize the disparity between it and justice. Popular morality believes in justice, but not in the law as able to achieve it. And with some reason. There is practically nothing in the law texts relating to the poor. The rights of fisherfolk might be noted in a decision, and generalities about the powerful not getting special treatment occur, but it is clear that the poor are involved in cases very rarely – there are no treatments of hired labor, for example. The law simply did not care very much about the very poor. And when they did get involved in a legal matter, they could count on coming out badly, as Jesus' advice indicates clearly:

For while you are going with your opponent to appear before the magistrate, on your way there make an effort to settle with him, so that he may not drag you before the judge, and the judge turn you over to the officer, and the officer throw you into prison. I say to you, you will not get out of there until you have paid the very last cent. (Luke 12:58–9)

Knowing the inefficacy of the legal system and of the justice of the powerful to protect them, the poor must resort to informal means of dispute resolution, or simply knuckle under.

On a daily basis, however, proverbs and fables advise strategies for dealing with the more powerful. They emphasize the futility of trying to get the better of the rich. No matter what you do, you will be eaten anyway, as 'The Wolf and the Lamb' teaches:

A wolf seeing one day a lamb that had wandered away from its flock did not attack him to carry him off by force, but rather sought a specious pretext to justify his hostility. 'Did you not slander me last year, small as you were?' he asked. 'I didn't slander you at all last year; I was only born *this* year,' was the reply. 'Aren't you grazing on grass that is mine?' continued the wolf. 'I have never touched any greenery.' 'Have you not taken up water which is mine?' persisted the wolf. 'Up to this very moment, it is only my mother's teat that nourishes me,' came the riposte. Then the wolf seized the lamb and said to it as it downed the meal, 'You can't keep a wolf from his dinner, even though you answer easily all my complaints.' (Babrius, *Fables* 89)

A good defense against the powerful was to avoid confrontation as much as possible, as in 'The Oak and the Reeds':

The wind having uprooted an oak tree made it fall from the mountainside into a river. The churning torrent carried along this giant ancient tree, planted by men of old. At the same time many rushes rose firm on both sides of the river, drinking water on the banks. The oak was astonished that plants so frail and weak were not torn away, since his own strong trunk had been uprooted. A rush spoke wisely to him, 'Don't be surprised. You fought against the wind and so you were vanquished. We, on the other hand, bend, disposed to adjust to our situation, whenever a light breeze moves our tops.' (Babrius, *Fables* 36)

But it is also helpful to be smart. Many fables emphasize how an intelligent analysis and appropriate response to a situation pays off handsomely. For example, 'The Lion and the Fox':

A lion got too old to go on the hunt. He lay stretched out toward the back of his cave as if he were kept there by illness. He pretended to have weak breathing and smoothed his harsh voice. This news spread through the haunts of the wild beasts. All were concerned about the weakness of the lion, and each entered the cave in order to see for himself. The lion had no trouble devouring them one after the other. So he had found a way to live plentifully in spite of his old age.

A clever fox suspected the situation and said, keeping his distance, 'O King, how are you doing?' The lion replied, 'Greetings, you who are most dear to me of all the animals. Why don't you come closer instead of looking at me from a distance? Come here, my friend, and by your various, colorful stories lighten my final days.' 'Watch after yourself!' replied the fox. 'But please excuse me if I must go. I am put off by the tracks of so many animals that go into your cave, but you don't show me any coming out.' (Babrius, *Fables* 103)

As hostile as the poor were to the wealthy and their power, wealth in and of itself, beyond its role in hierarchical strife, was important to the poor. They knew that wealth was power, but they also knew the risks. Poverty was not good. But the reality of riches and its appeal was somewhat fraught. Greed could lead to disaster, as in the fable of the mouse in the soup:

A mouse fell into a cooking pot full of soup that did not have a lid. Choked by the grease and on the point of death, he said, 'I have eaten, I have drunk, I have enjoyed all the pleasures of life; it is time for me to die.' (Babrius, *Fables* 60)

Proverbs are also ambivalent about wealth. On the one hand, it provides opportunities and so is welcome. But on the other, there is some suspicion of it, for example for the borrower. There is also the common implication that wealth is gained by treachery, theft, and other antisocial means. So the basic aim is to keep what one has, rather than to increase it greatly – the strategy is decidedly defensive, conservative, and aimed at self-preservation above all. The proverb 'better to be poor on land than rich at sea' (Diogenianus 2.62) catches the tone of caution. If you are poor, you make the best of it.

This view of wealth and poverty does not lead to questioning of the existing order of things; proverbs convey a very strong sense of hierarchy, as does, for example, the fable 'The Jackdaw and the Eagle':

An eagle snatched a sleek lamb in his talons to give to his offspring to eat. A jackdaw was spurred on to do the same thing. So he swooped down on a ram. But he entangled his claws in his fleece, and beat his wings in vain trying to carry off his theft. A shepherd came running up, seized him, and cut his wings. The bird then confessed, 'I am rightly punished. Why did I, being only a jackdaw, try to act like an eagle?' (Babrius, *Fables* 137)

But at the same time I note that the most frequent expression of the poor's attitude toward those more fortunate than themselves is illustrated by what Tyndaris says of them in Plautus' *The Prisoners* (583), '… *est miserorum, ut malevolentes sint atque invideant bonis*' ('it is the nature of the downtrodden to be discontented and to envy the wealthy'). If the poor had the time and inclination to dream, that dream and desire was not the overthrow of the rich, but to have what they have.

Survival

The tenuous economic condition of the poor guided their lives. Their position in the social hierarchy was bad and not likely to get better. But their strategies for survival served them well. A combination of cooperation and competition assured as much success as possible within their constrained circumstances. Fate provided a framework for understanding their universe. They dealt with subjection to the more powerful by accommodation and resistance. They could hope for a just world in which they would be in a better situation, but its unlikelihood did not keep them from working hard and, quite naturally, from envying those who had more than they.

4

COPING IN BONDAGE:
SLAVES

THE DOMESTICATION OF ANIMALS and the beginning of slavery go hand in hand, for a person is potentially the most useful of all animals. Thus from early times humans have tried and often succeeded in dominating other humans to further their own welfare. This longstanding, organic development of slavery in parallel with the more general use of animals subordinated to humans' needs explains why in antiquity the institution of slavery was never seriously contested as being other than a normal, acceptable way of relating to other human beings. Slavery was omnipresent in the Romano-Grecian world. Its specific forms and applications varied according to local factors, but its existence was not questioned in any practical way. The physical and psychological toll that slavery visited upon individual slaves occasionally came to the attention of masters; the fundamentally arbitrary ways of demarcating a difference between 'slave' and 'not slave' troubled philosophers. But except for a few rare and uninfluential outliers, neither those who thought about slaves and slavery, nor those who just used slaves, nor those who had dealings with others' slaves in their daily lives, considered the merits or practicality of abolition; the story of slavery is one of accommodation to it or attempts to escape or avoid it, not to overthrowing the condition itself within society.

This cultural reality provides the guide to seeing slaves living out their lives. Slavery does not so much reduce the slave to a dehumanized

9. Into slavery. A sad procession of men, women, and children is led into slavery, to be sold by the trader Aulus Caprilius Timotheus, who proudly boasts of his unsavory (even to the ancients) profession on his tombstone.

'thing,' as it creates a different order of existence, an environment in which the slave is 'rehumanized' in a social or cultural role. Romans never denied the 'humanity' of slaves, their 'personhood' as men, not beasts, no matter how much they compared them to beasts as chattel property, or spoke of them as morally inferior, weak human beings. They just wanted them to be socialized to their slavish role. From the slave's perspective, his or her life as negotiation of that slavish role reveals what it meant to be a human in an enslaved condition.

Coming to a general picture of slaves in their slave experience is complicated by the complexity and variety of that experience. The evidence for the slave's mind world, scanty as it is, is never entirely coherent. Challenges also arise because the Westerner tends to use knowledge or impressions of New World slavery to make sense of what is known of Romano-Grecian slavery. As I will show, there are important, revealing points of comparison, but the differences are stark as well; I mention here only the most obvious, the lack of race as a basic element in ancient slavery and the much wider diversity of slave life in antiquity.

A slave voice?

Are there actual slave voices in ancient sources? A few authors who wrote for the elite had begun or spent part of their lives as slaves:

Plautus, the comedic writer of the Roman Republic; Diogenes, the Greek founder of Cynic philosophy; Epictetus, the Roman Stoic philosopher of the early empire; and the fabulists Aesop and Phaedrus all claimed or have been claimed directly or indirectly to have begun life as slaves, or to have been enslaved during a portion of their lives. What is most striking is that no author who demonstrably is or was a slave explicitly takes on the task of writing about his experience *as a slave*. Epictetus and Plautus come the closest, for the former's use of slave examples and the latter's use of slave characters in his plays clearly address the three main concerns of a slave's outlook. Still, one might expect to find among the tens of thousands of pages of Latin and Greek works one that was explicitly written by a slave about the slave experience – or at least among the thousands of titles of ancient Latin and Greek works that once existed but no longer survive. After all, we know that many slaves were educated. For example, one, Phlegon of Tralles, wrote history and other matters during the time of the emperor Hadrian, while another, Q. Remmius Palaemon, once he gained his freedom was a famous professor of literature at Rome. But there are no nonfiction works that even claim to be by slaves about slaves, and only one piece of fiction: *The Life of Aesop*, written by an unknown author. There are fictional works that famously foreground the 'slave experience': Petronius' *Satyricon*, Apuleius' *Golden Ass*, various ancient romances, and Lucian in *The Runaways* and some other tales speak at various times and in various ways from a slave's perspective. *Satyricon* and *The Golden Ass* are certainly written by elites – Petronius was of the imperial court and Apuleius a provincial elite. The background of the authors of the romances is unknown. *The Life of Aesop* would seem from its simple language and style to come from the pen of an ordinary person, while Lucian was raised in an artisan family and has some claim to firsthand knowledge of nonelite life and outlooks.

Of course historians and other elite literary and legal sources mention slaves. Traditionally, these have formed the backbone of all discussion of ancient slavery. My project, however, is to seek the slaves' mind world without the cultural bias and contamination that inevitably exists when these elites touch on slaves and slavery. It can be argued, quite properly, that the standard elite sources can be used if care is taken to account for their social point of view; many scholars have done just that. But I wish to leave them aside in order to emphasize the picture that can be painted without them. It is an experiment of sorts, but I believe a more immediate experience of the slave mind world is accessible without their interference. As a result, although I use some elites such as agricultural writers and the novelists Petronius and Apuleius who are striving to see the slaves' world, standard elite historians, biographers, and letter-writers only occasionally figure in my narrative.

There might be some hope of finding slave voices in Christian literature given the participation of slaves in early Christian worship and social groups. In the Gospels there are forthright examples of slavery in action, as well as some understanding of slave attitudes. But in the New Testament epistles only the First Letter of Peter seems to speak of slaves from a slave's point of view, despite all the rhetoric about slaves being a significant part of the Christian community, and if the author was a slave, he has disguised this well. Later Christian literature is also unhelpful. So in Christian as in pagan literature the voice of the slave is hard to find.

At a slight remove, the many references to issues of concern to slaves, particularly those relating to sexuality and to running away, show that dream interpretation and astrological works were responding directly to slaves and their concerns. And fables, while applicable to a wide range of statuses, were rightly seen in antiquity, as now, as in many cases expressing genuine attitudes and strategies of slaves. But this makes it puzzling to realize just how unexamined the life of a slave was in other popular literature. In proverbs and gnomic sayings, slavery is virtually invisible. It remains strange that fables should seem to evoke the situation of slaves, while proverbs and other popular literature do not.

Outside of literature, certainly slaves left their own voices as epitaphs, mostly very short, on their graves. These gravestones are more easily imagined as the true voices of slaves and are a valuable window onto their slave experience; I use them extensively. Other archaeological evidence for slavery is rather limited, and what does exist is difficult to relate to the slaves' mind world. Thus material culture does not add much to the discussion here. Papyri, though, offer a very useful source for thinking about slaves, providing demographic as well as contextual evidence that greatly enriches our understanding.

Numbers and sources of slaves

The demography of slavery helps to provide some background for the slaves' mind world. Slavery was not the predominant form of rural labor in the empire; there were heavy concentrations on a relatively few broad estates, mostly in Italy and Sicily, plus a higher than average percentage of slaves in larger towns and cities. Although the regional variation was obviously great, overall perhaps only one household in seven owned a slave, with most of these being owned by the elite and employed not in agriculture or trade, but in domestic work. Very many subelite economic units would not have been able to afford a slave, or make slave labor economically viable (as Aristotle from an earlier age put it, 'Because they have no slaves, it is necessary that the poor use their wives and offspring to do what slaves would normally do' (*Politics* 5.1323A)). An educated guess – and the sources, scattered and fragmentary as they are, allow little more – would put the number at about 15 percent of the entire population, and much less in many places. As I look at the slaves of the Romano-Grecian world, it is important to keep these facts in mind. Slaves lived in a society with many other slaves, but their numbers and importance varied from place to place. This truth does not mitigate the often terrible conditions of ancient slavery, but it does mean that slaves' lives might be less restricted, less oppressed, and less close-ended than would have been the case had society depended on many more of them.

Besides the importance of understanding the relative paucity of slaves and their concentration in the hands of the more well-off city-dwellers, it is also relevant to point out that slaves in large measure shared the same basic somatic features, cultural assumptions, and often language with their masters. Slaves with radically different skin color and facial features were always rare, although sub-Saharan Africans were enslaved and appear in the Romano-Grecian world, as do tall, blond, light-skinned Germanic types, for instance. The ability of the majority of slaves to blend into the physical 'look' of society as a whole, combined with the fact that in most instances slaves dressed exactly like ordinary people of similar occupation, meant that there was no easy, visible signal of slavery unless a brand, haircut, tattoo, slave collar, or other purpose-specific marker existed. Thus during slavery it was easy and natural for slave and free, especially recently freed slaves, to associate with one another – and if a slave ran away, it was easy to blend into the population while attempting to escape detection. The lack of physical and somatic markers of slavery created opportunities for life that were lacking in some other historical societies with slaves.

People could come into slavery in a variety of ways. While war captives provided the most spectacular and perhaps even most numerous slaves during the expansion of Roman rule in the days of the republic, by the time of Augustus massive wars that produced large numbers of captives were relatively few and far between. Another source involved raising offspring slaves to adulthood. Births to slaves were of course slaves themselves, so children born to slaves were raised in slavery. Unwanted births to free persons could be and were abandoned, and anyone taking in such a child could raise it; although Roman law asserted that such foundlings always remained freeborn, in fact if raised in slavery it was virtually impossible to prove 'original freedom.' Thus foundlings were a steady source of new slaves.

The fourth main, though less important, source was enslavement of grown men and women. Although occasionally still war captives, these came primarily from bandits and pirates who were ready to kidnap travelers and other vulnerable people in towns or the countryside. Augustine attests to the horror of their indiscriminate raids on free populations in isolated areas and across the imperial borders:

> So great is the number in the province of Africa of those who are called in common parlance 'slavers,' that they practically clear the province of human beings by carrying off people to sell in places across the sea – and almost all are free persons. For very few are discovered to be sold by parents – and even these are not sold as indentured for twenty-five years as is allowed by Roman law, but indeed they are sold as true slaves and sold across the sea as slaves. The slave traders buy real slaves from their masters only very rarely. Moreover, because of this mob of slavers a throng of predators and kidnappers is so out of control that in hordes fearsomely dressed like soldiers or wild men they swoop down on certain underpopulated rural areas screaming like banshees and forcibly drag off the people whom they then sell to the slave dealers. (*Letter* *10)

10. A slave on the block. The man stands on a dias for display during the auction. An auctioneer and bidder stand nearby.

Gaius Tadius was one such unfortunate, as his grave attests:

Dedicated to Gaius Tadius Severus, son of Gaius, kidnapped by bandits at age 35, and his son Proculus, 6 years old. Limbricia Primigenia, freedwoman of Lucius, set this monument up for her husband and son. Alas, the son ought to have put up the gravestone for the mother! (*ILS* 8506)

Despite the fact that the Roman *Lex Cornelia* forbade the sale of

11. Auctioning a slave. The auctioneer is at left, while the portly bidder turns the naked slave to examine him closely.

citizens into slavery, slave dealers were notorious for not asking any questions. And regardless of the existence of a legal 'plea for restoration of freedom' before a magistrate, it must have been fairly rare for a person once kidnapped and sold to be able to assert his freedom through the legal process. In addition a father, who had total legal control over offspring, could sell a child into slavery, often to pay a debt or stave off starvation; although Roman law fussed about this, it is clear that both in the case of Roman citizens and provincials, children continued to be sold throughout our period; the quotation from Augustine above is one of the many confirmations. And there was also legal self-enslavement. While debt slavery – selling a free person into slavery to pay that person's debts – was illegal, and technically at least a Roman citizen could not sell himself into slavery, a person could, in fact, 'contract' himself to become a slave, giving up his rights as a free man in return for money. 'Many men being free sell themselves over into slavery, with the result that they are "contract slaves," at times on difficult terms, or rather on the most harsh imaginable' (Dio Chrysostom, *Oration* 15.2). Evidently, sometimes whether legally or not, a free person voluntarily became a slave. Finally, ordinary people condemned for especially heinous crimes could be punished with slavery. The relative numbers from these sources cannot be known, but each would have its own effect on the psychology of the slave. A child raised as a slave could easily have a different outlook than an adult captured and enslaved later in life, after having lived as a free person for years. A kidnapped person must have felt the injustice of it all even more, while a self-enslaved person presumably knew what he was getting into.

Life enslaved: subjection

Despite the range of reactions to slavery it is possible to imagine arising from the various origins of individual slaves, the central fact of servitude was the total subjection of the slave to the master; they were available at all times and had to labor at the master's will. Surely it is highly probable that Augustine got it right: 'All slavery is filled with bitterness: everyone locked in slavery at once does what he has to, but does it grumbling' (*Commentary on Psalm* 99.7). Lucius in his asinine form describes the hard lives of slaves in a bakery:

Great gods! What miserable, pitiable creatures! Their entire bodies were a welter of inflamed bruises; their backs scarred by the rod were shaded more than covered by their sorry, ragged garments; some had a slight covering over their private parts; all wore such wretched tunics that their bodies showed through the tatters; their heads were half-shaved; they bore letters branded into their foreheads and their feet were in shackles. Eyelids scorched by the steamy dank of the dusty darkness, they were half blind in all their sallow ugliness. Just like boxers who fight sprinkled with dust, these men were white with a dirty flour ash. (Apuleius, *The Golden Ass* 9.12)

And, Apuleius tells us, the owner of these slaves was 'a decent and very sober person'! Harsh treatment was synonymous with slavery. In a letter from Egypt, one brother chides another for treating their mother 'harshly, as if she were a slave.' And in another a woman complains to the authorities that her husband has treated her and their children 'as if she were his bought slave,' abusing them and locking them away.

Of course, it was always possible that fate found a particular slave in the possession of a thoughtful master. An example may be Servandus:

Valerius Servandus, freedman of Lucius, Gaius, and Sextus Valerius, age 20, lies in this grave. His patrons set up the monument in recognition of his many merits. 'Servitude, you were never hateful to me. Unjust Death, you took freedom from this wretched man.' (*CIL* 13.7119, Mainz, Germany)

As it was part of the master's ideology to suppose that slaves could be content to serve, one must wonder if it was Servandus himself who thought his slavery happy, or only his patrons. And 'kind' or 'good' would perhaps be too generous a term for these owners; their motivation was purely practical – but some actions did make their slaves' lives better than they might otherwise have been. The agricultural writer Columella offers his practical approach to managing slaves well. He saw and tried to avoid at least some of the pitfalls of slave ownership, especially by setting reasonable goals for work and sufficient levels of outfitting and feeding, by controlling cruel overseers, and by having venues for slaves to bring problems to him to be resolved (*On Rural*

Matters 1.8.17–19; 11.1.13–28). One can wonder if many estates or households were run on these principles of enlightened self-interest, but at the very least it is possible that some slaves found themselves in situations that while still grossly exploitative, were at least mitigated with regard to the worst of the many possible abuses.

And abuses abounded. Physical abuse was the most frequent and violent form of degradation. The legal material in the *Digest* repeatedly makes allusion to all sorts of violence against slaves, with very few notices that repercussions might follow for the masters. Slaves could be and were beaten in the normal course of things either to encourage good behavior or punish bad, or both at once – or simply out of anger, frustration, or sadism. There was in practice no control over the master's powers to physically abuse out of all proportion to any act: 'Is not a penalty of many years' confinement imposed on the slave who has provoked his master with a word, or has struck him a blow that is quickly over?' (Augustine, *City of God* 11) The old standbys were flogging (perhaps the favorite routine punishment) and confinement in chains to a cell (*ergastulum*); Aesop's master, for example, refers to these (*Life*, p. 123). But there were an unlimited number of specific abusive behaviors, often accompanied by long-term marks of degradation such as branding: 'Eumolpus covered both our foreheads with huge letters and wrote with a rough hand the stigmatic mark of runaway slaves all over our faces' (Petronius, *Satyricon* 103). This sort of abuse was a constant theme in fiction involving slaves, as is easily seen from the many examples in the plays of Plautus or the novels of Apuleius and Petronius. There is no indication that Christian slave holders engaged in such behavior any less than polytheists; indeed, the defenselessness against physical abuse was everywhere the preeminent marker of slavery. The evidence of early modern Brazil and North America paints a similar picture:

> At the beck and call of his master day and night, the domestic servant had no regular hours. Added to the long hours was the discomfiture of constantly being under the watchful eyes of the whites and being subject to their every capricious, vengeful, or sadistic whim. Domestic servants frequently had their ears boxed or were flogged for trifling mistakes, ignorance, delinquent work, 'insolent' behavior,

or simply for being within striking distance when the master was disgruntled (W. Blassingame, *The Slave Community*)

Apuleius tells the story of a cook who feared death as punishment for allowing a deer's haunch to be stolen (*The Golden Ass* 8.31); Martial notes another cook who was whipped because a rabbit was not prepared correctly (*Epigrams* 3.94). And beyond the beatings and brandings, the general physical living conditions of most slaves were abysmal, although these varied especially between rural and urban household slaves. They were dependent for food and clothing on the master; despite repetitious advice from agricultural writers and philosophers, denial of adequate supplies in all likelihood was rife.

As for living conditions, there is very little evidence for slave quarters in houses, although such have been identified at a few rural estates in Italy; it seems probable that, as occurred in the slave society of Brazil, slaves must often have lived in the hallways and under the stairs of great houses, pulling their cots out at night and putting them away during the day. There is an example of this when Lucius, not yet in his donkey-form, waits for his love, Photis, in his bedroom. He notes that 'the slaves had their floor-space arranged as far as possible away from the door; I imagine that this was so that they would not be near enough to overhear our chat during the night' (*The Golden Ass* 2.15). So not only the beatings, but the general living conditions could be abusive. One of the most desired privileges would be to have one's own living space, however humble. Small cells have been identified in some great houses as probably slave quarters; even a makeshift shack on the grounds must have been welcome.

Just as bad as the physical abuse was the mental abuse: '"Aesop, lay the table. Aesop, heat the bath. Aesop, feed the livestock." Anything that's unpleasant or tiresome or painful or menial, that's what Aesop is ordered to do' (*Life*, p. 116/Daly). The author Athenaeus gives a peek into the slave's demeaning world:

Epikrates, in 'The Hard to Sell Slave,' makes a slave indignantly say: 'What is more hateful than to be summoned with Boy, Boy! to where they are drinking; to serve, moreover, some callow youth or bring him a piss-pot, and to see things laid out in front of us – half-eaten cakes and pieces of chicken which, although left from the meal, the women forbid us slaves to eat. But what *really* makes our blood boil is to have them call any of us greedy gluttons when we do eat some of those things! (*Intellectuals Dining* 6.262(d))

And Hermeros in Petronius' novel emphasizes the demeaning treatment that accompanied the slave servant's life: 'I bought out of slavery my slave wife, so that no one could wipe his hands on her bosom' (*Satyricon* 57.5–6).

Leaving aside wider cultural and personal reasons for such behavior by the masters, the practical goal of the physical and psychological abuse was submissiveness training. The ideal was to get the slave both to obey without question, and to use his abilities positively to perform whatever the master needed. While one might wonder about the efficacy of beatings and mental torture in creating a willing, thinking slave, this disjunction did not normally occur to masters. The burden of willing obedience was rather transferred mostly to the slaves, as Paul emphasized to the Christians at Colossus:

> Slaves, obey in everything those who are your earthly masters, not with eye-service, as men-pleasers, but in singleness of heart, fearing the Lord. Whatever your task, work heartily, as serving the Lord and not men, knowing that from the Lord you will receive the inheritance as your reward … Masters, treat your slaves justly and fairly, knowing that you also have a Master in heaven. (Colossians 3:22–4:1)

And the unknown author of 1 Peter even drops any admonition at all to masters, and puts the entire burden on the slaves:

> Servants, be submissive to your masters with all respect, not only to the kind and gentle but also to the overbearing. For one is approved if, mindful of God, he endures pain while suffering unjustly. For what credit is it, if when you do wrong and are beaten for it you take it patiently? But if when you do right and suffer for it you take it patiently, you have God's approval. (1 Peter 2:18)

Others such as Apollonius were in total agreement in placing the responsibility on slaves, regardless of what sort of terrible person the master was:

> What is more, though masters would incur no reproach for neglecting slaves, for whom they probably may feel a contempt because they are not good, yet the slaves who did not devote themselves wholly to their masters, should be destroyed by them as cursed wretches and chattels hateful to the gods. (Philostratus, *Life of Apollonius* 4.40/Conybeare)

The worst was perhaps that combination of physical and psychological: sexual abuse. This most usually stood outside the sadism and submissiveness training of the run-of-the-mill abuse. It, of course, could be rape as an act of violence against the victim, but the casual, deeply 'normal' assumption by slaves and free alike that slaves were available as sexual objects meant that overt violence often was not involved. A bit later than the period covered in this book, Salvian wrote in the fifth century AD, 'Female slaves are forced unwillingly to service their most shameless masters; these sate their lust on them, trapped as they are by their condition, unable to resist' (*On the Government of God* 7.4). And it was not only women who suffered. Petronius tells the tale of Glyco's slave, who was forced by his master's wife into her bed. 'The slave did no wrong; he was forced to do it' (*Satyricon* 45). Male slaves were also the subject of their master's sexual ravishing. Despite the fact that characters like Trimalchio boasted that they had advanced from master's favorite in pederasty to his favorite in the household ('For fourteen years I was the object of my master's sexual attentions – it is not a base thing to do what your master commands'), to freedom and wealth, the reality of rape must have been very much on boys' as well as girls' minds. As the Elder Seneca put it, shameful sexual behavior is criminal in a freeborn person, a necessity in a slave, and a duty in a freedperson (*Declamations* 4, Preface 10). Nothing in the New Testament speaks out against this sexual abuse. Rabbinical literature describes when it is all right to have sex with one's female slave. Even the enlightened Roman philosopher Musonius Rufus wrote, '[E]very master has full authority to use his slave as he might wish' (*Discourse* 12.88). The expectation that slaves would be sexually available anytime, anyplace was well-nigh universal, and so they had to take this into account in their own lives.

In the face of even the most violent physical abuse, slaves had little recourse. While good masters might hear a slave's complaints and actually do something about them, the very poor opinion of slaves held by the vast majority of masters led them not only to initiate violence against their slaves, but to condone it in their overseers, all in the name of obedience. In theory a slave could take refuge in a temple or at a divine statue, using the ancient right of asylum as a protection against an abusive master. And they did, as a number of anecdotes mention. One must wonder, however, how often this desperate recourse met with long-term success. True, slaves had various legal rulings in theory limiting the almost unlimited arbitrary action of masters. Through the period covered in this book, laws and decrees were issued to prevent owners from throwing their slaves to the beasts, from retrieving abandoned sick slaves if the slaves recovered, from killing a slave with impunity, and against the castration of slaves. There is legal evidence of slaves pursuing justice with regard to such things, but surely it was the rare slave who would find success in a complaint against his master – through a representative, of course, because the slave was not a person at law. The only legal action that seems to have been fairly common and sometimes successful related not to slavery, but to freedom: processes to determine if a person was free born and illegally in an enslaved condition. So the matter at hand was not treatment of a slave, but treatment as a slave of a person claiming to be free. Society in general had some sympathy for people who claimed to be free but were in slavery. The issue was very different from a slave claiming abusive treatment as a slave, and was treated as such. But in any case, an attempt at law ending in failure would most surely also lead to heinous punishment for the slave who tried this. The law therefore offered scant to no aid to a slave in an abusive situation. In fact, the law was a primary tool of control for masters. The fear of gruesome capital punishment meted out to 'criminal' slaves on a routine basis by magisterial judgments – crucifixion, burning alive, being torn apart in the arena by wild beasts – was very real. Only the most confident and the best-connected slave would have dared try the magistrate's judgment. Almost all would have thought about the legal system in terror, not in hope.

A slave identity was a combination of what was imposed upon him, and what he could fashion for himself. The naming of a slave by the master is the most symbolically laden act of identity management. The act of naming reidentifies the slave as the property of the new owner; it embodies the attempt to eliminate that person's former self and to show that identity is under the control of the new master. But the new slave did not simply forget all that had gone before. In the case of a person sold into slavery by force as an adult, the memory was vivid and remained. One epitaph records this in the case of a Parthian who was captured when young and sold as a slave; he ended up in Ravenna, where eventually he was freed and set up a marker that noted this fact:

> Gaius Julius Mygdonius, born a free man of the Parthian race, captured at a tender age, carried over into Roman territory into slavery, then made a Roman citizen thanks to Fate … (*CIL* 11.137 = *ILS* 1980)

Another enslaved captive, Claudia Aster, ended up in Puteoli (Puzzuoli) on the Bay of Naples, was freed but remembered her origins as a captive in Jerusalem at the end of the Jewish War of AD 70 (*CIL* 10.1971). A third, one Arrius Capito, a financial manager while a slave and a moneylender upon gaining his freedom, recalled his origins in Pannonia, across the Danube:

> Capito the freedman of Arrius, a moneylender of the Pannonian nation, lies here having lived 35 years. (*CIL* 13.7247, Mainz, Germany)

While yet another recalls his father's name even after years in slavery:

> Gaius Ducenius Phoebus, freedman of Gaius, son of Zeno, was born in Nisibis in Syria, and made a freedman in Rome. (*CIL* 6.700 = *ILS* 3944, Rome)

Finally, a man taken across the imperial borders and sold into slavery in Gaul eloquently speaks of his enslavement and winning his freedom:

> Gaius Ofilius Arimnestus, freedman of Caius, of the Palatine voting

district, while still living set up this monument to himself and to Mindia Prima daughter of Marcus, his wife, and to Gaius Ofilius Proculus, his son. A barbarian land gave me birth. Profit handed me over to undeserved slavery so that my whole being changed. Yet I did all that I could to honor the name received from my father. When I could not prevail with entreaties, I obtained my freedom with my own money. I won over my master through carrying out my duties – I never had to be beaten, I received no rewards … (*CIL* 12.5026, Narbonne, France)

While such documentation is scarce, the slave's memory of life before slavery surely remained clear; certainly slaves in the American South and in Brazil, as a comparison, vividly recalled their lives in Africa before capture and slavery. I would fully expect the same retention of memories as a form of maintaining an identity beyond that imposed by the masters.

In a stimulating retrieval of the voices of invisible Romans, Sandra Joshel has emphasized how important occupation was to the formation and maintenance of identity among slaves. Her careful, convincing study highlights how in epigraphy slaves mention occupation far more than free persons do, and how this is the slaves' decision, not the masters'. In work the slave could establish an identity because occupational excellence served to satisfy the master, who valued and even rewarded skillful slaves; to mark off one's excellence in relationship to fellow slaves; and to garner money that might ultimately be used to purchase freedom for himself and, perhaps, also for loved ones among the other slaves. There was simply no downside to being good at your occupation, so given the opportunity slaves could work hard and be proud of it.

Not that I for a moment think a slave's work was sweetness and light. Many slaves never had a chance to learn a trade or skill, so could not take advantage of excelling in it. Others neglected opportunities when they arose. Masters worked slaves very hard, both as a practical matter of getting necessary jobs done and as a way of maintaining order and submission. Still, pride in work was possible on various levels, and many slaves were able to center themselves through focusing on this element of their lives over which they had some control, for a master was not likely to tell a slave to stop doing an excellent job, and there was at least the chance of reward.

Thinking in slavery

As slaves thought about their lives and its limited possibilities, slavery itself channeled their thinking. The most fundamental aspect of this thinking was a lack – the lack of any possibility of a changed or alternative society, one without slavery. There was simply no social existence conceivable that did not have slavery as an accepted, integral part of it. Whereas from the mid eighteenth century AD in the West the concept of the intrinsic wrongness of slavery gained ground and spread to the slaves themselves and abolition movements steadily gained steam, nothing of the sort ever happened in the Romano-Grecian world. So one aspect of slave thinking, the hatred of slavery as an institution and the belief that not only could one escape personally, but the whole edifice could and should be dismantled, was entirely lacking to slaves of the period covered in this book. Thus the most radical thought was to escape slavery – never to end it unconditionally for all. This outlook framed all other thought. When slaves thought about their situation and the ways to deal with it, considerations were exclusively practical.

Insecurity was always on a slave's mind. The very fact of being owned created this fundamental condition. Nothing was assured. One might do everything the master wished, and do it well, and still be sold, or be separated from loved ones, or grow sick and be abandoned, or old and be left to wither away in neglect, or worse. Some solace and guidance could be found in homespun wisdom, popular philosophy, and other attempts to reconcile the human condition with the reality of a slave's existence. Groaning, grumbling, and dissatisfaction were weak resorts; in the end, recognition of the unfairness of life and resignation to the lot that fate had spun must usually have been the only mental defense against the angst produced by the inherently insecure and stressful situation. The guard in Plautus' *The Prisoners* (196–197) had advice, cold as it was: 'Now, you men … if it's gods' will that you have to be the unlucky ones [to be enslaved], the best thing you can do is to take it patiently; that way, it won't seem so hard.'

The slave community

Slaves' thoughts also turned to trying to take some control to relieve the stress and to bring a measure of normality to their lives. The place to begin this process was within the slave community itself. Although the master sought work and obedience, all understood that slaves, as human beings, interacted with each other. A master might isolate 'troublesome' slaves, and in particularly dangerous conditions such as mining the possibilities for community were severely attenuated. But under normal conditions, whether in a great house, a smaller establishment, or in a rural situation, slaves formed bonds and negotiated interrelationships that gave meaning to their lives, despite the underlying insecurity and brutality of it all. There is much evidence of solidarity and friendship among slaves. Here one ex-slave recalls a lifelong friendship reaching back into common slavery:

> Aulus Memmius Urbanus set this up to Aulus Memmius Clarus, fellow freedman and companion most dear. Between you and me, my most valued fellow freedman, I know there never was ever a quarrel. I also with this inscription bring the gods above and below to witness that you and I, bought at the same time as slaves in the same household, were freed together as well. No day ever separated us except that of your fateful death. (*CIL* 6.22355a = *ILS* 8432, Rome)

The case of Jucundus in the household of Taurus is another example:

> Jucundus, slave of Taurus, a litter-bearer, was a real man as long as he lived. Throughout his life he watched out for himself and for the others. Callista and Philologus, fellow slaves, set this up. (*CIL* 6.6308 = *ILS* 7408d, Rome)

The use of the word for 'real man' (*vir*) captures the fact that this slave and others like him were able to see in themselves and others the trait prized in the culture as a whole, manliness. And Jucundus' habit of watching out for his fellow slaves embodies the solidarity of the slave community, which is often seen, although, as I will discuss shortly, often subverted as well. An example is the fact that when the Roman senator Pedanius Secundus was murdered by his slaves, not a single fellow slave tried to stop it, or betrayed who had done it, despite the most savage punishment (Tacitus, *Annals* 14.43). And in the *Life of Aesop* his fellow slaves act as a group in their opposition to him as an outsider, as well as trying to make him take the blame for their own wrongdoing.

Groups of slaves also acted together in religious life. A votive set up in Gaud (southwestern France) states:

To the God Garris. Geminus, a slave, paid the vow freely also on behalf of his fellow slaves. (*CIL* 13.49, Gaud, France)

As a further example, slaves often organized themselves into burial societies, either within a household, if it were large, or across households or as fellows in a common endeavor, for example as the gold miners in Dacia, or wool workers in Italy:

The wool combers set up this monument to Acceptus, slave of Chia, their fellow. (*CIL* 5.4501, Brescia)

In Luceria, in Italy, slaves buried one of their own under this headstone:

To the Gods of the Netherworld and to Gelasmus the slave of Sittia. His colleagues from the Hercules and Apollo Association set this up. He lived 25 years, 3 months, and 21 days. (*AE* 1983.213)

But as in the case of Aesop, there could also be competition within the community. Rivalry for the master's favor naturally occurred. The fictional Hermeros describes this:

I tried very hard to satisfy my master, who was a dignified and august man. And in the household I was dealing with people who tried to trip me up whenever they could. But in the end I won out, thanks be to my master! (Petronius, *Satyricon* 57)

Among the slaves there could be vicious gossip, quarreling, and sabotage of each other's work, as is well illustrated by the stressful household Augustine describes in his *Confessions* in which the slaves were drawn into the strife between family members. It was necessary to have dispute resolution mechanisms in place to settle quarrels that could arise over just about anything – in the case of Aesop, the women of the household argued over who would get his sexual favors. Perhaps the most insidious undercutting of slave solidarity were the *silentiarii*, those slaves whose job it was to keep order among them.

> They fear their fellow slaves, the drivers and the informants [*silentiarii*] among them to enforce their submission, as well as the overseers set to manage them. Indeed, slaves are slaves to these almost as much as to their actual masters: any of them can flog or kill them, any can grind them down. What more can be said? Many slaves take refuge at their master's feet, since they fear their fellow slaves so. For this reason we ought not blame those slaves who flee such a situation; rather look to those whose treatment compels them to become runaways. (Salvian, *On the Government of God* 4.3)

The general way slaves were organized invited abuse of slave on slave; for example, Aesop states that a handsome slave would make sexual advances on another who 'caught his fancy' (*Life*, p. 125). Free men were not hired as overseers and managers; rather, slaves were given these responsibilities. This was true whether the household needed the managing slaves, or it was a rural property with an absent owner. As in other slave societies, such foremen were deeply hated by the other slaves. Especially if they were unsupervised by the master, they had no restriction on the punishments they could inflict, their assignment of slaves for their personal benefit, and their sexual depredations – not to mention cheating the master by cooking the books, conducting personal business, and the like. One of the strongest admonitions of the agricultural writers is to keep close track of the slave overseers to be sure they do not treat the slaves cruelly. Slaves could in theory appeal to the master against the abuses of overseers and fellow slaves, and a good master is advised to facilitate such appeals. But as the quotation from Salvian above attests, often the only escape from a fellow slave was to run away.

Besides the powerful and hated overseer, slaves feared also their fellow slaves who were torturers and punishers. While routine floggings and other sorts of corporal abuse took place at the hands of fellow slaves under the master's direct authority, it was common practice to outsource more serious physical punishment simply because to do it 'in house' was much more disruptive to life in the slave community. There were, therefore, professionals who specialized in dealing with slaves that masters considered exceptionally recalcitrant or vicious. A good example can be found in Matthew 18:21–34. In this story, Jesus tell of the king who forgave a servant of his a great debt; the servant then went to a man who owed him money in turn – but refused the poor man's plea for mercy in collecting the debt and sold him and his family to meet the obligation. When the king learned of this, he 'turned him over to the torturers, until he should pay back all he owed.' And Apuleius in his novel has slaves punishing other slaves.

Life in the slave community was complex: individual slaves had to make judgments about their fellows, form friendships and alliances, and ward off as much grief as possible. The same complexity extended to life beyond the immediate slaves around him to the free population outside the household. The basic issue to decide is whether slaves and those free in the world at large were fundamentally divided from one another by the free persons' feeling of superiority over slaves simply from the fact of being free. While there is no doubt that the elite and in all probability the fairly well-off felt such a disdain and maintained a huge psychological barrier between themselves and any slave, we have to ask if most ordinary people would feel that way. Modern opinions differ. Some think that any free person would have marked himself off from slaves, proud in his freedom and sure in a superiority it gave him over slaves, even if a given slave had more money, influence, and prospects than he did. Others point out that the actual lives of ordinary people were very similar to those of many slaves, and so there is every reason to suppose that slave and free persons in the same conditions thought more about the things they had in common than a designation 'slave' or 'free.' They also had in common a huge distance from the elite and could easily share a resentment, even hatred, toward the tiny ruling minority. When the senator Pedanius Secundus was murdered by his slaves, for example, and the whole of the household slaves were condemned to be crucified as a punishment and object lesson, since none had divulged the plot nor prevented its carrying out, the common people slave and free formed a large, angry mob and at first prevented the punishment from being inflicted; only Emperor Nero's assignment of troops to clear the way allowed the executions to proceed (Tacitus, *Annals* 14.42–5).

Even if one wished to separate slaves from ordinary people, it would have been hard. I have noted that for the most part slaves looked and spoke like freemen. Slaves as a rule wore no distinctive clothing. There were exceptions, of course: branded slaves, or those with a 'slave cut' – closely cropped hair, or those wearing a master's special livery. But apart from those in business and formal wear – the toga – all men looked pretty much the same in daily life. Petronius has his character Hermeros say, 'I was a slave for forty years and nobody knew whether I was slave or free.'

Slaves were active outside the doors of households and often lived outside. They were entrusted with duties great and small by their masters that free persons also performed at times, such as work in construction and carrying, artisanry, mercantile trade, and moneylending. Given the similarity in background, culture, and occupation, it is no wonder that slave and free belonged to the same religious and secular organizations. There are many examples of freeborn, ex-slaves (freedmen), and slaves belonging to the same association. Some with a recent past of slavery held no empathy for those still enslaved; one such was Larcius Macedo, son of a freedman, who was especially cruel to his slaves and was killed by one (Pliny, *Letters* 3.14). Many more maintained ties with slaves on an equal basis in professional and religious associations whose purpose was ostensibly funereal but, in fact, were social gatherings. At Praeneste an association of fullers was mixed: several slaves are listed as well as a freedman; at Ostia a society of freedmen and slaves of the town set up a monument to the divinity Bellona; at Lanuvium they participated with freeborn in the cults of Antinous and Diana, although masters' permission was required. Slaves were challenged to negotiate a world in which at times they lived and acted with and almost as free persons; but they were always aware that a run-in with the authorities would reveal their fundamental difference in civil and criminal law, particularly with regard to swift recourse to physical punishment in the case of a slave, even if the only charge was littering:

> Marcus Alfius Paulus, city manager, orders this: Whoever might wish to throw away excrement in this place, take warning that this

is not allowed! If anyone act against this proclamation, let him if a free person pay a fine – if a slave, whip his ass as a warning! (*AE* 1962.234, Herculaneum)

Slaves and their masters

In the midst of life as a slave among other slaves and among the free population, four topics were always on his mind. These are revealed by three questions which appear in the *Oracles of Astrampsychus*, and which are particularly appropriate for thinking about slave attitudes – 'Will I come to terms with my masters?'; 'Am I going to be sold?'; and 'Will I be freed?' – and a fourth question asked not by slaves but by masters, which is indirectly related: 'Will I find the fugitive [slave]?' Thus slaves were concerned about relationships with their masters, about being sold, and about being freed, while the masters' focus on fugitives indicates a slave's mind was frequently on running away. These concerns are reflected in much the same way in various dream interpretations found in Artemidorus. The commonest reference is to gaining one's freedom, to various relations with a master (good, bad, changing), and to running away; being sold seems to appear only once as a topic. If these concerns are combined with those interpersonal behavioral traits mentioned on gravestones, it would seem that a reasonable sweep of a slave's mind world was focused on survival in the moment, with hope alternating with fear about the future. What is missing is much indication of dwelling on the status of 'slavehood' itself, of any of the interiority that one might assume must have occupied a slave's mind. And there is little outcry against the injustice of this slavery, only recognition of the personal situation a slave might find himself in – although the epitaph from Rome of a slave is evocative:

Here I, Lemiso, lie. Nothing save death ended my toil. (*CIL* 6.6049 = *ILLRP* 932, Rome)

Still, it is reassuring to know that the slaves themselves, with their own voices, offer at least a general delineation of what was paramount in their minds. The picture that emerges is one of active slave lives forging spaces of action and, if possible, working for their freedom.

Negotiating relations with masters consumed much of a slave's thinking. *The Life of Aesop* takes as fundamental the conflict between slave and master, and shows how the slave could effectively deal with this. Some masters were better to their slaves than others; some slaves were more entrepreneurial in their adjustment to slavery than others. The permutations were potentially infinite, but each slave had to develop specific responses to his specific situation.

First of all, there were various ways that a slave could accommodate himself to his circumstances. The simplest was to accept the fate of slavehood and make the best of it. 'There's no need to go on wailing. It's clear enough that you are unhappy. In bad situations it is best to keep your spirits up' (Plautus, *Prisoners* 202). So the guard advises the prisoners of war who have just been sold into slavery. The sentiment is echoed by a saying of Publilius Syrus (Maxim 616): 'The slave who pulls against the bit makes himself miserable – but he is still a slave.' Making the most of a bad situation was therefore one accommodation: 'The slave who serves shrewdly holds a share of his master's role' (Maxim 596). This would be easier if the master had some sense and took the advice of the agricultural writers to maintain as positive and reciprocal a relationship with slaves as was practicable.

It might also be easier if the master took a fancy to you, and the relationship developed into something other than just sexual abuse. Illegitimate children of slave owners might not only be loved, but even be bequeathed money: Steia Fortuna, a slave of Publius Steius Felix, inherited one-sixth of his property – she was probably his illegitimate daughter (*CIL* 14.1641, Ostia Antica, Italy). Fiction is full of slaves who advanced from sexual favorites to more important roles in the household and, ultimately, to successful lives as freedmen; Hermeros and Trimalchio in Petronius' *Satyricon* are famous examples of this ilk. And many masters had favorites among the slaves. One adopted a slave as his son and set him up in a successful tavern business:

> Vitalis, a household slave and also a son of Gaius Lavius Faustus, lies here. He lived 16 years. As manager for the Aprianas tavern, the patrons loved him – then the gods summoned him away. You passers-by, if I ever gave you short measure so that I could add to my father's profit, forgive me. I ask in the name of gods above and

below: take care of my mother and father. Farewell! (*CIL* 3.14206.21 = *ILS* 7479, Amfipoli, Greece)

Another recalled with affection a favorite little slave girl:

Celerinus the master set up this grave monument to the most unfortunate Valentina, his nursling and dearest delight, daughter of the slave Valentio, his steward, who lived but 4 years. (*CIL* 3.2130, Salona, Croatia)

Pliny the Elder gives a real-life example of a slave who was propelled to the heights of wealth through the favor of his mistress:

[Corinthian bronze was famous and dear.] Once in offering for sale a candelabra of this material an auctioneer named Theron threw in as a free bonus a slave named Clesippus, a humpbacked fuller, and a fellow of surpassing ugliness. A wealthy woman named Gegania bought the candelabra for 50,000 sesterces and along with it came the deformed slave. So pleased was she with her acquisitions that she threw a party to show them off. There, just to give the guests something to make fun of, Clesippus came out stark naked. Shameless lust swept over Gegania and she took him to her bed, then soon after included him in her will as an heir. Wildly wealthy at the woman's death, Clesippus worshiped that candelabra as a guardian god ... Their immoral behavior was nevertheless avenged by the elaborate sepulcer Clesippus set up through which the memory of Gegania's shame lived on above the earth ever after ... (*Natural History* 34.6.11–12)

Pliny's story is somewhat unusual for it involves a female master taking a male concubine. Male masters keeping female concubines from among the slaves is much more frequently attested; women could have found a certain security in this relationship, although they were always susceptible to bad treatment either by the master or his wife. And evidently a fair number of such liaisons turned out to be permanent, for they are noted with some frequency in the funerary epigraphy. For example:

This monument is set up to the Gods of the Netherworld and to Septimius Fortunatus, the son of Gaius, and to Septimia his concubine,
first a slave and then freed. (*CIL* 5.5170 = *ILS* 8553, Bergamo, Italy)

Most slaves, of course, did not have long-term sexual relations with
their masters. Habits that kept a slave in the good graces of the master
included variations on what the master most wanted in a slave: efficient
labor, profit, obedience, and faithfulness. Obedience meant control,
so whether real or feigned, some level of obedience was the best way
to adjust to the situation and avoid punishment. Paul advised Christian slaves to be genuinely obedient, 'not in the way of eye-service, as
men-pleasers' (Ephesians 6:6) and so recognized the reality of feigned
obedience as well as the desirability (in the slave owner's eyes) of the
real thing. Faithfulness was closely allied. So, again, either genuine or
simulated demonstrations of trustworthiness were a fairly sure way to
keep on the right side of the master. And flattery was always in order,
whether of a master or of a slave overseer. Some might even genuinely
love the master they flattered, obeyed, and worked faithfully for. All of
this was easier with a kind master, of course. In such a situation it might
actually seem preferable to remain a slave than to be freed. The ex-slave-
turned-philosopher Epictetus has this observation about the perils of
freedom as opposed to slavehood with an enlightened master:

The slave wishes to be set free immediately. Why? Do you think that
he wishes to pay money to the collectors of twentieths [tax on manu-
missions]? No; but because he imagines that hitherto through not
having obtained this, he is hindered and unfortunate. 'If I shall be set
free, immediately it is all happiness, I care for no man, I speak to all
as an equal and, like to them, I go where I choose, I come from any
place I choose, and go where I choose.' Then he is set free; and immediately having no place where he can eat, he looks for some man to
flatter, someone with whom he shall dine: then he either works with
his body and endures the most dreadful things; and if he can obtain a
manager, he falls into a slavery much worse than his former slavery;
or even if he becomes rich, being a man without any knowledge of
what is good, he loves some little girl, and in his happiness laments
and desires to be a slave again. He says, 'What evil did I suffer in

my state of slavery? Another clothed me, another supplied me with shoes, another fed me, another looked after me in sickness; and I did only a few services for him. But now a wretched man, what things I suffer, being a slave of many instead of to one.' (*Discourses* 4.1.34–7/ Long)

The author of *The Life of Aesop* puts it more succinctly:

If you are good to your slaves, no one is going to run away from what is good to what is bad and condemn himself to vagrancy with the prospect of hunger and fear to face. (p. 122/Daly)

A smart master appreciated the hard and diligent work of 'good,' i.e. faithful and obedient, slaves and rewarded it. The rewards could be small – presents at Saturnalia, an occasional day off – or large, for example the opportunity to acquire funds with which to buy out the master and become free. The slave's purse, called his *peculium*, was always technically the possession of the slave's master, just like everything the slave 'owned,' including his very person. But in reality slaves accumulated sums small and large which they could spend on the same range of things free persons did. For example, they could make votive offerings, as this epigraph from Pesaro in Italy indicates:

Faustus, the slave of Publius Versennius, paid for a statue and shrine to the god Priapus out of his *peculium*. (*CIL* 11.6314 = *ILS* 3581)

Others might spend on material improvements to their lives, or save to eventually purchase their freedom or the freedom of a loved one – or on wastrelry. Slaves of all sorts had a *peculium*, even, if we can believe Plautus, shepherds: 'The keeper of sheep who pastures another's flock has a little money of his own put away, upon which rides his hopes' (*The Comedy of Asses* 539). They would use every opportunity to increase this. For an urban slave, the opportunities were great. These ranged from selling his own food, to stealing and selling a master's possessions on the street, to accepting bribes for contracting the various services needed or for access to the master or mistress of the house, as in this instance:

> Right away, then, a person calls, presenting a dinner invitation – and not a clueless house servant, either, and to keep him obliged, you slip him at the least five drachma, smoothly, mind you, so as not to seem awkward. (Lucian, *On Salaried Posts in Great Houses* 14)

A slave could also make goods or conduct business on the side, and sell these for his own income. The opportunities for town slaves were much greater because they had both more 'free time' and more access to resources and sales outlets. But even on the farm, the overseer (*vilicus*) usually did his own side business, as Columella acknowledges when he warns that an unsupervised overseer is likely to do business for his own benefit because the master is absent (*On Rural Matters* 1.8.14).

Slaves were also commonly used as extensions of the master in business dealings. The *peculium* was the great motivator for a slave to be an effective agent, for he could garner money in straightforward and not-so-straightforward ways as he carried out his master's business, whether that was in trade, moneylending, or artisanry.

The slaves of the Pompeiian Lucius Caecilius Jucundus even had seals to use in business transactions, with their own names. The New Testament story of the faithful slaves clearly illustrates how the system worked. The master went on a journey and left each of three slaves varying amounts of money to manage in his absence. Two slaves invested the money and gave the profit to the master upon his return; the third, fearing repercussions if he invested and lost money, simply buried his allotment. When the master came home, he praised the slaves who had invested well, but was angry with the one who had played it safe. He rewarded the first two, but stripped the third of any further responsibility and, presumably, any hope of advancement within the household (Matthew 25:14–28). So trusted slaves were free to use their entrepreneurial skills to increase the master's wealth; at the same time these slaves were making network contacts and otherwise positioning themselves for future profit, whether benefiting from added trust from the master or making money 'on the side' in various related transactions. One of Trimalchio's favorite slaves developed resources in just that way. He was young and handsome – clearly an attraction for Trimalchio – but also talented and resourceful:

I kissed the boy not because he is pretty, but because he is trustworthy. He can do division and read books at sight, from what he earns he has bought a suit of Thracian armor, purchased a fancy chair with rounded back, and two braziers from his own money. (Petronius, *Satyricon* 75)

While one might question the wisdom of his purchases, he has an education suitable for commerce, and has earned money and purchased objects while still a slave.

Sometimes, as in the parable above, things could go terribly wrong for the master; even more than just failure to invest, the slave might take advantage of the situation to cheat and flee. A Roman legal text (*Digest* 14.5.8) tells of one Titianus Primus who appointed a slave 'to put out loans and accept pledges as security for them.' However, the slave went further: on his own (using his master's funds?) he took to taking over debts owed to grain merchants by purchasers and then paying them off at a profit. Accumulating a tidy sum in this way, he absconded. This shows the position of trust a slave could be given, as well as how a slave might take the chance to accrue wealth. The only exceptional thing here is that the slave ran away rather than waiting until he was freed to set himself up in, presumably, financial dealings.

Such a picture should not delude anyone into thinking that the opportunities for most slaves were great. Only a select few would be purchased or chosen to be trained to be agents and so on for the master. But even for the run-of-the-mill slave in a household and for agricultural slaves there were opportunities to accumulate a small *peculium* and with it lighten the burden of slavery somewhat.

Resistance

The constraints and abuses suffered in slavery naturally led slaves to paths of resistance; it was in a combination of accommodation and resistance that slaves were able to achieve their identity, and the mix of the two varied infinitely in the slave community as each slave adjusted to his or her peculiar situation, talents, and psychological disposition. Slave owners fully expected resistance, which they thought of as disobedience, faithlessness, and hostility. Whether in rural or urban settings,

12. Slaves at work. Here two women slaves making roof tiles left imprints of their shod feet, and their names scratched into the yet soft clay. The scratches read (in Oscan) 'Delftri, the slave of Herrenneis Sattis, signed this with her foot'; and (in Latin) 'Amica, the slave of Herreneis, signed this, while we were setting out the tile to dry'

masters were perfectly aware of the (to their minds) negative actions of slaves, and that such actions were endemic. *The Life of Aesop* is full of examples of this sort of self-assertion. Slaves talked among themselves, gossiping, inciting each other to disobedience, talking back to the master if they dared, casting disrespectful glances his way if they did not. Masters might try to mitigate such chatter by having slaves work under close supervision, as Columella recommends, or by encouraging quarreling, as Cato urges, or by punishing slaves who tried to intimidate their masters with threats and hostile gestures, but collusion to get the better of the master could not be stopped. Masters often branded slaves as inveterate liars – and indeed they often were, for lying was frequently a way to try to avoid charges against them, real or false, and the accompanying punishments. As Salvian remarked, 'Slaves lie in order to escape punishment. Why would anyone wonder that a terrified slave would prefer to lie rather than to be flogged?' (*On the Governance of*

God 4.3). Slaves complained whenever they could get away with it, and weeping and wailing in the presence of the master was a standard tactic (Apuleius, *The Golden Ass* 9.21), as was the 'slow-down.' Slaves could shirk work by skulking around and hiding to avoid notice, going slowly, failing to complete tasks, and doing their assignments poorly. Masters sometimes thought this was due to fatigue or simple laziness – but the tactics are well documented in other societies holding slaves. Feigning illness was another standard recourse: slaves could hope to be allowed to lie abed, or be sent to the 'sick house' for a time. Pretending ignorance was also attempted – although it, as the other strategies, could end in a flogging.

More serious were overt acts against the master's interests. Theft was a constant possibility. There is ample evidence from the documents from Egypt that slaves were not trusted, and often earned that distrust. Mistresses as well as masters and overseers had to assume that slaves would steal. Food was particularly tempting:

Slaves are accused of having greedy mouths and bellies. And this is nothing astonishing. He who often starves, craves satiety. And obviously, anyone would prefer to take care of his hunger with delicacies, rather than with plain bread. So we should forgive if a slave goes for food he is normally denied. (Salvian, *The Governance of God* 4.3.13–18)

Theft was endemic, whether to supply a real want, such as food, material to sell or trade to increase one's *peculium*, or just to show defiance of the master.

Property damage was a form of theft, for it deprived the master of his possessions. Carelessness could always be pretended, and sabotaging equipment was a good way to avoid work, at least for a time. Failing to serve conscientiously was another way of retaliating – if the slave didn't get caught:

Who then is the faithful and wise servant, whom the master has put in charge of the servants in his household to give them their food at the proper time? It will be good for that servant whose master finds him doing so when he returns. I tell you the truth, he will put him in charge of all his possessions. (Matthew 24:45–7)

So far so good – the faithful servant. However:

> … suppose that servant is wicked and says to himself, 'My master is staying away a long time,' and he then begins to beat his fellow servants and to eat and drink with drunkards. The master of that servant will come on a day when he does not expect him and at an hour he is not aware of. He will cut him to pieces and … there will be weeping and gnashing of teeth. (Matthew 24:48–51)

It would be a rare but sweet revenge for a slave to do as Callistus did: His master had sold him as a worthless slave; his new owner made him a doorman, responsible for controlling entrance to his mansion. When his old master sought entrance, he turned him away, in turn, as unworthy (Seneca, *Letters* 47).

Often, slaves were tempted to harm. In Egypt they are attested as showing disrespect to masters, shouting at them and otherwise insulting them. They are even seen participating in assaults and physical violence in the streets. Such was the extent of this behavior that a life for a slave owner could carry some risk on a regular basis. Actual murder of masters was probably rare, although, living among slaves, the elite were always potentially the target of extreme violence and there were enough actual examples to keep the possibility fixed in their minds. Besides various instances given in elite literature, an inscription from Mainz tells a story of slave revenge:

> Jucundus, freedman of Marcus Terentius, a cattleman, lies here. Passerby, whoever you might be, stop and read. See how I complain to no avail, undeservedly taken from life. I was not able to live more than 30 years. A slave tore life from me and then cast himself headlong into the water below. The River Main took from that man what he had taken from his master. Jucundus' patron erected this monument. (*CIL* 13.7070 = *ILS* 8511, Mainz, Germany)

From Clunia (Peñalba de Castro) in Spain comes another:

> Atia Turellia, daughter of Gaius Turellius, age 27, was slain by a slave. Gaius Turellius and Valeria [erected this monument] … (*AE* 1992.1037)

Violence against masters on a grand scale did not occur; slave rebellions practically cease before the empire, although escaped slaves provided a continuous feed for outlawry, which itself sometimes amounted almost to rebellion. Classic revolt conditions did not exist, however: the slave population was not heavily male, recently imported into slavery, or greatly more numerous than the free population. Nor were there proximate places to escape to even if there were rebellion. It is unlikely that slaves thought much about this ultimate violence.

They might, however, consider violence against themselves. From comparative material it is safe to assume that suicide was an accepted avenue of escape from the horrors of slavery. Slave suicides are mentioned in legal materials, and apparently one part of a standard description of a slave for sale included a statement of whether he had ever tried to commit suicide. Just above I have given the case of the slave who murdered his master, then threw himself into a river. But beyond this, there are surprisingly few examples of slaves committing suicide, although it is instructive that Lucius in *The Golden Ass* thinks of suicide as a way out of his plight – even if he never follows through.

What slaves did think about and do in large numbers – and this is clear from the dream interpretation and fortune-telling evidence noted above – was escape by running away. The main cause was abuse; the main constraint consideration of family and social ties that would need to be left behind. In *The Life of Aesop* there are constant references to running away as a logical act by a slave to escape a beating or other abuse, whether at the hands of the master or a fellow slave. Egyptian material documents the frequency of runaways and the worry this act caused masters. Epigraphy leaves us with the rather pathetic measure masters sometimes took to thwart running away: a slave collar. These collars were inscribed with such things as:

I am a slave of my master Scholasticus, an important official. Hold me so that I don't escape from the mansion called Pulverata. (*AE* 1892.68, Rome)

And:

Seize me because I have fled and bring me back to my master, the highly estimable Cethegus in the Livian market, third region of the city of Rome. (*CIL* 6.41335, Rome)

And:

I am Asellus, slave of Praeiectus, an aide of the prefect of the grain supply. I have gone outside the walls. Seize me because I have run away. Bring me back to the place called 'At the Flower,' next to the barbers. (*CIL* 15.7172 = *ILS* 8727, Vellitri)

The *Carmen Astrologicum* of Dorotheus of Sidon has all the appearance of being used by slaves planning to or actually running away. The chart castings relating to their situation are eloquent: the runaway will 'travel far away' or 'stay close by'; he 'sticks to the street and does not stray and is not confused so that he arrives in his place which he wishes'; he 'sheds blood in the place which he comes to so that because of this he will be seized by force so that he might be sent back to his master'; he 'has caused suspicion and committed a ruse so that because of this he has fallen in chains'; 'the runaway has lost the goods which he stole when he ran away, he wandered away from them, and the runaway will be seized and sent back to his master, and misery and chains will reach him in this running away of his.' In six castings the runaway escapes successfully; in eight he is caught – perhaps in the house of a powerful person and retrieved only with great difficulty by the master, or returned but forgiven by his master, as seems to be the scenario desired by Paul in his letter to Onesimus' master. On the run, life may be hard or even disastrous for the runaway: he could die in his flight, perhaps by burning or by the knife, or at the hands of men, or by an animal, or a building falling on him and killing him, or drowning in a flood, or suicide, or having his hands and feet cut off, or being strangled or crucified or burned alive, or drowning at sea. These predictions in sum cover just about anything that could happen to a runaway and are vivid evidence of many a slave's focus on taking the radical step of escape from a master.

Once away, as the astrologer indicates, a slave might escape detection. One way to insure this was to have recourse to magic. Among the magic papyri is one that states that if a runaway carries three specified

Homeric verses inscribed on a small sheet of iron, 'he will never be found.' On a more practical level, because most would look and speak like the population they were running to, there would be no obvious way to identify a runaway. If challenged, how would anyone know a man was not free, unless a master or someone with a clear physical description appeared to accuse him of being a runaway? If they lacked the standard documentation of freedom, a person could only be proved to be 'free' or 'slave' by such things as distinguishing features, friends' witness, and their own evidence. So, too, documents from Egypt include authorizations to seek out and punish runaways, while Pliny the Younger tells of detecting slaves who had sneaked into the Roman army – many others presumably did this undetected (Pliny, *Letters* 10.29–30).

While on the run, a slave might take shelter with friends or former slaves of the household, take on work as a hired laborer, try to (illegally) join the army, become a robber, attach himself to a landowner as a tenant, or do just about anything a poor free person could in society. He might have a very hard life, and he might eventually be recaptured. But the harping of the elite literature on runaways; the detailed indications of intense interest in running away which the fortune-telling literature reveals; and the practical ease with which a runaway could melt into the population combine to show that running away was a very live choice for a slave in hard circumstances.

I have so far looked at the slave voice with regard to those who control their lives, whether slave (e.g. a foreman) or a free master, and have seen that voice in the material related to runaways. Next I turn to slaves voicing their fears that they will be sold away. Some few slaves might view being sold as a positive thing, a way to escape a bad master, but for most it was a thing to be dreaded: conditions, while they might be better with a different master, might also well be worse. But more than concern for their own well-being, the specter of sale meant the potential disruption of close, positive, supportive ties within the slave's community.

Marriage, sex, and family

The closest ties were those of family. Although in law slaves could not marry – someone who had no 'personhood' could not be legally joined to another – in fact they routinely developed long-term relationships. Indeed, a look at the evidence from inscriptions noting slave unions shows how hard it is to distinguish them from free unions in terminology or formulas. From time to time the mate is called a *contubernalis*, a 'tentmate,' the conventional term used to describe a partner in a slave union:

> To the Netherworld Gods. Anna, slave of Quintus Aulus, lived 19 years. With no warning at all sudden death snatched her away in the flower of her youth. This is dedicated to the best mate (*contubernalis*). (*AE* 1976.173, Cosenza)

> To the Underworld Gods. Hermes Callippianius set this up to Terentina, slave of Claudius Secundus, who lived 22 years, 3 months. She was the dearest, most dutiful, most deserving mate. (*CIL* 6.27152, Rome)

However, traditional words for 'spouse,' *uxor* and *coniunx*, appear more frequently than does *contubernalis*:

> To the Netherworld Gods. Mercurius her fellow slave set this up to his well-deserving wife (*coniunx*), Fortunata. (*AE* 1973.110, Rome)

> This is set up to Primus, slave of Herennius Verus by Hilarica, his wife (*uxor*). (*CIL* 3.11660, Wolfsberg, Austria)

And these words even appear in legal texts, clear evidence that they were accepted as descriptors of slave unions. Evidently, slaves could be thought of as 'married' by both slaves and free, whatever their juridical condition technically. Sometimes these unions were encouraged by the masters, as Varro advises: 'Make the overseers more eager in their work by giving out rewards, and see to it that they can accumulate personal savings, and that each has a female fellow slave, so they can bear children together' (*On Agriculture* 1.17.5). Other times, the slaves themselves initiated the unions without specific encouragement. These could be fraught, and certainly sex was not restricted to such unions.

Indeed, it is hard to disentangle a broad description of sex among the slaves. The masters' assumption was that slaves, if left to themselves, would turn to dissipation, which included profligate sex among themselves and in brothels (Columella, *On Rural Matters* 1.8.9–10). The main factor encouraging a loose attitude toward sexual mores among slaves was that masters male and female were free to treat men and boys, girls and women as available sexual objects who had no justification for or means of resistance to advances. Any right to sexual integrity was eliminated a priori by the very nature of the slave's enslavement. A slave might strive to maintain that integrity in the face of powerlessness to resist rape, but for the woman so treated or for the man unable to prevent it, the divorce of sex from its usual context of self-directed recreation, procreation, or profit meant that any social rules governing acceptable sex were extremely weak.

For many, the degradation produced only misery. For the most successful, sex became just another weapon in the arsenal of accommodation or resistance. As I have shown, sexual relations with a master might mean master-slave offspring who would normally be treated better than other slaves, and perhaps even result in a better place in the household for the mother/concubine. In some instances, a master even freed and married such a concubine. For a boy – and here Petronius' Trimalchio is the fictional example par excellence – the male master's favor might win long-term benefits, even after boyhood charms faded. A favorite male slave might catch the eye of his mistress, and turn out well. Despite these outliers, the usual slave expectation would have been to be used and cast aside, all a part of the degradation of slavery.

How would this situation have affected the creation and maintenance of long-term 'marriage' relationships among slaves? To judge by the evidence of the inscriptions, slaves worked around it. Unable to prevent abuse, impervious to their masters' degrading views of their sexuality, they still formed lasting bonds.

These bonds produced children – and an epigraphic record that is impossible to distinguish from the expressions of affection and appreciation seen on the gravestones of free persons. The evidence of children is extensive; for example:

To the most unfortunate Pieris, slave of Gavianus, who lived 24 years. What it was proper that a daughter do, her unhappy parents,

Anteros and Gallitana, did instead. They set up this monument for themselves – and for their daughter. (*CIL* 9.955, Troia, Italy)

To the shades of Primulus, the babe of Sequens and Primula. This is set up to their slave son. (*CIL* 13.4199, Hetzerath, Germany)

This is the grave of Martialis age 10, Loveus age 9, and Paternus age 4, slaves in the Laediensian house. Gemellinus slave of Florus set this up to his children. (*Hispania Epigraphica* 6.636, Lugo, Spain)

So, too, mention of parents:

To the Underworld Gods. Priscus and Primigenia, his parents, and Theophile, his wife (*coniunx*), set this up to Primitivus, slave of Violentilla, an eye doctor. He lived 18 years, 7 months, and 16 days. (*AE* 1953.59, Rome)

And of siblings:

Sacred to the Underworld Gods. Antinoe and Phoebe are two sisters and fellow slaves of the Volusii, Marcus and Aemilianus. Here lie Phoebe who lived 6 years, 10 months, 15 days, and Antinoe, 1 year and 20 days. Phoebus and Rhodope set this up to their most dutiful daughters, and Tertius did as well. (*AE* 1984.347, Pagus Interpromium, Italy)

In the following example, grandparents, who along with the father are still slaves, are mentioned, while the mother has gained her freedom:

To the Underworld Gods. Anthus slave of the Marci, his grandfather, Rhoxane his grandmother, Terminalis his father, and Julia Euphrantice his mother set this up to their son, Tiberius Julius. (*CIL* 6.35530, Rome)

Of course the children of slaves belonged to the master as slaves themselves. Slaves with children tended to be more cooperative with masters because of a desire not to be separated. In addition, if the master so chose, a woman could be freed from work or even set free if she produced three to five children. Slaves suffered the same torments of parenthood that the free did, including loss of a young child:

Novesis slave agent and Juventilla set this up to Surisca their most unfortunate daughter who lived well-deserving, but only 2 years and 3 months. (*CIL* 3.2126, Salona, Croatia)

And a child and mother lost in childbirth:

To the Underworld Gods. To Candida my well-deserving wife, +/- 30 years old, who lived with me +/- 7 years. She was tortured in childbirth for four days and could not give birth. And so she died. Justus her fellow slave set this gravestone up. (*CIL* 3.2267, Salona, Croatia)

The breakup of such slave families could only cause great pain and suffering for the slaves involved and for their close friends. There is some evidence of some sympathy on the part of authorities late in the imperial period regarding the separation of slave families through sale. In AD 334 the emperor Constantine decreed:

Regarding the Sardinian imperial estates, see to it that the new possessors of land which has been distributed to different owners do not separate slave families. For who would tolerate children being taken from parents, brothers from sisters, husbands from wives (*sic*)? Therefore if anyone has dragged off rent families to different owners, compel these separated families to be reunited … Take great care to see that hereafter there be no complaint in the province about the distribution of loved ones among different masters. (*Theodosian Code* 2.25.1)

The decree, of course, highlights that fact that rending families was routine. And, indeed, records of sales from Egypt seem to indicate that in most cases owners paid no attention to selling slave couples or families as a unit, and from an owner's standpoint there is scant reason why they should. Women of childbearing age, children, strong young men:

all met different markets and would normally be sold individually. The rending of families must have been the most dreaded result of being sold.

Social and religious connections

Slaves also developed close attachments through sharing social interaction. Despite the advice of the agricultural writers to keep slaves working from dawn to dusk in order to make them so tired that all else they can think about is eating and sleeping (Columella, *On Rural Matters* 1.2.9–10), slaves found time to themselves. If nothing else, the accusations of masters bear witness to this: Columella, for example, complains that urban slaves have far too much free time on their hands. Echoing a commonplace of elite authors, he talks of slaves who have 'spent a lot of time in frivolous, dissolute activities prevalent in cities. These lazy and sluggish sorts of slaves are usually hanging around doing nothing, idling about the Campus Martius, or in the circus, theaters, gambling dens, low eateries, and whorehouses, and generally daydreaming about them all the time they are not actually there' (*On Rural Matters* 1.8.2). This situation was the result of 'overstaffing' in urban conditions. Whereas on the farm slaves could (and the agricultural writers urge this strongly at numerous points) be kept working from dawn to dusk, exhausted so that they didn't have time or inclination for slacking, city slaves were more for show than for necessity; there were not nearly enough chores to be done to keep the slaves busy, and they were kept for conspicuous display and status as much as for the particular services each provided. Encolpius in his charade at Croton pretends that all his slaves have been killed in a disaster at sea. He says, 'His recent shipwreck had added to his sadness – he had lost over two million sesterces, but this loss did not affect him nearly so much as the loss of his slaves, for without them he couldn't even recognize his own high status' (Petronius, *Satyricon* 117). He kept his slave entourage not because they all had important things to do, but because their very presence added to his dignity. Thus on a daily basis many slaves in households indeed had time on their hands to socialize.

Slaves could also look forward to festival days as well as to whatever time they could sequester for themselves in the course of daily duties. Masters were well aware of the value of occasional opportunities for diversion and letting off steam, both of which helped slaves to live more happily in their menial condition. Columella advises that on holidays a master should reward his slaves with little monetary gifts and associate with them in a friendly way, even eating with them; as early as the writings of Aristotle these strategies had been recommended. To judge from a slave rental contract from Egypt, a slave could expect eight days a year as holiday; the contract states that if more than this number of days is taken, pro rata deductions of rental would be made.

These sorts of festival days presumably varied from place to place, according to local customs. In Rome there were three 'slave festivals': the Saturnalia (late December); the Festival of Female Household Slaves (*ancillarum feriae*) (July 7); and the 'Slaves' Festival Day' (*servorum dies festus*) (August 13). The Saturnalia was celebrated widely in the empire while the other two were local festivals; other festivals would have been celebrated elsewhere. In addition, slaves certainly participated in festival life during nonslave-centered celebrations, and at times the holiday would have been very local and even individual – for the spirit (*genius*) of the master, for example, or for the household protective deities (*lares*), or for the dead. During these festival times, slaves could look forward to laxity of rules governing their work and behavior, to better food, to wearing the nicest clothing they had, to socializing – and often to heavy drinking, and general carousing.

Not only social but also religious connections were sometimes broken by sale. But while some religious activities were grounded in local household and family units, others transcended these. In *The Life of Aesop*, Aesop shows piety toward the goddess Isis, an example of worship that transcended the local. Inscriptions give examples of slaves worshiping a wide range of traditional 'greater gods' such as Minerva, Mars, Mercury, and Jupiter, as well as Mithra, Isis, and the Christian deity. Not surprisingly, Fortune figures as an object of devotion as well, and Silvanus is particularly popular; Jupiter 'The Free' seems especially appropriate since the dedication appears on Delos, a major slave marketplace:

Marcus Granius Heras, freedman of Marcus, Diodotus Seius, slave of Gaius and Gnaeus, Apollonius Laelius, slave of Quintus, Prepon Alleius, slave of Marcus, Nicandrus Rasennius, slave of Marcus, erected this statue of Jupiter the Free. (*CIL* 3.14203.3 = *ILS* 9236)

And of course magic and superstitious practices abounded, as they did throughout the culture, slave and free. Columella recommends that the owner be sure that the slave overseer prevent soothsayers and witches (*haruspices* and *sagaes*) from the estate because these folks 'appealing to empty superstition push ignorant minds first to waste their money, then finally to engage in immoral acts' (*On Rural Matters* 1.8–9). Interestingly, however, the Greek magical papyri do not have a single charm or reference to a magical practice directed particularly at a slave's situation or needs, except the one quoted above to protect runaways and ones directed at professionals who happened to be slaves, such as charioteers. From New World analogy, I would expect such spells (a curse on an overseer, for example), but none appears. I must assume that slave witches and wizards had their own spells, which, not surprisingly, were not a part of the magical manuals – or, at least, not of the ones that survive. Fortune-telling is another matter, however. As noted, Artemidorus' dream book has many interpretations related directly to slaves. Clearly the customers Artemidorus has, and anticipates for his son, include slaves as regulars. It is not hard to imagine that less scrupulous 'professionals' such as soothsayers would have also done a brisk business among slaves whether in town or in the country. Consultation with them was one popular way to deal with the insecurities of slave life.

Freedom

In the midst of ties and emotions of family, friends, and religion, the slave always feared separation through sale. The fear was real, a constant presence in his life. The best way out was to gain freedom. The desire for freedom consumed slaves. Despite the potential loss of some security, as the guard in Plautus' play *The Prisoners* (119) says, 'I'm sure we'd all rather be free than slaves.' In *The Life of Aesop*, Aesop is constantly asking his master to free him – the master, Xanthus, promises repeatedly, but reneges just as frequently. As I interpret Lucius' adventures as an ass in Apuleius' novel to be a palimpsest for a life of slavery, the rose that Lucius needs to eat in order to regain his human form (and, as it turns out, salvation at the feet of Isis) is freedom itself. The *Carmen Astrologicum* gives many castings that indicate that a slave will be freed;

13. Free at last. A public manumission ceremony declares a slave free. Note the freedman's cap.

Artemidorus interprets dreams to promise the same thing. There are many inscriptions set up by freed slaves and many references in elite literature to them. In this one, an ex-slave gives thanks for divine help:

> Dedicated to the Spirit of the Annii Macer and Licinianus. I, Alphios their slave, set this up to fulfill my vow – I am now free! (*CIL* 12.619, Auriol, France)

Manumission was the route to freedom. Masters controlled this almost completely – the only exception was being able somehow to prove your improper enslavement and so free status before a magistrate. The masters often held out the promise of freedom as an incentive to get slaves to do what they wanted them to do – although it is interesting to note that the agricultural writers do not include this promise among the rewards they suggest to encourage slaves. Slaves could be freed through the declaration of the master before friends or before a magistrate, through self-purchase, or by testament. If officially manumitted before a magistrate they received a document proving this (*Digest* 3.2.8.1). Although contracts for manumission are known from Egypt, the actual document proving freedom has rarely been found. There are a few examples in Greek; here is a Latin one:

> Marcus Aurelius Ammonion, son of Lupergos, son of Sarapion, from Hermupolis the Greater, ancient and splendid, declares in the presence of his friends that Helen, his house-raised slave, age about 34 years, is no longer to be a slave and to now be free. He received as the price of her freedom 2,200 Augustan drachmas from Aurelius Ales, son of Inarous, from the Tisicheos district of the Hermupolite nome. Ales, son of Inarous, gave the money to Helen the aforementioned freedwoman and will make no claim for it against her. Done at Hermupolis the Greater, ancient and splendid, on the seventh day before the Kalens of August, when Gratus and Seleucus were consuls, in the third regnal year of Caesar Marcus Aurelius Antoninus Pius Fortunate Revered. (*M.Chr.* 372)

In theory a freed slave could produce a document like this, but it was written on perishable material – an incised waxed tablet enclosed by wooden plates inscribed in pen and ink – so it was unlike another type of 'manumission,' the discharge of a solder from service, which was written in bronze. There does not seem to be any reference in fiction or elsewhere to a manumitted slave producing a document as proof of his freedom. When a master does try to reclaim a runaway, the man is identified by physical features, and the statement that he could not produce a liberation document is never mentioned. Thus although in theory this sort of identification could have made it harder for a runaway to escape successfully – or easily forged to prove freedom – it does not seem to figure importantly. Freedom itself, however, was celebrated happily when it occurred. In one club that had both free and slave members, the newly freed slave was to bring an amphora of wine to the next meeting – the equivalent of three cases of the stuff – to lubricate a fine celebration of a great event (*ILS* 7212, Lanuvio, Italy).

Certainly not all slaves were eventually freed; many died in harness. Probably few males were freed before the age of thirty (although the

Egyptian evidence may contradict this), and few females before the end of their childbearing years (early forties). And to judge by comparative material, slaves in urban households were much more likely to be freed than those in the countryside. Still, slaves could see freedmen around them; the possibility of manumission could be real or remote, but at the very least, to judge from fiction and nonfiction sources and, most of all, from the slaves' voices reflected in the fortune-telling material, it figured prominently in a slave's mind as he contemplated his life and options.

Conclusion

A slave's outlook was bounded by his possibilities. He focused on managing in his current condition vis-à-vis the master, up to and including escaping in flight; he developed strong ties with other slaves, even to the point of forming a family, and feared the disruption of being sold; he longed for a freedom that might eventually come. Slavery deprived the slave of self-determination, but it did not deprive him of self-identity. He remained a thinking, feeling, acting human being, and lived within slavery coping as best he could.

AFTER SLAVERY:
FREEDMEN

THE FREEDMAN, THE EX-SLAVE, is an ordinary Roman very difficult to imagine because there is not even a remotely similar category in
Western societies. Freedmen have attracted a good deal of attention in
Roman social history because the elite interacted with them in significant and often negative ways. Ironically, their visibility in prejudiced
elites' sources has made their actual lives quite invisible. Freedmen or
freedwomen are much like other free ordinary folk, but their situation
and possibilities are different enough, and the animus and misunder-
standings regarding them misleading enough, to call for a separate
treatment.

The animus comes out in the elite's literary portrayal of the freedmen,
a portrayal that has often been taken as a true description of freedmen in
general. The treatment of such authors as Juvenal, Martial, Tacitus, and
Suetonius depicts freedmen who were insulting at least and anathema
at most to the ruling men of the empire, and to their literary mouth-
pieces. The origin of this attitude is in the dynamics of slavery and freed
slaves within the elite household. I will describe in detail below the
circumstances and life of freedmen; in summary here I just note that
ex-slaves, like slaves, were absolutely essential to the 'leisure class' life
of the aristocracy. And more than just a source of labor, ex-slaves in particular represented the most successful of an elite's slaves. These were
the slaves who had been put in charge of affairs in the household and on

rural estates. These were the slaves who had been financed in business ventures on behalf of the master. It was only through such dependent men (and at times women) that a master could manage and control the resources to produce the wealth that produced the leisure. In return for the 'privilege' of being a slave or ex-slave in the master's household, the slave or freedman owed obedience and duty to the master and his interests. As far as the master was concerned, the position was one of perpetual dominance (for a slave) and subalternship (if a freedman). If they accepted this position, then all was well. But, in fact, a man was often employed in a responsible task because he was exceptionally talented; with freedom could come an assertion of that talent for his own purposes, leading to significant or even vast wealth. With the talent and wealth came the challenge to and extreme tension for the aristocracy that always arose when 'outsiders' qualified by ability and money challenged the existing elite for influence and power. But with freedmen it was much worse than had the challenge come from mere nouveaux riches – these were men who had once been *slaves*, a condition inherently and inextinguishably degrading in the eyes of the leaders of society. It is this revulsion at status-crashing that turned what might have been mere disdain into active loathing.

And worst of all were the ex-slaves of the imperial family. I do not include these freedmen in general here as they are set apart from other ordinary freedmen by their special relationship to the imperial household, but their role in creating the perception of the elites must be noted. The imperial freedmen derived prestige from association with the ruler of the rulers. They were relied upon to run the machinery of the empire (for the empire was thought of as a great household by the emperor, to be managed like any other 'estate'). They could take advantage of their position to assert themselves (as agents of the emperor) blatantly at the expense of the elite, who had to do as the emperor wished or suffer the consequences. So the irksomeness was doubled: the elite had to bow to the emperor, and also to his agents, who once had been *slaves*.

The hatred of imperial freedmen especially, but uppity freedmen in general, brought scathing opprobrium to focus on this societal group. To keep them at bay, they were disparaged as forever despised, inferior; they were marked by law and custom as unworthy of mixing with the elite in politics or marriage or anything. All this is understandable given the mentality of the elite. But what all too often happens is that this assessment of freedmen is generalized to provide the context and even details of lives of freedmen in general. I seek to retrieve the outlook of ordinary freedmen and to show how large the gulf was between their lives and negative descriptions of freedmen provided by the elite.

Alongside the alleged ancient hostility toward ordinary freedmen lies the modern misunderstanding that sees the freedmen as the bourgeoisie. Just as the ancient aristocracy limned freedmen according to their prejudices, over the past two centuries many have tried to find a 'middle class' in the freedmen because they were often engaged in commerce and industry. But they are no such 'class' in any sense that fits the actual conception of a 'middle,' nor do they fit the sociopolitical implications of a bourgeoisie. Fortunately, many scholars now avoid such descriptions, but they are found in older works, and in careless popular accounts.

A more pernicious nuance to the discussion of freedmen comes with racist overtones. Moderns have taken their cue from the vehement accusation of Tacitus and Juvenal about 'Orontes flowing into Tiber.' Starting with a conviction that peoples of the Eastern Empire (the Orontes is a river in Syria) were effeminate, intriguing, loathsome folks in general, the elite was convinced that slaves mostly came from there (or, at least, the ones who became uppity freedmen) and were displacing native-born, virile, moral Italians in Rome. This was leading to a definite decline in the quality of Romans as a whole, they thought. Early in the twentieth century the great ancient historian Tenney Frank wrote an extremely influential article in which he used epigraphic evidence from Rome to 'prove' the ancients right; he concluded that during the empire only 10 percent of Romans had 'pure' Italian blood and that fully 80 percent of the city of Rome were freedmen and their descendants from the eastern, 'oriental' part of the empire. Read today, his analysis is blatantly Eurocentric, racist, and a paradigm of orientalism. But his statistics and conclusions so fit the ancient elite's own prejudiced views that they were not seriously questioned by A. M. Duff in his fundamental 1928 treatment of freedmen ('It seems, then, that freedman and their descendants in a great measure ruined Rome ... Manumission, if it has been directed aright, need not have worked with such deplorable effects upon the population ... The influx of Oriental blood would not have been so overwhelming'); Frank's premises and 'evidence' were influential even as late as the 1960s. It is time once and for all to eliminate such thinking from any discussion of freedmen.

Freedom

When I talk about freedmen I actually restrict myself to a specific group: slaves that have been freed by masters who were Roman citizens. Manumitted properly, these slaves became Roman citizens, although citizens with some disabilities, which I will discuss. Freed slaves of any other citizenship (and remember that there was no universal Roman citizenship until early in the third century AD) did not gain citizenship in either their local towns or in the Roman body politic upon gaining freedom; rather, they became just like any other noncitizens in their communities – Athens, Alexandria, Antioch – and in the empire. Of demographic necessity, therefore, freedmen were concentrated in Italy, where citizens were concentrated, and to a lesser extent in the western areas of the empire; Roman citizens and therefore Roman freedmen were rarer in the eastern regions. Moreover, it seems that most freedmen lived in urban rather than rural areas since the opportunities to gain one's freedom were apparently more abundant in the urban household setting.

Manumission was what made a person a freedman. As I discuss in Chapter 4, manumission was always a possibility. Probably most emancipation took place for men by around age thirty and for women toward the end of their childbearing years, say their mid forties. Exceptions were always possible, of course, but relatively young men of talent would be most useful to their ex-masters and now patrons; older women might be of little economic use to the master, and could well be gotten out of the household. But there are no statistics, and clearly many slaves were never freed at any time in their lives. A master's calculus might include personal as well as economic considerations; the matrix of decision-making is unknowable in detail.

The legal aspects of manumission can be briefly summarized. There were a number of ways to perform the act. These ranged from public and formal procedures before a magistrate to a very informal declaration of freedom in front of friends, to testamentary grants of freedom. It might have made a difference if a person were freed formally or informally, for informal manumissions did not technically carry Roman citizenship; only an inferior species of citizenship called Junian Latin status was granted. Although it might seem logical that many more slaves would be freed informally, and so with disabilities, than formally, the relative numbers are unknown; estimates have ranged as high as 40 percent or more being Latins, but it is impossible to know. Freedmen themselves do not make any distinction either in epigraphy or in fiction. No one identifies himself as a 'Latin freedman'; Latins are almost completely absent from Roman legal documents. The absence in the evidence probably reflects a lack of concern in people's minds to distinguish between freedmen with full citizenship and those with Latin citizenship. After all, they both had mostly the same economic, social, and legal rights. The main Latin disability was the inability to leave children an inheritance in Roman law. The only other 'problem' with being a Latin citizen within the Roman citizenship world was that you could not hold political office in Rome, or other place that was composed of Roman citizens. As I have repeatedly stressed, the inability to hold political office was not a worry in the minds of ordinary people, and certainly would not be in the minds of most freedmen. They had no hope, and no ambition, no thought to break into the ranks of the local, much less the imperial, elite. While occasionally the Latin status was important in an elite context, it was never so in the lives of most ordinary Romans. It is fully justifiable to treat freedmen who gained freedom formally in the same discussion as those who were informally manumitted, and the groups are conflated in the discussion below.

As I have mentioned, the elite cultural, social, and economic paradigm could only be sustained through the employment of capable, trusted slaves in positions of supervision and management. Although free labor was hired when help was needed on a seasonal or specific project, there is little evidence that free persons were hired to do the supervisory work that a slave or freedman could do, and they literally could not be a business representative. A prime example of a reliable freedman is Cicero's indispensable Tiro, first his slave and then his freedman. Among the local elite, Lichas of Tarentum is a wealthy merchant in Petronius' novel, who owns ships, has estates, and uses quite a number of slaves to carry out the household's business transactions; it is these who might expect ultimately to be freed. Legal authorities Ulpian and Gaius make it clear that both male and female slaves could

14. Freedom at the death of a master. Frequently a master would reward faithful slaves with their freedom at his death, thereby keeping their service for his lifetime and harming only his heirs, who lost valuable property. In this relief, mourners surround the bier. Note the woman wearing a freedman's cap at the lower right.

be used by masters as agents. This would pave the way to freedom with skills learned. And, indeed, some freedmen's freedom comes after being witnesses or agents in their masters' poisonings, murders, and crimes. The historian Dionysius of Halicarnassus wrote of freedmen 'who having been confidants and accomplices of their masters in poisonings, receive from them their freedom as a reward' (*Antiquities* 4.24). This sort of unethical behavior should not surprise, for freedmen served their former masters, and if those were engaged in nefarious activities, it is only natural to suppose that their freedmen would have been as well.

The same usefulness extended to more ordinary people holding slaves. Here an owner has freed a slave and set him up in the business of engraving in gold and silver:

> This is dedicated to the spirits of Marcus Canuleius Zosimus, dead at age 28. His former owner set this up to a well-deserving freedman. He in his life spoke ill to no one and did everything according to his ex-master's wishes. He always had in his possession a great amount of gold and silver, but never ever did he covet any of it. He surpassed all in the art of engraving in the Clodian technique. (*CIL* 6.9222 = *ILS* 7695, Rome)

This usefulness to the master as a slave is the formative fact of a freedman's life. It is perfectly conceivable that a master might free a slave out of kindness and consideration for a job well done, or to demonstrate generosity, or to create free dependents who would enhance his social status, or to profit from a slave purchasing his freedom, or even just to get rid of deadwood he no longer wished to spend money on for living expenses. But the most rational progression was from selection of a young slave as especially talented and responsible (and perhaps sexually appealing, as in the case of Trimalchio), to assigning the slave duties, to promoting the slave to management of an aspect of the master's business affairs, to freeing the slave and continuing to benefit from his services once a freedman, thus retaining economic return without the expense of maintaining a slave.

This brings us to a central observation about freedmen, long noted: Freedmen appear in business of various sorts in large numbers. Not only is this attested to in epigraphy; the phenomenon appears in elite descriptions as well as in novels and documents. The reason for this is that in the Romano-Grecian world the ability to raise capital for a new venture was extremely limited. An ordinary person could not borrow start-up funds easily on reasonable terms because of the comparatively underdeveloped banking and finance system. Incremental growth, i.e. growth funded from direct profits, was always possible, but margins did not facilitate this. On the contrary, freedmen clearly came into business in large numbers with the financial backing of their masters either in operations as a slave, or later as a freedman, or both. For the masters this made perfect sense because they needed reliable persons to act on their behalf. By using slaves, who were legally part of the master, so to speak, and freedmen, who had obligations and ties to the master, a master could be as certain as possible of good management. The legal authority Gaius affirms this: 'A reasonable cause for freeing a slave is if he frees him for the sake of having an agent' (*Institutes* 1.19). Through slaves and freedmen, an elite's business activities could be conducted without trusting free partners or agents, and without the social reprobation of direct business dealings.

For the slave-to-become-freedman, the master held out two inducements to hard work: the promise of freedom for a job well done, and the chance to earn and keep private money, the *peculium* or 'stash' that slaves were allowed to accumulate, looking forward to the day of freedom. For a slave with ambition and talent, these inducements coupled with a future in business and hope for a decent life, possibly even wealth, were very appealing. The ongoing relationship of a freedman to his patron ranged widely. There might be none at all (if the patron was dead, or if payment for freedom had severed all important ties), or a very close one if the freedman remained physically in the patron's household. But the origins of the freedman's success in freedom were directly bound to his experience under his master, and to opportunities that afforded.

The Brazilian evidence gives us a striking parallel:

> Slaves who handled such supervisory positions with skill and responsibility were often rewarded for faithful service. Their owners permitted them to acquire property for their own use, including land and other slaves, and eventually to earn their freedom by buying themselves. Such freedpersons often continued in a client relationship with their former owners; and thus a slave's ownership of his or her person and of other slaves did not threaten a slave owner. Rather, the success of the slave tended to increase the slave owner's status and position in society, since command over people was a function of high status in the society. (Karasch, *Slave Life*)

A freedman's life began and was formed within the master's household, his *familia*, as a slave, a nonperson. Upon manumission he was 'born again' and his manumitter, the master, became his 'patron,' a word from the same root as *pater*, 'father.' In legal texts a freedman is equated with a son. The *Digest* states, 'By freedman or son the person of patron or father should always be honored and held sacred.' In the official nomenclature of a Roman citizen, the filiation – naming the father – is replaced with libertation – naming the freeing master, the patron. The restrictions, duties, and obligations of a son were much like those owed by a freedman, although in important ways a freedman was freer than a son who was under the authority of his father. For example, although a son could not marry, or keep his earned money, or hold property in his own right, a freedman could do all these things. But a freedman could not bring lawsuits or bear witness against his patron, as a son could not against his father. Most of all, both were supposed to honor and obey the father/patron as the source of their being; indeed, obedience was the highest good in a slave-become-freedman, as it was in a son or daughter. The burial of freedmen with other family members emphasizes the close connection to the household. The epigraphic record has hundreds of examples of this habit, for example:

> Sextus Rubrius Logismos, silversmith, ordered in his will that this grave monument be built for himself and Rubria Aura his freedwoman and Sextus Rubrius Saturninus his son and all his freedmen and freedwomen and their descendants. (*AE* 1928.77, Rome)

> Eutychia his daughter set this monument up to the Spirits of the Dead and to Titus Labienus Patavinus her well-deserving father and to their freedmen and freedwomen and their descendants. (*CIL* 5.2970, Padua, Italy)

From the relationship in slavery and manumission sprang variations of specific obligation, going beyond whatever a possibly ersatz father–son relationship might have supposed. These were of two kinds: unwritten, open-ended ones called *obsequia* (loyal behavior) and *officia* (bounden duties), continuing the ideals of obedience and dutifulness in a slave; and specifically listed ones called *operae* (tasks or specified owed services). The *obsequia* and *officia* expected by the cultural norms might include, in general, anything that would contribute to positive standing in society such as loyalty in disputes with others, publicly acknowledging the social importance of the patron by being a visible client, or helping out if the patron hit a rough patch. A freedman's owed services that he agreed to overtly upon manumission might differ quite substantially, depending on whether he stayed in the household, or operated outside it in business or other affairs. Owed services might include such things as a specified number of hours of labor in the patron's interests or household. And it should be noted that not all slaves had any duties at all to a former master since a slave who purchased his freedom outright might have no ties beyond what he perhaps retained as a purely emotional matter as a former member of the household. In reality both formal and informal kinds of obligation could vary widely, but as they existed they fulfilled a former master's desire to control and benefit from the existence and labor of his former slave. The direct benefit to the freedman was that performing his duties kept him in the good graces of the patron, and so assured support he might get in life (for example, help in legal troubles) and in business, such as continued capital investment by the patron. The patron benefited both socially and financially. The arrangement was mostly advantageous to both parties.

Abuses quite naturally were common in the system. The freedman might get 'uppity,' especially if he was successful in business, and renege on the dutifulness a patron felt was his right. Elite literature is full of railings against ungrateful freedmen, and legal decisions attempt to deal with it as well. Clearly the aristocracy of the empire perceived overpowerful freedmen to be a problem. But for ordinary freedmen the problem was abuses by patrons. One was to demand excessive *operae*. A patron might compel work past the agreed-upon number of years, for example. The *Digest* states that a freedwoman over fifty years old could not be forced to provide labor for her patron, so clearly this had happened; also, a woman who had been freed could not be forced to marry her patron (although if the woman when a slave had promised to marry him upon manumission, she was compelled to follow through on the promise).

Another was to impose on the bonds of loyalty and demand that tasks be done that were inappropriate because of the age of the freedman, or his physical condition, or the time required to perform the task and so take the freedman away from his own gainful employment. Sometimes the master tried to control future behavior of the freedman by forcing him to accept a large loan, thus binding him to the patron through debt; he might also force him to remain unmarried so that the patron would inherit the freedman's estate, rather than having it go to offspring. In the case of informal manumissions, the patron could and did threaten to retract the grant of freedom even though this might not be strictly legal; a simple denial that the grant took place would suffice, especially if the patron had been clever and granted the freedom without any witnesses present. The authorities were likely to side with the patron in any dispute, as evidence from Egypt shows: the prefect of Egypt informs a freedman that he will be flogged if the prefect hears any further complaints about him from his patron (*P.Oxy.* 4.706). In short, patrons often used whatever means they had, illegal and legal, to bind freedmen; as Artemidorus wrote, '… many freed slaves nonetheless continue to act as slaves and to be subject to another' (*Dreams*, 2.31).

Because freedmen figure so prominently in elite literature and in the legal writings, it is easy to think that they were numerous. But trying to identify just who is a freedman is a tricky business. To be sure there are some self-identified freedmen, those who announce the status on their tombstones, and some literary examples as well, most notably the cast of Trimalchio's dinner in Petronius' *Satyricon*. But taking a lead, as so often, from elite literary references to freedmen in every nook and cranny, historians have sought freedmen in large numbers. The search methodology is based upon the fact that there is a reasonable correlation between a certain set of names, mostly of Greek origin, and freedman status as overtly attested to in inscriptions. This fair correlation is then expanded into assertions based upon most if not all persons carrying such names being freedmen, and demographic statistics then follow. Without going into statistical detail, it can be said that this procedure is highly suspect. In fact, there are many apparently freeborn persons with 'freedman' names, and announced freedmen with names not on the 'freedman list.' The end result is that it cannot be known with any certainty whether a person is a freedman or not unless he tells us so, most normally by using the epigraphic formula 'freedman of X' to indicate he was freed by a particular owner.

The difficulty is increased because 'freedman' was not a category of the street; that is to say, ordinary people did not go around identifying themselves as 'freedman,' nor, apparently, did others so identify them, unlike the readiness to identify someone as a slave. In the New Testament, for example, there is a single possible reference to people who are freedmen (although the status of freedman is used metaphorically to describe followers of Christ); allegations that, for example, Lydia, the dealer in purple of Acts 16, was a freedwoman or that Paul was the son or grandson of a freedman have no proof in the texts themselves. In *The Golden Ass* a single episode in the novel (10.17) involves a person identified as a freedman, and I know of no reference in the Greek romances. People designated as freedmen are rare in the papyri. Mention of them is also rare in Artemidorus' *Interpretation of Dreams*; there is one reference, for example, to whether the dreamer will marry a freedwoman, but this is definitely an outlier. Unlike many social types such as women and slaves, 'freedman' is not a trigger for meaning in dreams – there is no connection made, for example, between arrogance and freedmen, or ungratefulness and freedmen; they just do not appear as meaning-carriers. Given that Artemidorus was assembling interpretations from his dossier of dreams dealt with, this means that the clients were not dreaming dreams with freedmen in them and, even more, without traits of freedmen as noted in elite literature carrying dream meaning. While a contributing factor might be that Artemidorus is writing for an audience in the Greek East, where freedmen were far fewer than in Italy. When evidence from dreams is added to other material, it is clear that people were not terribly interested in 'freedman' as a defining category.

This indifference starkly differed from the freedman's own sense of accomplishment in gaining freedom. A clear indication of this is that freedmen often identified themselves as ex-slaves on their gravestones by naming their ex-master.

> *Freeborn:* C. Cornelius Cai filius Lupulus = Gaius Cornelius Lupulus, son of Gaius.

> *Freedman:* C. Cornelius Cai libertus Lupulus = Gaius Cornelius Lupulus, freedman of Gaius.

Gaius Lupulus the freedman could have easily omitted 'freedman of Gaius'; there was no need to put it there, just as there was no 'requirement' that a filiation ('son of Gaius') be added. The important thing to emphasize is that a person who had won his freedom was very much aware of the feat and voluntarily wished to display the fact on his gravestone. He was proud of winning his freedom and dying a free man. But at the same time, to all appearances, other ordinary folks did not particularly care on a daily basis whether a person was a freedman or not.

How many freedmen were there? I have noted that the status is intrinsically limited because it can apply only to slaves freed by Roman citizens. These citizens accounted for just 10 to 15 percent of the total population in the empire before universal citizenship in AD 212. Their freedmen numbered perhaps half a million. Remember that freed status disappeared after the first generation; at any given time among a numerous citizen population such as in Italy or a Roman citizen colony, perhaps only one in twenty was a freedman or freedwoman; in areas with few Roman citizens, a person would probably have to meet well over a hundred people to find himself dealing with a single citizen freedperson. These numbers are of necessity very gross estimates, as demographic information is lacking. But they do give some indication of the scale of the situation. And that scale is very small indeed, especially as compared with slaves, who constituted perhaps 9 million (15 percent) of the total population, varying, of course, by time and place. There is no question of a freedman population overwhelming a free population, or even of being numerically very visible. This conclusion stands directly against the impression of 'Orontes flowing into Tiber' of the elite sources and the supposed evidence of the names of freedmen that I have critiqued above.

Freedmen's voices

It is time to let the freedmen speak for themselves. But before I do that, it is useful as a transition to look at the voice of an actual freedman's son. This is Quintus Horatius Flaccus, the famous poet Horace. In his *Satires* (1.6.65–88), Horace tells of how his father had been a slave, probably enslaved during the civil tumults of the early first century BC. He was freed, and worked as a tax collector living in Venusia. He wanted his son to be educated. He did not send him to the local school in Venusia, however; rather, he took him to school in Rome and watched over him. According to Horace, his father just wanted him to be successful in the same frame as he himself was. But his father's care paid off more than that. Horace's talents landed him a place in the circle of Maecenas, patron of the arts at Rome. Horatius, therefore, is a clear example of an ambitious freedman father. There is no hint that he was ashamed of his freedman status, or of his profession – although he wanted his son to rise in society through a good education and connections. Horace stresses the general (he assumes) tendency to disparage someone whose father was a freedman. But it was only his attempting to rise that laid odium on the son at the hands of the elites he now cavorted with. And that son did not disown the father, but respected all that his freedman father did for him, raising him in a strongly moral fashion and helping him to better himself. Had Horace remained a merchant or an auction-eer, or a tax collector, Horace's father would not have complained, he says. So in Horace's father we have a freedman proud of who he was, eager for the betterment of his son, content in his place.

It is important to keep freedmen like Horace's father in mind when scholars speak of freedmen belonging to a 'marginal subcommunity'; or aver that 'he had been a slave and neither he nor others could forget it.' As I have shown, there is scant evidence for this, except as wealthy freedmen relate to elites. Indeed, the mere fact that there was no prohibi-tion on intermarriage between freeborn and freedmen should be clear evidence that ordinary people didn't care; the complementary restric-tion on the marriage of freedmen and members of the highest elite, the senatorial class, emphasizes that any 'disgrace' was in the eyes of that aristocracy alone. I can also point to the fact that freedmen were exempt from property taxes, just as freeborn citizens were; had they been sec-ond-class citizens surely this would not be the case. Nor was a freedman identifiable on the street. Upon manumission traditionally a freedman's cap was worn, and there are illustrations of this. But this cap was a ceremonial one and not an everyday head covering. Freedmen looked and dressed just like everyone else on the street. A freedman lived as freeborn Romans did, and restrictions on his social standing were deter-mined by economic circumstances, individual ability, and ambition, not by social restrictions.

There were legal disabilities, but these were not of much account. As I have noted, freedmen could not hold office in Rome or in munici-palities, but how many would want to? They were barred from some Roman priesthoods, but how many aspired to them? They could not join the legions, although they were eligible for other military and quasi-military units. But as most male slaves were freed around age thirty, not many would have wanted to set out from there on a military career. In sum, these legal disabilities would not have touched the lives of ordinary freedmen in any significant way.

As most freedmen came to their freedom through their accomplishments under their master but, as the culture demanded, the master expected deference and material benefit from the freed slave, there were bound to be different feelings toward a master depending on the personality of the freedman, and that of the master. Some freedmen would respect and appreciate their patrons, as Hermeros says to Encolpius in Petronius:

> I made every effort to please my master, a really high-class and dignified person whose little finger was worth more than your whole body and soul. (*Satyricon* 57)

Grave epigraphy has abundant evidence of this sort of honor given to a patron by a freedman; while it is possible to discount a few such occurrences as post-mortem sycophancy, or as required by a codicil of testamentary liberation, the frequency of positive remembrances must reflect good relations in many situations. For example:

> Lucius Servilius Eugenes and Lucius Servilius Abascantus and Servilia Lais, the freedwoman of Lucius, set this up of their own free will to the best of patrons. (*CIL* 5.7955, Cimiez, France)

> To the Spirits of Tiberius Claudius Onesimus, who lived 65 years, 6 months, and 5 days. Aurelia Dioclia his wife and Tiberius Claudius Meligerus his freedman set this up to the best of patrons. (*CIL* 6.15172, Rome)

> To the Spirits of Quintus Fabius Theogonus, a paint dealer doing business in the Esquiline area near the statue of Plancus. Fabia Nobilis set this up to the very best and most thoughtful patron, well deserving of her greatest loyalty, and to herself. (*CIL* 6.9673, Rome)

Such good relations could be powerfully important to a freedman as he could derive not only material benefit from a favoring patron, but also prestige from association with him, should he be a pillar of the community.

Others might harbor resentments real or imagined against their ex-master and try, as I noted above, to avoid the formal and informal obligations owed, even to the extent of being hauled into court by a patron demanding that *operae* due be performed. Naturally these would not leave an epigraphic record and so remain anonymous. But there is evidence of a patron's anger at an ungrateful freedman:

> Marcus Aemilius Artema made this monument for Marcus Licinius Sucessus his well-deserving brother, and for Caecilia Modesta his wife and for himself and for his freedmen and freedwomen and their offspring EXCEPT the freedman Hermes who I forbid to have any entrance, approach or access to this monument because of his wrongs against me. (*CIL* 6.11027, Rome)

Legal sources list some of these 'wrongs' that freedmen did to their patrons: failure to carry out duties to a former master; insolent behavior; physical attack; spreading malicious rumors; inciting someone to bring legal action against them; or publicly accusing them at law.

Circumstances varied depending on whether the freedman remained in the patron's household or set up in his own home and establishment. In the household, the freed slave would receive food and lodging, but would lack the freedom of action inherent in living on his own. On the other hand, being put out of the household upon gaining freedom could turn out to be much less happy than imagined. Epictetus, a freedman himself, holds up with not a little philosophical piquancy the possibility that a freed slave would find himself out in a world much less kindly than the one he left as a slave; I have quoted the passage in full in Chapter 4 (*Discourses* 4.1.34–7).

It is curious, and perhaps just a result of literary intent, that in almost all instances the freedmen in the 'Trimalchio's Dinner' episode of the *Satyricon* cannot be shown to be either independent of or dependent on their patrons. The patrons are, in fact, invisible. Perhaps this is just so that the freedmen can be put on display, rather than because their patrons really did not figure in their daily lives. But at any rate, there would be freedmen who had no patron and so no patron to be involved.

These would operate without the support but also without the interference of an ex-master.

Freedmen formed close relationships with other freedmen. For example:

> To Aulus Memmius Clarus. Aulus Memmius Urbanus set this up to his fellow freedman and partner most dear to himself. Between me and you, O best of the best, my fellow freedman, I know in my heart there never was a hint of disagreement. And with this gravestone I bring the gods of heaven and hell to witness that you and I bought together at auction were freed together from the household, nor did anything ever come between us except your fatal day. (*CIL* 6.22355a = *ILS* 8432, Rome)

Naturally rivalries between freedmen existed at the same time as friendships. The gravestones of freedmen testify to the competition for recognition among themselves. Their very frequency coupled with an emphasis on accomplishments dear to freedmen's hearts – success in family and business – bear witness to this. Such rivalries were normal within the context of the honor-driven culture. It seems, though, that normally freedmen associated with each other despite the competition. Freedmen at times formed their own associations, but this does not appear to have been a common phenomenon; few such groups are attested to in epigraphy. As might be expected from the fact that ordinary freedmen were not stigmatized or disabled in significant ways, they associated not only with their fellow freedmen but with freeborn as well. Thus much more commonly than 'freedman' associations, we find associations of mixed condition, very commonly free and freed, and often enough including slaves as well. Sometimes free, sometimes freed are leaders; there seems to be no pattern indicating that freedmen were discriminated against in any way; there is no 'freedman milieu.' Freedmen also mixed with slaves not only in the associations but also in other things, as can be seen in this dedication of an altar to the *Lares Augusti*:

> When Gaius Caesar, son of Augustus, and Lucius Paullus were consuls, these cult officers set up an altar to the Augustan Lares: Quintus Numisius Legio, freedman of Quintus; Lucius Safinius,

1. A street in Pompeii. Where ordinary people lived and worked. Imagine the sidewalks and street filled with the hustle and bustle that was the lifeblood of a town.

2. The town's busy market. A cutlery merchant has his wares spread out on a temporary table in the forum of Pompeii. The intense activity all around would be typical of a market day.

3. Merchants selling cutlery. The needs of everyday life were bought in stalls along the street or in the mercantile center (forum) of a town.

4. Vibrant religion. Ordinary men carry a bier in a religious procession at Pompeii. The protecting divinity stands in front, with the men's carpentry profession modeled behind.

5. Consulting a corner sorceress. Many professional and amateur magicians and soothsayers were ready to meet the demand for using the supernatural to understand and control the world.

6. Religious procession. The whole population turns out to honor the Great Mother goddess Cybele at Pompeii – elites, priests, and ordinary people.

7. Slaves and ordinary free men gather animals from the hunt to ship to the city for popular arena games.

8. Prostitutes advertise their wares. Scene from the dressing room of a Pompeian bath-and-brothel show risqué acts as a perhaps playful reminder to those disrobing or robing that sexual services are available. The boxes portray clothes hampers for bathers.

9. Entertainment. Gambling was popular with ordinary men, whether with dice or other games of skill and chance. Here two men play at a table, probably in a tavern.

10. An everyday woman. The lack of jewelry and plain garment indicate that this is an ordinary woman, pensively looking out at us.

11. Another ordinary woman.

12. Nursing mother. Although wetnurses were available, many ordinary women nursed their children.

13. Midwife delivers a baby. The birthing chair was standard, as was the use of a midwife while in labor.

14. Letter in a woman's own hand. Thermouthas writes to her mother telling her about her pregnancy, sending news, and asking about her father's health.

15. Their daily bread. Workmen construct a wall.

16. A peasant at work. The farmer takes his local produce to market.

17. Poor fishermen with their rods.

18. A beggar with his dog at his side seeks alms from a wealthy woman.

19. Punishment of a slave. A man strikes a slave with his fist, probably enacting a scene from drama, but certainly reflecting real life.

20. A slave is beaten. Striking a slave with a rod was a common form of punishment and control.

21. Slaves serving in an urban household. In preparation for a Dionysian festival feast, a slave carries bread in a flat basket.

22. Slave collars meant to assure the return of a runaway. FVGI. TENE ME. CVM REVOCAVERIS M(EO) D(OMINO) ZONINO ACCIPIS SOLIDVM. I ran away. Hold me; when you bring me back to my master Zoninus, you get a gold coin.

23. A procuress. Go-betweens, both male and female, facilitated the trade of prostitutes by supplying (mostly) women to customers, and managing those women if they were part of a brothel.

24. A brothel cubicle. The small room indicates it was intended only for the business at hand. The concrete bed presumably had a mattress and coverings of some sort. There may have been a stool or other wooden furniture as well.

25. Courtesans. High-class prostitutes of the elite were participants in elaborate entertainments in the homes of the wealthy. Here they wear typical dress, a tunic which slips easily off the shoulders, and a pallia, or cloak, of fine cloth which, too, falls away easily.

26. The Colosseum (Flavian Amphitheater) in Rome was the most famous venue for arena entertainments and executions. It was completed in AD 80 and seated around 50,000 people.

27. Provincial amphitheaters. There were over two hundred amphitheaters scattered throughout the empire. Some were small, some were temporary wooden structures, but many were large and elaborate, as this one at Pompeii shown in a fresco which also narrates the riots between citizens of Pompeii and Nuceria in AD 59.

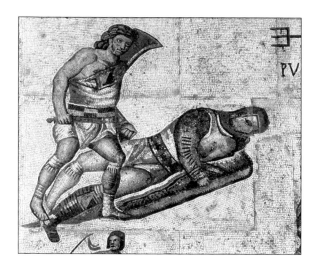

28. Gladiatorial contest. The *retiarius*, a fighter with a net and short sword, has cast away the net to deal the final blow to his adversary, a *secutor*, or 'pursuer'. *Retiarius* vs *secutor* was a specialty paring in the arena.

29. A beast hunt. A local magnate named Magerius celebrated his beast-hunt games with a grand mosaic. In the center is a slave holding a tray of prize money, rewards for the willing *bestiarii* (wild beast fighters).

30. Gladiators duel in these two mosaics now in Madrid. A *secutor* gets the best of a *retiarius* while the judges observe to insure the rules are followed.

freedman of Lucius; Hilarus and Sodalis, slaves of Gaius Modius Cimber; Aeschinus, slave of Octavius Marcus. (*CIL* 10.1582 = *ILS* 3611, Pozzuoli, Italy)

It is worth noting that these slaves and freedmen were not from the same owner and so had formed relationships outside their respective households.

The two most significant social accomplishments of freedmen were freedom itself and family. Although fictional, and buried in a narrative of an outrageously excessive freedmen's dinner, Petronius' Hermeros offers a defense of the dignity and pride in winning his freedom in his speech to Encolpius:

We only seem ridiculous to *you*. Behold your school master, an older man: We are pleasing to *him*. You are a child fresh off your mother's breast, hardly able to utter 'mu' or 'ma,' a clay vessel, a soaking leather strap, softer, not better. You think you are better off? Then eat two breakfasts, dine twice a day. I prefer my good name to gold. *And* I might add, who has ever had to ask anything of me more than once? I was in bondage for forty years. Through it all, no one knew whether I was slave or free. I was a boy with long hair when I came to this town – they hadn't even built the town hall yet. But I really worked to keep my master satisfied – a much-respected man and full of dignity, whose little finger was worth more than our whole being. There were, of course, those in the house who now and again tried to trip me up. Nevertheless – thanks be to the master! – I won through. *These* are the real accomplishments, for being born free makes life as easy as snapping your finger. (*Satyricon* 57)

Probably the first deed on the part of a newly freed slave was to try to free in turn the woman he had been living with in slavery and any children they might have had; as Hermeros states, 'I bought out of slavery my slave wife, so that no one could wipe his hands on her bosom.' Of course, not all freedmen would have had such a relationship in slavery, but if it did exist, freeing wife and offspring must have been of paramount importance. Otherwise, a freedman might marry after gaining his or her freedom. There were some disabilities for the wealthiest freedmen, especially relating to the prohibition against marrying into the senatorial class, but ordinary freedmen had the right to marry whom they pleased; if they had children, these possessed the same testamentary rights as freeborn. And there could still be some children for a freedman's family even if, as is likely, freedom came for a man about age thirty and for a woman even somewhat later in life. In either case – children freed from slavery or children had later in life – a freedman's family was far less taken for granted than a freeborn person's might have been. The clearest evidence of families' importance comes from freedmen's gravestone inscriptions and, especially, relief sculptures. On these reliefs are found not the mythological themes and heroized portraiture familiar from grave reliefs of the elite. Rather we have ordinary people staring out from the grave, proudly dressed in the citizen garb of the toga and stola and often with a child between or beside the parents.

Dear bonds between freedman husband and wife are illustrated by the famous gravestone of Aurelius Hermia and his wife, Aurelia Philematio, quoted also in Chapter 4:

> I am Lucius Aurelius Hermia, freedman of Lucius, a butcher working on the Viminal Hill. This woman, Aurelia Philematio, freedwoman of Lucius, who went before me in death, my one and only wife, chaste of body, faithfully loving a faithful husband, lived equal in devotion with no selfishness taking her from her duty. [*Image of Philematio looking lovingly at Hermia.*] This is Aurelia Philematio, freedwoman of Lucius. I alive was called Aurelia Philematio, chaste, modest, ignorant of the foul ways of the crowd, faithful to my husband. He was my fellow freedman, the same now torn from me – alas! He was in truth and indeed like and more than a father to me. He took me on his lap a mere seven years old – now after forty years I am dead. He flourished in all his doings among men on account of my faithful and firm devotion. (*CIL* 6.9499 = *ILS* 7472, Rome)

Many other inscriptions, while brief, express a respect for a lost spouse:

> For the Spirits of Gaius Octavius Trypho, freedman of Marcella.

Aelia Musa set up this monument to her well-deserving husband. (*CIL* 6.23324, Rome)

Another shows the respect a son had for the wish of his parents to be united in death as in life:

Marcus Volcius Euhemerus, freedman of Marcus, requests that after his death his remains along with those of Volcia Chreste, his wife, be placed in a single burial urn. Marcus Volcius Cerdo, Marcus' son, did as his father asked. (*CIL* 6.29460 = *ILS* 8466, Rome)

These expressions of love and memory mirror similar declarations of fidelity, loyalty, and so forth commonly found on free persons' grave markers.

In the *Satyricon* we have an example of a proud father ambitious for his children, much as Horace's father was for him. Echion, a rag dealer, has two sons. One is of an intellectual bent and he is engaged in preliminary studies of Greek and literature. The other has completed his preliminary studies and now masters a bit of law and is being trained to take over Echion's business, or to embark on another one such as law, or barbering, or auctioneering. An inscription gives another case of parental devotion. This time, a mother grieves for her daughter:

Posilla Senenia, daughter of Quartus, lies here. Quarta Senenia, freedwoman of Gaius, also. Passerby, stop, read what is written. A mother was not permitted to enjoy her only daughter. Some god – I do not know which one – envied her and made it not to be. Since it was not possible that she while living be dressed by her mother, after death her mother did this properly when her time on earth was up. She has clothed her finely with this tomb, she whom she loved all through her life. (*CIL* 9.4933, Monteleone Sabino, Italy)

Parents grieve for their children. Here a parent bemoans the fact that the child will never enjoy the parent's hard-won freedom:

Sacred to the Spirits. I do not say his name, nor how many years he lived, lest the grief be alive in our hearts when we read this. You were a sweet little baby but death shortly took your life. You never enjoyed freedom. Alas, alas! Is it not grievous that he whom you love perish? Now death everlasting gave the only freedom he will know. (*CIL* 8.25006, Carthage)

How many children freedmen had is impossible to say. I might speculate that many children born in slavery were not redeemed, that the freed slaves were too old to have large families. But it is simply impossible to know. Nor can it be known what happened in the next generation, for the marker of freed status, the 'patronymic' giving the name of the patron in place of the biological father, disappears, of course, in the nomenclature of the offspring of a freedman. This inscription illustrates how a couple, Atticus and Salviola, identify themselves as having emerged from slavery with the notation 'freedperson of Eros,' while they give their son, a child of now-free parents, the traditional filiation of a freeborn person, 'son of Atticus':

Gaius Julius Atticus, freedman of Eros, while living set up this monument. Julia Salviola, freedwoman of Eros, deceased, and Gaius Julius Victor, son of Atticus, dead at age 18, lie buried here. (*CIL* 13.275, St-Bertrand-de-Comminges, France)

As I have noted before, freedmen found their identity not only in their freedom and families, but in their work. Although there would naturally have been stratification within the category of freedman according to the success of work – the difference between a shopkeeper and a grand international trader – the focus on work and on fellows who made a living working is remarkable; perhaps half of all inscriptions of freedmen mention a craft or profession, a much higher percentage than on the epitaphs of freeborn and remarkably different from the focus of the elite on a life of leisure, avoiding notice of actual work as much as possible and competing for public office and recognition. At the very top of freedmen were the *Augustales*, in origin priests of the imperial cult, but whose office opened the way to active participation in a range of local duties and so to some extent substituted for the municipal offices freedmen were ineligible for. As the equivalent of the local freeborn elite, sharing their ambitions, these men are of no concern

15. A freedman family. The couple holds hands in the symbol of legitimate marriage; their two children are in the background.

here. I mention them only to indicate that for a small subset of freedmen there was the local recognition that the elite in general craved as part of their *raison d'être*. Almost all freedmen, like almost all freeborn, cared not at all for office-holding and public life beyond neighborhood offices in professional and social clubs and associations, and found their satisfaction in their work, families, and friends.

A freedman coming out of slavery most often had a trade or occupation that he had learned or trained in as part of his slave experience. A good example of the process is the slave baker and cook in Apuleius' *Golden Ass* (10.13–16). These brothers had been set up by a wealthy master in an establishment away from the slave household and operated independently. Although we do not know the end of their story, it is likely that they were eventually freed and went on to run food services as freedmen. Such was the normal pattern that found so many freedmen in business of one sort or another. The variety of this work was extensive. Trade and industry were primary foci since these businesses would be logical ones for masters to put their slaves to work at. Echion's aspirations for his sons list occupations as barber, auctioneer, lawyer; Horace's father listed merchant, auctioneer, or trader. The friends of Trimalchio at the dinner have the following occupations: porter, undertaker, petty trader, clothes dealer, huckster (or porter, again), pleader, innkeeper, state performer, stonemason/monument maker, perfume dealer, barber, auctioneer, muleteer, itinerant hawker or performer, cobbler, cook, and baker. Other sources note freedmen who were gladiators, actors, lawyers, doctors, artists, and architects. So they were active in a wide range of occupations. I would suppose that the higher mortality rate of towns and cities, where most freedmen lived, combined with smaller families to start with, probably meant that the constant replenishment of freedmen through manumission did not produce more merchants, artisans, and small-time professionals than the economy could bear.

In their social and economic world beneath that of the elite, freedmen had a rich religious life. Traditionally discussion of this focuses on the *Seviri Augustales*, the six-man board charged with the worship of the emperor mentioned briefly above. But all the others turned their attention to mundane religious activities in their daily lives too. Many, both men and women, were involved in religious associations in common with slaves and free men, especially in households as in this example:

> Dedicated to Scribonia Helice, freedwoman, by the worshipers of the Household Gods and Fortune of Lucius Caedius Cordus. (*AE* 1992.334, Castelvecchio Subequo, Italy)

While the early Christian communities composed of a cross-section of ordinary people have been seen as, if not unique, at least extraordinary in the Romano-Grecian world, in fact that world was heavily populated with similar associations meeting social needs in various contexts – household, vocational, ethnic, locational, and, especially, religious. Freedmen were full participants. Freedmen even figured in the priesthoods of traditional Roman deities. Contrary to the usual assumption that only one, the Bona Dea, was open to freedmen, epigraphy shows activity and even leadership involving much other cultic activity. Indeed, priests of the Bona Dea do appear:

Maenalus, attendant official, dedicates this to Philematio, freedman of the emperor, priest of the Bona Dea (*CIL* 6.2240, Rome)

Gaius Avillius December, contractor of marble, rightly fulfilled his vow to the Bona Dea along with his wife Vellia Cinnamis. Erected when Claudius Philadespotus, imperial freedman, was priest and Quintus Iunius Marullus was consul, the sixth day before the Kalends of November. (*CIL* 10.1549, Pozzuoli, Italy)

But priests of other divinities do as well. For example, from Chieti comes a dedication of a freedman priest of Venus:

Gaius Decius Bitus, the freedman of Gaius, priest of Venus, dedicated this to Peticia Polumnia, freedwoman. (*AE* 1980.374)

While elsewhere we find freedmen related to the cult of the Vestal Virgins:

Decimus Licinius Astragalus, freedman of Decimus, priest of the Vestal Virgins [dedicated this]. (*CIL* 6.2150, Rome)

And to Ceres:

Publius Valerius Alexa, freedman of Publius, lived piously 70 years, a priest of Ceres; he lies here. (*ILTun* 1063, Carthage)

Helvia Quarta, freedwoman, priestess of Ceres and Venus while alive set up this monument for herself. (*CIL* 9.3089, Sulmona, Italy)

Thus freedmen were active in many cults. Of the approximately 250 Latin inscriptions indicating vows to gods I examined, over half, leaving aside clearly local divinities, are to gods of Roman religion: Jupiter in his many guises, Hercules, Mercury, Silvanus, Juno, Diana, Apollo, and Fortuna. Isis is the only 'foreign' religion represented, although other evidence makes it clear that another 'foreign' cult, that of the Phrygian Great Mother (*Magna Mater*), was also much used by freedmen, some of whom are attested as priests. This spread of traditional and newer gods is typical of the record of devotion for the population in general. Once again, freedmen do not stand out from their free counterparts in the religious aspect of their social and cultural lives.

Nor do they in death. There is a cemetery filled with the graves of ordinary Romans at Isola Sacra between Rome and Ostia. In this cemetery the graves of freedmen and freeborn Romans are indistinguishable and are intermixed. There is neither 'freedman art' nor 'freedman habit' nor a 'freedman section' which would separate freedman's tombs from others. As in other aspects of religion, honoring the dead was done in conformity with general standards and habits of the population. Freedmen single themselves out on grave monuments in being especially proud of their families and their freedom, but otherwise they acted just like those they had associated with while living.

Conclusion

A freedman lived with the constant incubus of a previous servile existence hovering over him. Or so we are told: The general view is that they lived under a stigmatic cloud because of their formerly servile status, and that this stigma stayed with them for life, no matter how successful. To the elite, fixated on a 'free' life as the only one worth living – i.e. a life ideally, if not really, free from subjection to another – the mere fact of servile origin seemed an ineradicable mark of Cain, one that doomed the bearer to a life of angst and insecurity, if not self-loathing. But the evidence does not indicate that this was, in fact, the case at all. Freedmen seemingly without blush and often with evident pride declare themselves 'ex-slaves' on their tombstones. While the elite might emphasize the servile origins, the freedman rather would find pride in his success as a good slave that had earned him his freedom. He had, in fact, in most cases been promoted (i.e. freed) because he was good at what his master wanted done. His previous servile condition was no fault of his, and his progression out of it a sure sign of his qualities as a human being, for he had made the most of the situation. His servile life had been his home; he normally retained good feelings for his former slave community after 'promotion' and once free moved easily between the two worlds, a liminal figure but not a conflicted one. Likewise, as presumably his freedom owed some if not all to a good relationship with his owner, he could also navigate in the world of the masters, knowing when to be obsequious, when to offer advice, when to hold back, and when/how to push, whether in relations with elites or subelites, or merely with powerful freeborn foremen or other freedmen. Selected for a variety of survival and success skills, the typical freedman was multifaceted, socially savvy, and economically prepared. He was a dynamic player in the world of ordinary Romans.

A LIVING AT ARMS:
SOLDIERS

LEGIONS MASSED TO CRUSH THE SLAVE REVOLT of Spartacus; a fiery charge against shrieking barbarians: images of the Roman soldier are inextricably linked to the visuals of novels, film, and television. But aside from the brief moments of battle discipline, carnage, bravery, and death, what was it like to live the life of a Roman legionary? The sources, however broadly tapped, do not allow the story of the common soldier to be told at any single time during the first three centuries AD. However, it is possible to construct a composite picture based on material from this entire period. Massed legions, screaming barbarian hordes, bravery in battle all existed, but I will lay out the rest of the legionary's existence in all its limitations, promise, banality, and excitement.

The legionary soldier, like other invisibles, is virtually never noted individually by the main classical sources. He appears in a mass – 'the army' or 'a legion', or some other grouping; only in exceptional and frequently semi-fictionalized situations does a soldier appear as an individual in elite writers. For these authors, the army below the command level is except in very rare situations an undifferentiated mass playing a role in the elite drama that they called history. When the elite deigned to think about common soldiers, they liked to spotlight heroic efforts, but in the end saw mostly a dangerous body, ignorant, low born, and motivated by base instincts. Looked at from the social, economic, and cultural level of the common soldier, however, his life, although it could

16. The army at war. Here two soldiers advance, one with the short sword (*gladius*) at ready, the other with his spear (*pilum*).

be hard and even at times deadly, was in many ways privileged with a stability and benefits that few other ordinary men could hope to find. This becomes clear as I look at the soldier on his own terms.

Recruitment

The actual number of new recruits each year was fairly small. Thinking about the legions scattered over the empire, it is easy to forget that the term of service was long, and loss by war minimal; around 7500–10,000 or so new soldiers each year would have sufficed to keep the legions up to strength. All had to be freeborn Roman citizens; freedmen were recruited to only a few specific units, and slaves were completely ineligible during the empire – indeed, as Artemidorus states, for a slave to dream that he is a soldier means that he will be freed, because only free men could be in the legions (*Dreams* 1.5). But the number of necessary recruits is not large assuming a citizen general population of around

9 million. Legions were not kept at their full 'paper' strength of 6000 men, but this was for financial reasons, not because there is any evidence that it was difficult finding the necessary number of recruits. The evidence for forcible recruitment, conscription, during the empire is scattered and slight. As the *Digest* 16.4.10 notes, 'Mostly the number of soldiers is supplied by volunteers.'

Almost all were between seventeen and twenty-four years of age; twenty was probably the usual age at enlistment. Elite sources liked to imagine that they all were down-and-outers. As Queen Elizabeth referred to her impressed soldiers as 'thieves who ought to hang,' so Tacitus talks about the needy and homeless that represent the dregs of society entering the army (*Annals* 4.4). To the elite, the rough world of the ordinary and the poor could only be painted in disdainful strokes. In fact, most if not all these were young men who had grown up with their families, had learned a trade, even if this was only farming, and had now determined to set out on a new life. As the normal cultural habit was for women to marry young, in their teens, and men to marry old, in their late twenties, few recruits had started a family of their own. *Simplicitas* (simple-mindedness) and *imperitia* (ignorance) were desired qualities. Clearly, idiots were not sought out – but a person with few ideas of his own could better be molded in the appropriate ways. There were exceptions, of course. Even at the level of the common soldier, some literacy might be desired in a subgroup of recruits since these men would more easily rise to the positions of clerks in the legion (Vegetius 2.19).

Both ancients and moderns have chosen to emphasize the arduousness of service. But a picture of hard life is misleading if taken at face value by moderns. Once any thought of comparison between the living conditions of the Romano-Grecian world and the Western world since 1800 is put out of mind, it is clear that a soldier had a good life by ancient standards. Even if the peasant recruit went from his hard farm life to a hard soldier's life, he labored in much better, more promising conditions than he ever could have experienced had he stayed on the farm, because in major ways the soldier's life ameliorated the harshest aspects of that life.

In light of this, it is not surprising that recruits were not wanting. As one document from Egypt puts it, 'If Aion wants to be a soldier, he only need come, since everyone is becoming a soldier' (*BGU* 7.1680). Although some parents might object, most would agree with these Jewish parents who in a Talmudic story seem eager to have their son enlist:

> A man came to conscript someone's son. His father said: look at my son, what a fellow, what a hero, how tall he is. His mother too said: look at our son, how tall he is. The other answered: in your eyes he is a hero and he is tall. I do not know. Let us see whether he is tall. They measured and he proved to be small and was rejected. (*Aggadat Genesis* 40.4 / Isaac)

The general assumption is that parents wanting a son in the army were unusual. But there is no reason to suppose that these parents' attitude is weird or rare – indeed, the source misses the opportunity to inform us of this, if true. On the contrary. This random mention clearly shows that service was something that could be and was sought after by parents for their children. Both parent and child realized that prospects in civilian life were overall extremely bleak, and that the army was a bright possibility in the midst of that bleakness.

So many a young man was easily attracted by the possibility of military service. Of course, such a choice would not be for everyone. Leaving the family farm or business could have its disadvantages as the known was traded for the unknown, the stability and support of a family for a new life in a different environment. The family might object. In a letter from Egypt a wife scolds her husband for encouraging a son to become a soldier:

> Concerning Sarapas my son, he has not stayed with me at all, but went off to the camp to join the army. You did not do well counseling him to join the army. For when I said to him not to join, he said to me, 'My father said to me to join the army.' (*BGU* 4.1097 / Bagnall & Cribiore)

Not only was there the factor of emotional loss of a son; there was also the practical difficulty of the loss of manpower in the home in the short term, and the loss in the long term of support in old age by a grown son. There could be (although not necessarily would be, especially later in the empire) travel distant from home. There certainly would be separation from the physical support of family, and even from news of any immediacy, given the slowness of correspondence. Letters from Egypt show that soldiers posted to distant locales continued to maintain those family ties. Presumably separation from home and kin was often not easy at the beginning, or even throughout the years of service. Apion, an Egyptian enlisting and posted to the fleet at Misemum, in Italy, although not a legionary, expressed this situation well:

> Apion to Epimachus his father and lord, very many greetings. First of all I pray for your good health and that you may always be strong and fortunate, along with my sister, her daughter, and my brother ... Everything is going well for me. So, I ask you, my lord and father, to write me a letter, first about your welfare, secondly about that of my brother and sister, and thirdly so that I can do reverence to your handwriting, since you educated me well ... Give all my best wishes to Capiton and my brother and sister and Serenilla and my friends. I have sent you through Euctemon a portrait of myself ... (*BGU* 2.423 = Campbell, no. 10)

The psychological links of family probably kept many a young man from enlisting. But the rewards awaiting were potentially great, and many others left family for a new life. In a world of chronic underemployment, a dearth of food during late winter months, and the hazards of physical disaster which could seriously disrupt the rhythm of life, the army offered the only full-time, fully employed, regularly salaried opportunity. Artemidorus took this reality and used it in his dream interpretation:

> Taking up a career as a soldier portends business and employment for the unemployed and needy, for a soldier is neither unemployed, nor in want (*Dreams* 2.31)

This sailor's implicit experience that service raised him from poverty was certainly shared by soldiers:

Lucius Trebius, son of Titus, father [dedicated this monument]. I, Lucius Trebius Ruso, son of Lucius, was born into abject poverty. I then served as a marine at the side of the emperor for seventeen years. I was discharged honorably. (*CIL* 5.938 = *ILS* 2905, Augusta Bagiennorum, Italy)

Being a soldier was considered a profession both by the soldier himself and by the civilian world. When Paul wishes to give examples of people who work at a job and deserve to be paid for it, he includes soldiers.

Who serves as a soldier at his own expense? Who plants a vineyard and does not eat of its grapes? Who tends a flock and does not drink of the milk? (1 Corinthians 9:7)

A soldier appears in Horace, *Satires* 2.23–40, alongside a farmer, innkeeper, and sailor as an example of someone who works hard, looking forward to a retirement. And the possibilities for material gain were manifold. First of all there was the paid salary. A soldier made about a good daily wage for a laborer in the civilian world – but he made this every day of the year whereas the civilian laborer was often unemployed, underemployment being the norm for the ancient world as a whole at all times. Despite stoppages of various sorts and spending by soldiers, documents from Egypt indicate that as much as 25 percent of annual pay was saved. As a soldier continued in service he might well advance in grade, and with such advancement came higher salary – usually 1.5 times and sometimes twice the common soldier's pay; if one was promoted to be a centurion – admittedly a rare event – pay was perhaps fifteen times the raw recruit's. In addition, under the emperor Septimius Severus, all soldiers' pay doubled. If soldiers were transferred, they received a travel allowance (*viaticum*); if they were led on a long march, they got 'boot nail money' (*clavarium*), the residue of which would also be put into the savings bank. Then there were the periodic liberalities from the reigning emperor. These donatives were paid directly to the soldiers on a pro rata basis determined by the grade in the army. In addition, upon the death of an emperor, soldiers could expect a bequest to reach them. Finally, at discharge the soldier was paid a bonus. At first this bonus was paid in land, but the combination of a lack of suitable land and complaints from soldiers about being, in essence, cheated through distribution of poor and distant land led to the substitution of a monetary bonus. This deposited money and bonus were not under the control of the soldier's father according to a rule going all the way back to Augustus. In fact, the jurists were very clear that being a soldier meant that the most important aspect of a father's power over his son was severely attenuated: whatever money a soldier acquired through being a soldier was not subject to control by his father. Not only could a father not have access to it, it could also be bequeathed independently of a father's wishes. This provided a soldier with an economic freedom unheard of in the civilian population.

Besides monetary gain, the soldier looked forward to special privileges at law. In his private life, the soldier could, as I noted, make a will independent of his father's wishes. In interpersonal relations, the essence of those privileges was that the soldier was always favored both by the circumstances of trial and legal procedures. Military courts had sole jurisdiction over soldiers; this included soldier-on-soldier crime and any acts a soldier might commit as a soldier. If a civilian made an accusation against a soldier, it was tried in the camp by a military tribunal made up of centurions. In addition, any civilian wishing to charge a soldier had to follow him; a soldier could not be charged *in absentia*. Neither could he be called to a distant venue to act as a witness. And if a soldier were away on army business, he could not be sued. If a soldier made an accusation against a civilian, it was tried in a civil court. But a soldier's suit had precedence and had to be heard on a date set by the soldier. If a soldier were unfortunate enough to be convicted of a serious crime, he was exempt from torture, or condemnation to the mines, or hard labor; if of a capital crime, he could not be executed as a common criminal – no hanging, crucifixion, or being thrown to the wild beasts.

Considering all of this, it is not surprising that some thought of the army as a way to evade legal problems in their civilian life; after all, it would be easier to pursue a suit or fight one if enjoying military privileges. A third-century jurist addresses this sort of scam:

 Not everyone who joins the army because he has a lawsuit pending should then be cashiered, but rather only those who join up having the court case specifically in mind, doing so to make himself more formidable to his adversary through military privileges. A person who enlists while engaged in litigation should be carefully scrutinized: If he gives up the litigation, leniency is in order, however. (Arrius Menander, *On Military Matters* 1 = *Digest* 49.16.4.8)

Such shenanigans were only to be expected; faking the privileged position of soldiers was a tempting route to success at law.

There were also disabilities at law that a soldier suffered, for example he could not accept gifts of items that were in litigation; he could not act as an agent for third parties; and he could not purchase land in the province where he was serving (a prohibition evidently evaded with regularity). But these were minor indeed compared to the advantages. It is easy to see why recruits were not hard to find.

Enrollment and training

Upon presentation to the recruitment officers, a recruit's vital record was taken. This was simply his first name, family name, father's first name, surname (*cognomen*) if he had one, voting district, place of birth or origin, and the date of enlistment. It is notable that age was not taken down. The date of enlistment was crucial, however, for from that date was figured the years of service required before discharge. That date must have been a part of the permanent record that followed the soldier, for dead servicemen much more regularly give the number of their *stipendia* – years of service – on their tombstones than they do their age.

Finding a mind uncontaminated by fancy ideas (*simplicitas*) as well as steeped in ignorance (*imperitia*) was relatively easy. Finding recruits with a useful skill was another matter. Smiths, carpenters, butchers, and huntsmen were, according to Vegetius 1.7, examples of the sort of expertise the army could use; men coming into service already trained were highly valued.

After a trial period during which the recruitment officers determined if the recruit had the proper physical and mental attitude to become a good soldier, the man was officially inducted. He was given the 'military mark' – an indelible brand or tattoo on the hand – and then posted to a legion, where basic training took place for the first four or five months. Initiated into the legion, the soldier began a new way of life.

If he came illiterate, and most would, he found that the life of the army was to an astonishing degree paper driven. All sorts of records were kept on a daily and annual basis and required literacy of a number of soldiers. Especially if one wanted to advance, the ability to read, write, and do sums was essential. Vegetius 2.19 notes that literate recruits were sought:

> The army seeks in all its recruits tall, robust, quick-spirited men. But since there are many administrative units in the legions that need literate soldiers, those who can write, count, and calculate are preferred. For the entire record-keeping of the legion, whether of obligations or military fatigues or finances, is noted down in the daily records with even greater care than the taxes-in-kind accounts or the records of various sorts kept in the civilian world.

In Vindolanda, near Hadrian's Wall, writing tablets were found that because of their unusual preservation environment could still be read. These tablets showed literacy among not only unit leaders such as centurions and decurions, but also rankers. One scholar even claims these show greater general literacy than in the civilian population. Even if a soldier came illiterate, he might learn on the job. For those, a rough 'military' literacy was probably all they ever possessed; the literate, literary, cultured world of the officer class remained inaccessible to them.

On a daily basis there was enough food to eat. There were no non-military persons except, perhaps, for families of officers and of a few soldiers (see below). The prevalence of small-time thieves and hooligans that cursed civilian towns was totally absent; what little crime there was would be soldier-on-soldier. But it is perhaps in sanitary conditions, medical care, exercise, and general concern for good health that the soldier's life benefited the most. In the army, every large encampment had a bath complex that provided a place for less-structured exercise as well as some cleanliness. Engineered latrines with flushing water flowing through got rid of the human waste, care being taken to discharge this into a river or lake away from where water was taken for the legion. Vegetius writes:

> Now I will give advice about something which must at all cost be

looked to: how the health of the army can be protected ... The army should not use bad or swampy water, for drinking bad water is like taking poison and makes those drinking it ill. And indeed when a common soldier falls ill, all officers, from the lowest to the commander of the legion, should do his utmost to see that he is made well with proper diet and medical attention. For it will go badly for soldiers who must deal with both the demands of war and of disease. But it should be noted that military experts agree: daily exercise at arms leads more to the health of the soldiers than anything the doctors can do. (*On Military Affairs* 3.2)

While the goals of Vegetius might not always have been met, the soldier was better fed, and lived in a decidedly cleaner, better-aired environment that was better equipped with sanitary facilities, than the population at large.

Life in the camp

Most of army life is a routine of sleeping, eating, fatigues (i.e. daily, menial chores around the camp), and drilling. It was crucial that the legion operate efficiently as a unit and obey commands unquestioningly. This was achieved by constant exercises. For recruits, twice-daily drills were the order; for experienced soldiers, once daily. Here the soldiers learned to move as a body through practicing marching and maneuvers; they learned how to use their weapons, the shield, the sword, and the spear; they built up endurance so they could march long distances daily with heavy packs. They also apparently took care of their own sanitation and other needs, having latrine details and such like.

Barracks provided living space for each soldier. Soldiers lived together in their units: each barrack had a larger room with its own antechamber for the centurion, and eight to ten rooms for a *contubernium* of eight men. Each *contubernium* room was divided into an anteroom and sleeping chamber. It is certain that a centurion could have his mate (and, presumably, children) living in the camp with him; although there is evidence that some soldiers did as well in a few camps, the norm was to have only the men in the camp itself; 'wives' lived outside with the family, visited regularly by the soldier who had to live in the camp itself.

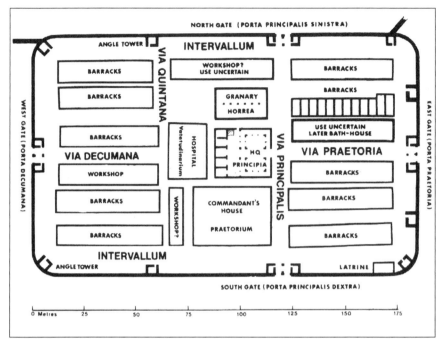

17. A Roman fort. This plan of the Housesteads fort on Hadrian's Wall in northern England is arranged in a typical fashion. The soldiers' barracks are on the left and right sides, the commander's place in the lower center.

This living situation might seem cramped, but it was probably no less private that most civilian living conditions for ordinary folk. The sense of comradeship inherent in this dormitory life was enhanced by the fact that the unit prepared its own food and ate together – there was no mess hall and central kitchen, except, perhaps, for the ovens to bake bread.

Medical treatment for the Roman population as a whole was a rather hit-and-miss affair. The first recourse for any ailment was home cures, whether at the hands of family members or local 'experts' in the community. Doctors were professionals who had to be paid; although the elite used them extensively, access to them was limited for large portions of the population. In the army, though, loss of manpower through disease or injury was taken very seriously. As in armies down to modern times, more losses were incurred through physical disabilities than through warfare itself. Doctors needed to be at hand to treat wounds but also,

18. Life in a fort. This is what a common soldier's barracks looked like.

more regularly, diseases and injuries incurred in the line of duty outside of warfare itself. Although medical practice was a curious mixture of invasive actions (surgery, etc.), harmful procedures, home cures (diet, exercise, adequate sleep, etc.), drugs, and prayers, it constituted the best the Roman world had to offer. A well-trained doctor had at least a better chance of diagnosing properly an affliction and so increasing the chances of offering effective cure. I would suppose, although no proof is possible, that more men survived through being treated by doctors than would have if left to their own devices.

As the passage from Vegetius above shows, the first defense against disease was good diet, exercise, hygiene and sanitation. Army fare was simple, but as healthy as was available. The diet of soldiers was more varied and nutritious than the usual: there were plenty of calories from the 880 grams a day of unground wheat; 620 grams of vegetables and pulses, fruits, cheese, and fish supplemented this. Cereals were healthy and could be stored easily for long periods of time. The favored cereal was wheat, although barley could be used in a pinch – and as a punishment. It was ground and cooked in gruel or baked into loaves in camp, or into small biscuits on campaign. Although meat was never a central part of the Roman diet, the archaeology of camps shows that there was also quite a bit of it, probably above the average fare; especially at times when there were sacrifices made during festivals and feast days, meat was part of the diet. There is also evidence that domestic animals were

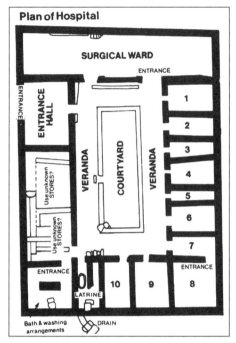

19. Hospital at the Housesteads fort. Good medical treatment for soldiers was an important part of their care, as disease and accident were much more deadly than the occasional skirmish or battle.

killed and eaten, fish and seafood caught, and hunted meat eaten. Vegetables and legumes were also added as available. Of course, wine was a staple and salt was added to food.

Like other ordinary Romans, legionary soldiers enjoyed getting together to socialize. The basic organizational unit, the century, formed a natural, cohesive group both at the most basic level, the eight-man barracks unit, and in the larger group represented by the century itself. In armies that moved about with some regularity, or lived in temporary quarters, the fluidity of the situation itself meant that larger social networks were slower to form. But the army became more and more sedentary from the later first century AD, the time of the Flavian emperors. The legions were increasingly posted to permanent camps. In this setting, associations of various sorts among the soldiers and officers sprang up. This is unsurprising since, as I have noted in describing the life of ordinary civilian Romans, people enjoyed joining together in associations with others who shared some common focus, whether that was religious, geographical, or business. The military authorities were ambivalent about these associations, just as civilian authorities were about organized groups in their towns. There was always the suspicion that antisocial, if not downright nefarious things, were going on in and through the meetings. Marcian, a legal expert of the early third century AD, noted that the common soldiers could not join in associations:

> At the order of the emperor it is decreed that the governors of the provinces not permit fraternal associations in general and, specifically, not permit common soldiers to form associations in the camp. (*Digest* 47.22.1 pr.)

Based on the authorities' customary suspicion of organized groups, I judge that this notice reflects a long-standing prohibition, not something recently initiated. Presumably this reiteration of the prohibition indicates that they were already widespread among common soldiers, despite the fact that this was formally banned. The easiest conclusion is that soldier associations gradually developed in the army as the army became more and more sedentary after the Flavians, that the commanding officers did not like this, but that they continued anyway, in spite of repeated attempts to curb them, as reflected in the notice found here in the *Digest*.

In a sense the army itself was the common soldier's 'association.' For these soldiers, the baths were their place of leisure and relaxation beyond the barracks. Every camp had baths, sometimes in the camp itself, more commonly just outside. Besides the hygienic benefits of bathing (probably compromised by unhealthy water), the social atmosphere replicated the importance of baths in the social life of the civilian world. Common soldiers could go here, chat with friends, and generally goof off; it was an important venue for relaxation and relief from the routine of the camp, and soldiers relished their time there.

The soldier had social insurance of two sorts. First of all, forced savings in cash were collected from their pay and from special donatives; this was then made available to them upon discharge or, in the case of death on duty, to a father or heir. In addition, soldiers were compelled to contribute an unknown amount to a personal burial fund administered by the legion (Vegetius 2.20).

Beyond the resources of the camp and the associations, soldiers also had access to the settlements that grew up near every legionary fortress and camp. These *canabae* served many important functions, but in a soldier's somewhat routine life one of the primary attractions was the watering holes and whorehouses (often conjoined). Here, too, a soldier technically prohibited from marriage would keep a woman as a 'wife' or just as a 'live-in' (*focaria*), as well as a family and perhaps even a slave or two, a topic treated in detail below. It is not clear how regular contact might have been maintained. Presumably at the fairly frequent festivals soldiers could leave the camp; but there was no day off on a regular basis and certainly no regular permission to live off base. However it was managed, it is clear from the extent of these *canabae* that frequented they were. They allowed an important dimension of the soldier's life, whether or not he had a 'family,' which mitigated what on paper looks like a very isolated life in a camp.

The routine could also be broken by being sent off with a detachment to do police duty in a town or rural area, or to purchase or otherwise acquire supplies for the camp, or for some special task such as escorting a dignitary through dangerous lands. Service on such duty would have been desirable as it provided variety and offered opportunities to interact with and exploit the civilian population.

Further aspects of a soldier's life

Once in the army the soldier had an opportunity to learn a skill, for the bane of all armies is leisure time and the Roman army was no different in trying to keep soldiers busy. Lucius Marius Vitalis joined the praetorians at age seventeen and although already literate, his intent was to learn a skill:

> I, Lucius Marius Vitalis, son of Lucius, lived seventeen years, fifty-five days. I did well in my studies and persuaded my parents that I should learn a profession. I had left Rome in the praetorian guard of Emperor Hadrian when, while I was working hard, the fates envied me, seized me, and removed me from my new calling to this place. Maria Marchis, my mother, set up this monument to her wonderful, luckless son. (*CIL* 6.8991 = *ILS* 7741, Rome)

Part of the appeal of the army was that by learning new skills the young soldier could hope for advancement to higher rank, responsibility, pay, and exemption from daily fatigues. There are many inscriptions that record careers, sometimes simple, sometimes extensive with many promotions and transfers from place to place around the empire. Some men were recruited who could step directly into higher grades and the centuriate; in other cases common soldiers advanced to these posts in the course of their careers. Sometimes, though, death forestalled that coveted promotion:

> … an adjutant of the century of Lucilius Ingenuus, expecting promotion to centurion, who died by shipwreck lies buried here. (*ILS* 2441, Chester, England)

Advancement was not on merit alone. The soldier had to arrange for two things: letters of recommendation and bribes. In fact, bribes were the order of the day, as a letter of Claudius Terentianus shows:

> I beg you, father, to write to me at once about your health, that you are well. I am anxious about things at home unless you write to me. God willing, I hope that I shall live frugally and be transferred to a cohort. However, nothing gets done here without money, and letters of recommendation are no use unless a man helps himself. (*P. Mich.* 8.468 = Campbell, no. 43)

Despite the hazards of life, bribes, and influence, promotions were an exceptionally important part of the appeal of the military life.

A soldier also advanced in status in the eyes of the civilian world in a way impossible for men who did not enlist. Artemidorus is witness for this, as he says a dream of being a soldier portends for the dreamer 'being thought well of' (*Dreams* 2.31). This was recognized in law as soldiers were freed from the increasingly onerous local duties loaded on civilians as the years of the empire progressed. But even more, the soldier gained great standing because he was the local representative of imperial power, and because he alone was professionally equipped with quality weapons and skilled in their use. The mark of his position was the soldier's sword belt; his uniform and equipment advertised his special status and function.

20–23. Common soldiers. These men who served along the northern frontier of the empire adorn themselves on their gravestones with typical weaponry (the *pilum*, or thrusting spear, the *gladius*, or short sword, the *scutum*, or shield, and *sagum*, or cloak. The sword and its belt were the most powerful symbol of his status and authority.

The same privileged and powerful position that brought esteem or even envy could also bring hostility. Civilians might loathe him, so long as they feared him; the end result was the same. The literature of the elite and of ordinary folk repeatedly notes the overbearing attitude of soldiers and the resentment-cum-fear this inspired in the civilian population; many soldiers in all likelihood relished this power to intimidate, extort, and generally terrorize at will. The sentiment of the *Historia Augusta* was perhaps overly optimistic:

> A soldier is not to be feared as long as he is properly clothed, well armed, has stout boots, and there is something in his purse. (*Life of Severus Alexander*, 52)

The jurist Ulpian, for example, assumes that soldiers will try to steal from the civilian population. Inappropriate requisitions were rampant. The pathetic attempts to stop it were ineffectual, if well intended. Here is an example from Egypt:

> Marcus Petronius Mamertinus, prefect of Egypt, declares: I have been informed that many of the soldiers, while traveling through the country, without a certificate requisition boats, animals, and persons beyond what is proper, on some occasions appropriating them by force, on others getting them from the commander by exercise of favor or deference. Because of this private persons are subjected to arrogance and abuse and the army has come to be censored for greed and injustice. I therefore order the commander and royal secretaries to furnish to absolutely no one any travel facilities at all without a certificate, whether he is traveling by river or by land, on the understanding that I shall punish severely anyone who, after this edict, is caught giving or taking any of the things mentioned above ... (*PSI* 446 = Campbell, no. 293)

Forced billeting (as noted, for example, in Pliny's letter to Trajan, *Letters* 10.77–8) was a common abuse, as were blackmail, extortion, and other methods to extract money from the civilian population for personal use. When soldiers ask John the Baptizer what they should do to be good, he tells them, 'Don't extort money and don't accuse people falsely – be content with your pay' (Luke 3:14). In Egypt a man entered significant bribes in his account books as a 'business expense'!

A most graphic and extensive example of a soldier abusing his authority comes from the novel of Apuleius, *The Golden Ass* (9.39–42). Here a gardener is riding along a road in Thessaly on Lucius, the man-turned-into-an-ass protagonist of the novel. A centurion traveling alone meets them coming from the other direction. In the initial encounter, the legionary soldier is recognized both by his uniform (*habitus*) and by his demeanor (*habitudo*). He behaves haughtily and arrogantly (*superbo atque adrogant sermone*), addressing the gardener in the army's official language, Latin, although they are in a Greek-speaking area, and block-ing his path. He invokes his right to requisition transport and comman-deers the ass to carry his unit's baggage and equipment. The centurion takes umbrage both at the gardener trying to force his way past him, and at the failure to respond to his Latin query; he displays his inbred arro-gance (*familiarem insolentiam*), and resorts immediately to violence, strik-ing the gardener with his centurion's staff, knocking him to the ground. The gardener clearly recognizes the unequal power relationship and tries to placate the soldier by being obeisant (*subplicue*) and offering the excuse that he didn't understand the Latin. The soldier repeats that he is commandeering the ass for state use and begins to lead him off to his fortlet. The gardener again tries begging – he addresses the soldier in an obsequious tone and beseeches him to be more kindly. All to no avail. In fact, the gardener's pleas only increase the violence of the soldier, who prepares to kill him with further blows from his staff. But the gardener tackles the soldier and beats him to near death, then heads for the nearest town. The soldier recovers and enlists the help of fellow soldiers who in turn summon the civil magistrates of the town to find and execute the gardener for attacking the soldier; these officials are motivated by fear of the soldier's commander if they don't act. The gardener is arrested by the magistrates and held in jail pending, presumably, execution without trial, at the behest of the soldier. The soldier gets away scot-free, despite his excessive violence against the gardener. He loads up Lucius with his military gear prominently displayed to terrorize anyone he might meet on the road (*propter terrendos miseros viatores*), and progresses to the next town, where he thrusts himself on a local magistrate for billeting, rather than staying at an inn. So in this encounter are seen the negatives civilians experienced from the soldiery: arrogance from which there was no recourse, unauthorized requisitioning, billeting on the civilian population, violence from which there was no effective protection, and manipulation of the civil judicial system in favor of the soldiers.

An episode in Petronius illustrates similar haughty behavior. Encolpius, deserted by his lover Giton, buckles on his sword and goes looking for revenge.

> As I rushed about, a soldier noticed me, some sort of con man or thug, and he said to me, 'Hey, fellow soldier, what's your legion? Who's your centurion?' When I bravely lied about my century and legion, that fellow said, 'Come on now, do soldiers in *your* army go around in fancy footwear?' My lie betrayed me at that point by the look on my face and my trembling. 'Hand over your sword, or it'll be the worse for you!' Despoiled, I had neither sword nor revenge. (*Satyricon* 82)

From the soldier's perspective, therefore, being in the army encouraged a sense of superiority over the civilian population, an experience of power that could at once allow and exculpate almost any excess. There was no check on this other than self-policing (surely extremely ineffective) and the fruitless bleatings of Roman officials, for example:

> The Governor of a province must see that persons of limited resources are not treated unjustly by having their only lamp or small supply of furniture taken from them for the use of others, under the pretext of the arrival of officers or soldiers.
>
> The governor of a province shall see to it that no action be authorized favoring persons claiming unfair advantage for themselves by the assertion of their military status. (*Digest* 1.18.6.5–6)

The arrogance that Apuleius describes was a normal part of being a soldier. A member of a group set apart, answerable only to its superior officers, who were likely to be complicit, the soldier relished his position of power in a world where relative power was the only way to get things done – or to prevent them from being done to you. For the soldier, this was definitely a positive aspect of the job.

The one major soldierly act not mentioned in the tales of Apuleius and Petronius is bribery. Presumably the poor gardener was in no position to offer a bribe to the soldier; many others in civil society were in such a position, however. In the Easter story, soldiers are bribed:

> While the women were on their way [from the empty tomb], some of the guards went into the city and reported to the chief priests everything that had happened. When the chief priests had met with the elders and devised a plan, they gave the soldiers a large sum of money, telling them, 'You are to say, "His disciples came during the night and stole him away while we were asleep." If this report gets to the governor, we will satisfy him and keep you out of trouble.' So the soldiers took the money and did as they were instructed. And this story has been widely circulated among the Jews to this very day. (Matthew 28:11–17)

A soldier assumed that bribe-taking was part of his privileges and supplemented his pay accordingly, generally ignoring advice such as that quoted above from John the Baptizer to not take any more than his due, and be satisfied with his pay.

Soldiers, women, and marriage

The most controversial aspect of military life both for common soldiers in antiquity and for scholars in modern discussions was the so-called 'marriage ban.' Augustus had passed two laws of seemingly conflicting content. On the one hand, the *Lex Papia Poppea* encouraged the formation of families and the bearing of children. On the other, a law or decree of unknown name prohibited soldiers from marrying, thus preventing them from forming a legitimate family. This juxtaposition of measures reveals two conflicting goals of the Augustan arrangements for the Roman community.

During the early and middle republic, the army was recruited from families and only for temporary service. The ideal of the peasant-soldier was ingrained in practice and in myth: the farmer who leaves his home, family, and fields to serve his community, sometimes in far-flung places for extended periods of time, and then returns to take up the plow

24. A soldier and his wife adorn their gravestone; their son is before them. As he grasps a sword in his left hand just as his father does, he was probably a soldier, too.

25. A soldier's extended family. This gravestone was set up after the ban on marriage was lifted in the early third century AD. It reads: To the Underworld Powers. Aurelia Ingenua, the daughter, set this up at her own expense to most dear parents, Aurelius Maximus, veteran of the Second Auxiliary Legion, her father and to Aelia Prima, her mother; as well as to Aelia Resilla, her grandmother. Aurelius Valens, a soldier of the Second Legion, also dedicated this to the kindliest of in-laws.

again. As this became more myth than practice during the second century BC, soldiers became less and less peasant recruits serving and returning home, and more and more tied to their generals as the source of rewards both in battle and after extensive campaigns. Culminating in the civil wars of Pompey, Caesar, Octavian, and Antonius, soldiers came to represent the rending of the community rather than its bedrock foundation.

In this situation, Octavian-become-Augustus saw that he needed to control the army in every way possible to keep it from continuing to be the juggernaut for disruption that had, indeed, brought him to power. He managed this at the managerial level by controlling personally or through trusted lieutenants the recruitment, deployment, and command of virtually all the legions in the provinces; this essentially eliminated the ability of others to raise and lead an army against him.

Besides cutting off the possibility of new military warlords rising against him through military commands, Augustus also had to deal with the soldiers' expectations of rewards from their generals, which had risen hugely following the promises of bonuses as an enticement to service during the civil wars of the first fifteen years of his ascendancy. After deactivating large numbers of those soldiers and paying them off with cash and land, he realized that his newly envisioned community could not afford politically or financially to continue with the soldiery essentially blackmailing him with expectations of extensive, expensive, and unpredictable rewards for service. His solution was to break cleanly with the myth of the peasant-soldier family and to establish the military family separate from the civic family as the basis for the future army's recruitment, organization, and loyalty. Artemidorus catches exactly what was happening in his interpretation of the dream 'Taking up a career as a soldier':

> To be enrolled as a soldier or to serve in the army indicates death for those suffering from any sort of illness. For an enlisted man changes his very life. He ceases to be an individual making his own decisions and takes up another way of life, leaving behind the other. (*Dreams* 2.31)

In a real sense, the solution of the *Lex Papia Poppea* and of Augustus' military reform was the same: recreate or create a basic unit of life and responsibility in both the civilian and military spheres.

This new army (never openly conceived as such, of course) had everything Augustus saw was lacking in the army of his youth. Creating the units ceased to be a process of disrupting the civic family with large conscriptions carried on with regularity; the twenty to twenty-five years of service for a soldier meant that only around 7500 new soldiers had to be recruited from all Roman citizens each year. Loyalty of the recruited soldiers was to him, or to him through his lieutenants, alone. An explicit reward system of expectable lines of advancement, regular pay, and discharge bonus was in place, eliminating the propensity for and expectation of ad hoc rewards. Overall commitment to military duty was assured by walling off the soldiers from civilian expectations and focusing on fellow soldiers, not on civil families, for social support and interactions. They were often removed far from their natal homes and families, and remained away for many years – not infrequently for the rest of their lives. The clearest evidence for the success of this process is the large number of funerary dedications by soldiers to other soldiers. Here are two examples:

> Gaius Julius Reburrus, soldier of the Seventh Legion, Twinned and Lucky, born in Segisama Brasaca, lies here having lived 52 years and served for 24 of those. Licinius Rufus, soldier of the same legion dedicated the gravestone. (*CIL* 2.4157, Tarragona, Spain)

> This is a memorial to Aurelius Vitalis, a soldier of the Third Flavian Legion, who served 7 years of his 25-year life. Flavius Proculus, a participant in the German incursion, a soldier of the legion just noted, and Vitalis' heir in the second degree, set this up to his fine fellow soldier. (*CIL* 13.6104 = *ILS* 2310, Speyer, Germany)

This is very different from the family dedications that dominate in the civilian world; the soldiers are family to the other soldiers, and this is exactly what the marriage ban was intended to produce.

Central to the creation of that military family was cutting off the basis of the civic family, the procreation of children – and thereby the projection of that civic family as a unit into the future. Just as children and the passing on of inheritances both real and social was the key *raison d'etre* for the civil family, procreational celibacy was the key to the continuance of the military family; only by eliminating the possibility of creating legitimate children could a soldier's connection with the civic family's civil orientation be broken, and a steadfast focus on the military family assured. Tertullian correctly saw that such celibacy sets a man apart from society and creates a society within a society, in his case Christian, in the Roman case, military.

It is clear that procreational celibacy along with its radical goal of the creation of a military society had nothing to do with sex, women, or children in the broader sense. Soldiers were always free to find sex where they could and to create liaisons with women; there were no prohibitions. The prohibition was against forming *legitimate* families; it was intended to and perhaps succeeded in keeping these relationships outside the core life of the soldier. An unforeseen consequence of the significant decrease in extensive wars of aggression after Augustus was that the legions became increasingly garrison forces; the boon of the absence of permanent women and children (wives and children) in a peripatetic soldier's life became a curse once the legions became more and more sedentary. The progressive loosening of the rules regarding procreational celibacy – permission for soldiers to have the rights of married men (Claudius), testamentary and inheritance rules that increasingly allowed soldiers' illegitimate children to inherit like legitimate children (Flavians, Trajan, Hadrian) – culminating in the removal of the marriage ban by Septimius Severus parallels the increasingly immobile posting of the legions and the rise of permanent, stone-built legionary camps and outposts. The system of a separate military society breaks down. By the third century AD all traces were gone of Augustus' attempt to thwart would-be warlords through the creation of a military family loyal only to the *pater familias militum* – the 'father of the soldiers' family.' It is perhaps not surprising that the acknowledgment of this through the elimination of the marriage ban by Septimius Severus took place at the beginning of a century of renewed discord, warlordism, and the dominance of soldiers' demands in the political life of the Roman community. Augustus' experiment broke up on the rocks of human nature.

Whatever the variety of relations with women was during service, it is clear that upon discharge the soldier's woman could, if the soldier so wished, be accepted as *uxor*, a legal wife, with full privileges of a married woman, thus making any de facto situation during a soldier's enlistment official upon discharge; no punitive action was taken for the soldier having 'violated' the anti-marriage rule. The legal disability was significant, however, for a liaison during active duty. Most particularly, without legal Roman marriage, passing on one's name and possessions through family inheritance was impossible. The child could not be enrolled on the birth album (proving Roman citizenship). Regardless of the legal status of father and/or mother, any child was illegitimate and could not inherit as a legitimate son until the loosening of the inheritance rules. Of course, the child could be named an heir, but that did not have the same social force as a son inheriting as a son. If a soldier had a wife and child at the time of enlistment, the marriage was dissolved and the child (probably) declared illegitimate; certainly any subsequent children suffered this diminution in status. Another disability arising from lack of legitimate marriage was the elimination of a dowry from the wife. Also, there could be no prosecution for adultery, since there was no marriage at law.

Despite all this, marriage and family were clearly important in the personal lives of many soldiers. The percentage of men who established unions and, indeed, whom they chose as companions must remain unknowable. Perhaps if the names of wives given in inscriptions are good evidence, most soldiers preferred Romanized women. Here are two examples:

Lucius Plotidius Vitalis, the son of Lucius, of the Lemonia voting district, a soldier in the Fifteenth Legion Apollinaris, lies here. He lived 50 years and served 23. Annia Maxima set this monument up to a most dear husband. (*AE* 1954.119, Petronell, Austria)

To the Underworld Gods. Aurelius Victor, soldier of the First Italic Legion, lived 36 years and was a soldier for 18. Valeria Marcia his wife and Valeria Bessa his daughter, his heirs, set this up to one who was well-deserving. (*CIL* 3.13751a, Kherson, Ukraine)

Other evidence indicates that many of the wives were freedwomen, so a slave girl was the origin of the relationship.

Gaius Petronius, son of Gaius, from Mopsistum, lived 73 years and served 26 in the cavalry wing Gemelliana. He lies here. Urbana, his freedwoman and wife, set this up. (*ILS* 9138, Walbersdorf, Austria)

There are also numerous inscriptions noting a soldier on active duty with a wife and family. Here is one:

To the Nether Gods. This is dedicated to Marcus Aurelius Rufini-
anus, who lived 10 years, our son. Likewise to our daughter, Aurelia
Rufina, still living. Marcus Aurelius Rufinus, a soldier in the First
Legion Adiutrix, and Ulpia Firmina his wife, their parents, set this up
for them and also for themselves. (*Die römischen Inschriften Ungarns*
5.1200, Dunaújváros, Hungary)

What is clear from all this is that soldiers openly formed marriages
and had offspring, whatever the official rules said about it. This openness would not have been possible if the anti-marriage regulations had
been strictly enforced. So Augustus' attempt to force an exchange of a
civil family for a military one ran up against the deepest cultural drive
in the civil population, the propagation of the family; not surprisingly,
both flaunting of marriage ban and agitation for its amelioration began
immediately and lasted until soldiers were at last officially allowed to
marry in the early third century.

What did common soldiers do for heterosexual sex? Certainly, there
was no attempt to enforce or encourage celibacy among the legionaries.
Sex with women was part of being virile, and being virile was fundamental to being a soldier. Violent rape, a practice fully condoned by the
officers when conducted under battle circumstances, was assault akin to
slaying male enemies, not a 'sexual' act; it should not be confused with
soldiers seeking sexual outlets. However, there were two easily accessible nonviolent outlets that had no long-term repercussions: prostitutes
and slaves – who were often one and the same person. The *canabae* near
the camps probably had prostitutes along with other merchandise. In
addition, one's own female slave was available willy-nilly at any time,
and many soldiers had slave girls while on active duty.

A different kind of relationship could easily develop with local girls
from near the military postings. A soldier might take up a liaison with
a girl who would set up house for him and provide him with sexual
gratification as well as other household duties; these were called *focariae*
('hearth girls'). One even left a grave inscription documenting her relationship with a marine:

Marcus Aurelius Vitalis was a soldier from Pannonia who served 27
years in the praetorian fleet at Ravenna. Valeria Faustina, his *focariae*

and heir, set this monument up to a fine person. (*CIL* 11.39 = *ILS* 2904, Ravenna, Italy)

As these inscriptions attest, women often had relationships that led to the informal marriage so many soldiers enjoyed, along with the resulting children. So one way or another, the common soldier did not need to lack for sexual gratification with women.

The first serious treatments of homosexuality in the imperial Roman army appeared only a few years ago. Other treatments belabor the apparently severe punishment of homosexual behavior in the republican army, using the examples that elite sources provide about officer culture, which are heavily colored by vanities of 'honor' and 'virility.' At the least, such violent punishments (even if probably seldom meted out) reveal that homosexual behavior existed in those early armies. However, for the army of the high empire there are not even elite sources for attitudes or action regarding homosexual behavior among common soldiers in the legions. A few bits and pieces of evidence can help to form at least a general picture, however.

Male relations with male slaves and with male prostitutes, while perhaps frowned upon by the elite in a hypocritical sort of way, were widely accepted as a fact of life. As common soldiers, and especially centurions along with other officers, held slaves, this sort of relationship existed in the army as well. In Plautus' *Pseudolus* (1180–81) a soldier's slave is accused of as much: 'At night, when the Captain was going on guard, and when you were going with him, did the sword of the officer fit your scabbard?' In *Epigram* 1.31 and elsewhere, Martial speaks of the sexual relationship of a centurion, Aulus Pudens, with his boy slave Encolpus. Likewise relations with male prostitutes were presumably acceptable. It seems highly unlikely, then, that soldiers having become used to sexual satisfaction with male slaves and paid partners always drew the line if a fellow soldier might make an advance or indicate availability.

The one thing that might have inhibited homosexual behavior between social equals (i.e. both common soldiers) would be a cultural position that is well attested for both the elite and the nonelite: the passive or 'receptive' partner in a relationship was stigmatized as effeminate, and being effeminate was the opposite of what a male should

be, masculine. It was part of soldierly culture to be manly, not effeminate. Therefore, a soldier might resist a sexual relationship because of
its negative cultural overtones – in a word, guilt at transgressing an
important cultural norm of manhood. It does seem that this taboo held
for the citizen army of the middle republic and perhaps even for the late
republic, which is the period from which all the elite testimony about
the horrors of male homosexuality in the army appears. Then the anecdotes disappear. During the imperial period there is no tale of officers
debauching subordinate soldiers; no indication of rules and regulations
governing homosexual relations among the soldiers; nothing. Why this
is the case has been variously explained. One historical incident provides a clue: When two soldiers were accused of being part of Saturni-
nus' plot to kill the emperor Domitian, they said they could not possibly
have been because their known condition of being 'penetrated ones,'
i.e. passive partners in homosexual activities, marginalized them so
much that no one would have included them in a plot (Suetonius, *Life of
Domitian* 10). This presents a picture of soldiers who know that some of
their confrères engage in the passive role in male-to-male relationships,
mark this down as a stigma, but do nothing further; there is no 'outing,'
no punishment beyond a certain marginalization within the soldiers'
community. While such social pressure would have had some effect
at the very least to make soldiers careful to hide their activities with
each other from their fellow soldiers as much as possible, clearly these
activities persisted. But for the most part, as long as a soldier maintained
either the outward trappings of masculinity or, if for whatever reason
he appeared 'feminized' to his fellows, he continually demonstrated his
ability to act like a man in exercises, fatigues, and war, nothing would
happen beyond a bit of sniping from those around him.

Religious life

One of the ways a soldier was acculturated into the military life was by
shifting religious focus. Deities worshiped before becoming a soldier
were, of course, not banned once military service began. But instead
of a panoply of local/ethnic gods, the soldier was encouraged to focus
on two overriding manifestations of the divine – the emperor; and the
'official' Roman divinity Jupiter Optimus Maximus along with the rest

of the pantheon – as well as Eternal Rome and Augustan Victory as embodiments of the Roman State.

The emperor was warlord-identified-with-the-State. The official religion emphasized the unity of the armed forces as well as the centrality of the emperor in its life. This was the private army of the emperor as the embodiment of Rome. Augustus advanced from the status of his warring predecessors and contemporaries to claim not preeminence in the State, but quasi-divine leadership and, ultimately and increasingly in his successors, synonymy with it. So loyalty to Rome and loyalty to the personified Rome, the emperor, became conflated completely in the soldier's mind. Loyalty to the emperor was central to the soldier's life: 'For the soldiers swear continually throughout their service that they will place the safety of the emperor above all else' (Epictetus, *Discourses* 1.14.15). From Vegetius 2.5 and other snippets a reasonable outline is possible: Soldiers swear by the majesty of the emperor to strenuously do all that the emperor might command, protect his and his family's well-being (*salus*), never desert the service, nor refuse to die for Rome. Certainly the oath was repeated annually; probably it was repeated each day at reveille; at any rate, its creed was omnipresent. Soldiers took this oath seriously:

This dedication is for the safety of the emperor. As a new recruit I, Lucius Maximius, son of Lucius Gaetulicus, of the Voltinian voting district, from Vienne, made a vow in front of the Twentieth Legion Valeria Victrix in the name of Augustan Panthean Victories most holy. Now after 57 years of service and advancement to the rank of chief centurion in the First Italic Legion I have fulfilled my vow. Dated in the year of the consuls Marullus and Aelianus (AD 184). (*AE* 1985.735, Swischtow, Bulgaria)

The emperor was present in many quasi-religious elements of the soldier's life. Imperial names were given to subunits of the army; the emperor's image was in every camp on a standard, carried by a special 'image bearer' (*imaginifer*); his face graced armor and other equipment; all coins bore his visage; all rewards and medals came from him (via the local commanders). The emperor was the source of largess, not just the regular salary but occasional donatives and gifts at death. The emperor in turn played the dual role of *commiles* – fellow soldier – and divine leader, a sort of god-with-us.

In the ordered life of the camp, cultic ritual was ordered as well. This order was something foreign to civilian life, where cultic activity was available but entirely voluntary. From Dura-Europos there is a calendar of sacrifices – a trans-empire calendar meant to inculcate in the soldiers the old gods and the imperial house as fonts of being. Here are listed, day by day, religious actions to worship specific gods, to offer supplications to the emperor, to celebrate birthdays of the imperial family with sacrifice, to give thankful remembrance for past victories, and to celebrate the sacred standards of the legion. Besides the obvious use of such occasions to emphasize the focus of the army on the emperor and Rome, the ceremonies themselves regardless of their declared purpose provided occasions for unity, for example parades and festivals, and for diversion. Celebrations were also an opportunity to let go of the tight discipline of the camp. They were drunken, excessive affairs when rules were forgotten at least for a moment. So the ceremonies provided unit identity for the common soldier, and gave his life both relief from the normal routines, and meaning.

As with the marriage rules governing soldiers, the religious aspect of his life helped to create a new allegiance separate from those of civil life. His original enrollment has all the marks of an initiation into a new religious world – the declaration of personage, the tattoo with which he was marked, setting him apart from the unmarked, and the sacred oath to the emperor all refocused the recruit, while the regular religious events of the year reinforced both otherness vis-à-vis the civilian population and unity of the initiated.

All of this is not to say that soldiers did not have private religious lives as well. If it can be said that cultic activity as a group focused on the official religion of the legion and individual cultic activity indicated personal religious beliefs outside this official activity, then the evidence of individual dedications points to the lively existence of private religious life. But this should not be exaggerated. There were no 'private' soldierly cults; the two most often associated with soldiers, Mithra and Jupiter Dolichenus, in fact are attested to by far more nonsoldiers' dedications than soldiers'; in the case of Mithra less than 20 percent of dedications are by soldiers; for Dolichenus it is less than 40 percent. But

26. Soldier religion. A soldier makes a small sacrifice at an altar.

although not specifically 'military,' these and other cults were a comple-
ment to the religious focus of the legion itself.

Soldiers and social mobility

While it is certain that not all recruits were poor, a substantial portion
must have been. The benefits of service detailed above, combined with
the continuing status accrued as a veteran, meant that the army was the
only institution in the Roman world that could more or less guarantee
social as well as financial advancement if one worked hard and lived
long enough. Not only did it provide the financial resources (whether
well or ill gotten did not matter); much more importantly (for others
could make money), it provided a mechanism to move between social
classes, something that was virtually impossible in the civilian world.
A common soldier could advance to high rank and then, as a veteran,
become a town councilor.

This monument is for Gaius Julius Valerio, son of Gaius, of the Papirian district, a veteran of the Thirteenth Severan Twinned Legion, formerly a special assignment soldier, who became a town councilor and presiding magistrate of the colony of Sarmizegetusa. Gaius Julius Valerianus, also a special assignment officer, Carus, a military provisioner and councilor of aforesaid colony, Fronto, a soldier of the First Praetorian Cohort and secretary to the Prefect of the Guard, also a councilor of the same colony, Valeria, and Carissima, their children, set this up to the memorial of their father. The town council allotted the place for the monument. (*AE* 1933.248, Sarmizegetusa)

Such mobility among nonsoldiers was almost unheard of and was yet another reason why the army had a great appeal to ambitious, poor, or even not-so-poor, twenty-year-olds.

Negatives of service

Despite all the advantages a man would have seen in military service, there were negatives as well. Most profoundly, a soldier accepted willingly a serious diminution of his personal freedom and rights. His oath put him under the control of his masters, i.e. of his military officers, even to the point of being subject to summary capital punishment. As Artemidorus says, 'Many freed slaves nonetheless continue to act as slaves and to be subject to another, just as a soldier is a "free man," but nevertheless is under the command of his superiors' (*Dreams* 2.31). Like others who voluntarily subverted their freedom to another's will, people such as indentured servants and gladiators, soldiers made a calculation and decided loss of freedom was a price worth paying. But, still, they did give up something that civilian men valued highly.

Of course, the primary day-to-day dangers were from disease – always by far the most lethal element in premodern armies – and actual military action whether in war or in 'peacekeeping' operations. Artemidorus says that if an old man dreams of enlisting as a soldier, it often portends his death (*Dreams* 2.31). A soldier might live his entire life without fighting in a line battle, for example if he was posted to the III Augusta in North Africa or the VII Gemina in northern Spain. Legionaries along the Rhine and Danube and in the East might expect more action during a lifetime of service. And some died:

> Marcus Domitius Super, soldier of the Second Legion Adiutrix, who lived 32 years and 6 months and died in the German War. Also Aurelius Julius who lived 26 years and 5 months and Revocata their mother who lived 50 years. Concordius their freedman set this up. (*Die römischen Inschriften Ungarns* 5.1228, Dunaújváros, Hungary)

> Aurelius Victor, soldier of the Second Italic Legion, was lost in battle against the Gothic host. He lived 30 years. Aurelia Lupula made this for a most dear husband. (*CIL* 3.11700, Dobrna, Slovenia)

> Canius Otiorix, soldier of the Second Legion Adiutrix, died in Parthia. Canius Speratus, his son, set this up also for himself while living and for his wife, also still alive. (*CIL* 3.3628, 3630, 10572, Szanto, Hungary)

Any units could be called upon to do bandit-duty at any time. A force list from a garrison at Stobi (Macedonia) names men who died accidentally by drowning and at the hands of bandits; the latter fate befell a soldier of the Twenty-Second Legion:

> Januarius Vosenus, soldier of the Twenty-Second Legion … was killed by bandits … (*CIL* 13.2667, Lyon, France)

But for most soldiers, the hours of training and drudgery were not followed with any frequency by actual use of their weapons in dangerous situations.

Another disadvantage of being a soldier was the constant possibility of transfer. When men dream of being a soldier, it means that they will suffer 'vexations, unpleasantnesses, instability, and being away from home,' so Artemidorus tells his reader (*Dreams* 2.31). But the biggest challenge and the most constant stress of life under the standard was to make the culture of the service work for the soldier. Although in theory duties were assigned and regulations enforced with an equal hand, the regular experience of the soldier was likely to be far different. Vegetius

2.19 alludes to the possibility of 'unjust, excessively heavy assignments or exemption from duties.' The centurion was the focus of authority for the common soldier; it was he who could make life good or a hell for the soldiers under him. Fear and instilling it in soldiers was a fundamental element of Roman discipline – one terrible centurion was nicknamed *cedo alteram* – 'bring me another' – referring to his staff, which he broke over the backs of his soldiers as he beat them for discipline (Tacitus, *Annals* 1.23). Besides flogging, the *Digest* lists other military punishments: reprimands, fines, fatigues, transfer to another branch of the army, reduction in rank, and dishonorable discharge. For lesser infractions a soldier might be fed on barley instead of wheat, or made to suffer some psychological punishment such as standing in front of the commander's headquarters all day, in plain sight of his fellows, wearing only a tunic and without the signifying sword belt. For desertion of a post in battle, or betrayal or desertion from the army, the penalty was severe: execution. Bribery was rampant as a way to avoid excessively harsh treatment, or to gain some privilege. Tacitus notes the need to bribe centurions (*Annals* 1.17), and I have already noted the letter from Claudius Terentianus in which he claims that 'nothing gets done without money.' Bribery could secure a leave, or a longer one (Tacitus, *Histories* 1.46). It could also gain relief from daily fatigues, and increase chances for advancement. Clearly, a soldier had to be ready to bribe if he hoped to keep on the good side of his centurion.

Did harsh conditions of service lead soldiers to mutiny? The historian Tacitus (*Annals* 1.16–67) has a famous passage in which mutineers in Pannonia complain about the awfulness of their soldiering. Their issues include abusive centurions and officers, low pay (although Tacitus cites here a denarius a day, surely a good wage at the time), frequent and vicious corporal punishment, many and dangerous military expeditions, compulsory extension of their legal tours of duty, and officials reneging on promises of land as a reward after service was ended. Assuredly, the dangers of service are well taken: war, difficult conditions, and the harshness of discipline. Although in certain circumstances, and if the right leader appeared, mutinies occurred, these are reported only very rarely in the sources. And it is to the point to note that as soldiers became increasingly sedentary and nonwarring, the harshnesses were mitigated but the benefits were not decreased. Vegetius 3.4 notes the 'idleness and luxury' (surely a relative thing!) that soldiers at their home base experienced – as welcome for many soldiers as annoying to the commanding officers once they needed soldiers for a real campaign.

After service was over

A common soldier who joined the legions at age twenty could reasonably expect to complete his service and live on after discharge. Of course, he could extend his service, and inscriptions show that many did. But after the normal twenty years' service, at about forty years of age, he could live at least a few years, given ancient life tables. In other words, one of the appeals of service would be the expectation of honorable discharge and continued life with the status of a veteran; about half of all recruits lived to be veterans, receiving special treatment from the imperial government.

Soldiers were discharged in three categories: honorable, medical (= honorable, with prorating for time served), and dishonorable. Only the first two gained the soldier the rewards, rights, and privileges of being a veteran. Perhaps 6000–7000 veterans were produced each year, with a total of perhaps 50,000–60,000 veterans alive at any given time. Exclusively veteran settlements existed, but were uncommon; there were about fifty founded in the first century of the empire and they become increasingly less common thereafter; fully 300 would have been needed to house all the available veterans during that time period.

Some veterans, especially in the eastern part of the empire, returned to their hometowns; some others settled near the place where they had last served – this is true especially in the western part of the empire. Still others ended up in widely disparate locations. There is an interesting set of inscriptions that illustrates this scattering. *Diplomata*, bronze discharge documents, have been found for five soldiers from a single unit that was to have been settled at Paestum in southern Italy. Although the soldiers involved were noncitizen troops of the fleet, not citizen legionaries, what happened to them is striking. The five documents were found widely dispersed in Kavala (Philippi, Macedonia), Daldodeltzi (Thrace), Pompeii (Italy, north of Paestum), Agaiola (Corsica), and Slamac Slavonski (Pannonia, modern Croatia), thus indicating how these veterans settled throughout the empire. On the other hand some veterans did settle in the *canabae* right next to the camps where they served. Valerius Pudens did this:

> To Jupiter Optimus Maximus for the health and safety of Emperor Hadrian. The veterans and Roman citizens settled in the *canabae* of the Fifth Macedonian Legion dedicated this when Gaius Valerius Pudens, veteran of the Fifth Macedonian Legion, and Marcus Ulpius Leontius were chief magistrates of the inhabitants of the *canabae*, and Tuccius Aelianus was aedile. (*CIL* 3.6166 = *ILS* 2474, Iglita, Romania)

As a whole, veterans were well treated. At the point of discharge they collected not only their savings from years of service, but also the monetary bonus awarded to all veterans; more money came in if their petty officers' association paid out. A high-ranking common soldier such as a centurion would walk away with enough capital to enter the elite of a town and qualify for membership in the local town council and for holding the highest local magistracies. Two examples suffice. A centurion returned to his hometown in Macedonia and held the highest office there:

> In honor of Publius Mucius, son of Quintus, of the Voltinian voting unit. He was centurion of the Sixth Armored Legion, then a chief magistrate of Philippi. Gaius Mucius Scaeva, son of Gaius, set up this monument. He did this in accordance with the will of Gaius Mucius Saeva, son of Quintus, of the Fabian voting unit. (*AE* 2004.1335, Krenides, Greece)

Another returned to his hometown in Spain after service:

> Laeta, his daughter, set this up to honor Gaius Julius Scaena, son of Lucius, of the Sergian voting district. He was a commander of cavalry and legionary head centurion in the Fourth Legion, then subsequently a chief magistrate [of Tucci]. (*CIL* 2.1681[5], Martos, Spain)

A ranker would have less money, of course, but still by the standards of the subelite culture, he would be well off. A veteran soldier (not, apparently, a centurion or petty officer) from Faventia in the Po Valley held a chief magistracy in the North African town where he settled:

Quintus Annaeus, son of Quintus, of the Pollian voting district, a native of Faventium [Italy], lies here, dead at age 53 having lived honorably. He was a soldier in the Fifth Legion, decorated twice, then a chief magistrate of Thuburnica [North Africa]. Quintus Annaeus Scapula supervised this. Hail to you, too [passerby]! (*CIL* 8.10605 = *ILS* 2249, Sidi Ali Ben Kassem, Algeria)

And just above I have given an example of a ranker who rose to be a magistrate of the *canabae* next to his former legionary camp.

Other veterans had enough money to set themselves up in business. Here, a man became a pottery merchant:

To the Underworld Spirits and Eternal Memory of Vitalinius Felix, veteran of the First Minervan Legion, a most wise and honest businessman from Lyon who dealt in ceramic goods. He lived 59 years, 5 months, and 10 days. He was born on a Tuesday, was sworn as a soldier a Tuesday, became a veteran on a Tuesday, and died a Tuesday too. Vitalinius Felicissimus, his son, and Iulia Nice, his wife, set this up and dedicated it. (*CIL* 13.1906 = *ILS* 7531, Lyon, France)

And Gentilius Victor dealt in swords, appropriately enough:

Dedicated to the Health and Safety of Emperor Commodus and the Successful Return of the Twenty-second Legion Primigenia Loyal and Faithful. Gaius Gentilius Victor, veteran discharged honorably from the Twenty-second Legion Primigenia Loyal and Faithful, sword dealer, ordered in his will that this monument be set up at a cost of 2000 denarii. (*CIL* 13.6677 = *ILS* 2472, Mainz)

Naturally some soldiers threw away their resources on bad investments or on wild women and drink. Perhaps Titus Cissonius was one:

I am Titus Cissonius, son of Quintus, of the Sergian voting district, a veteran of the Fifth Gallic Legion. While I lived I drank freely. You all drink who still live! Publius Cissonius, son of Quintus, Sergian district, his brother, set this up. (*CIL* 3.293/6825 = *ILS* 2238, Yalvaç)

But many others clearly prospered as veterans.

A variety of special privileges and exemptions was added to their financial advantage. A document from the time of Octavian (*c.* 32/31 BC) states that '... [veterans] are to be exempt [from taxation].' Another from the emperor Domitian states that they are '... free and exempt from all public taxes and toll dues.' They were also exempt from charges associated with shipbuilding and from being required to collect taxes due the government. They were not, however, exempt from all taxes. They had to pay the inheritance tax and the property tax, and special assessments, for example, for road repair.

Not only did veterans not pay important taxes, they were also exempt from various obligations to perform service. The same documents cited above affirm this: veterans are '... excused from the performance of compulsory public services' and are '... not to be appointed against their will to other magistracies or as ambassador or superintendent or tax farmer' (Octavian) and '... [veterans] should be free and immune with total exemptions' (Domitian). Should a veteran become entangled with the law, his status also stood him in good stead. In the most extreme cases, he, like town magistrates and other important local persons, was exempt from the degrading forms of capital punishment, and from being condemned to the mines (a virtual death sentence).

As veterans have preferential treatment in other things, so too with regard to their crimes:

> They should not suffer punishments as others do ... Therefore they are not to be condemned to the mines nor other state labor camps, nor to be thrown to the beasts, nor to be beaten to death with clubs. (Arrius Menander, *On Military Matters* 3 = *Digest* 49.18.1)

When these immunities conflicted with obligations they might legally be bound to perform, or protections they might have in view of their position in a civil post, Ulpian says that the veteran's immunities remain, even if he becomes a councilor:

> Anyone given an honorable discharge is granted immunity from required duties and taxes even in a city in which he is resident, nor

does he lose this immunity if he voluntarily takes on a duty or tax burden (Ulpian, *Opinions* 3 = *Digest* 49.18.2)

With all these privileges and exemptions, it is small wonder that the benefits of veteran status would have been before the eyes of the common soldier as he went through his years of service. Far from being unceremoniously discarded or fobbed off with a small bonus, the discharged Roman soldier could enter into a new phase with reasonable assurance that he would have a decent life in whatever town he wished to settle in.

Conclusion

There is no diary of a common soldier, nor even a fictionalized account of his mind world. But by piecing together material from a wide range of sources, and in particular by using the soldiers' voices left in stone on grave markers and monuments, it is possible to catch a glimpse of their fears, hopes, and dreams. In a social world that was both quite inflexible and often economically insecure, being a soldier was a good option for a healthy young man, especially if the possibilities at home were not promising. He had to sign away some important elements of civilian freedom and serve his military superiors unquestioningly; there was the disruption of living far from where he had spent his youth; but the pay was regular and the basic needs of life – housing, decent food, comradeship – were all assured in a way very difficult to find in civilian life. A skill could be learned or honed; literacy was a possibility. Should he get into trouble outside the camp, he had an advantage in the civilian legal system, such a peril to ordinary civilians. He was treated sometimes with fear, sometimes with respect, but always he had the feeling he was a special person in society. The army had to become a soldier's family, but even here there were leniencies that allowed a wife and children even if officially prohibited, and he was free of his father's power, and free to write his own will. Service was long, and there was no assurance that war, disease, or accident would not end life before he could collect on the benefits of veteran status. But the bet was in general a good one, and many men took it.

SEX FOR SALE: PROSTITUTES

'You with the roses, rosy is your charm; but what do you sell, your-self or the roses, or both?'

WHETHER SLAVE OR FREE, an invisible's abilities often determined their way in life. Bodily strength in construction, digging, or plowing carried a young man whether working for himself or as someone's slave. An older man might use a skill – cobbling, or blacksmithing, or vine tending – in his own interest or his owner's. A grown woman might keep house and raise a family, help out in a shop, or do cottage work, again either freely or as someone's slave. A child or young woman might look forward to marriage – or to sexual exploitation for some-one's profit. For like a young man using his physical strength to meet consumers' needs for hard work, a woman's body could be used for consumers' demands for sex. The life was often involuntary, dangerous, and degrading. But slavery and poverty alike demanded something productive from a young woman. Her ability to provide sex meshed with the lustful demands of men in a culture that jealously guarded the chastity of married women. This situation created a profitable business that many slave owners, as well as free females – and their families – could not neglect.

Although I refer here to women, it needs to be noted that there is explicit testimony in ancient sources that male whores did exist, catering, presumably, both to male and female clients; for example, the legal authority Paulus notes that a male prostitute can be killed by a husband if found having sex with his wife (*Sententiae* 2.26.4). There are, however, no special notices, nor any norms or laws, that apply to males only, or to males in a different way from females. In an effort to streamline the narrative, I have therefore not treated male prostitutes as a separate category. It is, however, important to recognize that they did exist and plied their trade as the women did.

There must be no romanticizing the life of a prostitute. For every woman who chose that life, there were many others forced into it. Slaves, in particular, were helpless and exploited. And this included children, male and female. Although masters could restrict future prostitution of a slave by a clause in a contract for sale, there is no reason to suppose they did this very often. In fact, there is no reason to suppose masters would have anything but maximum profit in mind when it came to prostituting slaves, some of whom were bought specifically for that purpose. Children would have been particularly vulnerable to such exploitation. Free women, too, must frequently have been in desperate situations, with poverty biting at their heels and perhaps family pressure to bring in a small income. While a slave owner might step in to prevent the worst sort of gang rapes, since his property would be damaged, free women had not even that weak protection, unless a pimp could intervene. Physical abuse by customers surely was common; excessive sex must have led to vaginal and anal injury, and to urinary tract infections. It was a hard if not desperate life. It is necessary to always remember this when thinking about the mind world and options of prostitutes, slave and free.

I am concerned here only with women who become ordinary prostitutes, and with their customers. Therefore I do not treat two other types of prostitutes, those purportedly engaged in temple work, and 'high class' women who served the wealthy. Despite a few references that seem to indicate the existence of sacred, temple prostitution in the Romano-Grecian world, a recent very careful and encompassing study has shown conclusively that it existed neither at Corinth (the prime candidate) nor any place else. Therefore sacred prostitutes do not figure in the lives of ordinary people, or of anyone else. On the other hand, high-class prostitutes were a significant presence. The elite erudite Suetonius wrote a book, *Lives of Famous Prostitutes*, which is regrettably lost. He and other writers were fascinated with these courtesans, mostly because of the titillating details of sexual excess among a class that supposedly held morals in high regard – the combination of outright debauchery, hypocrisy, and, often, court intrigue was irresistible. So Suetonius, for example, has the emperor Gaius (Caligula) setting up a whorehouse in his palace:

> And lest any type of plunder go untried, in his palace he set up a number of small rooms just like in a brothel and decorated them sumptuously. He had married women and freeborn stand in the cells, again just like in a brothel. Then he sent heralds around to the markets and places of public business to invite young and old to indulge their lusts. He had money available to offer at interest to those who came – and men at the ready who openly wrote down their names, as contributing to Caesar's income. (*Life of Gaius* 41)

Suetonius and Tacitus both luridly tell of imperial women engaged in something like prostitution, but their very emphasis on this highlights how uncommon it was. On a more realistic level, courtesans did exist and served elite males. The plot of Plautus' *Comedy of Asses*, for example, revolves around a wealthy person seeking to contract for the services of a virgin courtesan, and Lucian's *Dialogues of the Courtesans* imagines the life of such high-class prostitutes. Although upon examination few actual names appear in the historical record, it is safe to assume that such courtesans could influence events; they often became long-term accouterments as concubines. And, of course, elites would on occasion use ordinary prostitutes, as the emperors Caligula, Nero, and others were alleged to have done. But the combination of access to one's own slaves and the resources to keep a woman as a concubine mostly took care of any need to resort to common prostitutes.

I leave the mythical temple prostitutes and the very real elite courtesans aside, to take up ordinary prostitutes. Roman law defined such a person as 'any woman who openly makes money selling her body' (*Digest* 23.2.43, pr. 1). The law did not punish prostitution. It was legal and a prostitute could not be prosecuted for her profession. Sexual relations with a prostitute did not constitute adultery, nor could an unmarried whore be a party to adultery, much less be guilty of adultery herself. *Stuprum* (illegal intercourse) was the term for sexual relations with an unmarried girl/woman (or widow), or boy/man, but it was inapplicable to sexual relations with whores. The key here is inheritance and family inviolability. Sex with a prostitute (at least, a female prostitute) would not endanger the bloodline of the family, nor compromise the sexual purity of a potential wife. Some legal disabilities did, however, adhere. Prostitutes were *probrosae*, meaning, according to Augustan marriage laws, that they could not marry freeborn Roman citizens. They also suffered from *infamia* per the Praetor's Edict – they could not write a will or receive full inheritance. But these restrictions were probably often flouted or ignored and, at any rate, the stigma disappeared if a prostitute married. The Roman legal system basically left prostitutes alone.

So as far as is known, authorities did not care about the moral aspect of prostitution – after all, intercourse with a whore did not break any laws, or even any moral strictures as far as the man was concerned, since it did not constitute adultery. For the woman there was some disgrace arising from sexual license but, again, there was no legal prohibition or penalty. It is unlikely that prostitutes at first had to register with the authorities; since the elite cared not a whit about 'controlling' prostitutes, there would be no reason to go to the trouble to register them. But it did eventually dawn on them that the service was potentially taxable. And by the mid first century AD prostitutes did, indeed, pay a tax. As such a tax was previously known with certainty only at Athens, it is likely that the inspiration for the Roman tax originated from that experience. The first documentary attestation is under the emperor Nero, but the emperor Caligula instituted it

> … on the proceeds of the prostitutes at a rate equivalent to the cost of one trick; and it was added to this section of the law, that those who had practiced prostitution or pimping in the past owed the tax to the treasury, and even married persons were not exempt. (Suetonius, *Life of Gaius* 40)

Thus the tax, as Suetonius notes, amounted to the value of one trick, and could not be evaded by claiming to have quit the business. In order

27. A brothel. The only archaeologically identified brothel in the Romano-Grecian world is at Pompeii. Here the prostitutes had the use of small chambers; erotic scenes decorated the wall above each opening.

to collect this 'service tax,' officials would have had to keep some track of who was a whore. The tax (and so responsibility for oversight) was collected in various ways in various parts of the empire, sometimes by tax collectors, sometimes by public officials, most often, it seems, by soldiers detailed for the task. These were supposed to exact the tax, but often engaged in extortion, as well; I think of John the Baptizer urging soldiers to collect no more than their due and to be satisfied with their pay – clearly something that usually did not happen. Prostitutes working independently perhaps presented something of a challenge to tax men; on the other hand, those in private brothels could be registered and tracked, and the municipal brothels would have made it even easier, but that did not stop imperial officials from extorting still more money, as is attested by a document from Chersonesus on the Black Sea coast. The abuses this system worked on the prostitutes themselves can only be imagined.

There was one further way that prostitutes came into contact with the authorities. When there was a festival or other day, perhaps a special market, which brought more people than usual to a town, a one-day permit to prostitutes was issued, presumably with a fee attached, although this is not explicitly attested to. From Upper Egypt comes one such permit:

> Pelaias and Sokraton, tax collectors, to the prostitute Thinabdella, greetings. We give you permission to have sex with whomever you might wish in this place on the day given below. Year 19, the 3rd day of the month Phaophi. [signed] Sokraton, Simon's son. (*WO* 1157/ Nelson)

Despite lacking the details of just how such a mobile product as sex could be kept tabs on, clearly the Romans managed it. The rate, as we are told by Suetonius, was based on the value of a single trick. A document from Palmyra, far to the eastern end of the empire, actually gives three amounts: a per-trick rate of one denarius or more paid one denarius, a per-trick rate of eight asses (eight-tenths of a denarius) paid that rate, and a per-trick rate of six asses (six-tenths of that coin) paid that rate. Just how much was collected cannot be established, however. The relevant details are unknown, such as how often the tax was collected (daily? Monthly?). So, for example, if a whore charged one denarius, turned five tricks a day, and paid the tax daily, then she would pay 20 percent of her 'take' in taxes. But if the tax were assessed monthly and she worked steadily at the same rate, then over, say, twenty days' work in the month she would earn 20 × 5 = 100 denarii, of which only one would be paid in tax for a 1 percent rate; the lower is much more probable, however, since taxation rates in other environments were usually in the 1–5 percent range. The pimp or even the owner of several brothels might be the person who actually paid the tax, rather than the whore herself. Streetwalkers were probably harassed unmercifully by officials seeking bribes or payment in kind, as were, we can imagine, women who might easily multitask in prostitution and some other technically tax-exempt profession – chambermaids, tavern workers, entertainers. The evidence gives us examples of the tax from far-flung areas of the empire; clearly this tax was widely collected. From Egypt there are even a few receipts, for example:

Pasemis, to Senpsenmonthes, daughter of Pasemis, greetings. I have received from you for the tax on prostitutes at Memnonia for the first year of Nero, the Emperor, four drachmas. Dated the fifthteenth day of the month of Pharmouthi.' (*O. Berl* Inv. 25474/Nelson)

A tax register, regular collection, a system for granting daily permits – this tax of prostitutes was collected assiduously and, it is reasonable to suppose, brought in quite a good income to the government.

This was, however, the only way the state intervened in prostitutes' lives unless there was wild disorder or actual injury done in the course of business. And, of course, prostitution could cause or accompany rowdiness. As such, the magistrate responsible for local public order – the *aediles* in Rome, for example – kept some watch on their activities. But since it was not illegal to ply their trade, only disruption of public order could bring down any action by officials.

Indeed, such was the lack of concern for the trade that there was no attempt to 'zone' for prostitution – no 'red-light' district. Venues for prostitution were scattered helter-skelter throughout a city or town. Naturally there would be more activity in some areas than in others – around the forum and temples for example, or, in Rome, in the infamous Subura section – but a whore could be found just about anywhere in a town. As to health considerations, there was absolutely no concern on the part of officialdom. Nor was there much of any practical repercussion to being a prostitute beyond taxation and the social stigma some might attach to the profession.

In the abstract, prostitution must have been very appealing to a person of marketable age and/or desperate condition. The income was potentially good, girls deemed likely prospects were lured with promises of clothing and other enticements, and they had no other skill or product that could bring nearly so much cash – certainly neither weaving nor wet-nursing, the other two primary cash occupations of women. But although some prostitutes operated independently, as is known because they paid the prostitution tax, the system was not geared to favor individual entrepreneurial prostitution. The pimp, a standard character in plays and stories featuring whores, was omnipresent. He (or she; certainly there were female pimps) organized, controlled (when he did not actually own), and exploited the prostitutes. He personally or as an agent for a wealthy investor collected a large portion of the income from a girl, certainly a third, very possibly more. If quarters or clothing or food were provided, this was all paid for at a premium from earnings. The woman was powerless to resist (literally in the case of a slave, de facto if a free person). Despite the prospect of income, it is easy to believe that a typical prostitute ended up with relatively little take-home pay and, of course, the whole low-life, earn-and-spend atmosphere of brothels and public houses and street-corner solicitation did not encourage foresightful savings plans. But we should not sell the prostitutes short. In the longer run, it seems that many prostitutes were freedwomen, so they must have not only earned enough to buy their freedom from slavery, but continued in the trade after gaining their freedom; a few might become madams and continue their profession indirectly. One Vibia Calybe began as a slave in prostitution and rose to manage her mistress's brothel as a freedwoman:

Vibia Chresta, freedwoman of Lucius, set up this monument to herself and her own, and to Gaius Rustius Thalassus, freedman of Gaius, her son, and to Vibia Calybe, her freedwoman and brothel manager. Chresta built the memorial entirely from her profits without defrauding anyone. This grave is not to be used by the heirs! (CIL 9.2029 = ILS 8287, Benevento, Italy)

And in a risqué poem in honor of the phallic god Priapus, another slave prostitute's success is recognized:

Telethusa, famous among the whores of the Subura district
Has gained her freedom, I think, from her profits.
She wraps a golden crown around your erection, holy Priapus,
For women like her hold that to be the image of the greatest god.
(Priapeia 40)

It is telling that Artemidorus notes that seeing a prostitute in a dream portends success:

Thus in dream symbolism the prostitutes have nothing at all in common with the brothel itself. For the former portend positive things; the latter the opposite. To see in a dream street whores plying their trade profits a man. The same goes for prostitutes waiting for business in a brothel, selling something and receiving goods and being on view and having sex. (*Dreams* 1.78, 4.9)

On the other hand, many must have died poor, miserable, and forgotten, a fate not unusual for many other ordinary people once their ability to earn even a small income disappeared through age or circumstances. Artemidorus has another interpretation which hints at this:

A woman eating her own flesh means she will become a whore, and thus be fed from her own body. (*Dreams* 3.23)

A slave skeleton was found at Bulla Regia in North Africa with a lead collar around her neck intended to make whoever came upon her outside of the town capture her and return her. It read: 'This is a cheating whore! Seize her because she escaped from Bulla Regia!' (*AE* 1996.1732, Hammam Derradji, Tunisia). It is impossible to imagine that her life was anything but horrible.

There was no shortage of prostitutes. Some were forced into prostitution, perhaps by a family on the edge of starvation, something that is illustrated by a document from Egypt. It tells of how a certain Diodemos, a town councilor of Alexandria, takes a liking to a prostitute and spends many evenings with her, but then murders her. He is arrested and eventually confesses.

And the mother of the prostitute, a certain Theodora, a poor old woman, asked that Diodemos should be compelled to provide for her a subsistence allowance as a small recompense [presumably, for the loss of her daughter's life]. For she said, 'It was for this reason that I gave my daughter to the brothel-keeper, so that I should be able to have sustenance. Since I have been deprived of my means of livelihood by the death of my daughter, I therefore ask that I be given the modest needs of a woman for my subsistence.' The prefect said [to Diodemos], 'You have murdered a woman who makes a shameful reproach of her fortune among men, in that she led an immoral life but in the end plied her trade ... Indeed, I have taken pity upon the wretch because when she was alive she was available to anyone who wanted her, just like a corpse. For the poverty of the mother's fortune so overwhelmingly oppressed her that she sold her daughter for a shameful price so that she incurred the notoriety of a prostitute.' (*BGU* 4.1024, col. VI/Rowlandson, no. 208)

Diodemos was found guilty, executed, and a tenth of his property turned over to the mother, 'who, because of the poverty which constricted her, dragged her own daughter away from the path of virtue, on account of which she has lost her ...' (It is worth noting in passing the sympathy the magistrate had for the mother and, posthumously, for the daughter forced into prostitution – so much so that he was willing to punish a fellow elite.) In literature, too, mothers turn their daughters to prostitution in order to bring money home; Lucian's *Dialogues of the Courtesans* features a number of such mothers.

Others ran away into the profession. Still others were raised in slavery, and many were enslaved for the work. A standard motif in the romances is a girl who is kidnapped by bandits or pirates and sold into slavery. In *The Golden Ass* Charite, a girl from a provincial elite family captured by bandits, faces such a prospect. The bandits have voted to kill her for trying to escape, when one comrade (actually Charite's lover in disguise) urges a different path:

But if you cruelly kill the girl, you will have done nothing more than vent your anger without gaining anything in return. Now what I think is this: We should take her to a nearby town and sell her. For such a sweet young thing will bring a pretty price, for sure, especially since I myself have pimps of long acquaintance there – one surely will be able to make a good offer for such a high-born lass. There, she must display herself in a brothel and won't be able to escape like she almost did just now. Seeing her service men in a whorehouse will be sweet revenge for you. (*The Golden Ass* 7.9)

Another standard theme in literature is raising foundlings for prostitution; other ancient evidence corroborates this source as well.

Prostitutes were, quite literally, everywhere. It has been estimated that perhaps one in every hundred people (men, women, children) in

Pompeii was a prostitute (based on an estimate of a hundred prostitutes in a population of 10,000). It would have been much higher for women in the prime ages of, say, sixteen to twenty-nine. Premodern comparative material points to something like 10 to 20 percent of 'eligible' women who worked at least intermittently as prostitutes. With an average of around ten customers a day, not a high figure using comparative data, this would mean 1000 tricks a day in Pompeii alone. Such figures might seem at first blush very high, but the combination of strong demand, a relatively low health risk (see below), and an absence of alternative ways for women to make money pushed many into prostitution. While the elite would have automatically considered any whore unsuitable for marriage, and certainly strongly disapproved of husbands overtly or indirectly allowing or coercing a wife to take up prostitution, not all ordinary people would necessarily have shared this view. A husband might well sexually abuse his wife, prostituting her:

> A man dreamed he had brought forward his very own wife in order to offer her as a sacrifice on an altar, sell the sliced up flesh, and gain a great profit for himself. He further dreamed that he rejoiced in his deed and attempted to conceal the profits because of those standing around watching him. Now this man brought his own wife into a shameful life of prostitution and earned his living from her work. The deed was most lucrative as a means of gain for him, but it was properly to remain hidden. (*Dreams* 5.2)

In addition, the presence of slavery and the good return prostitution brought on investment meant that the market was constantly supplied by slave owners as well. So the sex industry had a steady source of workers not only in the slave owners using their possessions to reap profits, but in pimps ready to employ free women in brothels, inns, or baths.

> A person is a pimp if he has slaves working as prostitutes; but he also is a pimp who provides free persons for the same purpose. He is subject to punishment as a procurer whether he makes this his main business or conducts it as an ancillary activity of another business, as for example if he were a tavern owner, or a stable master, and he

had that sort of slave working and taking advantage of their opportunity to make money, or if he were a bath manager, as happens in
certain provinces, having slaves to guard the clothes people leave
and who also offer sex in their workplace. (Ulpian, *On the Edict*, in
Digest 3.2.4.2–3)

Brothels were the most organized locales for prostitution. Combining what can be learned from the only certainly identified purpose-
built brothel known, the Lupanar in Pompeii, with literary references, a
picture can be drawn. There might be a reception area open to the street
except for a curtain; inside, prostitutes walked about gauzily dressed
or naked for inspection by prospective customers, or they might sit on
chairs or couches; each had a small room furnished with a bed, whether
wooden or brick. Women were advertised by what their expertise was,
and perhaps by what they charged for their services; this might be set
and posted either in the reception area or above the chamber door. There
was scant room for loitering in the individual cells; they seem to have
been for business only. Privacy seems not to have been a concern; there
is little evidence for a fabric barrier at the door of the individual rooms,
and none for a door. In other words, the brothel does not seem to have
been a place of socializing, entertainment, or the like, followed by sex. In
all likelihood the brothel was poorly lit and dirty – but then, that would
be the condition of most places where ordinary people congregated.

The *Satyricon* contains a vignette about such a brothel. Encolpius has
lost track of his lover, Ascyltos. Searching for him, he asks an old woman
selling vegetables on the street, 'Do you know where I live?' The clever
hag says she does, and takes him … to a brothel.

I noticed some men and naked women walking cautiously about
among placards of price. Too late, too late I realized that I had been
taken into a whorehouse … I began to run through the brothel to
another part, when just at the entrance Ascyltos met me … I hailed
him with a laugh, and asked him what he was doing in such an
unpleasant spot. He mopped himself with his hands and said, 'If
you only knew what has happened to me.' 'What is it?' I said. 'Well,'
he said, on the point of fainting, 'I was wandering all over the town
without finding where I had left my lodgings, when a respectable

person came up to me and very kindly offered to direct me. He took me round a number of dark turnings and brought me out here, and then began to offer me money and solicit me. A whore demanded a fiver for a cubby, and he was already pawing me. The worst would have happened if I had not been stronger than he.' (*Satyricon* 7)

So here two different people took the opportunity to direct strangers to a whorehouse, presumably for a tip from the house; the house had resident prostitutes, but also rented rooms 'by the hour' for customers who, like Ascyltos' masher, brought their own entertainment. It is interesting to note that once he realized it was a whorehouse, Encolpius covered his head – a traditional motion when one entered such a place.

Some prostitutes operated not in a brothel, but out of a dwelling. In Plautus' *Comedy of Asses* a higher-class whore has her own place. To it she can admit whom she pleases. There is a placard which she can hang out stating 'engaged.' She has erotic paintings up to excite her caller. She has entertainment facilities so she can throw a party, if she wishes to have more than one potential customer. Although such cannot have been the norm, it is useful to recall 'high-end' work. Opinion varies, but we may see an ordinary prostitute in real life working from a dwelling in the House of the Vettii at Pompeii. Here there is a back room off the kitchen decorated with explicit erotic art in a style reminiscent of the paintings in the known brothel, the Lupanar, in that city. At the entrance of the house is a graffito which states, 'Eutychis, a Greek lass with sweet ways, 2 asses' (*CIL* 4.4592).

Taverns and eateries were regular venues for whores – a room or two at the back or upstairs served the purpose. The distinction, universally shared, was that an innkeeper might be a reputable person, while a barmaid was nothing but a prostitute serving food and drink. Literature regularly assimilates barmaids to whores, and Roman legal texts concur:

> We say that it is not only the woman who openly sells herself in a brothel who earns a living (from her body); so, too, if (as is usual) she does not spare her modesty in an inn or tavern, or other such place. And moreover we understand that 'openly' means that such a woman takes on men randomly, without discrimination, and so

28. A prostitute serves an individual. A woman in a pose typical of Venus and meant to show off her figure entertains a customer while a servant looks on, ready to assist as needed.

supports herself as a prostitute, unlike a woman who commits adultery or fornication, or even a woman who has sex with one or two men for money, who do not seem to make money openly with their bodies. Octavenus nevertheless most correctly states that even the woman who gives herself openly for free ought to be counted among the prostitutes ... We moreover call the women 'madams' who offer women for hire, even if they carry on this commerce under another name. If anyone running a tavern has women for hire (and many are accustomed to have female prostitutes under the guise of having tavern maids), then she also is properly called a 'madam.' (Ulpian, *On the Edict*, in *Digest* 23.2.43. pr. 1–3 and 7–9)

And so, as in every age, bar girls attracted men:

Successus the weaver loves the bar girl named Heredis – who

certainly doesn't give a damn for HIM. But a rival scribbles on a wall that she should have pity on him. Come on! You're just spiteful because she broke off with you. Don't think you can better a more handsome guy – an ugly guy can't best a pretty one. (*CIL* 4.8259)

But another graffito from Pompeii perhaps illustrates that the difference between innkeeper and maid was not honored: 'I fucked the innkeeper' appears on a wall (*CIL* 4.8442, *Futui coponam*). There were, however, presumably some establishments that were not disreputable. The bar owner Haynchis, for example, runs a beer shop with the active assistance of his daughter, whom it would be nice to think maintained her honor while doing so (Rowlandson, no. 209).

There is a marvelous description of paid sex in a public house in the Christian story of 'St. Mary the Whore.' Although brought up carefully, Mary was seduced by a treacherous monk. In shame, she fled her hometown and became a prostitute in a bar. Her uncle, a very holy man named Abraham, looked for her and after two years finally found her. He disguised himself and went to the town.

So then, arrived at the town, he stepped aside into the tavern and with anxious eyes he sat looking around him, glancing this way and that in hopes of seeing her. The hours went by, and still no chance of seeing her appeared; finally he spoke jestingly to the innkeeper. 'They tell me, friend,' he said, 'that you have here a very fine girl; if it is agreeable to you, I would like very much to have a look at her.' The innkeeper … replied that it was indeed just as he had heard – she was an extremely pretty girl. And indeed Mary had a beautiful body, almost more than nature had any need of. Abraham asked her name, and was told that it was Mary. Then Abraham merrily said, 'Come now, bring her in and show her to me and let me have a fine supper for her this day, for I have heard the praises of her on all hands.' So they called her. And when she came in and the good old man saw her in her whore's garb, his whole body practically dissolved in grief. But he hid the bitterness of his soul … and so they sat and drank their wine. The old man began to jest with her. The girl rose and put her arms around his neck, beguiling him with kisses. … The old man spoke to her genially. 'Now, now!' he said. 'Here am I come to make merry ...' So then the old man produced a gold piece he had brought with him and gave it to the innkeeper. 'Now, friend,' he said, 'make us a good supper, so that I can make merry with the girl; for I have come a long journey for love of her.' When they had feasted, the girl began to urge him to come to her room to have sex with her. 'Let us go,' he said. Coming in, he saw a lofty bed prepared, and straightaway sat down gaily upon it ... So then the girl said to him, as he sat on the bed, 'Come, sir, let me slip off your shoes.' 'Lock the door carefully,' he said, 'and then take them off.' ... 'Come close to me, Mary,' said the old man. And when she was beside him on the bed he took her firmly by the hand as if to kiss her, then taking the hat from his head and his voice breaking into weeping, 'Mary, my daughter,' he said, 'don't you know me?' ... Laying her head at his feet, she wept all night ... When dawn had come, Abraham said to her, 'Rise up, daughter, and let us go home.' And answering him, she said, 'I have a little gold here, and some clothes, what would you have me do with them?' And Abraham answered, 'Leave all those things here ...' (Ephraem, Deacon of Edessa/Waddell)

Of course, Mary is released from her life of sin, but her experience gives us the best picture we have of the tavern as a venue for sex.

Public baths were also a favorite haunt of whores, as this remark by the historian Ammianus Marcellinus makes clear:

If they [the bathers] suddenly learn that a previously unknown prostitute has appeared, or some whore of the common herd, or an old harlot whose body is up for cheap, they rush forward jostling, pawing the newcomer, and praising her with outrageously exaggerated flattery like Egyptians laid on their Cleopatra ... (*History* 28.4.9)

The nudity – and all the more if men and women bathed together, as could occur – provided, like drink in a tavern, a stimulant propelling clients toward willing sexual partners; food and various other services were also available, such as massages. Just as a masseuse could easily move on to provide sexual services, bath staff easily could and did combine routine tasks, such as watching over customers' clothing while they bathed, with access to sex should a customer desire it. Indeed at the Suburban Baths in Pompeii, the most fully excavated example, there are explicit paintings illustrating progressively more audacious (or humorous) sexual participants and positions located above the shelf where clothes were deposited preparatory to bathing. There were also rooms for prostitutes above the bath, and even a separate entrance from the street in case customers just wanted sex, without bothering about the bath. A graffito on the wall outside states:

> Whoever sits here, read this above all: if you want to fuck, look for Attis – you can have her for a denarius. (*CIL* 4.1751)

All of these places – brothels, dwellings, taverns, baths – catered to ordinary people, along with the occasional elite who was slumming. Often a lit lamp in a niche signaled prostitution within, although lamps adorned other business facades as well. Such establishments were scattered throughout the city, as was housing and population in general, and in addition prostitutes could go out to serve at dinner parties or local festivals.

Besides work in specific places, whores also worked the streets. The emperor Domitian proclaimed prostitutes could not use litters; one might guess that this was to prevent mobile servicing of clients as much as to deny a mark of the elite to whores and the protection of enclosed curtains against the lewd remarks of fellow citizens. But even without enclosed litters, there were plenty of opportunities. T. Quinctilius Atta, a Roman author of the first century BC from whom we have only a single literary fragment, described audacious prostitutes in his *Aquae Calidae*: 'they whored through the streets like wolves looking for their prey.' They could hang out in any quarter, but their choice of station was related to the traffic that could be expected, and sometimes produced a nickname for whores. Festus 7L states:

> *Alicaria* is a word for prostitutes in Campania because they were accustomed to make their money hanging around the mills grinding grain (*alica*), just as those who took up position in front of stables were called 'fore-stablers' (*prostibula*).

They might work public areas that had more or less hidden spaces for discreet sex. Markets and areas with public buildings had lots of potential customers; in a pinch, tombs outside the city could be and were used for business. The arches (*fornices*) of large public buildings such as theaters and amphitheaters – arches that give the word 'fornication' – were popular spots. As at the baths, the arousing activity of the places – in the case of the theater, often salacious performances; in the case of the arena, the excitement and blood lust of gladiatorial contests – provoked sexual arousal that local prostitutes could take advantage of. Somewhat more private than the local archway but very much in its spirit was the one-room cubby opening onto the street with a masonry bed either used by a whore on duty there, or rented cheaply to bring a client to.

The theater was related to prostitution both directly and indirectly. The area around a theater teemed with people before and after a performance; this provided opportunities for prostitutes. But more than that, some productions in the theater were as provocative as any wall paintings in a brothel. These were the mimes, a favorite with the people. They were performed by actors assumed to be of low character and, unlike in other theatrical art forms, women were allowed. Even if those actors themselves were not immediately involved in prostitution, their characters' actions encouraged sexual fantasies. While a performance of a Greek tragedy or a Roman historical drama would not incite such, this more popular form of stage production did. Mime performers used a combination of gestures and acrobatics – rather like risqué ballet – as well as some singing and verbal play to tell rude stories of everyday life or mythology. At the Tavern on the Street of Mercury in Pompeii a series of highly erotic scenes from mimicry were painted on the wall – clearly these appealed to the imbibers' enchantment with these theatrical displays. It is not surprising that these mimers not only stimulated demand for prostitutes, but multitasked in that profession as well.

The Floralia in Rome was a lewd festival of spring; named for a whore of yore, it could hardly have been otherwise. A parade of prostitutes and performance of mimes were central to the celebration. Tertullian describes it with disgust:

> The very prostitutes, sacrifices on the altar of public lust, are brought out on stage, quite unhappy in the presence of other women – the only people in the community from whom they keep out of sight;

they are paraded before the faces of every rank and age; their abode is proclaimed, their price, their specialties, even before those who do not need to be told; and yet more is shouted out, what ought to lie hid in the shadows and in their dark caves – but I'll keep silent about that. Let the senate blush, let everyone be ashamed! These women themselves, assassins of their very own decency, blush this once a year, fearful of having their deeds brought to the light before all the people. (*On Spectacles* 17.3–4)

On stage, mimic adventures acted by whores were set to the lives of ordinary people – tailors, fishermen, weavers – in compromising situations, as adultery was a favorite theme. These theatrical displays, as was normal with mimes, featured the usual obscene dialogue, singing, dancing, gestures, and suggestive movements of bawdy comedy. The final act often featured complete nudity on stage as the actors complied with the audience shouting 'Take it all off.' A Christian author, aghast, describes the goings-on:

Those games are celebrated with all moral restraint thrown to the winds, as is suitable to the memory of a whore. For besides the out-of-control, filthy language and the outpouring of every kind of obscenity, harlots are even stripped of their garments at the rhythmic demand of the people, and then they play the part of mimes, and are kept on stage before the appreciative audience until even shameless eyes are sated with their shameful gestures. (Lactantius, *Divine Institutes* 1.20.10)

The appearance of both mimes and whores at the Floralia emphasizes their popularity among ordinary people as well as their similarity as part of the sex industry: mimes, like prostitutes, performed on street corners, in performance-specific spaces, like brothels, and for private parties. Their openly raunchy moves and sex-soaked themes must have approximated strip shows in many instances. And like strip shows, the segue to prostitution was a brief one.

Temples as well as theaters were popular hangouts for prostitutes. In Plautus' *Curculio* the whorehouse visited is next to the Temple of Aesculapius; in front of the house is an altar to Venus. And in Plautus there is a description of the prostitutes congregating at the Temple of Venus:

> The altar area is mobbed right now. Surely you don't want to hang around there among those whores on display, playthings of millers, and the rest of the harlots – miserable, dirt-smeared, filthy little slavelings, stinking of the whorehouse and their profession, of the chair and bare bench they sit on to solicit, creatures no free man ever touched, not to mention married, five-dollar sluts of the vilest little slaves. (*Little Carthaginian* 265–70)

There is a tantalizing detail of this activity from real life. South of Rome at the eightieth milestone along the Via Latina, at an ancient sanctuary of Venus, four women set up a cookshop:

> Flacceia Lais, freedwoman of Aulus; Orbia Lais, freedwoman of Orbia; Cominia Philocaris, freedwoman of Marcus; and Venturia Thais, freedwoman of Quintus, built a kitchen at the shrine of Venus in a leased space. (*AE* 1980.2016)

Now these women, all freed slaves, have names that are typical of prostitutes. Thais and Lais are both names of famous high-class Greek prostitutes; they would be grand names for Roman harlots. Indeed, it was common for a whore to take an appropriate name. A good example is a prostitute who became a Christian saint of the fifth century AD:

> My father and mother gave me the name Pelagia at birth but the citizens of Antioch call me Margarita ('Pearl') because of the abundance of pearls they've given me as my sins' reward. (Jacobus, *Vita* 7)

Thus when Pelagia became a whore she took the name Margarita ('Pearl'). Furthermore, the association of prostitutes and taverns/cookshops combined with the use of temple locations as spots for solicitation makes it almost irresistible to speculate that this roadside restaurant next to a temple of Venus also served sex. However these four women came to be freed – perhaps through saving their money and purchasing freedom – they had enough capital to set out on their own.

As they went about their business in these various places, prostitutes were supposedly compelled to wear 'official garb' – the toga. Or so scholars have deduced from remarks by elite authors Horace (*Satires* 1.2.63, 82) and Sulpicia ([Tibullus] *Elegies* 3.16.3–4), and from references better suited to a requirement, clearly quickly dropped, to have women convicted of adultery wear the toga. And while it is clear that prostitutes were not to wear the sartorial badge of respectable womanhood, the stola, it is just as clear from other references that their normal garb was hardly the toga. In fact, ancient sources in general do not describe a working whore dressed in this way – not Plautus, not Apuleius, not Petronius. And in addition, there is not a single illustration, erotic or otherwise, in sculpture, reliefs, wall painting, or graffiti that can be identified as a prostitute in a toga. It is hard to say if this supposed dress code was ever widely implemented, or whether it was mostly a confusion with the pallia, a cloak worn by women, including whores. Elaborated descriptions of prostitutes that do appear in literature are rather more the expected: women tarted up in fine, colorful, diaphanous clothing, wearing rouge and other makeup – or parading about in a brothel dressed either in skimpy clothing or none at all. The moral advice in a letter from Egypt is typical in that it urges a wife to be the opposite of a prostitute, shunning 'garments woven with purple and gold threads,' dressing modestly so as to 'look shapely to her own husband, but not to her neighbor,' and not using rouge and white lead as face makeup (Rowlandson, no. 260). In erotic paintings women are shown either as naked (sometimes with a breast band), or clothed (in various stages of dishabille) in normal female garb; unfortunately it is impossible to tell which might be lusty wives and concubines, and which out-and-out whores. But a painting from the Tavern of Salvius at Pompeii can reasonably be seen as showing a prostitute and her prospective client. Here the woman is dressed in a long gown of colorful orange-yellow material, with fancy slippers. She is kissing a man and he says, 'I don't want to [screw] with Myrtalis'; presumably the joke is that he rejects Myrtalis in favor of the lovely woman he is with presently. There is also a hint of the dress distinction here, since in the next frame of the painting a barmaid appears wearing the same long gown as the whore, but in plain white, and she has normal footwear. In short, prostitutes advertised their wares; selling sex meant selling something alluring. Their clothing created that allurement – and Roman officials had little interest and no effect in dictating what they should wear, much less requiring that that be a toga.

One of the primary reasons to use a prostitute was that the sexual services offered were more exciting, adventurous, and varied than what was expected of a wife or even of a discreet lover. An example of this proficiency in described in Achilles Tatius' novel, *Leucippe and Clitophon*. Clitophon, stating that his experience 'has been restricted to commercial transactions with women of the street,' graphically describes that experience:

> When the sensations named for Aphrodite are mounting to their peak, a woman goes frantic with pleasure; she kisses with mouth wide open and thrashes about like a mad woman. Tongues all the while overlap and caress, their touch like passionate kisses within kisses … When a woman reaches the very goal of Aphrodite's actions, she instinctively gasps with that burning delight, and her gasp rises quickly to the lips with the love breath, and there it meets a lost kiss … (*Leucippe and Clitophon* 2.37 / Winkler)

Along these lines, I can also point to the prospective contractor of the services of the courtesan in Plautus' *Comedy of Asses* (788): when the lamp is extinguished, she is, he insists, to be 'lively.'

Erotic art from Pompeii offers graphic examples of what a prostitute had to offer. In particular, sex acts that were seen in the general culture as polluting were on display. Fellatio and cunnilingus – there are also decorated lamps combining the two into the '69' position – both involved the mouth and were considered unclean and degrading in the extreme to judge by numerous insulting remarks abounding in elite literature and in graffiti. Another sex act displayed is intercourse from the rear-entry position. But exactly for the reason that these enticing acts were forbidden to 'nice girls,' they were probably available for sale to willing buyers. A word of caution is needed, however. Scenes in paintings and on lamps that depict 'unnatural acts' (as Artemidorus would put it), i.e. oral sex, are in fact rare. And many such erotic scenes may be intended at least as much to display the female body as to catalog possible sex acts with prostitutes.

Sex acts more acceptable to women in general, such as intercourse in the 'riding' position, with the woman on top, still proved popular when provided by professionals, to judge from the paintings. Whatever else the Roman viewer, male or female, may have seen in these illustrations, their basic eroticism is unmistakable. Among all the themes possible, surely the choice of erotic scenes in a dressing room of a bath that appears to have rooms available for sex in the story above is no accident. A viewer might chuckle at the acrobatics of some of the figures illustrated, but his or her last thought is likely to have been erotic, of the possibilities existent upstairs, as surely it was intended to be.

As I have emphasized before, prostitutes were available to anyone who could and would pay; there was little shame in using their services. As Artemidorus states, 'But having sex with a woman working as a whore in a brothel signifies only minor disgrace and very little expense' (*Dreams* 1.78). Plautus has a character proclaim that there is no stigma, much less a negative legal repercussion, in using a whore – contrary to the social and legal risks of adultery. As a character readies to enter a brothel:

> No one says 'no,' or stops you buying what is openly for sale, if you have the money. No one prohibits anyone from going along the public road. Make love to whomever you want – just be sure you don't wander off it onto private tracks – I mean, stay away from married women, widows, virgins, young men, and boys of good family. (*The Weevil* 32–7)

Prostitutes charged a wide variety of prices for the same sex act, or for specific requests. A common price was around a quarter of a denarius, or somewhat less than a full day's low pay for a workman. The evidence comes from graffiti at Pompeii. So, 'Optata, household slave, yours for 2 asses' (*CIL* 4.5105) and 'I'm yours for 2 asses' (*CIL* 4.5372). Few charged less, and a common insult was to refer to the very small coin, the *quadrans*, a quarter of an ass, and call someone a *quadrantaria* – a 'five-cent whore.' Some prostitutes thought they were worth a lot more, however, as Attis, mentioned earlier, who is 'yours for a denarius,' or Drauca, immortalized in a scribble on the wall of the Pompeiian brothel: 'On this spot Harpocras spent a denarius for a good fuck with Drauca'

(*CIL* 4.2193). The prices are given in the 'ass,' a tenth of a denarius – what is interesting is that even in multiples of the ass that form a larger coin available for use, such as the sesterces (= 2½ asses) or the denarius (= 10 asses), prices are almost always quoted in asses. This is because the small coin was the common money on the street – two asses would buy one's daily bread or a cup of decent wine, or a chunk of cheese. Ordinary people carried their money in this coin, its multiple the sesterces, and its dividers (a half ass, a quarter ass), and spent it that way. So whores naturally priced their services in this coin. If a person wanted to splurge, it looks like eight asses (i.e. close to a full day's good wage) would purchase food, a room, and sex in a public house. Naturally, cash up front was required.

About two to three asses per day was enough to scrape by on during most of the empire. A person paid by the day for work could expect between five and ten asses; however, regular daily work for anyone besides a soldier, who got perhaps two to three asses per day as spending money in addition to salary sequestered for required deductions (food, shelter, equipment, savings), was very unlikely. Thus a prostitute who could work regularly and bring in even the low price of two asses a trick could earn twenty or more asses per day. This is far more than a woman could earn in any other wage-earning occupation, and twice what a well-paid male worker could expect.

I would emphasize, though, that most prostitutes would have worked through a pimp, who would have taken much of a free prostitute's income. A slave prostitute would turn over most if not all of her gain to her master. To get an idea of how that worked, look at the anger Paul aroused in the owners of a slave girl:

> Once when we were going to the place of prayer, we were met by a slave girl who had a spirit by which she predicted the future. She earned a great deal of money for her owners by fortune-telling. This girl followed Paul and the rest of us, shouting, 'These men are servants of the Most High God, who are telling you the way to be saved.' She kept this up for many days. Finally Paul became so troubled that he turned around and said to the spirit, 'In the name of Jesus Christ I command you to come out of her!' At that moment the spirit left her. When the owners of the slave girl realized that their hope of making

money was gone, they seized Paul and Silas and dragged them into the marketplace to face the authorities. (*Acts* 16:16–19)

Just so, the owner of a slave girl in prostitution regarded her as a profit-maker, sent out into a brothel or onto the street to bring back money at the end of the day. A document from Egypt notes, 'Drimylos bought a slave-girl for 300 drachmas. And each day they went out onto the streets and made a splendid profit' (Rowlandson, no. 207). And a literary epigram captures fictionally the grave inscription of a pimp who specialized in evening companions at banquets:

> Psyllus, who used to take to the pleasant banquets of the young men the venal ladies that they desired, that hunter of weak girls, who earned a disgraceful wage by dealing in human flesh, lies here. But cast not thou stones at his tomb, wayfarer, nor bid another do so. He is dead and buried. Spare him, not because he was content to gain his living so, but because as keeper of common women he dissuaded young men from adultery. (*The Greek Anthology*, *Epigrams*, 7.403/Paton)

Women on the streets meant that passing men felt free to make lewd remarks and advances – and they did. A married woman from a prosperous family would wear appropriately modest clothing, advertising her condition, when she went out. A girl from such a family was always dressed to display her status and was accompanied by a female slave or older woman charged with keeping prying eyes and remarks at bay. But ordinary girls and young women had to go about whatever business took them onto the street without such a constraint – after all, their presence there was not for show, or to take a stroll, but for some specific task, and their resources did not allow the luxury of delicate clothing or a private guard. The very fact that ordinary prostitutes were unprotected pronounced them reasonable prey in the eyes of men, whether for direct approach, or just as the butt of remarks. In sum, any girl or woman dressed commonly, as slaves, too, dressed, was fair game. And all the more if the woman was dressed to draw attention to herself, as a whore might well do. Ulpian in the *Digest* is eloquent:

If anyone proposition a young girl, and all the more if she is dressed like a household slave, there isn't much harm done. And even less, if she is dressed like a prostitute, not in the garb of a respectable matron. (*Digest* 47.10.15.15)

We therefore know that an insult from a male, or an unwelcome advance, received scant protection from authorities. Prostitutes had to look out for themselves.

This might not be easy if ruffians decided to set upon you. When C. Plancius, a friend of Cicero's, was a young man he was involved in the gang rape of a female mime:

They say you and a bunch of young men raped a mime in the town of Atina – but such an act is an old right when it comes to actors, especially out in the sticks. (*In Defense of Plancius* 30)

Surely prostitutes fared no better if hoodlums or dissipated boys or men attacked.

As I have noted, once in prostitution, most prostitutes were managed by a pimp. The opportunities for exploitation and physical abuse were rampant, and a whore had little or no recourse; she was in many respects like a slave, even if freeborn. This condition must often have meant a mean, abusive, depressing life from which there was, in practice, no escape. Social abuse was added to physical. Although disgrace is exaggerated as a 'scarlet letter' worn by prostitutes, there certainly was some stigma attached to selling sex. A graffito from Pompeii reads:

The lass to whom I wrote and who accepted my message at once is my girl by right – but if she responded with a price, she is not MY girl, but everyone's. (*CIL* 4.1860)

I have already noted that prostitutes were *probrosae*, meaning they, according to Augustan marriage laws, could not marry freeborn Roman citizens. They also suffered from *infamia* – they could not write a will or receive full inheritance. But on the one hand, prostitution was not an irredeemable condition; one could quit the profession, marry, and live happily ever after. On the other hand, the moral stigma was not so great that it prevented many women from staying in the business. When faced with a number of bad choices, it is no wonder that 'disgrace' alone did not keep women from turning to prostitution.

And practical concerns were certainly higher in the prostitute's mind than supposed shame. For example, getting pregnant was very inconvenient. As Myrtium says in Lucian's *Dialogue of the Courtesans*, 'All the good I've had from your love is that you've given me such an enormous belly, and I'll soon have to bring up a child, and that's a terrible nuisance for a woman of my kind' (282/Harmon). Insofar as preventing pregnancy was concerned, a favorite method was magical spells, for example this instruction for a charm to prevent conception: 'Take a pierced bean and attach it as an amulet after tying it up in a piece of mule hide' (*PGM* 63.26–8/Betz). The rhythm method was also tried. Doctors *thought* they understood female ovulation, but in fact had it all wrong – the periods recommended as safe for intercourse were in fact a woman's most fertile times. Pessaries and ointments were more practical; these were thought to 'close' the uterus and so prevent conception. Oil was a favorite component of these, whether olive or some other, mixed with ingredients such as honey, lead, or frankincense; they were probably ineffective. Potions were recommended as well, such as a combination of willow, iron rust, and iron slag, all ground finely and mixed with water, or mixing male or female fern root in sweet wine and drinking it. And there is archaeological as well as textual evidence for the use of sponges and other intercepting materials by women for contraception with common vinegar as an active sperm-fighter (which it is); these were used extensively. Of course, the desired outcome – conception prevention – may often have occurred coincidentally after resorting to one of the many methods touted by folk and professional medicine, thus encouraging prostitutes to resort to such methods, but in fact contraception must have been a very hit-and-miss affair.

During pregnancy, abortion was an option. As a medical procedure it was rare, and recommended against by medical writers as being extremely dangerous. However, there were various potions that were guaranteed to produce an abortion. These were taken orally or as a vaginal suppository; in both instances, misunderstood physiology rendered the techniques of dubious value, although some oral concoctions may have actually worked. Once a child was born it could be disposed of by infanticide or abandonment.

In modern times, prostitution carries with it very real dangers of sexually transmitted diseases to the health of both prostitute and customer. The Romano-Grecian prostitute had a bit less to worry about in this regard. Of course, the most deadly STD of all, HIV-AIDS, did not exist in antiquity. And syphilis was unknown. Although there has been a lively discussion among medical historians over the years, some claiming syphilis as a New World disease brought to America as part of the 'Columbian exchange,' some claiming Old World evidence from antiquity, still others claiming both origins concomitantly, bone analysis done on ancient skeletons has proven conclusively that there was no syphilis in Western antiquity. Whatever symptoms some have attributed to that disease can be explained by other diseases that present in similar ways. So a whore did not have to worry about this particular scourge of brothel life. Gonorrhea, the second-most-feared sexually transmitted disease, may have existed in the Roman world, but as it does not leave a mark on bones, osteology cannot help us here, and the references by medical writers are inconclusive. However, it is certain from these authors that two less-serious (but nonetheless painful and damaging) venereal diseases did exist, namely genital herpes (chlamydia) and genital warts (condylomas); oddly, however, no medical writers actually connect these or any other infections directly with sexual intercourse. As irritating as the latter diseases might be, a prostitute could reasonably expect to practice her trade free of life-threatening sexually transmitted disease. In this small way, at least, ancient life was safer than modern.

We must imagine prostitution as widespread among ordinary people in the Romano-Grecian world – a possibility for children, women, and some few men, and a normalized sexual outlet for males. Women through choice, necessity, or compulsion, both free and slave, worked in this oldest profession. Walking down the street of any town, you would have seen the whores standing around the forum, beckoning you from a doorway, or soliciting you leaving the theater. They were a familiar and popular aspect of the lives of ordinary folk. But being a prostitute was often dangerous, and exploitation was widespread. There was some disgrace, although none comparable to the vilification they receive in the elite literature. In good circumstances, prostitutes could lead a reasonable life, perhaps even a bit better than average among ordinary folk. In bad conditions, the vicious exploitation would have led to abuse and an early death.

FAME AND DEATH: GLADIATORS

OF ALL ORDINARY ROMANS, gladiators probably have the highest profile in the modern imagination. Their representation in ancient settings, as well as in later mythical, metaphorical and artistic incarnations, intrigues and excites. But like other ordinary folk, the men (and a few women) who became gladiators lived real lives. Those lives, focused on the arena as a venue for one of the most popular entertainments in the Romano-Grecian world, were hardly typical. But balanced between glory and the finality of death, they made their way.

The arena was, as its name implies, a sandy surface. It could be in a gigantic edifice like the Colosseum at Rome, or in one of the very many more modest amphitheaters scattered around the empire, or in a converted theater, or even in a town plaza blocked off temporarily for a local event. Gladiators were trained entertainers who fought with swords and other weapons in pairs (except in very rare cases) in the arena for the entertainment of a crowd. But before discussing these gladiators in detail, it is important to identify carefully the demographics of the arena. In particular, it is important to separate the arena as an execution venue from the arena as a contest venue. Romano-Greeks firmly believed in the necessity and efficacy of painful, brutal death for those ordinary people condemned for serious antisocial behavior such as murder. Thus crucifixion, burning alive, and condemnation to be torn to pieces by wild beasts or killed by fellow prisoners featured strongly in their capital-punishment universe. In these cases the combination of spectacle meant to deter others and the reestablishment of social order by brutalizing those who had brutalized that order appealed very strongly to their sense of justice and order. Executions in the arena typically took place at the 'noon break' between wild-beast hunts in the morning and gladiators in the afternoon; they were advertised as part of a normal event, as this painted notice from Pompeii demonstrates:

> Twenty pairings of gladiators and their back-ups will fight at Cumae on October 5th and 6th. There will also be crucifixions and a wild-beast hunt. (*CIL* 4.9983a)

They involved a completely different group of people – condemned criminals – and they were not in any way a 'contest' or a 'sport,' as the other two events could at least be presented as being. Criminals were sometimes executed outright, as when beasts were set upon tied-up victims, sometimes as faux gladiators or wild-beast hunters, sent into the arena to fight each other or beasts without training and without protective armor. Also, on occasion a criminal might be condemned to a gladiatorial school, in which case, after training, he would perform in the afternoon, with the same chance of survival as any other gladiator. If he lived through three years of fighting and two more of service in the school, he was freed. But in discussing gladiators it is important to remove criminals from our imaginations; their circumstances, prospects, and fates were altogether different.

In fact, gladiators were drawn from two groups: slaves and free volunteers. A slave, as the possession of another, had no choice about becoming a gladiator. There were two motivations for the slave owner: retribution and gain. The owner might wish to get rid of a misbehaving slave, and sell him to a gladiatorial agent. He also might wish to take advantage of the special physical condition and abilities of a slave, and sell him to be trained for the arena. Volunteers, on the other hand, freely contracted themselves to become gladiators. A Pompeiian graffito gives an example:

> Severus, a freeborn man, has fought 13 times. 'Lefty' Albanus, also freeborn, fought 19 times – and beat Severus! (*CIL* 4.8056)

Putting oneself under contract – *auctoratus* was the Latin term – was a legal transaction in which the volunteer received a signing bonus and the prospect of prize money if successful, and in return agreed to be trained and to fight. Quite specifically, he swore he would give up his rights to protection under the law, promising to allow himself to 'be burned, chained, beaten, or killed' in his contracted position. This is not, however, reduction to slavery. The closest (although still imperfect) equivalent is joining the army, where enlistment is also for a specified time, legal rights are given up, and an oath is taken which includes a promise to die for the emperor. Petronius replicates the gladiatorial enlistment oath in his novel. In order to trick the sympathy of possible patrons, the anti-hero Eumolpus offers a plan:

'Make me your master, if my idea pleases,' Eumolpus said. No one dared criticize the suggested artifice. And so, in order that the false-hood remain safe among us all, we took an oath to obey Eumolpus. We swore 'to be burned, bound, beaten, and slain by the sword' – as well as whatever else Eumolpus might order. Just like *real* gladiators, we pledged ourselves body and soul to our new master. (*Satyricon* 117.5)

The gladiator volunteer's contract was for a specified time and although the contractee agreed to very severe terms, presumably he would be released if the contractor failed to live up to his side of the bargain, especially in the matter of the signing bonus and pay for appearances.

The relative proportion of slaves and volunteers in gladiatorial events is unknown. In the few and mutilated lists of gladiators that survive, there seems to be a preponderance of slaves, although both slave and free figure in all lists. Most epitaphs are of free or freed men, but these gravestones must represent only a small portion of all the gladiators who fought. Furthermore, it is more likely that free or freed fighters would have the resources and relationships necessary to have a monument set up. Free gladiators in general were thought to be better fighters than slave, because they had entered voluntarily into the profession. But that does not mean that they outnumbered slaves in the arena. In the end, the proportion is simply unknowable.

Some women became gladiators. A relief from Halicarnassus

(Turkey) shows two, 'Amazon' and 'Achillia,' fighting each other; it is now in the British Museum. The inscription states that they fought to an honorable draw, so presumably they fought again. Elite literature mentions a number of times the disgrace of noblewomen fighting in the arena, and of shows put on by emperors featuring women (and dwarfs). An inscription from Ostia boasts of fielding ordinary women:

> Hostilianus, Head Town Councilor, Treasurer, and Chief Priest of Ostia, put on the Youth Games by decree of the town council. He was the first from the very founding of the city to put on gladiatorial games featuring women. He did this together with his wife Sabina. (*CIL* 14.5381)

Such displays always remained a rarity, however. No woman gladiator memorializes herself in a gravestone inscription. Nothing is known about these entertainers or their lives.

There were many players in the creation, organization, management, and provision of gladiators. The *lanistae* were the most infamous. These men acquired, trained, and rented out gladiators. However, individuals and groups (priests, associations) also played a role in the industry, as did, on a very large scale, the imperial government. In all cases, the gladiators had to be housed, fed, prepared, treated if sick or injured, and leased out for fights. They represented a significant, ongoing investment, and an elaborate business.

A slave who was chosen by his master to be trained as a gladiator, of course, had no choice in the matter. But the volunteer certainly did. While the elite's rhetoric stigmatized free men who chose the gladiator's profession by claiming that they were degenerates, bankrupts, desperate men driven to desperate choices, the persistence of the rhetoric and even of official and legal attempts to discourage or even to prevent volunteers shows the strong pull of the arena for both men and the occasional woman as well. And, of course, the elite concern was only for those of their own class. If men and women from a cultural background of superiority found the arena nonetheless appealing even though emerging onto the sand brought the opprobrium of their peers, what must the pull have been for ordinary people who stood to win all the glory and gain, while leaving their previous life behind them entailed only a modest loss in

29. Female gladiators. Although quite uncommon, women did fight. Here two, Achillia and Amazon, fight to an honorable draw on a relief from Halicarnassus in Asia Minor.

rights, and a gain in prestige? The risk was great, that could not be denied. If the training regimen went well and a man escaped the normal life-threatening experiences of disease and accident, there was a one in ten chance of dying in the first bout, assuming he was pitted against another tiro. If a person survived, his chances in a second round were probably not any better. However, if he managed to fight through, his chances improved just as his prizes and glory did. And even if he were a slave forced into gladiatorial work, the same calculus was at work in motivating him. The basic premise was that a slave who served his master well at least had some chance of freedom; this would play out in the arena as well as in other aspects of a slave's life. In winning, a gladiator gained a purse which (allowing for all the potential risks of the *peculium*) he hoped could be accumulated to buy his freedom. The living conditions in gladiatorial slavery were better than field work, certainly, and perhaps equaled those of favored household slaves, for the investment in a slave gladiator was great. In the case of a volunteer there was no initial cost beyond the signing bonus, whereas with a slave the manager had to recoup not only the cost of training and maintenance, but that of acquisition. He had every reason to keep the slave gladiator not just alive but healthy and, ideally, committed to his role in the arena, for a willing slave gladiator was like a volunteer: much more likely to prevail, or at least put up a good fight and so enhance the manager's reputation and the prices he could command for future leases for future games. The promise of freedom was the best motivation – and the fact that freed slave gladiators continued as volunteer fighters shows that for some, at least, the career was not merely from compulsion but freely worth the risks.

It is not surprising that freeborn ordinary young men, presumably healthy and strong, volunteered for the gladiator's life. This career offered opportunities that no other did. By being a gladiator, a person succeeded in the recognition game that emphasized the importance of the ego-individual. The hierarchical Romano-Greek social structure meant that it was very difficult to jump the status queue either in wealth or social standing. As a gladiator, however, a young man possessed currency valued by all levels of society: excellence in courage, physical prowess and skill (especially at weapons), and perseverance. By showing himself to be 'manliness-positive' he could propel himself to heights of social adoration, for outstanding manliness (what Romans called *virtus*) trumped even money and birth and education when it came to gaining awe. From the elite standpoint, this fact explains at least some of the anxiety felt about gladiators – they gained a position of renown and recognition that could outshine the elites.' Not that the young man contemplating a gladiatorial career would care about such things. What he cared about was that he had not only a guarantee of being fed and housed, and of earning money on a regular basis, but the possibility of recognition, of becoming a star:

> Men train and exert themselves for the worldly contest and think it their honor's glorious day if they win through with the people looking on and the emperor himself present. (Cyprian, *Letter* 58.8)

Gladiators' epitaphs often stress their fixation on glory: 'I am famous among men fighting with arms'; 'I did not lack for fame among all men'

(Robert, nos. 69 and 260). They gloried in their strength, skill, daring, and victory over all rivals. They knew the appeal such glory had. It did not escape actual and potential fighters that, as Tertullian remarks (*On Spectacles* 22), 'men surrender their minds and spirit – and the women! – *they* give up their very bodies as well' to gladiators.

The feeling of self-importance, enhanced especially by the pomp and circumstance surrounding the pageantry of the fights in the arena, fed this very natural desire for fame. The day before a fight there was a parade of the men who were to perform. Their enthusiasm and good looks were enough to inspire others, as they did the friends Lucian features in his tale *Toxaris*:

> The next morning, while walking about the marketplace he saw a sort of procession of high-spirited, handsome young men. These had been enrolled to fight duels for hire and were to settle their combats on the next day but one. (*Toxaris* 59/Harmon)

The friend is inspired to try to earn money in this way, and signs up. While that was not a very likely scenario – gladiators were trained fighters, not picked up from the street – the inspiration of the men parading through the marketplace before a gladiatorial display certainly was. The day after this procession, the combatants reclined on couches – not the usual stools at table – and ate a ceremonial meal together, the *cena libera*, literally the 'unrestricted meal,' meaning they could eat anything they wanted, breaking from their usual training regimen. Indeed, the whole day was a release from rules and regulations, culminating in the feast. Not all gladiators were so blasé about the dangers that awaited them in a few hours that they simply enjoyed the excess of the day of liberation; rather, they took thought for their family and possessions:

> Why even among the gladiators I observe that those who are not utterly bestial, but Greeks, when about to enter the arena, though many costly viands are set before them, find greater pleasure at the moment in recommending their women to the care of their friends and setting free their slaves than in gratifying their belly. (Plutarch, *Customs*, 'A Pleasant Life Impossible' 1099B/Delacy and Einarson)

At the last feast, as part of the pageantry and advertising, the public was allowed in to watch and mingle. The last meal of (soon to be) St. Perpetua, before she was to be executed as a criminal (criminals also shared this *cena libera*), illustrates this:

> The day before the games it was customary to feast at a last meal, which they called the 'unrestricted dinner.' But Perpetua and Saturnus made this into a Christian Last Supper feast (*agape*), not a 'last meal.' And with the same steadfastness, they taunted the people standing around, threatening the judgment of God, bearing witness to the good fortune that was their suffering, ridiculing the curiosity of those pushing and shoving about them. And Saturnus said, 'Is tomorrow not enough for you? Why are you so eager to look on those you hate? Are we friends today, enemies on the morrow? Take a good look at our faces, so you can recognize us on that day!' Thunderstruck, all then departed – and not a few believed. (*Passion of Saints Perpetua and Felicity* 17)

The public could thus vicariously participate in the pageant by tossing comments to the gladiators and generally engaging in a personal way with the upcoming event. Presumably if autographs had been part of the culture, they would have had miniature swords or clay helmets signed as souvenirs.

And so the gladiator's career would generate passionate enthusiasm and recognition that he excelled in manliness among fellow men. Gladiators themselves reveled in this effect. Their epitaphs record such sentiments as 'great shouts roared through the audience when I was victor'; 'I was a favorite of the stadium throng' (Robert, nos. 55 and 124). One Pompeiian gladiator even took as an 'arena name' Celadus, which is derived from the Greek word for 'clamor.' Augustine has a vivid account of how the arena seized hold of a young man named Alypius:

> Not wishing to lay aside the worldly career set down for himself by his parents, he had gone ahead of me to Rome in order to study law. And there he was utterly swept away by an unbelievable passion for the gladiatorial games. For despite the fact that he was opposed to – even detested – such things, a fatal meeting with friends and

30. Souvenirs. Gladiator memorabilia was very popular. It ranged from vastly expensive engraved glass beakers to common lamps with battle scenes embossed. Here are two more laborate lamps in the shape of gladiators' helmets.

fellow students – he met them by chance returning from his midday meal – changed everything. With friendly urging they brought him, strongly objecting and resisting, into the amphitheater, seat of the savage and deadly games. He said to them, 'Although you drag my body into this place, do you think you'll be able to turn my spirit and eyes to that spectacle? I am here – but I'm *not* here. And so I'll get the best of both you *and* the games.' When they heard this, they hastened all the more to coerce him along with them, eager to find out if in any way he was able to do as he said. When they got there and had gotten settled into their seats, everything seethed with unimaginable raw emotion. Alypius, eyes tightly closed, forbade himself to get involved in such monstrous evil. Oh, if only he had closed his ears as well! For at a critical moment in the fight, when a huge clamor wildly pulsated from the whole crowd, overwhelmed by curiosity and thinking himself ready to condemn and control whatever might be happening, even gazing on it, he opened his eyes. That was it.

His spirit was stabbed with a more severe wound than the gladiator whom he longed to see received in his body, and he fell, more miserable than the fighter whose fall had brought the roaring crowd to its feet ... As soon as he saw the blood, he drank in at once the fierce cruelty of it all. He did *not* turn away, but rather stared, rooted to the spot, imbibing the madness, and didn't even realize what was happening. He took wicked delight in the contests; he was drunk with the gory excess. Now he was not the person who had entered the amphitheater; now he was one of the mob he had joined, a true fellow fan of those by whom he had been dragged in. He looked on; he shouted; he threw himself into it completely – and he left consumed by that insanity that would impel him to return again not only with those friends who had first brought him, but even without them, inducing others to come along. (*Confessions* 6.8)

The enthusiasm of the crowd could easily spill over into disorder. Elite literature is sprinkled with examples of the crowd shouting insulting things at the emperor from the protection (which sometimes proved illusionary) of the mob. Indeed, the assembling of ordinary people in such venues as the amphitheater or theater provided perhaps their best opportunities to confront their leaders. Beyond local ramifications, gladiatorial contests could become proxies for local competitions, jealousies, and rivalries. The most famous example of this is the rivalry of Nucerians and Pompeiians from two small cities in Campania, Italy. The historian Tacitus describes the riot this rivalry brought about in the course of gladiatorial games attended by spectators from both towns:

About this same time a terrible mayhem arose from a really inconsequential beginning. It all happened at gladiatorial games given by Livineius Regulus, a local Pompeiian bigwig recently expelled from the Roman senate. Locals from the neighboring towns of Nuceria and Pompeii were hurling insults at each other the way small-town rivals often do. Words became stones; then swords were drawn. The Pompeiians got the best of it – they were the home crowd, after all. As a result, many wounded Nucerians were carried up to Rome, and many wept over the death of a parent or child. The emperor referred the matter to the senate, the senate to the consuls. They, in turn, put the question again in the senate's lap. That body decreed a ten-year moratorium on gladiatorial events at Pompeii, and the clubs, which had been formed illegally, were disbanded. Livineius and the others who had fomented the riot were exiled. (*Annals* 14.17)

Quite amazingly, a fresco painting from Pompeii survives that illustrates this very riot. Some citizens fight inside the arena, while outside Nucerians and Pompeiians are attacking each other with clubs and fists. Elsewhere a graffito adds immediacy to the painting: 'Campanians, by this victory you've been destroyed with the Nucerians' (*CIL* 4.1293). Other graffiti express similar thoughts, probably unrelated to this specific event: 'Bad luck to the people of Nuceria!' (*CIL* 4.1329); 'Good luck to all the people of Puteoli, good luck to the people of Nuceria, and down with the people of Pompeii!' (*CIL* 4.2183). Passions clearly ran high, and not just regarding who was going to win a particular gladiatorial combat.

In addition to the adoration of the crowd, a gladiator was likely to gain access to unlimited sexual partners, for the adoration, not to say lust of women for gladiators – virtually naked, muscular, shining with *virtus*, notoriously available – was common knowledge. The graffiti of Pompeii reveal the pull of sexual conquest that went along with victory in the arena. The successful gladiator Celadus boasts in a couple of scribbles, 'Celadus, one of Octavius' Thracian gladiators, fought and won three times. The girls swoon over him!' (*CIL* 4.4342 = *ILS* 5142a) and 'Celadus the Thracian gladiator. Girls think he's magnificent!' (*CIL* 4.4345 = *ILS* 5142b).

But it would be a mistake to assume that every gladiator became a crowd favorite. For every man who won the heart of the crowd, there were many others who slogged along in the profession, trying to stay alive and not especially admired. Petronius in his *Satyricon* records a fictional critique of such fighters. After praising a future game that will feature free, not slave, gladiators, and ones who won't shy away from fighting, Echion adds:

After all, what has Norbanus [a wealthy Pompeiian] ever done for us? He put on a two-bit gladiatorial show, decrepit men who would have fallen down if you breathed hard on them. I've seen better *beast fighters* than those guys. He killed off some caricatures of mounted fighters – those castrated cocks, one a feckless spawn, yet another bandylegged, and in the third match a man as good as dead, already hacked up badly. There was, I'll admit, a *thrax* who had some gumption, but even he fought strictly by the rules. In short, their manager flogged each and every one after the matches – and the crowd hollered for him to beat them more! They were little better than runaway slaves! (*Satyricon* 46)

Not everyone became a star.

Beyond the arena, gladiators were the objects of popular culture. There were lamps and fancy glass jugs featuring gladiatorial motifs; Trimalchio had expensive cups illustrated with scenes from an apparently epic contest between two very famous gladiators, Petraites and Hermeros, and he planned to have further scenes from Petraites' victories carved on his tomb monument (*Satyricon* 52, 71); and children dressed up and played as gladiators. With all the hype and cultural popularity, it is small wonder that once in the service, a gladiator yearned to fight:

> But among the gladiators in the emperor's service there are some who complain that they are not put up against anyone or set in single combat, and they pray to God and approach their managers begging to go out to single combat in the arena. (Epictetus, *Discourses* 1.29.37)

It was in fighting that the gladiator gained and maintained his luscious fame.

But despite the draw, a gladiator also knew that he was betting everything. One speaks from a Cretan grave: 'The prize was not a palm branch; we fought for our life' (Robert, no. 66). And things did not always work out so well. A gravestone tells it all:

> I, who was brimful of confidence in the stadium, now you see me a corpse, wayfarer, a *retiarius* from Tarsus, a member of the second squad, Melanippos [by name]. No longer do I hear the sound of the beaten-bronze trumpet, nor do I rouse the din of flutes during one-sided contests. They say that Herakles completed 12 labors; but I,

having completed the same [number], met my end at the thirteenth. Thallos and Zoe made this for Melanippos as a memorial at their own expense. (Robert, no. 298/Horsley)

The scanty evidence from epigraphy indicates that perhaps 20 percent of participants were killed; if all fought in duels, then one in ten duels would end in a death, although other scholars have put the fatality rate at 5 percent, or one in twenty matches. On either calculus, fighting in more than ten duels would be pushing the odds severely. In all likelihood most gladiators were killed in their first or second fights (George Ville makes an arresting comparison to World War I aerial combat), while survivors went on to win many more. In exceptional cases every fight would end in a death, but this was an expensive result, and a games' sponsor who lost a lot of valuable property thought it worth boasting about:

Here at Minturnae [Italy] over a four-day period Publius Baebius Iustus, Town Mayor, in honor of his high office put up 11 fighting pairs of first-rate gladiators from Campania; a man was slain in each of the combats. (*CIL* 10.6012 = *ILS* 5062)

But once a gladiator hit his stride, his career could be long. There are inscriptions boasting of between fifty and a hundred-plus victories. One example of a gladiator with a long career can be found in the epitaph of Flamma (meaning 'Flame'), a *secutor*, i.e. a heavily armed man who normally fought against a *retiarius*, a man with sword and net:

Flamma the *secutor* lived thirty years and fought thirty-four times. He won outright twenty-one times; fought to a draw nine times; was honorably defeated four times. He was from Syria. Delicatus ['Delightful'] made this to his well-deserving fellow-at-arms. (*ILS* 5113, Palermo)

Flamma therefore fought for around thirteen years (about age seventeen to thirty), and so on average 2.5 times a year. This is more frequent than most. Of the fifteen gladiators whose records are known, most fought less than twice a year; perhaps a few gladiators fought more than three times a year – although for some, fighting was much more frequent, as a graffito recording a summer's games demonstrates:

> Florus won at Nuceria on July 28th. On August 15th he came out on top at Herculaneum. (*CIL* 4.4299, Pompeii)

Chances of survival might actually increase as the fighter progressed, not only because his skills were honed by experience, but because his owner/manager would protect his investment as the price per fight increased. Perhaps he would create matches against easier opponents, perhaps he would have the other gladiator 'throw' the match, perhaps he would manage a 'draw with honor' (*missio*) rather than a mortal defeat. But the evidence of gladiators who earned the official release from service, the wooden sword (*rudis*), offers an impression of relatively numerous victories: The three examples epigraphy gives of their victories detail numbers ranging from seven to eighteen. These men thus earned their release fairly quickly. With so little data to go on, I can only say that some successful gladiators had long careers, some short; it is impossible to know the reason why this would be so in individual cases, or even what an overall, generalized picture might actually be.

The life of a gladiator was significantly shorter than ordinary people's in other occupations, that is for certain: While a person who reached the age of twenty might expect to live to forty-five or so, on average, of the fifteen gladiators just noted, only two lived past age thirty, and while most seem to have died in the arena, not all did. This evaluation is confirmed by the gladiator graveyard discovered at Ephesus, Turkey, in 1997: Almost all the sixty-seven skeletons were males under thirty. To judge by the descriptions of the physical deformities of gladiators the physician/researcher Galen examined as a medical assistant to gladiators, and the traumas discovered on the Ephesus remains, those who lived suffered from serious injuries, which probably helps to explain why even those who survived fights did not live long lives.

The gladiator did not make his life worse in pursuing this career. The trade-off is clear: life at immediate risk in return for a life not otherwise accessible. But even the life risk has its positive side: By training and innate physical ability – 'athleticism' as it is called today – a man could have a greater degree of control over his fate than, say, as a day-laborer or even as a soldier. That control might be chimerical, but a strong young man, perhaps already predisposed to thinking himself indestructible in the way of youth, could be forgiven for believing in it, especially in the face of a world with so few options for propulsion into the stratosphere of public recognition and (at least relatively) good living conditions.

In spite of this reality, ancient elite sources and modern sources emphasize, one could almost say fixate on, the stigma – what the Romans called *infamia* – attached to becoming a gladiator *auctoratus*, voluntarily; the same dishonor, it is claimed, came to the voluntary beast fighter (*venator, bestiarius*). This fixation arises from the ancient elite's obsession with status and dignity and a modern willingness to accept this obsession as a guiding light in interpreting the lives of gladiators. It is true that this attitude existed among some of the ordinary people as well. For example, the dream interpreter Artemidorus interweaves this in a dream analysis:

> A man dreamed he was being carried aloft by some people in a bread-kneading trough filled with human blood, and he ate some that had congealed. Then his mother confronted him and said, 'My child, you dishonor me.' Then he further dreamed that the men carrying him set him down and he went to his home. Then in reality he enrolled as a gladiator and fought many years in fights to the finish. For to feast on human blood portended his would be the raw and unholy nourishment of human blood, and the words of his mother foretold the dishonor of his life. The bearing in a kneading trough portended the constant and unceasing danger he would be in, for everything put into such a trough must be consumed. His good luck in his fights might have run out, except that he laid down his profession and returned to his home. For after a long time, with some of his friends strenuously pressing him, he gave up being a gladiator. (*Dreams* 5.58)

Infamia was an inchoate concept at best, and certainly not a legal formula; nonetheless it was used as a catch-all to label many forms of behavior that seemed to undermine the basic social contract. For example, conviction in criminal court or, in many cases, civil court, led to *infamia*. Reprehensible actions such as bankruptcy, personally harming someone else (*iniuria*), and dishonorable discharge from the army produced the same result. Certain occupations did as well, specifically being a pimp or prostitute and, what is of interest here, being a 'gladiator pimp' (*lanista*) or an actual gladiator.

From elite literature one could be forgiven for thinking that the infamy of gladiators was a terrible thing to experience. Tertullian, carrying here both the animus of the elite and of the Christian, writes:

> The [elite] sponsors and managers of the spectacles bring out the charioteers, actors, athletes, and gladiators – men arousing the greatest passion to whom men give their souls and women their bodies as well. On account of such men the organizers commit themselves to the very things they criticize [in their salons] and the very skills they glorify; they then take as an excuse to denigrate and put down the men who exhibit them. Indeed, even more – these elites openly condemn them through social stigma and restricting their civil rights, keeping them from the senate, the public speakers' platform, the senatorial and equestrian orders, from all other positions and from certain other distinctions as well. What perversity! They adore whom they punish, they despise whom they approve, they praise the talent to the skies, but harshly criticize the talented. (*On Spectacles* 22)

Gladiators are sentenced 'to some rocky outcrop of infamy, with all vestiges of decent dignity stripped away' (*On Spectacles* 23).

But both legally and practically any stigma widely shared by the elite mentality is virtually meaningless in the lives of ordinary people; in truth for the gladiator the practical result of being labeled 'infamous' by action or occupation is small indeed. First of all, there is no conviction on a charge of 'infamy.' 'Infamy' accompanies a legally punished or socially disapproved action, but no one is brought up on the charge. Once 'infamy' adheres, however, there are legal repercussions. For example, a person could not represent someone else in a legal action, or be a witness in a prosecution, or have someone else represent him – he had to defend on his own behalf. Nor could he bring charges in court – but then, neither could minors, women, wards, freedmen (if their patron was involved), or sitting magistrates. Of course, as Tertullian notes, a gladiator could not be a senator or an equestrian or a local magistrate – but what gladiator would have dreamed, or cared, or even thought about that? The common people watching wouldn't care at all, either – after all, the social structure meant that in practice they were not eligible for such things, and they were not even infamous! 'Infamy' might get a gladiator excluded from a cemetery, but that would depend on the feelings of the owner, and how he felt about burials of tainted persons in his graveyard. If a gladiator were so careless or luckless as to be caught *in flagrante*, the abused husband could treat him like a slave, i.e. he could kill him on the spot – but this perhaps comes more from the assimilation to slavery that the gladiator's oath has wrought. Finally, a gladiator could not become a soldier ('infamous men don't serve in the army'), but a person would choose between going into the army and becoming a gladiator, so the issue of joining the army after becoming a gladiator was not a common problem; the few examples all appear in elite rhetorical exercises and are clearly created for effect. In sum, the practical ramifications of being declared 'infamous' because of being a gladiator touched no important part of most gladiators' lives – and certainly would not have lessened the pleasure of the audience, or their enthusiastic adoration of the stars of the arena.

These disparities between a supposed infamy and little evidence of it in the reaction of ordinary people come across most clearly in gladiatorial epitaphs. These are numerous, and provide much information. But what is most striking is that almost alone of those citizens supposedly infamous – morticians, slave dealers, whores, pimps, and gladiatorial managers – the gladiators' epitaphs are indistinguishable from those of other ordinary people in content and sentiments expressed; only the epitaphs of actors, another entertainer dear to the hearts of the crowd and again labeled 'infamous' by the elite, replicate this. In other words, gladiators made no effort to hide their profession, but rather foregrounded it. This is because they were proud of it, and its impressiveness overwhelmed any supposed stigma it might theoretically have carried.

That the stigma was fundamentally an elite concoction is revealed by a telltale notice in the legal material. The jurist Ulpian says that arena fighters who do not take pay do not gain *infamia*: '… those who fight in the arena for the sake of demonstrating their manly courage (*virtus*), doing this without pay, men of old held not to acquire *infamia*' (*Digest*

3.1.1.6). So the fundamental concern was not the pollution of blood, but the pollution of dependence – doing something for hire. It perhaps hardly needs to be pointed out that ordinary people worked for money all the time; their lives depended on it. There is no reason they should have shared the narrow vision of the elite when it came to stigmatizing the fighters on that ground.

For the gladiator slave who was freed by a Roman citizen in the course of his service, there was a more severe and very practical penalty than a supposed 'infamy' – he was denied the Roman citizenship that should accompany his freedom. Here the elite decree of stigma could be enforced, for freeing a slave could be a legal procedure. But the slave did not enter the profession of his own volition, as the *auctoratus* did. For the volunteer, any social penalty he might incur from fellow men who might either be taken up into the elite mentality or be genuinely disgusted at the blood and gore was light indeed, especially compared to the notoriety, even fame, he automatically possessed as a result of his chosen profession.

While in the service, a gladiator was associated with a *familia* unless he was a freelance operator. The *familia* (literally, 'household') was an organized living and training arrangement, sometimes housed, as at Pompeii, in a specially constructed building, sometimes with gladiators housed in a town and training and eating together. While it is not possible to confirm that the gladiator graveyard uncovered in Ephesus in 1997 was the property of a single *familia*, the fact that sixty-seven gladiators and probably a veteran fighter turned trainer – perhaps even manager as well – were buried together suggests that this might be the case.

The *familia* resembled, as gladiators did in so many other ways, military conditions. There were 'ranks.' A newcomer, having just sworn his oath and joined the establishment, was a *novicius*. As he trained, he gained the sobriquet of *tiro* – the word for a raw army recruit as well. This 'rank' remained until after the first fight, when normally one tiro was pitted against another. Not that this was always the case. An inscription from Pompeii tells of a tiro who went up against an experienced fighter – and won, not once, but twice in the same games:

Marcus Attilius tiro won. Hilarus of the Neronian *familia* who had fought 14 times with 12 victories was the loser. Marcus Attilius having fought once and won, won again. This time Lucius Raecius Felix, who before had fought 12 times and won 12 times, lost. (*CIL* 4.10236)

And another example of early success is:

Spiculus of the Neronian *familia*, a tiro, killed Aptonetus, a free volunteer, who had won 14 times previously. (*CIL* 4.1474, Pompeii)

Once spurs had, so to speak, been won as a successful tiro, a career was assured. The gladiator could fight as long as he was alive and marketable, whether with a manager or, if released, self-leased, on his own. But at least sometimes retired gladiators went on to be trainers, perhaps even managers; the old gladiator buried among the young ones at Ephesus seems to be an example of this.

Living conditions might or might not live up to high expectations. Some accommodations were cramped; men slept on cots or on the floor on mattresses. In other situations, conditions were probably better. The two gladiatorial training residences (*ludi*) extant now, both at Pompeii, are relatively airy, not enclosed – and weapons seem to have been unguarded. In other words, gladiators living there could come and go as they pleased, and the manager evidently was not concerned about the men seizing arms and leading a revolt à la Spartacus. Food was supplied abundantly, if rather boringly: the favored meal was a very carbohydrate-heavy gruel called *sagina*. Galen says that this was made of beans and barley – gladiators were sometimes nicknamed *hordearii* – 'barleymen.' Rabbinic sources also mention that beans were a staple of the gladiator's diet. This combination of grain and beans developed a strong frame and lots of musculature. Forensic study of gladiator bones found in Ephesus confirms the diet that the ancient sources describe; the intention was to 'bulk up' the men, and to provide fat as protection to the bones.

Trainers were on hand, likely veteran fighters themselves, to coach the specialized fighting modes such as the *thrax* or the *secutor*. And there were medical personnel. The most famous was the doctor/researcher Galen, who used his experience in treating gladiators' wounds to learn about human anatomy. In sum, the arrangements resembled very much those of a military camp – although the gladiators' food was reputed to be better.

Besides a context for training, the *familia* provided bonding. An inscription from southern Spain tells of how a *familia* took care to bury one of its own:

> A gladiator-fighting-from-a-chariot named Ingenuus, of the Gallician training camp, 25 years old, victor in 12 matches, a German by birth, lies here. His entire gladiatorial household (*familia*) set this up at their own expense. May the earth rest lightly upon you! (*CIL* 2²–7.362, Córdoba)

Another from Smyrna notes that the *familia* pooled resources and helped a fellow gladiator pay for the funeral honors of his little son. Yet another from Telmessos has one gladiator setting up a gravestone for the fellow he shared living quarters with in the gladiatorial school (*ludus*).

It is impossible to know how such bonding affected gladiators who were paired against their fellows of the same *familia*. When forty-nine pairings from a single *familia* fought, it is hard to believe that some contests did not pit friends against each other:

> Forty-nine pairings! The *Familia Capiniana* will fight at Puteoli in the Augustan Games, May 12th, 14th, 16th, and 17th. There will be awnings [over the arena]! (*CIL* 4.7994, Pompeii)

Some epitaphs do, however, recognize the inherent possibility for inner conflict when men of the *familia* were pitted against each other in the arena. Louis Robert gives the examples of Olympos, whose gravestone notes that 'he spared many in the arena'; Ajax 'saved many souls.' These sentiments mean that these men, and presumably others, fought with seriousness, but not with uncontrolled anger or blood-lust; they fought to win, not to kill, if it could be avoided. But even granted that the 'rules of combat,' if strictly adhered to, could produce both a good show and mutual survival of a pair, there was always the chance of a miscue. And, of course, just being in the same *familia* would not

31. A gladiator and his faithful canine. Many gravestones of gladiators feature a dog at the feet. With the stress of preparation and competition among fierce men, it was perhaps a gladiator's most trusted friend.

guarantee a friendly disposition toward all of one's fellow gladiators. Competition, pride, jealousy – many emotions could turn one member of the *familia* against another. The intricacies of friendship and rivalry must have been great. Perhaps the best friend was at times a dog: Robert has identified canines on more than a half-dozen grave reliefs set up for gladiators.

I have already quoted the material from Plutarch in which he states that some gladiators on the eve of combat took the opportunity to recommend their women to the care of their friends and set free their slaves. Suetonius notes in his *Life* of Emperor Claudius that Claudius freed an *essedarius* (chariot fighter) who had four sons. There are also many inscriptions which indicate that gladiators, whether slaves or free, had families. Their epitaphs are sometimes written by fellow fighters or other males, but the most usual by far is for a woman to dedicate the monument, often with expressions of endearment. Although in other ways gladiators were assimilated to the ways of soldiers, in this they are very distinct: soldiers' graves are almost always set up by a male, not surprisingly since soldiers, although they often formed liaisons, were long forbidden to marry. The dedications of gladiators thus clearly show that they belonged to the 'normal' world insofar as family was concerned. Indeed, a number of epitaphs give the names of children, so family life extended beyond just a wife. And it is worth noting that a term common for slave relationships (slaves could not legally marry), *contubernalis*, 'tent mate,' is almost entirely lacking from gladiators' dedications. Rather *coniunx* or *uxor* are found, both terms for a legal wife. There is no reason not to accept this at face value: Free gladiators were married, and slave gladiators seemed comfortable using the terminology strictly appropriate only to the free. Despite the disparagement of elite authors there is no reason to see these women as 'gladiatorial groupies' handed from one gladiator to the next as each was killed off, the lowest of the low, hardly better than long-term prostitutes. Just by looking at the epitaphs, it is impossible to distinguish their form and sentiments from those of any other ordinary people who set up monuments. And when we consider that a gladiator had not only the 'sex appeal' so notoriously mentioned in the ancient sources, but steady employment which yielded prize money once or twice a year, possibly in considerable amount, it is not surprising that some would form permanent relationships and have children.

While a good deal of time was taken up on an ongoing basis with training, gladiators must still have had quite a bit of time on their hands as they normally fought only infrequently. An intelligent manager must have looked for ways to make his investment pay. Renting out gladiators as bodyguards was an obvious option. Unfortunately, there are only rare mentions of this, and then always in relation to the elite. As in so many other aspects of his life, a gladiator's employment outside the arena remains something of a mystery.

Beyond the *familia* and family, gladiators found social contacts and relationships in professional associations. As with other such organizations, these *collegia* provided an opportunity to gather for a meal, discuss professional matters, gossip, and, perhaps, save up for the costs of a decent burial. We have a fine mosaic from North Africa that may show a club of beast fighters gathered at table. Inscriptions tell of associations

32. Nemesis. Gladiators and beast fighters (shown here) were under the protection of the goddess of vengeful fate – remorseless and fierce.

of other beast fighters, as well as of a *collegium* of retired gladiators at Rome.

Very little is known about the religious outlook of gladiators. This is surprising, since in such a deadly profession one might expect an interest in divinities that could provide protection. One gladiator makes a dedication to Venus, but this can hardly be related to the activity of the arena. Another dedicates to Mars, something that we might expect, as Mars was the god of war. A few others make dedications to Nemesis. This deity was closely associated with Fortune in the Romano-Greek mind, and as such was a power to be called on in parlous professions such as in military service and the arena. Nevertheless, it is striking that of almost 250 Latin inscriptions that mention Nemesis, only three, two by beast fighters and one by a gladiator, come from the arena professionals; the heaviest concentration by far is from soldiers of one rank or another. The Greek evidence concurs: Nemesis figures in only four or five of the documents.

While gladiators made bloody sacrifices to gain the protection of the supernatural, their mortal contemporaries in turn valued gladiators' own blood as a magical philter. The Roman antiquarian Festus (55.3L) states that 'the bride's hair used to be parted with the "celibate" spear which had been fixed in a gladiator's body that had been killed and thrown aside.' The blood on the spear was evidently thought to be a fertility potion. How else was the blood obtained? Evidently by rushing to the scene of death and collecting it. Tertullian tells that people caught the blood in cups and carried it off:

> Likewise what of those who, after a fight in the arena, carry off in their avid thirst the blood of the guilty slain – blood just then caught gushing from the neck. And this they use as a cure for epilepsy. (*Apology* 9.10)

Given Tertullian's animus against the games, I might suspect exaggeration. But years earlier the medical writer Celsus wrote, 'Some have freed themselves from epilepsy by deep drafts of the warm blood spilled from a gladiator's throat' (*On Medicine* 3.23.7). Pliny the Elder recommends the blood as a cure for epilepsy as well:

> Epileptics drink the blood of gladiators as though it were the cup of life ... They believe it is by far the most effective to gulp down the blood hot from the very man still gasping out his last breath, putting their lips to the wound, drawing out the essence of life itself. (*Natural History* 28.4–5)

And Aretaeus of Cappadocia describes exactly what Tertullian does: 'I have seen persons holding a cup below the wound of a man recently slaughtered, and drinking a draft of the blood! (*Treatment of Chronic Disease* 7.4.7–8). Besides insuring fertility and curing epilepsy, a gladiator's blood was useful in a potion to attract a lover:

> Love spell of attraction performed with the help of heroes or gladiators or those who have died a violent death. Leave a little of the bread which you eat; break it up and form it into seven bite-sized pieces. And go to where heroes and gladiators and those who have died a violent death were slain. Say the spell to the pieces of bread and throw them. And pick up some polluted dirt from the place where you perform the ritual and throw it inside the house of the woman

whom you desire, go on home and go to sleep. (*PGM* 4.1390–98/ Betz)

The gladiator's cultivated mystique of valor and violence made not only his life's essence coveted after death. It is an added curiosity to note that some people also, apparently, didn't stop with the gladiator's blood but cut out his liver as well: The Roman physician-pharmacologist Scribonius Largus reported that 'some people take a nine-times dosage of a small quantity of liver cut from a fallen gladiator' (*Compositions* 17). As Largus had earlier recommended as a cure for epilepsy the liver of a stag killed by a weapon that, in turn, had been used to kill a gladiator, it is safe to assume that the dose of gladiator's liver was for epilepsy as well.

Gladiators represent only one type of spectacle favored by ordinary Romans. Stage performances, chariot racing, athletic contests: All were a part of their lives. But the combination of fabulous popularity, bloody danger, and relatively extensive evidence for their lives makes those idols of the arena especially interesting. The lives of free, voluntary fighters were exceedingly dangerous, but that danger was part of the allure – that and the fame and, possibly, fortune. As a slave, of course, the gladiator had little choice, but even here the chance for freedom could be some motivation. In the midst of all the uncertainties and risks, men (and some women) carved out a life with friends and family even as they prepared for the duels on the sand. They were, in a way, just like other ordinary Romano-Greeks, doing their best to succeed in a world that was stacked against them.

BEYOND THE LAW: BANDITS AND PIRATES

AN OUTLAW IS SOMEONE WHO LIVES IN CONTACT with a society but who does not abide by the laws of that society. It is the very nature of stratified societies to create the possibility of outlaws. Stratified societies institutionalize and culturally enforce differential worth, power, and wealth; this provides the context for outlaws to appear. Simply put, there have to be laws before there can be outlaws, and hierarchically stratified societies regularly use laws to secure their structure. Their basis in exploiting some to the benefit of others offers motivation to some to escape the enforcing laws. One way to do this is to turn to outlawry.

The acceptance of a simple definition of outlaws – one who lives in contact with but outside society's laws – automatically eliminates from consideration two very prominent types of outlaw in the Romano-Grecian world: the tribal outlaws, routinely labeled by contemporaries as 'bandits' or 'pirates,' on the one hand, and the common petty criminal, on the other. The tribal type of outlaw is not operating within the sphere of Roman society; rather, these people might more accurately be labeled 'otherlaws,' because they are their own community, have their own laws, are organized in a stratified, hierarchical way, but simply do not abide by Roman laws. In this category belong such outlaws as the bandits of the Calycadnus Valley in Cilicia, the Maratocupreni of Syria, and, much later, the maurading Saxons in late antiquity. These are tribally based raider societies, which, like similar raider societies of other ancient times, such as the Cilician pirates and the Homeric chieftains themselves, and in later times, the Vikings, prey on anyone who has possessions to take. The geographer Strabo gives us an excellent description of such a raider society:

> After the Sindic territory and Gorgipia, on the sea, one comes to the coast of the Achaei and the Zygi and the Heniochi, which for the most part is harborless and mountainous, being a part of the Caucasus. These peoples live by robberies at sea. Their boats are slender, narrow, and light, holding only about twenty-five people, though in rare cases they can hold thirty in all; the Greeks call them 'camarae' … by equipping fleets of 'camarae' and sailing sometimes against merchant-vessels and sometimes against a country or even a city, they hold the mastery of the sea. And they are sometimes assisted even by those who hold the Bosporus, the latter supplying them with mooring-places, with market-places, and with means of disposing of their booty … they are well acquainted with wooded places; and in these they first hide their 'camarae' and then themselves wander on foot night and day for the sake of kidnapping people … the territory that is subject to the Romans affords but little aid, because of the negligence of the governors who are sent there. (*Geography* 11.2.12/ Jones)

Romans themselves, 'raiders' par excellence managing to conquer and loot the entire Mediterranean world, understood and dealt with this sort of bandit tribe as an opposing community.

The normal means of coping with these external 'otherlaws' is by an organized military action; in the example above, Strabo notes both the appropriateness and failure of Roman action against the raiders. Because both groups are playing by the same overall rules, the danger is clear: Either side victorious will try to attack and plunder, if not destroy, the other. Although the Romans themselves often do not rhetorically distinguish between 'otherlaws' and 'outlaws,' here I propose to make that distinction very clear. In the case of 'otherlaws,' the external dynamic creates a highly visible interaction that elites participate in and military and diplomatic leaders and so on document extensively. In the case of 'outlaws,' the elite are both less directly involved – of all members of society, they have the most capacity to protect themselves from outlaws – and more uncomfortable ideologically because of the critique of the hierarchical society that the outlaws represent. Uninterested and insulated, the elite at best pays attention to 'outlaws' when they approach the threat level that 'otherlaws' present; usually, outlaws are simply assumed as part of the landscape, measures are taken to avoid their depredations, and they are left to their lives in the usual silence of the sources reserved for groups considered unworthy of notice by the elite.

Another group I do not consider is the common criminal. These people – murderers, thieves, small-time racketeers – are predators on lawful society but emerge from it and go back into it without ever forming an alternative to it. Lucian gives a glimpse of their work:

> When I was going away from home to Athens by reason of my desire for Greek culture, I put in at Amastris, on the Black Sea; the city is a port of call for those sailing this way from Scythia, not far distant from Carambis. I was accompanied by Sisinnes, who had been my companion from childhood. After looking out a lodging near the port and transferring our effects to it from the vessel, we went shopping, without suspecting any mischief. In the meantime thieves pried the door open and carried off everything, so as not to leave even enough to suffice for that day. (*Toxaris* 57/Harmon)

The Gospels have a number of references to thieves and theft, as do novels and other sources. These petty criminals do not reject the norms of society but strike at it in the interstices, often with crimes of opportunity. Robbers had the capacity for making life difficult and dangerous for everyone, and they did so as they were able. But however obnoxious and worrisome, they posed no real threat, nor had any cohesive group identity.

Finally, I can safely ignore the metaphorical bandit – the use of the term 'bandit' and its cousins by Roman elites against each other in political competition. Broadly speaking, they mean by this epithet anyone who was not playing by the rules, and directed it at someone in order to win an argument or competition; it is a metaphorical use designed to smear an enemy, to criminalize them, and therefore to justify any action against them. These 'bandits' are not 'outlaws' at all; they are still operating within the elite political and social framework and have nothing to do with the reality of outlaws as people living outside the laws of society.

Discovering outlaws

Although I have discussed quite fully elsewhere the use of various sources, it is worthwhile to note here, in particular, the value of fictional narratives in retrieving the life of the outlaw of the Romano-Graecian world. As will become very clear, I rely heavily on these sources, although historians, inscriptions, and papyri provide material as well. The works of fiction, in particular Apuleius' *Golden Ass* and the Greek romances, limned a world that scholars have come to recognize as real. That is to say, the way the 'real' was arranged in the novels is fictional, but behind the fiction lie actual facts of social history, facts that can be retrieved and used by historians. I quote from the novels as though they are historical documents, but this is merely a narrative device; I fully understand that they are not history. My use derives from a confidence that what the characters are doing and saying in the episodes I describe is actually reflective of reality, although the words and situations themselves are constructed by the author.

Moving toward outlawry

The outlaws I restrict myself too – those living in contact with, but outside, lawful society – enact the ideology of that hierarchically stratified society. They form a community organized for the acquisition of power and possessions for some at the expense of others, but from outside that society's law framework, rather than, as the elite-run community, from within it. The Romans were very aware of the shared ideology of 'inlaw' rulers and 'outlaw' bandits. In one of the most extensive historical treatments of a bandit in classical literature, a historian has the bandit chief Bulla Felix make just this obvious point of comparison. When he is captured by the emperor Septimius Severus' men and set before the praetorian prefect Papinian, Papinian is said to have asked him, 'Why did you become a robber?' To which Bulla replied, 'Why are you a prefect?' (Cassius Dio, *Roman History* 77.10.7). Although the event itself may be fictional, the valid point is that both are robbers of a sort – the prefect within the law, Bulla outside it. Another metaphor comparing robbers and lawful citizens (this time doctors) is given by Galen:

> Robbers in our own country band together to harm others and spare themselves: similarly those [doctors] here combine against us, the only difference from bandits being that these men operate in the city, not in the mountains. ('Prognosis,' in *Corpus Medicorum Graecorum* V 8.1/Nutton)

The sharing of values, attitudes, and actions within the law and outside it was evident enough.

The condition of soldiers-as-bandits also illustrates the fuzzy line between 'lawful' bandits and 'outlaw' bandits. The depredations of soldiers are well documented, as is the (quite natural) segue of soldiers into banditry. In the first situation the long association of soldiers with violent solutions to problems, their possession of arms in a generally disarmed or at best poorly armed population, and the authority inherent in their position as Roman soldiers easily led to abuses which were simply robbery. The story in Apuleius of the centurion who requisitions Lucius in his asinine form, the anger this arouses, the violent attack on the centurion by Lucius' owner, and the final revenge of the centurion on that owner is a fine encapsulation both of the abuses possible and the anger of the civilian population at such abuses (*The Golden Ass* 9.39–42). The story in the Gospels of the 'extra mile' fits the same mould (Matthew 5:41), as does John the Baptizer's admonition to soldiers not to extort money and or accuse people falsely – and to be content with their pay (Luke 3:13–15). In the case of soldiers, it was perhaps logical to move into a life of outlaw banditry, given the possibilities for official banditry before. Skill in arms, a disposition to violence, and the poverty-stricken condition of some soldiers contributed to the transition of a certain number into full-time bandits, for despite the general advantages of being a soldier, some did not fare so well in their careers and deserted the standards in favor of brigandage. Here is a specific example in the historian Herodian:

There was a man called Maternus, an ex-soldier of notorious daring, who had deserted from the ranks and influenced others to escape service with him. Within a short time he had collected a large band of criminals and began to make plundering raids on villages and farms. (*Recent History of the Roman Empire* 1.10/Whittaker)

Maternus' enterprise succeeded beyond his wildest imaginings; he plundered whole provinces and plotted to kill Commodus and become emperor. His end came from betrayal by some of his men.

In similar fashion, pirates could evolve from wartime naval activities:

Having acquired a taste for rich plunder [as privateers in the service of King Mithridates VI], they still did not cease their activities when Mithridates was defeated, made peace and retreated. For, having been robbed of their living and their homeland on account of the war, and having fallen into hardship and poverty, they harvested the sea instead of the land, first in small ships, then in large ones, cruising around in squadrons, under the command of pirate captains just like generals in a war. (Appian, *War against Mithridates* 92/White)

Thus Mithridates had used what later would be called privateers to give him additional naval power; these captains turned to piracy after Mithridates was defeated, much as many pirates had their origins in the privateers of the early modern European wars.

In yet another crossover between lawful and outlaw worlds, bandits and pirates are entrepreneurs of a sort, trying to be successful in the resource acquisition approved of by society. Eric Hobsbawm writes,

As individuals, they are not so much political or social rebels, let alone revolutionaries, as peasants who refuse to submit, and in doing so stand out from their fellows, or even more simply men who find themselves excluded from the usual career of their kind, and therefore forced into outlawry and 'crime' … Banditry itself is therefore … a form of self-help to escape particular circumstances … [A bandit] is an outsider and a rebel, a poor man who refuses to accept the normal roles of poverty, and establishes his freedom by means of the only resources within reach of the poor, strength, bravery, cunning and determination … It sets him in opposition to the hierarchy of power, wealth, and influence: he is not one of them … At the same time the bandit is, inevitably, drawn into the web of wealth and power, because, unlike other peasants, he acquires wealth and exerts power. (*The Bandit*, pp. 19–20, 76)

In crossing back and forth, there are many instances of outlaws being on good terms with some group in lawful society. Although Bulla Felix is said to have eluded the authorities through bribes and cleverness ('he was never really seen when seen, never found when found, never caught when caught'(Cassius Dio 77.10.2/Cary), he surely enjoyed some protection from the wider population. He clearly had spies in lawful society, whether outlaws themselves or only fellow travelers is not clear; these spies gave him exceptionally good intelligence which aided in his raiding: 'He learned of everybody that was setting out from Rome and everybody that was putting into port at Brundisium, and knew both who and how many there were, and what and how much they had with them.' Likewise the outlaws in Apuleius blended into lawful society and returned intelligence to the group; this is noted once when a bandit stayed behind to see what actions the authorities took after the raid on Milo's house, again when a bandit was sent to scout out possible raids, and yet again when they mingled to find out where Chryseros kept his money (*The Golden Ass* 7.1 and 4.9). In the romance *Chaereas and Callirhoe*, Theron the pirate had 'thugs handily stationed with boats in harbors under cover of being ferrymen.' Outlaws often seem to be conceived of as wearing two hats, one a lawful occupation, the other banditry or piracy; in Achilles Tatius' *Leucippe and Clitophon* (5.7), Clitophon ran into mollusk fishermen who were actually pirates. When Bulla Felix captured people, he 'would take a part of what they had and let them go at once, but he detained artisans for a time and made use of their skill, then dismissed them with a present' (Cassius Dio 77.10.3). Such action softens any hostility of the population toward outlaws. When Maternus began his marauding, he freed prisoners and enlisted them in his band (Herodian 1.10.2); while this is not necessarily a socially positive step, it does hint at that. In Apuleius there is a close, symbiotic relationship between the outlaws and elements of the civil population. This is specifically noticed in at least two places. In this one, the gang is heading off for their lair after looting Milo's house:

> About midday, when the sun beating down was already making things very hot, we turned aside into a village where the outlaws had good friends among the elders. From the moment they met their voluble exchanges and kisses of friendship showed how close they were – even an ass could see it. And they also took some things from my back and gave them to the villagers as gifts, while in low whispers they seemed to be telling them that these were the fruit of their depredations. (*The Golden Ass* 4.1)

Such interaction was easy to maintain – it was mutually advantageous – and, of course, outlaws looked like everyone else and so could blend into the general population at will. Within this context, it is likely that the outlaws saw themselves as in some sense fitting in to society as a whole. Nevertheless, this 'fitting' was not to play the game according to the elite's rules, but rather to live a life against the normal grain.

Who becomes an outlaw?

Crossing over into outlawry was one way – perhaps the only and surely the quickest way – to break the heavy hand of the law and its enforcers which kept the poor poor, the oppressed oppressed, and resources safely in the hands of the already wealthy. With this perspective, it is easy to see that outlaw bands live out a genuinely alternative life within the heavily stratified society of the ancient Roman world. Their lifestyle does not seek change, nor is it a form of resistance. Rather, it is focused on a few very specific goals, and its social organization derives from the needs of fulfilling them. It is possible to recover what sort of person became an outlaw, as well as their goals and social organization, in the process revealing the perspective of outlaws on themselves and their world.

The ancient sources are clear about one group that yields outlaws: the desperados, i.e. those without hope. In Apuleius, for example, Haemus, the new bandit leader, notes that he can recruit many new men for the band because there are so many poor, desperate men out there (*The Golden Ass* 7.4). In Xenophon's *An Ephesian Tale*, Hippothous hopes to recruit 'able-bodied young men' in Mazacus, a town in Cappadocia (2.11–14). In *Chaereas and Callirhoe*, Theron goes around to the port brothels and taverns and there collects men for his crew. Strabo attests that the general poverty and ruggedness of the land gave people a reason to turn to piracy. And when Bulla the outlaw captured a centurion, 'he assumed the dress of a magistrate, ascended the tribunal, and having summoned the centurion, caused part of his head to be shaved, and then said, "Tell your masters that they should take care of their slaves, and then they wouldn't become bandits"' (Cassius Dio 77.10.5). Dio goes on to state, 'Bulla had with him, in fact, a very large number of imperial freedmen, some of whom had been poorly paid, while others had received absolutely no pay at all.' I have noted above the condition of ex-soldiers, which often provided motivation for outlawry. On the other end of the spectrum of possibilities, Xenophon notes in *An Ephesian Tale* a noble who, meeting with reverses in life, took up the life of a bandit: Hippothous started as a wealthy young man in Perintus, Thrace; after adventures revolving around a homosexual affair with one Hyperanthes (who dies in a shipwreck), Hippothous makes his way to Pamphylia.

> There, since I had no means of supporting myself and was distressed at the tragedy, I took to brigandage. At first I was only one of the rank and file, but in the end I got together a band of my own in Cilicia; it was famed far and wide, until it was captured not long before I saw you. (*An Ephesian Tale* 3.2 / Anderson)

Heliodorus also has a bandit of this sort. The outlaw captain 'came from a distinguished family and had taken up his present way of life only out of necessity'; he had been the son of a high priest of Memphis in Egypt, but had been illegally pushed aside by a younger brother and forced to flee to bandits 'in the hope of gaining revenge and regaining [his] position' (*An Ethiopian Story* 1.19 / Morgan). And it is safe to assume, although there is no mention of such a person by name, that there was a share of social misfits and ne'er-do-wells who could not or would not fit into the stratified society, and escaped into outlawry.

However, some must have become outlaws purely out of greed, not because of desperate circumstances. Apollonius claimed to have thwarted a recruitment effort, but the tale is illustrative nonetheless of the temptation that outlawry could put in the way of good citizens:

> But Apollonius replied: 'Since you tempt me to talk about pilotage, I would have you hear what I consider to have been any soundest exploit at that time. Pirates at one time infested the Phoenician Sea, and were hanging about the cities to pick information about the cargoes which different people had. The agents of the pirates spied out accordingly a rich cargo which I had on board my ship, and having taken me aside in conversation, asked me what was my share in the freight; and I told them that it was a thousand drachmas, for there were four people in command of the ship. "And," said they, "have you a house?" "A wretched hut," I replied, "on the Island of Pharos, where once upon a time Proteus used to live." "Would you like then," they went on, "to acquire a landed estate instead of the sea, and a decent house instead of your hut, and ten times as much for the cargo as you are going to get now? And to get rid of a thousand misfortunes which beset pilots owing to the roughness of the sea?" I replied that I would gladly do so, but that I did not aspire to become a pirate just at a time when I had made myself more expert than I ever had been, had won crowns for my skill in my profession. However, they persevered and promised to give me a purse of ten thousand drachmas, if I would be their man and do what they wanted. Accordingly I egged them on to talk by promising not to fail them, but to assist them in every way. Then they admitted that they were agents of the pirates, and besought me not to deprive them of a chance of capturing the ship, and instead of sailing away to the city whenever I weighed anchor thence, they arranged that I should cast anchor under the promontory, under the lee of which the pirate ships were riding; and they were willing to swear that they would not only not kill myself, but would spare the life of any for whom I interceded. I for my part did not consider it safe to reprehend them, for I was afraid that if they were driven to despair, they would attack my ship on the high seas and then we should all be lost somewhere at sea; accordingly I promised to assist their enterprise, but I insisted upon their taking an oath to keep their promise truly. They accordingly made oath, for our interview took place in a temple, and then

said: "You betake yourselves to the ships of the pirates at once, for we will sail away by night." And they found me all the more plausible from the way I bargained about the money, for I stipulated that it must all be paid me in current cash, though not before they had captured the ship. They therefore went off, but I put straight out to sea after doubling the promontory.' (*Life of Apollonius* 3.24/Conybeare)

How does the state respond to outlaws?

One of the most interesting aspects of outlaws and the authorities is that there is never even an attempt to end outlawry *tout court*. Measures are taken against outlaws, of course. The emperor Augustus, so his biographer Suetonius states, set up garrisons around the empire to help control brigandage; two centuries later Tertullian notes their existence still. In Egypt, Baebius Juncinus ordered that supporters of bandits be attacked in order to deny the bandits their bases in the villages. And also there, an official named M. Sempronius Liberalis at one time issued a three-month amnesty for bandits, stating that thereafter they would receive no mercy. Marcus Valerius Maximianus, a successful career military officer, boasted on his epitaph that among other accomplishments he had headed a detail that annihilated a band of outlaws in the lower Danubian basin. These measures were an ongoing response to an ongoing problem that never went away, but rather remained to fester and irritate the authorities, wherever they were. And it was only in case of personal concern or extreme disruption that the central authority invested extensive resources to actually annihilate an outlaw threat. Inscriptions give two illustrations of such action. From Syria comes:

By order of our Lords Constantine, the Triumphant Augustus and Most Noble Julian Caesar did Bassidius Lauricius, Most Outstanding Man, Companion, and Commander, seize by force a fort long controlled by a band of outlaws and threatening to the provinces; he then secured it with a garrison of soldiers so that Antioch could enjoy long-lasting and solid peace. (*CIL* 3.6733 = *ILS* 740)

And from Rome:

This is dedicated to the Strength of the Army which with faithful loyalty fulfilled the high hopes and prayers of Romans by wiping out the most savage outlaws. (*CIL* 6.234 = *ILS* 2011)

Apuleius gives a similar account, much elaborated, of course. Bandits made the mistake of attacking the entourage of a disgraced imperial official; the wife wrote to the emperor and the emperor ordered the troops to suppress the bandits – quite effectively, as it happens (*The Golden Ass* 7.7). Elsewhere in novels, the forces of the central government prove decisive in defeating large and dangerous outlaw bands. In the historian Dio, Bulla Felix became so threatening (he had perhaps a band of 600) that first a centurion with a force was dispatched to hunt him down and then, later, when that failed, a praetorian tribune: 'Severus … sent a tribune from his bodyguard with many horsemen, after threatening him with dire punishment if he should fail to bring back the robber alive' (Cassius Dio 77.10.6). In later antiquity (AD 354), Ammianus Marcellinus gave a lengthy description of a serious outlaw uprising in southern Asia Minor that was finally put down after extensive imperial resources had been deployed (*Histories* 14.2.1–20). These instances should not lead to the belief, however, that in reality the central authorities invested many resources in outlaw suppression. In most of the outlawry described in Apuleius, for example, the imperial power is nowhere to be seen. This is true for outlawry in the other novels as well, and nothing in other ancient sources contradicts it.

On the contrary, if any authorities are mentioned in regard to thwarting bandits and pirates, it is usually local authorities. It is the magistrates who are mentioned in Apuleius, for example, as organizing the search for Lucius after the bandits break into Milo's house (*The Golden Ass* 7.1–2). Strabo frequently mentions actions of local governments in trying to react to the piracy of the Cilician coast. These local authorities were limited in their effectiveness by the lack of a local police force, although Xenophon has an eirenarch of Cilicia, Perilaus, commanding a significant enough force to attack and annihilate an outlaw gang (*An Ephesian Tale* 2.11–14).

Vigilantism, either in the service of authorities or not, is rampant, however. Individuals took things into their own hands. In Dacia, for example, Bassus is avenged:

Dedicated to the Spirits of the Dead of Lucius Julius Bassus, son of Lucius, of the Sergian voting district, town councilor of the Dobreta and treasurer. He was killed by outlaws in his fortieth year. Julius Julianus and Julius Bassus set this up to their father, in cooperation with Julius Valerianus, his brother, who took revenge for his death. (*CIL* 3.1579)

And also in Dacia:

… [name is lost] was murdered by outlaws. Ulcudius Baedari and Sutta Epicadi, loving parents, set this grave marker up for their son. He was avenged. (*CIL* 3.1585)

Indeed, magistrates usually acted only when the citizenry had taken some vigilante action already. Typically, such action was of two sorts. First, a mob set upon someone whom they deemed had broken some law, whether it be through robbery, violence, sacrilege, or some other crime; the mob dragged the reprobate(s) to a place of assembly – usually the forum but sometimes the theater – and there the magistrates held a sort of court, which usually ended up in the punishment of the people seized. This happened to Lucius after he killed three men seeking to break into Milo's house and citizens set upon him for the deed (*The Golden Ass* 3.5–6). In the second sort of vigilante action, a gang is 'deputized' and heads into the countryside to deal with outlaws. Again, Apuleius provides us with a good example, as Tlepolemus returned to the bandit's cave after he had freed his love, Charite, and sought help from the villagers. Lucius narrates:

I went along willingly with a great crowd of citizens and other beasts of burden, for besides my usual, inveterate curiosity I strongly desired to see the outlaws taken captive. And indeed it was easy to seize them, held fast more by their drunkenness than by their bonds. The townsmen dug up all the treasure and carried it out of the cave, where they loaded the gold and silver onto our backs. Then they unceremoniously pitched some of the outlaws, still bound, headlong over a nearby cliff. As for the others, they beheaded them with their own swords, and left them sprawled there. Overjoyed at such vengeance, we returned happily to town. (*The Golden Ass* 7.13)

Here is pure vigilante action, right down to the summary execution of the criminals without even the pretense of a trial. A similar approach to banditry appears in the life of the emperor Maximinus: As 'a young man he was a shepherd and a leader among his peers; he would ambush bandits and so free his fellows from their attacks' (*Historia Augusta*, 'The Two Maximini' 2.1–2).

Another example also comes from rural life, for in those areas self-help against bandits was a given; there was no presence of a central authority. In this instance, Lucius was taken along when slaves fled their master; as they traveled at night, they were set upon by fierce dogs and attacked by the inhabitants of a farmstead, who assumed they were outlaws; they ceased their attack only after being convinced of the peaceable intent of the group.

> By chance we happened to be passing by a rural estate. Suddenly the tenants, thinking that our group was a band of outlaws, determined to bravely protect their possessions. They let loose howling mastiffs, huge beasts more savage than wolves and bears, that they had care-fully raised to protect their property. The dogs were further enraged by the shouts of their masters and driven even beyond their normal savagery by the uproar all around. So they rushed at us from every side, attacking, tearing at men and beasts alike until, thoroughly overwhelmed, most of us lay prostrate on the ground … It seemed like things could get no worse – but they did. The peasants suddenly began to hurl stones onto us from the rooftops and from a nearby hill. [The travelers eventually managed to show their attackers that they were not bandits. One of the attackers addressed them:] 'But we are not outlaws with robbing you on our minds! We were only trying to avoid just that fate at your hands!' (*The Golden Ass* 8.17)

Clearly, the inhabitants were quite prepared to protect their property from bandits with violence. This episode also illustrates another basic way to deal with outlaws, namely, to not go out at night. When Lucius is set to leave a town during the night, he is warned that he is crazy – that no one travels at night for fear of outlaws (*The Golden Ass* 1.15). In this case towns, especially walled towns, provided some protection in combination with solid gates and doors of houses within the town. Of course, as the attack by three ruffians on Milo's house shows, even being in a town and behind barred doors was no sure protection from outlaws (*The Golden Ass* 2.32).

By far the most effective means of dealing with outlaws has always been betrayal. In fact, this is the only means mentioned consistently in the sources. Perhaps Tlepolemus in Apuleius should not count, because he was a 'mole' in the outlaw gang in the first place – but it was his actions that laid the groundwork for the annihilation of the bandit gang (*The Golden Ass* 7.10–13). Bulla Felix was brought to earth through treachery: the authorities found out that he was having sex with another man's wife, and got both the wife and the man to help entrap Bulla through promises of immunity from prosecution. Bulla was taken captive while asleep in a cave (Cassius Dio 77.10.7). Maternus noted above was captured through betrayal as well, as was Jesus of Nazareth. Failing betrayal, it is safe to deduce that the success of authorities against outlaws was minimal.

Once an outlaw was caught, condign punishment followed. This was often preceded by the display of the criminals: Servilius Isauricus in the first century BC made a habit of parading captured pirates through the towns before execution.

> Publius Servilius (Isauricus) all by himself captured more pirate captains alive than all who had gone before him. And was anyone deprived of the pleasure of seeing a pirate in chains? On the contrary, wherever he went, he offered this most pleasing spectacle of conquered and captive to everyone. As a result, not only from the towns where the processions went but also from outlying places a throng came just to see the sight. (Cicero, *2 Verrine* 5.26.66)

Pirates obviously held great interest for the lawful population; note the crowd of townsmen who turned out to see the pirate Heracleo 'celebrate a triumph' as he tweaked the Romans' ears by sailing with impunity around the inner harbor of Syracuse (Cicero, *2 Verrine* 5.38.100).

The death penalty was normal for outlaws. This meant one of the two most humiliating executions in the Roman world: death by crucifixion or death in the arena, in the jaws of wild beasts. Strabo tells of Selouros, leader of a bandit band headquartered on Mount Etna in Sicily. He was captured and executed at Rome in the gladiatorial arena. Bulla Felix rescued two of his men from prison, where they awaited death by the beasts; when Felix himself was caught, he was thrown to the beasts as well. Presumably Apuleius is having fun with this punishment when he has the bandit Thrasyleon die *as* a beast (a bear, in this case), not *by* a beast – the irony is heightened by the fact that the bearskin which turns Thrasyleon into a bear comes from a bear kept to mangle criminals in the arena (*The Golden Ass* 4.13–24). Often after crucifixion the bodies were left on display, much as the bodies of hanged pirates and other criminals were in early modern times. The jurist Callistratus states that bodies of executed bandits should be left hanging in the place of their depredations to give solace to those they harmed and fear to those contemplating such a life.

The social life of bandits

Although there is no literature or other documentation written directly by outlaws, it is possible to reconstruct their social organization and general outlook. The ancient sources for such a reconstruction are the accounts of outlaw actions and attitudes found in documents written by nonoutlaw authors. As I have noted above, the fictional depictions of outlaws seem to have quite clear notions of the range of experiences and realities of the lives of real live bandits. The same can be said of other notices of outlaws in historians such as Cassius Dio and Herodian, and in New Testament references. As far back as Homer, an author was able to capture at least a verisimilar outlook of a pirate. But how far can these sources be pushed to reflect the actual life and attitudes of outlaws? There are two complementary approaches. First, it is necessary to determine a coherent picture of the outlaw's life and attitudes from the disparate ancient sources. Second, this picture can be compared with well-documented outlaw life from another time and place.

It is Apuleius who in Books 4 to 7 of *The Golden Ass* gives us the most detailed information about outlaws that appears in any ancient source; thus the following description is based upon his information, with other sources brought in as they prove illuminating.

In Apuleius, the outlaw community is composed entirely of males. The nakedness of the men at their banquet emphasizes the maleness of

the group, especially as the nakedness of the gymnasium comes immediately to mind; the general horseplay, uproarious songs, and smutty
jokes also emphasize an all-male camaraderie. Indeed, women are
excluded from the community; the old crone in the cave does not count
as female, and the woman Charite is a prisoner and a source of profit, not
a sexual object. The social origins of Apuleius' outlaws go unstated, but
they most likely began as the type of person the bandit leader Haemus
notes as potential recruits: the poor and desperate. Outlaws live in a
place apart from lawful society, in this case a cave rather than a pirate
ship or island base. It is in the mountains, a favorite haunt of outlaws in
any age because of their ruggedness and low population. Hippothous'
gang lives in a cave in Cilicia (Xenophon, *An Ephesian Tale* 3.3), and any
similarly isolated spot will do; the *boukoloi* of the Delta in Egypt used
islands in the marshes: '... it is almost impossible to run them to ground,
as they retreat into their dens and lairs in the marsh' (*An Ethiopian Story*
2.24). Pirates, of course, used the sea as well as coves and islands as this
sort of base – which made them harder to track down:

> While the bandits' plunderings on the land, being under the very
> eyes of the locals, who could discover the injury nearby and appre-
> hend them without much difficulty, were easily stopped, the plun-
> dering by sea had increased dramatically. (Cassius Dio 36.20.3–4)

At their base, outlaws live in an egalitarian community. In Heliodorus, an incidental event emphasizes this egalitarianism: The first
band of pirates takes the loot from the ship and divides it into equal-
weighted piles so that all ten will have an equal burden (*An Ethiopian Story* 1.3). They bind themselves by an oath, specifically to save a
comrade in trouble; in external comradeship they do not fight against
each other's bands. There is a secret, ritual greeting that identifies a
person as a member of the outlaws. While there is no explicit mention
of a set of rules governing the band, Cicero (noted above) refers to such
a contract in his *On Duties*: 'There even exist, it is said, bandit laws (*leges
latronum*) that must be paid attention to and obeyed' (2.11.40). A reference to a similar contract among outlaws appears in Achilles Tatius'
Leucippe and Clitophon (Leucippe is speaking):

'It was [Chaireas] who urged them to kill the woman and throw her overboard in my [Leucippe's] stead. The rest of the bandit band then refused to hand me over to him alone; he had now used up another body that might have been sold and brought them an initial profit. In place of the dead woman I was to be sold to benefit the common purse and not just Chaireas alone. When he objected, bringing up legal points and referring to their contractual obligations, how they were commissioned to kidnap me for his passion, not their profit, and even ventured to use some strong language ...' [one of the bandits cut off his head]. (*Leucippe and Clitophon* 8.16/Winkler)

The bandit 'laws' were also to some extent merely traditional. A narrative given by Heliodorus is illustrative of these traditional 'rules' (*An Ethiopian Story* 4.3.1–32/Morgan): Peloros the pirate, now in love with Charikleia, demands her as his reward for being the first into the Phoenician vessel; when he asks for it, Trichinos the chief refuses. Peloros says, 'Then you are overturning the pirate law that allows whoever is the first aboard an enemy vessel and the first to brave the danger of combat on behalf of all his comrades to choose whatever he pleases from the spoils.' Trichinos responds, 'I am not overturning that law, but I base my claim on another rule which says that subordinates must give way to their superiors.' Peloros turns to the band and says, 'Do you see how hard work is rewarded? One day each one of you will have his prize taken from him like this; one day you all will be the victims of this arbitrary and autocratic law.' A brawl then ensues. This passage illustrates well both the role of rules outlaws lived by and of the outlaw assembly in levelling the band.

Duties are chosen by lot among Apuleius' outlaws as, for example, sentinel duty and serving at table. They elect their leader: Haemus is so elected when their previous captain is killed in action. In Heliodorus' *An Ethiopian Story* the outlaw chief Thyamis makes a speech that sets out all the best traits of a leader: fairness in distribution of booty, not taking more than the rank and file, careful keeping of the common money fund, good recruitment, and proper treatment of women:

Comrades, you know how I have always felt towards you. As you know, I was born the son of the high priest at Memphis, but I did not succeed to the priesthood after my father's disappearance, since my younger brother illegally usurped the office. I took refuge with you in the hope of gaining revenge and regaining my position. You chose me to be your leader, and to this day I have made a practice of not giving myself a larger share than the rest of you. If it has been a case of sharing money, then I have been content with an equal portion, and if it has been a matter of selling prisoners, I have contributed the proceeds to the common fund in the belief that a leader as good as I hope I am should undertake the largest share of the work but receive only an equal share of the profits. As for prisoners, I have enrolled into our number those men whose physical strength was likely to be of use to use, and sold the weaker ones; I have never misused a woman, but I have set free the wellborn, either for ransom or from simple pity at their misfortune, while those of humble extraction, for whom slavery was a normal way of life rather than a condition imposed on them by their capture, I have distributed among you all as servants. (*An Ethiopian Story* 1.19/Morgan)

In *The Golden Ass* the bandits come to agreements by mutual consent, with all the outlaws in a council: They decide to kill Lucius by vote of the council; and they agree to Haemus' plan to sell the girl Charite after some deliberation and differing points of view. In Chariton's *Chaereas and Callirhoe* the pirates discuss what to do with Callirhoe; it is not exactly a council, but different ideas are expressed before the chief has his way. But in Heliodorus' *An Ethiopian Story* Thyamis, the chief of the outlaws, calls an assembly. 'By this time, they had reached the meeting place, and the rest of the [bandit] company had assembled. Thyamis took his seat on the mound and declared the island to be a parliament' (1.19/Morgan). When they accumulate booty, one of their number acts as a 'protector of the treasury' and advises regarding the best disposition of that booty; while Apuleius uses this term lightheartedly, the function is real. Equal distribution is essential to the maintenance of the band, as Cicero notes with reference to the gang leadership: 'Unless the pirate captain divides booty equitably, he is either murdered by his fellows, or deserted by them' (*On Duties* 2.11.40).

The egalitarian mode of life must have appealed to some; it is noted in lawful sources and even esteemed, as giving a true venue for merit.

A story in Lucian illustrates this attitude as Samippus reveals his wish of what he would be/have, if he could be/have anything:

> The gods can do anything, even what seems to be quite stupendous, and the rule which Timolaus laid down was not to hesitate to ask for anything, on the assumption that they will not say no. Well, I ask to be made a king, but not a king like Alexander, Philip's son, or Ptolemy or Mithridates or any of those who inherited their kingdom from a father. No, let me begin as a brigand with about thirty sworn companions, men absolutely trustworthy and full of spirit. Then let them grow by degrees to three hundred, a thousand, and soon ten thousand, until the total is some fifty thousand heavy infantry and about five thousand horse. I shall be elected chief by all, because they think me the most able leader and administrator. This very fact is sweet – to be greater than other kings, because I've been elected commander by the army on merit, and not inherited the kingdom after someone else has done the work – that would be like Adimantus's treasure and not so gratifying as when you see that you have won power by your own effort. (*The Ship* 28–9/Harmon)

On the other hand, the very hardness of the outlaw life put strains on 'normal' bonds between men. Heliodorus in *An Ethiopian Story* stresses how wealth acquisition is the preeminent characteristic of outlaws, surpassing both friendship and kinship in importance:

> Although they had lost so many of their friends, they [the winners] felt more joy in forming a respectful escort for the man who had slain them and yet lived than pity at the death of their comrades. So much more precious, evidently, do brigands consider money than life itself: friendship and kinship are defined solely in terms of financial gain. This was certainly the case here. (*Ethiopian Story* 1.32/Morgan)

Cicero also alludes to at least one source of friction among outlaws, and how it was resolved: 'For if anyone of the outlaw gang steals or sequesters anything, he loses his standing in the band' (*On Duties* 2.11.40). In fact, in Achilles Tatius' *Leucippe and Clitophon* an outlaw leader who does not distribute the booty evenly is killed by his crew.

In *An Ethiopian Story* the promise of equal distribution of booty is a prime motivator for an outlaw band. Since there is no internal division among outlaws in Apuleius, there is no picture of how conflict resolution was conducted. But in Achilles Tatius' *Leucippe and Clitophon*, cited just above, the contention between the leader and his men over the distribution of booty ends in the leader's beheading.

I now put next to this ancient picture of outlawry one particularly vivid comparison, the life of sea outlaws of the 'golden age of piracy,' the first half of the eighteenth century, in the Atlantic Ocean. Marcus Rediker presents an excellent account of these men in the book *Between the Devil and the Deep Blue Sea*. It needs to be stressed that whereas there were even in the eighteenth century and before accounts of pirates and pirate life, including a justly famous pseudonymous one by Daniel Defoe, the exceptional value of Rediker's approach lies in his use of evidence from the actual statements of pirates. These statements sometimes came after a pirate had 'reformed' and taken up writing memoirs (with not a little fiction thrown in, one might suppose), sometimes through investigations of authors, but the most valuable material comes from court records of trials of pirates. These trials were very public affairs and drew a good deal of attention as spectacle. In the course of them, pirates gave testimony of their deeds; their witness was recorded and preserved. Thus the very statements of pirates exist, which while not necessarily to be taken at face value in all cases, nevertheless give something totally lacking from ancient times.

Rediker's pirates live in a place removed from lawful society – the pirate ship and/or island base – and have a clearly articulated social order. This order seemed disorder to contemporaries, but upon examination it is revealed to be coherent, purposeful, and effective, given the origins, possibilities, and goals of the outlaw gang. What is more, 'this social order, articulated in the organization of the pirate ship, was conceived and deliberately constructed by the pirates themselves. Its hallmark was a rough, improvised, but effective egalitarianism that placed authority in the collective hands of the crew … egalitarianism was institutionalized aboard the pirate ship.' The origins of pirates were almost universally among the lower class poor; as is expectable, most had some seafaring experience, but this aspect would apply only to pirates, not to outlaws in general, of course. Almost all were male; of 521 pirates documented by Rediker (out of perhaps 5000 operating at the height of piracy), only two are female. In general, they came to outlawry free from close ties to lawful society: no wives or family were allowed; the politics of lawful society became irrelevant; established religion was actively rejected. They, in fact, rejected the entire structure of lawful society, and most especially the ideology of the stratified, hierarchical civil society captured and defined by its laws. In its place they substituted the egalitarianism just mentioned, and a new set of laws based upon that ideology. Internally, this egalitarianism meant that every outlaw had an equal voice, and that decisions were made communally. Externally, it meant that pirates did not prey on other pirates – there was a certain communitarianism that united the pirates in sentiment, even if there were few, if any, documented 'pirate alliances.' The feeling of being a member of a special community was perhaps enhanced by the use of a 'secret language' – a pidgin English mostly based upon extensive profanity and a limited vocabulary.

One of the most intriguing aspects of this new society was the existence of – even a requirement for – a written contract, called 'Articles,' which set out the constitution of the group. In a time before it was usual to think of government being based upon a concocted document rather than upon divine right and/or everlasting tradition (for example, the 'rights of Englishmen'), the pirates took their cue from contracts of business partnerships and laid out mutual obligations, governmental structures, laws of behavior, and economic rules. These documents had many elements in common, and so a 'normal' picture can be drawn.

Authority was in the band. An oath was sworn to work as a group. Each man had one vote and the majority ruled. Everyone was subject to the community's authority and had to obey its rules as laid down in the 'Articles,' even the captain. Indeed, 'the captain was the creature of his crew.' The governmental structure included mechanisms for legislating rules, executive action, and judicial decisions. The rules, as I have noted, were made in an assembly of the whole, called the council. The executive function was performed by this council (i.e. major decisions as to actions were voted upon), as was the judicial, when it sat as a court to deal with social or disciplinary problems. The chief executive, the captain, was elected by the council; in battle or other crisis he had full authority, but otherwise he had to lead by consensus, cajoling, and persuasion, as he could be deposed at any time by the council. The other elected official was the quartermaster. This man had the role of protector of the interests of the crew. In particular, he kept track of the booty and saw to its fair distribution. He was a sort of 'civil' magistrate alongside the 'military' captain.

Indeed, these two offices summarize well the basic leadership needs of the band: to get booty and to distribute it. The plunder was divided up into shares (the analogy with joint-stock companies is evident) and the shares distributed among the crew. The captain and quartermaster got more shares than others because of their responsibilities; each got 1.5 to 2 shares. Skilled men such as gunners also got more than a single share – 1.25 to 1.5 shares each. The rest of the men got a single share. Thus the egalitarian spirit was expressed in booty distribution; all were engaged in a 'risk-sharing venture'; no one was a laborer, no one a master.

Quite naturally the outlaw groups had their problems with discipline and maintenance of order. The men were most often deserters from the highly structured and disciplined life at sea found most strongly in the traditions of the British navy, but also in life on a merchantman. They had no inclination to recreate the life they had hated and fled. Thus, discipline was very loose. The basic goal was to discourage violence within the community; the basic methodology was to highlight a problem and bring a quick resolution by ejection from the community or death. Lashing was universally prohibited; the lash as the most painful symbol of the brutality of the navy and merchant marine was not allowed within the pirate community. If a dispute arose between two crew members, dueling was the accepted method of conflict resolution. In the case of conflict between the group and an individual, marooning was the normal punishment. Actual execution of a crew member was rare, and used only in the case of treason or introducing weakening elements into the group, such as women and young boys.

The similarities between Rediker's early modern pirates and ancient novelists' outlaw bands are striking. The same egalitarianism exists, and many of the same institutions and habits as well, such as a council for decision-making and agreed-upon rules of behavior. Of course, there is no complete correspondence. For example, whereas Rediker's pirates will have nothing to do with any religion, Apuleius' outlaws are committed to their protecting deity, Mars, as are Xenophon's in *An Ephesian Tale* (2.11–14). However, Plutarch notes irreligious or nontraditional religious behavior: 'They raided and violated places of refuge and holy sanctuaries … They offered strange sacrifices at Olympia and celebrated secret rites' (*Life of Pompey* 24.5/Perrin). An inscription records the results of just such a raid on a sanctuary:

> This statue of Venus is dedicated to Valerius Romanus, Most Outstanding, Guardian Overseer of the Most Splendid Colony Sicca Veneria, a man of wondrous goodness and integrity, because he restored the statue of the goddess damaged a long time ago by outlaws who had broken into the temple. May the memory of our steadfast patron last through the ages! (*CIL* 13.3689 = *ILS* 5505)

In another literary example, the cannibalism and bloody rituals found in Heliodorus and Achilles Tatius represent a total rejection of the 'decent' in normal religion, and so fall into line with the rejection of normal religion on the part of Rediker's pirates, but those pirates do not indulge in such unholy acts. On the other hand, in the ancient world the absence of monolithic religious establishments supporting the status quo removed the impulse to revolt against them felt by Rediker's pirates, but nonetheless, if one turned away from other aspects of lawful society, inverting them could still be a powerful statement of independence. It is not necessary to believe the lurid details of the novelists to accept their basic background, that outlaws were hostile not only to the legal norms of society, but also to its standard religious practices.

The shared traits and habits of Rediker's pirates and ancient outlaws as seen in history and fiction are a strong indication that the picture drawn here of Romano-Grecian outlaws reflects reality – a reality the sources do not privilege us to see very directly, but which can be retrieved by a careful use of ancient and modern sources.

Conclusion

Outlawry was one way – perhaps the only and surely the quickest way – to break the heavy hand of the law and its enforcers. With this perspective, outlaws are seen to live out a genuinely alternative life within the heavily stratified lawful society of the ancient Romano-Grecian world. Like Rediker's real pirates, Apuleius' fictional outlaws and the outlaws of the Greek romances live in a rough, cruel world, but also offer a kind of egalitarianism and democracy that stands in stark contrast to the hierarchical structure of the mainstream social system. Their community provides a – perhaps the only – alternative social structure in their respective worlds, and so it is a powerful, radical critique of those worlds. While the self-justifying and protective negative interpretation put on this critique by the elites might deceive one into thinking it is a cultural illusion, the ancient evidence and Rediker's pirates give strong indication that it was real in the eyes of the poor, the oppressed, and the outlaws themselves.

VALEDICTORY

'INVISIBLE' IS AN ADJECTIVE often used to describe the people I have talked about. These people, of course, were not invisible at all; they made up almost the entire population of the Romano-Greek world and were perfectly visible to each other. It is the elite's blindness to them that creates their historical penumbra, a shadowy world where brief illuminations only heighten the overall sense of their invisibility. This blindness is not so much to the literal existence of invisibles, but rather is an almost complete lack of interest in their lives on the invisibles' own terms. This bias makes using elite sources to discover the lives of ordinary folk very problematic. But given the significantly undersourced nature of ancient evidence for almost any aspect of history or life, muscling aside elite material in favor of lesser-known evidence might seem at least counterproductive and perhaps even foolhardy. I became convinced, however, that starting at the other end of the evidence, so to speak, would yield what the high-profile elite literature problematized or even obfuscated. And so I worked primarily with the lesser-known material of inscriptions and papyri, and used admittedly problematic insights from fiction, fable, Christian sources, fortune-telling, and magic.

These sources gradually revealed to me a world that once was invisible. It was a world of down-to-earth assessments, choices, chances, successes, and disasters. It was a world of limited options and limited opportunities for bettering oneself. But it was not a world of despair.

Fundamentally, people have always excelled at making the most of their situations; the race would hardly have survived if in the face of daunting challenges, manipulation, and oppression, people had just given up. Rather, people cope within the parameters of their lives. And sometimes even do very well. The visible that emerged was a tapestry of people working to make their lives as good as possible, struggling with all the emotional crosscurrents and enjoying all the satisfactions that came with it. Opening up their mind worlds was a revelation.

In the end, the people now made visible do not seem all that different from moderns. Not in the material ways, not in all moral norms, not in political sensibilities, or in the specifics of careers and possibilities. But in the gritty reality of dealing with what comes along, seeking solace and reward in interpersonal relationships and the supernatural, and carving out a place for themselves, they are much like other people, ancient and modern. While this banal reality stands far apart from the excitement of great deeds by great men, and certainly is not the engine of high-profile historical transformations, that does not mean it is inconsequential. There is a certain importance to the lives of the nonheadline makers; in them we glimpse the crowd in which the rich and famous move, and understanding them helps us to understand the whole culture and society. We can without hesitation turn from them to the Alexanders, the Caesars, the emperors and generals of the ancient world; we can study and be inspired by their philosophy, laws, literature, and architectural wonders. But behind all these accomplishments stood tens of millions who sustained the world of those accomplishments – ordinary men and women, slaves and freedmen, fairly wealthy and abysmally poor, even common soldiers, prostitutes, gladiators, and outlaws. They deserve to be made visible on their own terms, and I hope I have succeeded in making a start at doing so.

SOURCES

TRADITIONALLY, LITERATURE PRODUCED BY THE ELITE deserves pride of place in the discussion of the sources; its aesthetic as well as its richness deservedly mark it out for first attention. I try to extract evidence from this material. Thus when Horace writes in his work of freedmen, I can assume that entangled in whatever impression he wishes to give of freedmen are tidbits of the actual: Freedmen exist, they have patrons, they have attitudes that are intended to produce success. I need not accept Horace's presentation of freedmen, or his use of them for other rhetorical, poetic, or aesthetic purposes in order to extract plausible facts about 'real' freedmen and their attitudes from his work. He has taken these facts and arranged them for his purposes; social historians can do the same, taking the material and arranging it in a way that seems to fit with a broad picture of freedmen and their mind world. But it is a dangerous business: The historian can easily be deceived. Some literature is going to be more grounded in that world in immediate ways, some less. And some historians will start from here and some from there in seeing and being deceived. The challenge is to judge how much of the literary world is a construct of the author that hides the non-elite, and how much can be used to reveal them. The key is to work as carefully as possible to take the useful material and reject the narrative of dominance into which it is imbedded by the author. The social-history detail that can be extracted from ancient authors (mostly) intent on other things is amazing. Yet there are many aspects of daily life that the elite – the Ciceros, Tacituses, Martials, Juvenals, Plinys – could see if they wanted. But they simply do not care – they seldom even give a glance at the people enacting these details in their actual lives as people. High literature, therefore, provides not windows, but peepholes through which historians get glances at the ordinary Romans.

The drawbacks of this literature – the persistent point of view of the elite, the lack of overt treatment of ordinary people – make it less useful than another range of literature that is more relevant to my purpose. Lucian's work is one example. He was from Samosata, a city in Roman Syria, of an artisan family. His parents saw to it that he had a primary education; this was reasonably common in his day. After this, his father wanted him to do something useful with his life, but apprenticeship to an uncle sculptor was a complete failure and Lucian went on for more education and, eventually, the life of a professional rhetorician. In his work he shows sympathy for ordinary people including the poor, although there is no encouragement of antiestablishment action.

There are other works that also participate in this interest. The mere mention of using novels and romances (as they are called today; there are no such genres in ancient literary criticism) as a historical source might raise eyebrows, for what could be less useful for historical research than a consciously fictional recreation of ancient life, however artistically disguised as a 'real-life' drama or adventure? On the one hand it is possible to think of all history as fiction: 'History is not just a catalogue of events put in the right order like a railway timetable. History is a version of events' (A. J. P. Taylor). So, too, is overt fiction. Sorting out the 'real' from the 'fictitious' is equally challenging in both genres. Petronius can be used as a historical source – he must be used carefully, but the same applies to the need for cautious use of purely 'historical' sources. Ancient fiction will be an important well to draw from. I would point to three examples of how this can and should be done. First of all, Fergus Millar, inspired by a fellow scholar's attempt to extract the real world of the Japanese classic *The Tale of the Genji*, wrote in 1981 the pathbreaking article 'The World of *The Golden Ass.*' In this he showed beyond a doubt that Apuleius' novel of transformation and salvation is set in the identifiably real world of second-century imperial Rome. Keith Hopkins dissected the tale of Aesop's life to find many truths and insights into the world of the slave. And John D'Arms wrote with clarity about how Petronius' world of the *Satyricon* could be used intelligently to get at aspects of the later first-century Roman world below the elites. The Greek romances belong in this same range of sources. Although they are set in an imaginary world of black and white, good and evil, faith and betrayal, they too have their moorings in a real world and can be mined for useful observations and material. The use of Roman comedy for social history raises similar problems and requires the same solution as does the use of novelistic material. Comedy too had to be rooted in the understandable either in the form of known stereotypes or recognizable motifs of one's own society. Thus the theatrical world also produces bits and pieces of lives of the invisibles: soldiers, slaves, women, and the common run of men. In sum, literature remains a promising mine, albeit a hard and even dangerous one.

Some elite writings are not very 'literary,' i.e. their first intent is not artistry. These can have special uses in discovering the mind world of invisibles. In this category fall the agricultural treatises, such as Cato the Elder's *On Farming* or Columella's *On Rural Matters*. Such works are directed at wealthy agriculturalists, not peasants or small landholders, but imbedded in them are observations particularly important to understanding slaves. Other Romans as well wrote useful treatises on a wide variety of subjects. Galen wrote widely on issues related to medicine, and from time to time social history evidence appears. Epictetus, himself an ex-slave, leaves some traces of his servile origins in his recorded lectures. There are also works related to foretelling and controlling the future through skill and magic. Artemidorus of Daldus wrote *The Interpretation of Dreams*, in which he gives extensive treatment to a wide variety of dreams, all, he claims, based on actual experience. Likewise Dorotheus of Sidon, a slightly earlier contemporary of Artemidorus, wrote the *Carmen Astrologicum* (*Astrological Poem*). In it he details an elaborate astrological system and presents nativities (i.e. astrological predictions) for various configurations of the heavens. Finally, there are the magical papyri. These were again meant to guide professionals in using appropriate charms, spells, and prayers to help their paying audience. All three works were aimed at ordinary people. That is not to say that the elite were uninterested in dreams, astrology, and magic – quite the contrary. My point is that the main audience was a wide swath of the Romano-Grecian world, whoever wanted to pay a professional for 'psychic' advice or magical aides. Therefore scenarios, problems, tastes, prejudices, and enthusiasms found in these texts reflect actual concerns of real people. Examining the topics chosen for treatment in their works opens very clear access to the mind world of invisibles.

Roman legal texts would seem to be an excellent place to glean information about invisibles; they appear in many legal decisions. However, in the end the interaction of invisibles with Roman law is not as fruitful as one would have suspected. As John Crook wrote in *Law and Life of Rome* (p. 10):

> Roman society was very oligarchic. It perpetuated enormous differences in wealth and social power, and the upper class which determined its legal rules enshrined in them a code of values relevant to itself which cannot automatically be assumed to have been equally relevant to the lives and habits of the mass of the people. Furthermore, the intellectual power and subtlety and thoroughness of the great Roman jurists, which made their surviving writings a justly admired paradigm of law for later ages, was achieved at the price of concentration on certain groups of rules (those most relevant to the oligarchy of which they were members) and unconcern for what might in fact be going on below or outside that sphere.

Collections of fables and proverbs are also important sources. Proverbs are pithy statements offering an observation to describe a situation or as incentive to direct action. These are traditional, popular, anonymous, and instructive; they are repeated over time in essentially the same form. Fables are brief stories, usually involving animals and of an apparently homey, simple nature, offering a lesson of advice; as with proverbs, instruction is the key. All from (at least) Aristotle have thought of fables as a 'popular' genre, given their simplicity and appeal to children and the uneducated. However, fables also have a long history of being appreciated by the elite. Can they be considered 'popular'? Both fable collectors Babrius and Phaedrus address their collections to elites; both are elites themselves. The verses of the freedman writer of maxims Publilius Syrus also fall into this category. But the fundamental origin of the material in these genres can reasonably be called 'popular' and so excellent for this project.

In addition to these indirect sources, there are three direct sources of the invisibles' mind world, all of them rich with information: nonelite literature, papyrology, and epigraphy. In the New Testament material there is the single richest collection of literature written by what I call invisibles and expressing their outlook. The Gospels give us the world of the peasant. Here there is virtually no municipal life; it is a world without a middle, a world of the very rich and the very poor, a world of a small peasant economy and values. The perspective of the events and parables is one of limited good, distributive justice, and other reflections of a peasant's mind world, to judge from comparative material. On the other hand, the world of Acts and the Epistles is an urban one – the towns and townish attitudes of the Hellenistic East; this world is the world of a Strabo or a Dio Chrysostom. When Paul or other writers express attitudes toward wealth, women, slaves, the poor, the hierarchical structures, and the elite of society, it is reasonable to query them as representative of ordinary men of the towns, although an awareness of the shadings that their theological mission thrusts upon them is essential. Beyond the New Testament literature itself, patristic contributions can also offer material, although it is really not until after Constantine that there is a flood of surviving compositions, and increasingly Christianity was seized by an elitist mentality that in many ways comes to be the same as the pagan elite's. But all in all, early Christian literature is a rich source. In the same vein, Jewish literature has the potential to be useful, but I have not pursued this systematically for the present project.

Like the New Testament, epigraphic material speaks directly with the voices of ordinary people. There are problems, however. The very mass of inscriptions makes study difficult, for inscriptions are many, but distributed unevenly over time and space; adding to the challenge is the fact that discovery and publication of inscriptions is also erratic. Even without these issues of discovery and dissemination, there would be uneven demographic distribution. Long, elaborated inscriptions are almost exclusively the province of elite concerns – laws, official public inscriptions, elaborate epitaphs, and so on. Inscriptions that reveal the voices of invisibles are almost all very brief and either votive, offerings to the gods, or funerary, i.e. gravestones. Even for a person of quite modest means, an engraved stone was fully within his or her financial capabilities either through self-financing or perhaps through the support of a burial society. There is much evidence for social relationships and outlooks that ordinary folk wanted the world to know about. Relationships within the family based on the mention of kinship in dedications and the expression of hopes and fears in epitaphs are just two examples. And the graffiti from Pompeii, which add a variety and spice to the epigraphic record of ordinaries, are very valuable in thinking about their mind worlds.

Papyrology, like epigraphy, speaks with the direct voices of invisibles. Writing on papyrus was widespread in the Roman world, but only in a few places were dry conditions suitable for its survival through the ages. Papyri therefore present a geographical bias, because they come overwhelmingly from the desert areas of Egypt and some other parts of the Near East. This fact naturally leads us to ask whether papyrological evidence can be applied to areas outside Egypt. Once it was widely held that historians could not use papyrological evidence in this way because of Egypt's exceptionalism in the sociopolitical landscape of the Romano-Grecian world. This issue, once seemingly closed, has now turned 180 degrees. The idea that Egypt was a world apart and can be ignored in discussions of the rest of the Roman world is now very much out of vogue. As Roger Bagnall and others cogently argue, governmental practice and the use of documents within and outside Egypt was essentially the same, so that habits and items from Egypt can be taken as representative of habits in other areas of the empire.

Papyrus was a relatively inexpensive writing material. It was widely used to record governmental actions (tax, census records, internal correspondence) as well as receipts, contracts, and other financial documentation. In addition there are private letters, educational materials, and literary texts in fair number. Of course almost all of this material has long since perished. But letters and private documents that do survive most often come from the invisibles at hand, i.e. ordinary people below the elite, both male and (particularly astonishingly – and refreshingly) female. While it is often impossible to tell if the documents were actual autographs of these people – professional scribes and trained slaves were numerous and frequently employed – the origin of the documents from among the ordinary people is clear enough. Further,

government-generated documents – the vast majority of early imperial papyri – provide a very wide range of useful information, ranging
from census figures and extrapolations from them to the likely burden
of government, which would have directly affected ordinary people's
attitudes and views. Much like the graffiti of Pompeii and, to a lesser
extent, the inscriptions, the papyri show invisibles living their own
lives, without mediation through elite literature.

Beyond written evidence for invisibles, material culture adds
breadth and depth to the picture. Art is a message board for creators and
'readers' alike: Not created in a vacuum, both the creator and the audience are intended to get something out of the representations. It should,
therefore, be possible to 'read' art the way epigraphy or papyri or literature are read. There is much to work with: sepulchral images; graffiti
drawings; wall paintings in buildings and rooms meant for the use of
invisibles; images on fired-clay tableware such as terra sigillata – all
can be very revealing. Archaeological material beyond art also has great
potential for adding to our knowledge about ordinary people, although
it often has more to do with living conditions and arrangements than
mind worlds. However, as in the case of Jewish literature noted above,
I must confess that I have not used archaeology as much as would be
possible. Perhaps another more versed in the material will be able to
add to or correct the observations I make.

Finally, there is evidence from beyond the specified time and place of
the Roman empire. There is often a suspicion of the use of comparative
material. The problem of comparability is a real one: An inappropriate use of supposedly comparable material can lead one far astray. But
material from other times and places provides two invaluable things:
first, an inspiration to ask questions of ancient material that have been
asked elsewhere; and, second, ideas for links between the ancient material's often very sketchy and disjointed pieces of evidence. An ancient
fact or attitude cannot be taken as proven by comparative data, but its
probability can certainly be enhanced. In discovering the mind world
of invisible Romans, I use quite freely both the inspiration and the link-
ages drawn from mind worlds of other invisibles. This may make those
who feel that ancient history should be based on ancient evidence alone
a little nervous. But the Romano-Grecian world does not exist in some
sort of unique space separated by time and place from the rest of human

history. So my intent is not to compromise the purity of ancient history, but to reasonably build out from what little there is in order to answer questions – in this case about the mind world of invisibles – which the main sources themselves have virtually no interest in at all.

Taken together, all our sources make it possible to see the invisible Romans.

FURTHER READING

Introduction

There are two very sensible introductions to the challenges of writing ancient history: Michael Crawford (from whom the opening quotation comes) edited a strong collection of essays in *Sources for Ancient History: Studies in the Uses of Historical Evidence* (Cambridge, UK: Cambridge University Press, 1983); and David S. Potter's *Literary Texts and the Roman Historian* (London: Routledge, 1999) (from whom the final quotation comes) offers clear guidelines for using this sort of evidence. Susan Treggiari's *Roman Social History* (London: Routledge, 2002) has a good discussion of how to evaluate and use sources specifically for social history. Sandra Joshel's *Work, Identity, and Legal Status at Rome: A Study of the Occupational Inscriptions* (Norman, OK: Oklahoma University Press, 1992), pp. 3–15, presents an exceptionally apposite discussion of the issues involved in learning about invisible Romans from literature, epigraphy, and other sources; the whole book well repays careful reading.

Chapter 1

Works that succeed to some extent in treating ordinary men from a nonelite point of view include the essays in *The Romans*, ed. Andrea Giardina, trans. L. G. Cochrane (Chicago: University of Chicago Press,

1993), and Paul Veyne's 'The Roman Empire,' in *A History of Private Life, Volume 1: From Pagan Rome to Byzantium*, ed. Paul Veyne, trans. Arthur Goldhammer (Cambridge, MA: Harvard University Press, 1987), pp. 5–234. Peter Garnsey and Richard Saller's *The Roman Empire: Economy, Society, and Culture* (Berkeley: University of California Press, 1987) remains an excellent brief introduction to the period; Ramsay MacMullen's *Roman Social Relations* (New Haven: Yale University Press, 1974) and anything else by MacMullen provide good insights; and Nicholas Horsfall's *The Culture of the Roman Plebs* (London: Duckworth, 2003), while somewhat idiosyncratic, is stimulating. On early Christianity and Christians, see Bruce J. Malina, The *New Testament World* (Louisville: Westminster John Knox Press, 2001), and Wayne Meeks, *The First Urban Christians*, 2nd edn (New Haven: Yale University Press, 2003). Teresa Morgan's *Popular Morality in the Early Roman Empire* (Cambridge: Cambridge University Press, 2007) and Maureen Carroll's *Spirits of the Dead: Roman Funerary Commemoration in Western Europe* (Oxford: Oxford University Press, 2006), a pathbreaking treatment of epigraph as a rich source for the lives of ordinary people, together give background on how we can know what ordinary people thought. For magic, see Georg Luck, *Arcana Mundi: Magic and the Occult in the Greco-Roman World* (Baltimore: Johns Hopkins University Press, 1985), and Matthew W. Dickie, *Magic and Magicians in the Greco-Roman World* (London: Routledge, 2001); and on curse tablets, John G. Gager, *Curse Tablets and Binding Spells from the Ancient World* (Oxford: Oxford University Press, 1992). For astrology, see Ramsay MacMullen, 'Social History in Astrology,' *Ancient Society* 2 (1971), 104–16; and for dreams, Arthur Pomeroy, 'Status Anxiety in the Greco-Roman Dream Books,' *Ancient Society* 22 (1991), 51–74; for associations, see Philip A. Harland, *Associations, Synagogues, and Congregation: Claiming a Place in Mediterranean Society* (Minneapolis: Fortress Press, 2003); for street life, see Barbara Kellum, 'The Spectacle of the Street,' in *The Art of Ancient Spectacle*, ed. Bettina Bergmann and Christine Kondoleon (New Haven: Yale University Press, 1999), pp. 283–99; for law, see J. A. Crook, *Law and Life of Rome* (Ithaca: Cornell University Press, 1967).

Chapter 2

The following suggestions amplify the picture of women in the Romano-Grecian world. As always, most notices will spotlight elite women, but on a few occasions ordinaries are the focus, and in all there are insights into various aspects of the lives and outlooks of those women.

Sarah Pomeroy moved the study of Greek and Roman women onto center stage in the late twentieth century with her very readable and reliable *Goddesses, Whores, Wives, and Slaves: Woman in Classical Antiquity* (New York: Schocken, 1984; reissued with new preface and additional bibliography, 1995). Her treatment of the material is scholarly yet accessible, and important for a wide readership. For a recent, more modest but solid treatment there is now Eve D'Ambra's *Roman Women* (Cambridge, UK: Cambridge University Press, 2007). Jane F. Gardner's *Women in Roman Law & Society* (Bloomington: Indiana University Press, 1991) takes a more formalist approach, but contains much useful information. For late antiquity (a period mostly following that dealt with in this book), Gillian Clark's *Women in Late Antiquity: Pagan and Christian Lifestyles* (Oxford: Clarendon Press, 1993) has an excellent overview.

Sourcebooks are a very useful way to see what evidence is available. I mention especially Jane F. Gardner and Thomas Wiedemann's *The Roman Household: A Sourcebook*: (London: Routledge, 1991); Mary R. Lefkowitz and Maureen B. Fant's *Women's Life in Greece and Rome: A Source Book in Translation* (Baltimore: Johns Hopkins University Press, 1992); *Women in the Classical World: Image and Text*, ed. Elaine Fantham et al. (New York: Oxford University Press, 1994); and Suzanne Dixon's *Reading Roman Women: Sources, Genres, and Real Life* (London: Duckworth, 2001). For the legal condition of women there is Judith Evans Grubbs, *Women and the Law in the Roman Empire: A Sourcebook on Marriage, Divorce, and Widowhood* (London: Routledge, 2002).

Collections of essays abound and although usually focused on elite issues, especially literary and art historical studies, they still often contain good information about ordinary women. *Women's History and Ancient History*, ed. Sarah B. Pomeroy (Chapel Hill: University of North Carolina Press, 1991), stands out, and, for its useful chapters on 'invisibles,' *Women and Slaves in Greco-Roman Culture: Differential Equations*, ed. Sandra R. Joshel and Sheila Murnaghan (London and New York: Routledge, 1998).

Specific studies add greater context. The bibliographies of the works cited above will lead to many other interesting treatments. I have used a good deal of material from Egypt; several excellent studies have made use of the papyri and allowed this to happen. I mention especially *Women and Society in Greek and Roman Egypt: A Sourcebook*, ed. Jane Rowlandson (Cambridge, UK: Cambridge University Press, 1998). Roger Bagnall's work has been very valuable as well: Roger S. Bagnall and Bruce W. Frier, *The Demography of Roman Egypt* (Cambridge, UK: Cambridge University Press, 1994), and Roger S. Bagnall and Raffaella Cribiore, with contributions by Evie Ahtaridis, *Women's Letters from Ancient Egypt, 300 BC–AD 800* (Ann Arbor: University of Michigan Press, 2006). Studies on specific aspects of ordinary women's lives are rather rare. However, Susan Treggiari's 'Lower Class Women in the Roman Economy,' *Florilegium* 1 (1979), 65–86 and 'Jobs for Women,' *American Journal of Ancient History* 1 (1976), 76–104 are exceptional, as are Natalie Boymel Kampen's many contributions to seeing (and being unable to see) ordinary women in art: *Image and Status: Roman Working Women in Ostia* (Berlin: Gebr. Mann Verlag, 1981); 'Material Girl: Feminist Confrontations with Roman Art,' *Arethusa* 27 (1994), 111–37; and 'Social Status and Gender in Roman Art: The Case of the Saleswoman,' in Eve D'Ambra, *Roman Art in Context: An Anthology* (Englewood Cliffs, NJ: Prentice Hall, 1993), pp. 115–32. Beryl Rawson addresses ordinary women in 'Family Life among the Lower Classes at Rome in the First Two Centuries of the Empire,' *Classical Philology* 61 (1966), 71–83, as does Walter Scheidel in 'The Most Silent Women of Greece and Rome: Rural Labor and Women's Life in the Ancient World,' *Greece and Rome* 42 (1995), 202–17. Of some interest is also John R. Clarke, *Art in the Lives of Ordinary Romans: Visual Representation and Non-Elite Viewers in Italy, 100 B.C. – A.D. 315* (Berkeley & Los Angeles: University of California Press, 2003). I have not made much use of purely archaeological material; works like Penelope M. Allison's *Pompeian Households: An Analysis of the Material Culture* (Los Angeles: Cotsen Institute of Archaeology, UCLA, Monograph 42, 2004) and Lindsay Allason-Jones's *Women in Roman Britain*, 2nd edn (York: Council for British Archaeology, 2005) and *Daily Life in Roman Britain* (Westport, CT: Greenwood, 2008) give an inkling of the possibilities, which surely would repay more study.

Studies of the family and household often touch on the lives of ordinary women: K. R. Bradley, *Discovering the Roman Family: Studies in Roman Social History* (New York: Oxford University Press, 1991); Suzanne Dixon, *The Roman Family* (Baltimore: Johns Hopkins University Press, 1992); and Jane F. Gardner, *Family and Familia in Roman Law and Life* (Oxford: Clarendon Press, 1998). On motherhood and family, see Suzanne Dixon, *The Roman Mother* (London: Routledge, 1988, 1990); Beryl Rawson, *Marriage, Divorce, and Children in Ancient Rome* (Oxford: Clarendon Press, 1991); and Susan Treggiari, *Roman Marriage: Iusti Coninges from the Time of Cicero to the Time of Ulpian* (Oxford: Clarendon Press, 1991). I mention only a few articles that touch on specific topics; there is much more to be found in bibliographies. On sex, see Suzanne Dixon, 'Sex and the Married Woman in Ancient Rome,' in *Early Christian Families in Context: An Interdisciplinary Dialogue*, ed. David L. Balch and Carolyn Osiek (Grand Rapids: W. B. Eerdmans, 2003), pp. 111–29; on contraception and abortion, see J. M. Riddle, *Contraception and Abortion from the Ancient World to the Renaissance* (Cambridge: Harvard University Press, 1992), and E. Eyben, 'Family Planning in Graeco-Roman Antiquity,' *Ancient Society* 11/12 (1980/1), 5–82; on child exposure, see William V. Harris, 'Child Exposure in the Roman Empire,' *Journal of Roman Studies* 84 (1994), 1–22; on widows, see P. Walcot, 'On Widows and their Reputation in Antiquity,' *Symbolae Osloenses* 66 (1991), 5–26.

For evidence about females in early Christianity, particularly useful are Patricia Cox Miller, *Women in Early Christianity: Translations from Greek Texts* (Washington, DC: Catholic University of America Press, 2005); Gillian Clark, *Women in Late Antiquity: Pagan and Christian Lifestyles* (Oxford: Oxford University Press, 1993); Margaret Y. MacDonald, 'Reading Real Women through the Undisputed Letters of Paul,' in *Women & Christian Origins*, ed. Ross Shepard Kraemer and Mary Rose D'Angelo (New York: Oxford University Press, 1999), pp. 199–220; and Patricia Clark, 'Women, Slaves and the Hierarchies of Domestic Violence: The Family of St. Augustine,' in *Women and Slaves in Greco-Roman Culture: Differential Equations*, ed. Sheila Murnaghan and Sandra R. Joshel (London and New York: Routledge, 1998), pp. 109–29.

The Brazilian comparative material mentioned can be found in Mary C. Karasch, *Slave Life in Rio de Janeiro, 1808–1850* (Princeton: Princeton University Press, 1987).

Chapter 3

The basic work has long been H. Bolkenstein's *Wohltätigkeit und Armens-flege in vorchristlichen Altertum* (Utrecht, 1939), which is heavily used in A. R. Hands's *Charities and Social Aid in Greece and Rome* (Ithaca, 1968). Now there is also Marcus Prell, *Sozialökonomische Untersuchungen zur Armut im antiken Rome: Von den Gracchen bis Kaiser Diokletian* (Stuttgart: F. Steiner, 1997). Specific studies include J. Kolendo, 'The Peasant,' in *The Romans*, ed. Andrea Giardina, trans. L. G. Cochrane (Chicago: University of Chicago Press, 1993), pp. 199–213; and on pp. 272–99 of the same collection, C. R. Whittaker, 'The Poor.' Teresa Morgan's groundbreaking work, *Popular Morality in the Early Roman Empire* (Cambridge, UK: Cambridge University Press, 2007) provides much of the detailed discussion of fables and proverbs I have worked with; Greek popular literature is readily available in *Anthology of Ancient Greek Popular Literature*, ed. William Hansen (Bloomington, IN: Indiana University Press, 1998); fables are in *Babrius and Phaedrus*, ed. and trans. with commentary by B. E. Perry (Cambridge, MA: Harvard University Press, 1975). Comparative work in the ancient world includes Thomas W. Gallant, *Risk and Survival in Ancient Greece:. Reconstructing the Rural Domestic Economy* (Stanford, CA: Stanford University Press, 1991); G. E. M. de Ste. Croix, *The Class Struggle in the Ancient Greek World from the Archaic Age to the Arab Conquest* (Ithaca, NY: Cornell University Press, 1981); and G. Hamel, *Poverty and Charity in Roman Palestine, First Three Centuries C.E.* (Berkeley: University of California Press, 1990). Of wider comparative interest are Bronislaw Geremek, *Poverty: A History*, trans. Agnieszka Kolakowska (Oxford: Oxford University Press, 1994); Eric R. Wolf, *Peasants* (Englewood Cliffs, NJ: Prentice-Hall, 1966); and G. Sjoberg, *The Preindustrial City, Past and Present* (New York: The Free Press, 1960). Throughout my discussion I have benefited from the fertile ideas of James C. Scott, *Weapons of the Weak: Everyday Forms of Peasant Resistance* (New Haven, CT: Yale University Press, 1985).

Chapter 4

There are many good resources on Roman-Grecian slavery. Fundamental are Thomas E. J. Wiedemann, *Greek and Roman Slavery: A Sourcebook* (Baltimore: Routledge, 1990), and the numerous works of Keith Bradley such as *Slaves and Masters in the Roman Empire* (New York and Oxford: Oxford University Press, 1987); *Slavery and Rebellion in the Roman World, 140 BC – 70 BC* (Bloomington: Indiana University Press, 1989); and *Slavery and Society at Rome* (Cambridge, UK: Cambridge University Press, 1994), all of which provide much further bibliography. Now see also the excellent treatment by Sandra Joshel, *Slavery in the Roman World* (New York: Cambridge University Press, 2010). M. I. Finley's *Ancient Slavery and Modern Ideology* with a new preface by Brent D. Shawn (Princeton: Markus Wiener, 1998) remains very important. For a short general treatment, there is Yvon Thébert, 'The Slave,' in *The Romans*, ed. Andrea Giardina, trans. L. G. Cochrane (Chicago: University of Chicago Press, 1993), pp. 138–74. Jennifer A. Glancy's *Slavery in Early Christianity* (Oxford: Oxford University Press, 2002) has many good observations; Sandra Joshel's *Work, Identity, and Legal Status at Rome* (Norman, OK: University of Oklahoma Press, 1992) set studies in a new direction. For thinking about resistance and its embodiments, James Scott's *Weapons of the Weak: Everyday Forms of Peasant Resistance* (New Haven, CT: Yale University Press, 1985) is stimulating and his observations about peasants aid greatly the understanding of slaves' lives in slavery. For the archaeology, see F. H. Thompson, *The Archaeology of Greek and Roman Slavery* (London: Duckworth, 2003). For comparative material in the United States, W. Blassingame's *The Slave Community: Plantation Life in the Antebellum South* (Oxford: Oxford University Press, 1979) conveniently gathers much information, as does Mary C. Karasch's *Slave Life in Rio de Janeiro, 1808–1850* (Princeton: Princeton University Press, 1987) for Brazil; Jane Webster's 'Less Beloved: Roman Archaeology, Slavery and the Failure to Compare,' *Archaeological Dialogues* 15 (2008), 103–23, critiques archaeological and comparative evidence. Peter Garnsey's *Ideas of Slavery from Aristotle to Augustine* (Cambridge, UK: Cambridge University Press, 1996) treats elite concepts of slavery, while William Fitzgerald's *Slavery and the Roman Literary Imagination* (Cambridge, UK: Cambridge University Press, 2000) is most enlightening with regard to the elite's use of slavery in literature. Niall McKeown's *The Invention of Ancient Slavery?* (London: Duckworth, 2007) is a stimulating assessment of various approaches to Romano-Grecian slavery by modern scholars; he reveals how much a particular study of slavery is determined by the predispositions a scholar brings to it.

Of articles, Keith Hopkins's 'Novel Evidence for Roman Slavery,' *Past and Present* 138 (1993), 3–27, put *The Life of Aesop* on the map as evidence for slavery; Keith Bradley's 'Animalizing the Slave: The Truth of Fiction,' *Journal of Roman Studies* 90 (2000), 110–25, helps to understand the use of fiction to discover slaves. Patricia Clark's 'The Family of St. Augustine,' in *Women and Slaves in Greco-Roman Culture: Differential Equations*, ed. Sandra R. Joshel and Sheila Murnaghan (London: Routledge, 1998), pp. 109–29, describes Augustine's family's dysfunctional life, including interactions with slaves; late but still relevant material on Egypt is found in Roger S. Bagnall, 'Slavery and Society in Late Roman Egypt,' in *Law, Politics and Society in the Ancient Mediterranean World*, ed. B. Halpern and D. Hobson (Sheffield, UK: Sheffield Academic Press, 1993), pp. 220–40.

Chapter 5

The fullest treatment of freedmen and expression of the elite-skewed viewpoint is found in A. M. Duff, *Freedmen in the Early Roman Empire* (Oxford: Oxford University Press, 1928); for a succinct statement, there is Jean Andreau, 'The Freedman,' in *The Romans*, ed. Andrea Giardina, trans. L.G. Cochrane (Chicago: University of Chicago Press, 1993), pp. 175–98. Sandra Joshel's *Work, Identity, and Legal Status at Rome: A Study of the Occupational Inscriptions* (Norman, OK: University of Oklahoma Press, 1992) is fundamental to reassessing the skewed viewpoint; H. Mouritsen's 'Freedmen and Decurions: Epitaphs and Social History in Imperial Italy,' *Journal of Roman Studies* 95 (2005), 38–63, reorients against that traditional view as well; see his *The Freedman in the Roman World* (Cambridge, UK: Cambridge University Press, 2011), which appeared too late to be used here. On aspects of imperial freedmen, excluded from this essay, see Paul Weaver, *Familia Caesaris: A Study of the Emperor's Freedmen and Slaves* (Cambridge, UK: Cambridge University Press, 1972). For demographic questions, works by W. Scheidel are reliable; essays by Peter Garnsey, especially 'Independent Freedmen and the Economy of Roman Italy under the Principate,' *Klio* 63 (1981), 359–71, are always edifying. For 'freedman art,' see Lauren Hackworth Petersen's stimulating treatment in *The Freedman in Roman Art and Art History* (Cambridge, UK: Cambridge University Press, 2006). Brazilian comparative material is from Mary C. Karasch, *Slave Life in Rio de Janeiro, 1808–1850* (Princeton: Princeton University Press, 1987).

Chapter 6

It is appropriate here to pay homage to Ramsay MacMullen, who with his 1963 volume *Soldier and Civilian in the Later Roman Empire* (Cambridge, MA: Harvard University Press) paved the way for looking at soldiers as more than cogs in a fighting machine, worthy to be studied as a social as well as a military phenomenon. Good general treatments that deal with common soldiers as real people can be found in J. M. Carrié, 'The Soldier,' in *The Romans*, ed. Andrea Giardina, trans. L. G. Cochrane (Chicago: University of Chicago Press, 1993), pp. 100–137, and in B. A. Campbell, *War and Society in Imperial Rome 31 BC–AD 284* (London: Routledge, 2002), pp. 25–46, 77–105. R. Alston's *Soldier and Society in Roman Egypt: A Social History* (London: Routledge, 1995) is full of good material from Egypt which has wider application; Sara Elise Phang's *Roman Military Service: Ideologies of Discipline in the Late Republic and Early Principate* (New York: Cambridge University Press, 2008) offers a wealth of evidence. Basic sources are conveniently collected and translated in B. A. Campbell, *The Roman Army, 31 BC–AD 337: A Sourcebook* (London: Routledge, 1994). For demographic thoughts, see Walter Scheidel, 'Marriage, Families, and Survival,' in *The Blackwell Companion to the Roman Army*, ed. Paul Erdkamp (Oxford: Blackwell, 2007), pp. 417–34; and for much on marriage, sex, and family life, see Sara Elise Phang, *The Marriage of Roman Soldiers (13 B.C. – A.D. 235): Law and Family in the Imperial Army*, Columbia Studies in the Classical Tradition 24 (Leiden: Brill, 2001).

Chapter 7

The most direct and complete access to detailed material on prostitution in the Romano-Grecian world is found in the numerous works of Thomas A. McGinn: *Prostitution, Sexuality, and the Law in Ancient Rome* (Oxford: Oxford University Press, 1998); *The Economy of Prostitution in the Roman Empire* (Ann Arbor: University of Michigan Press, 2004); and, forthcoming, *Roman Prostitution*. Rebecca Fleming's 'Quae corpore quaestum facit ['She who makes money from her body']: The Sexual Economy of Female Prostitution in the Roman Empire,' *Journal of Roman Studies* 89 (1999), 38–61, is also fundamental. Briefer treatments are found in Jane F. Gardner, *Women in Roman Law and Society* (Bloomington: Indiana University Press, 1986), and Sarah B. Pomeroy, *Goddesses, Whores, Wives, and Slaves: Women in Classical Antiquity* (New York: Schocken, 1975), who gives a more generalized classical world context. For the nonexistence of sacred prostitutes, see Stephanie Budin, *The Myth of Sacred Prostitution in Antiquity* (Cambridge, UK: Cambridge University Press, 2008). John R. Clarke deals adroitly with the evidence of art for the study of Roman attitudes toward sex (and much else in the lives of ordinary folk); among his many works see especially *Looking at Lovemaking: Constructions of Sexuality in Roman Art 100 B.C. – A.D. 250* (Berkeley: University of California Press, 1998); *Looking at Laughter: Humor, Power, and Transgression in Roman Visual Culture, 100 B.C. – A.D. 250* (Berkeley: University of California Press, 2007); and *Art in the Lives of Ordinary Romans: Visual Representation and the Non-Elite Viewers in Italy, 100 B.C. – A.D. 315* (Berkeley: University of California Press, 2003); of a glossier nature is his *Roman Sex* (New York: Harry N. Abrams, 2003). For medical information, see Mirko D. Grmek, *Diseases in the Ancient Greek World*, trans. Mireille Muellner and Leonard Muellner (Baltimore: Johns Hopkins University Press, 1989), pp. 132–51; on contraception and abortion, see Plinio Prioreschi, 'Contraception and Abortion in the Greco-Roman World,' *Vesalius* 1 (1995), 77–87. The Egyptian material cited comes from *Women and Society in Greek and Roman Egypt: A Sourcebook*, ed. Jane Rowlandson (Cambridge, UK: Cambridge University Press, 1998).

Chapter 8

There has never been a lack of material on gladiators. All recent work goes back ultimately to two mid-century French studies, which accumulated most of the fundamental documentation: Louis Robert, *Les gladiateurs dans l'Orient grec* (Bibliothèque de l'Ecole des Hautes Études, Ive section, Sciences historiques et philologiques fasc. 278, Paris: Champion, 1940), and George Ville, *La gladiature en occident des origines à la mort de Domitien* (Rome: École Française de Rome, 1981(mostly written by

1967)). The best of the last twenty years includes Thomas Wiedemann, *Emperors and Gladiators* (London: Routledge, 1992); D. S. Potter and D. J. Mattingly, *Life, Death, and Entertainment in the Roman Empire* (Ann Arbor: University of Michigan Press, 1999); Alison Futrell, *Blood in the Arena: The Spectacle of Roman Power* (Austin: University of Texas Press, 1997); Donald G. Kyle, *Spectacles of Death in Ancient Rome* (London: Routledge, 1998); and Alison Futrell once again, *The Roman Games: A Sourcebook*, Blackwell Sourcebooks in Ancient History (Oxford: Blackwell, 2005). For readers concerned to know what the last twenty years have revealed about the postmodern cultural meaning of the arena and its players – an aspect of the games not treated here – these books will also provide useful bibliography in that regard.

Of the many articles on gladiators, of particular use are two by Valerie Hope, 'Negotiating Identity and Status: The Gladiators of Roman Nîmes,' in *Cultural Identity in the Roman Empire*, ed. J. Berry and R. Laurence (London: Routledge, 1998), pp. 179–95, and 'Fighting for Identity: The Funerary Commemoration of Italian Gladiators,' in *The Epigraphic Landscape of Roman Italy, Bulletin of the Institute of Classical Studies* Supplement 73 (2000), ed. A. E. Cooley, pp. 93–113. On female gladiators, Dominique Briquel's 'Les femmes gladiateurs: examen du dossier,' *Ktema* 17 (1992), 47–53, is fundamental while an English summary of the material can be found in A. McCullough, 'Female Gladiators in Imperial Rome: Literary Context and Historical Fact,' *Classical World* 101 (2008), 197–209.

Chapter 9

On bandits the best short introductions are Brent Shawn, 'The Bandit,' in *The Romans*, ed. Andrea Giardina, trans. L. G. Cochrane (Chicago: Chicago University Press, 1993), pp. 300–341, and his 'Outlaws, Aliens and Outcasts,' in *The Cambridge Ancient History*, 2nd edn, Vol. 11, ed. A. K. Bowman et al. (Cambridge, UK: Cambridge University Press, 2000), pp. 382–405. Werner Riess's *Apuleius und die Räuber: Ein Beitrag zur historischen Kriminalitätsforschung* (Stuttgart: Heidelberger Althistorische Beiträge und Epigraphische Studien 35, 2001) lays out fully the convincing arguments for being able to see 'real' bandits in Romano-Grecian history; his 'Between Fiction and Reality: Robbers in Apuleius' *Golden*

Ass,' *Ancient Narrative* 1 (2000–2001), 260–82, is an English summary of his main points. Thomas Grünewald's *Bandits in the Roman Empire: Myth and Reality* (London and New York: Routledge, 1999) denies an ability to see the 'real' bandits and argues for only a 'myth' being retrievable from antiquity. For piracy in particular, P. de Souza's *Piracy in the Graeco-Roman World* (Cambridge UK: Cambridge University Press, 1999) is a good introduction to the evidence. For a rather imaginative treatment of pirate life, see Nicholas K. Rauh, *Merchants, Sailors and Pirates in the Roman World* (Charleston, SC: Tempest Publishing, 2003). Groundbreaking work in seeing outlaws as a social phenomenon appears in Ramsay MacMullen, *Enemies of the Roman Order* (Cambridge, MA: Harvard University Press, 1967); comparative material for bandits in Eric Hobsbawm, *The Bandit* (New York: Delacourt Press, 1969); and for pirates, Marcus Rediker, *Between the Devil and the Deep Blue Sea: Merchant Seamen, Pirates and the Anglo-American Maritime World, 1700–1750* (Cambridge, UK: Cambridge University Press, 1989), Chapter 6: 'The Seaman as Pirate: Plunder and Social Banditry at Sea,' pp. 254–87. The romances are easily accessible in *Collected Ancient Greek Novels*, ed. B. P. Reardon et al. (Berkeley: University of California Press, 1989).

Sources

For Lucian, see C. P. Jones, *Culture and Society in Lucian* (Cambridge, MA: Harvard University Press, 1986); for the *Moretum*, William Fitzgerald, 'Labor and Laborer in Latin Poetry: The Case of the Moretum,' *Arethusa* 29 (1996), 389–418; for Apuleius, F. Millar, 'The World of *The Golden Ass*,' *Journal of Roman Studies* 71 (1981), 63–75, and William Fitzgerald, *Slavery and the Roman Literary Imagination* (Cambridge, UK: Cambridge University Press, 2000); for Aesop, Keith Hopkins, 'Novel Evidence for Roman Slavery,' *Past and Present* 138 (1993), 3–27; for the sensible use of Petronius as evidence, John H. D'Arms, *Commerce and Social Standing in Ancient Rome* (Cambridge, MA: Harvard University Press, 1981); for legal material, J. A. Crook, *Law and Life of Rome* (London: Thames & Hudson, 1967), and O. F. Robinson, *The Sources of Roman Law* (London: Routledge, 1997). Sources for popular morality are now readily available in Teresa Morgan's excellent *Popular Morality in the Early Roman Empire* (Oxford: Oxford University Press, 2007). Artemidorus is most accessible in *The Interpretation of Dreams: Oneirocritica by Artemidorus*, trans. and commentary by Robert J. White (Park Ridge, NJ: Noyes Press, 1975); Dorotheus of Sidon is found in *Carmen Astrologicum*, trans. David Pingree (Munich: K. G. Saur, 1976); magical papyri are in H.D. Betz et al., *The Greek Magical Papyri in Translation: Including the Demotic Texts* (Chicago: University of Chicago Press, 1986).

New Testament background can be found in A. N. Sherwin-White, *Roman Society and Roman Law in the New Testament* (Oxford: Oxford University Press, 1963), and for an anthropological and sociological perspective, see P. F. Esler, *The First Christians and Their Social Worlds* (London: Routledge, 1994). For an excellent introduction of what epigraphy can tell us, see *Epigraphic Evidence: Ancient History from Inscriptions*, ed. J. Bodel (London: Routledge, 2001) and now Maureen Carroll's outstanding study, *Spirits of the Dead: Roman Funerary Commemoration in Western Europe* (Oxford: Clarendon Press, 2006). Roger Bagnall has written a clear introduction to using papyri as evidence: *Reading Papyri, Writing Ancient History* (London: Routledge, 1995). On dreams, see Arthur Pomeroy, 'Status and Status-Concern in the Greco-Roman Dream Books,' *Ancient Society* 22 (1991), 51–74. For the use of art as evidence, start with T. Hölscher, *The Language of Images in Roman Art* (Cambridge, UK: Cambridge University Press, 2004 (orig. German, 1987)) and John R. Clarke, *Art in the Lives of Ordinary Romans: Visual Representation and Non-Elite Viewers in Italy, 100 B.C. – A.D. 315* (Berkeley and Los Angeles: University of California Press, 2003).

A WHO'S WHO AND WHAT'S WHAT OF LITERARY EVIDENCE

Achilles Tatius: Author (about the second century AD) of the Greek romance *Leucippe and Clitophon*.

Acts of the Apostles: An account of the first decades after the crucifixion of Jesus of Nazareth. Traditionally by Luke; written in the later first century AD.

Aelian: Claudius Aelianus (*c.* AD 175–235), author of *Various History*, a collection of observations and information about Romano-Grecian culture.

Aesop: Early and most famous recorder of fables. Traditionally born a slave about the sixth century BC, his life is told in the fictionalizing *Life of Aesop* of the first century AD. Collections under his authorship, such as those by Phaedrus and Babrius, were very popular.

Ammianus Marcellinus: Historian (*c.* AD 325–90s), portions of whose history of Rome in the fourth century AD survive.

Appian: Historian (*c.* AD 95–165) who wrote a history of Rome in twenty-four books, most of which survive.

Apuleius: L. Apuleius of Madaurus, North Africa (*c.* AD 125–80). Author of *The Golden Ass*, as well as other rhetorical and philosophical works.

Aristotle: Greek philosopher (384–322 BC).

Arrius Menander: A writer on military affairs in the early third century AD. Six extracts survive in the legal material.

Artemidorus of Daldus: Professional dream interpreter from Asia Minor who lived sometime in the first to second centuries AD and wrote *The Interpretation of Dreams*, which is a professional guide.

Astrampsychus: Pseudonymous author of *Astrampsychus' Predictions* (or *Oracles*), a popular guide to interpreting the casting of lots in order to foretell the future; written in Egypt in the third century AD.

Athenaeus: Author (second to third centuries AD) of *Intellectuals Dining*, an astonishing collection of cultural information in the guise of dinner-table observations.

Augustine of Hippo: Christian church leader, theologian, and philosopher who lived AD 354–430 and who wrote voluminously, his most famous work being his spiritual autobiography, *Confessions*.

Babrius: Produced a collection of 'Aesop's' fables in Greek. Exactly when he lived is uncertain.

Cato the Elder: Roman politician and military leader (234–149 BC) who wrote *On Farming,* a guide to successful large-estate management.

Celsus: Encyclopedist (c. 25 BC–AD 50). Only his *On Medicine* survives.

Chariton: Author (first to second century AD?) of the Greek romance *Chaereas and Callirhoe.*

Cicero: Roman rhetorician, politician, and philosopher (106–43 BC).

Collectio Augustana: Anonymous book of Greek fables of the second or third century AD.

Columella: Roman agricultural writer (AD 4 to c. 70).

Cyprian: Christian leader (c. AD 208–58) and writer of letters and theological treatises.

Digest: A comprehensive collection of material relating to Roman law, which was compiled at the order of the emperor Justinian I in the sixth century AD and contained essential legal material from the centuries before.

Dio Chrysostom: A Greek orator (c. AD 40–120), nicknamed 'Golden Mouthed,' who wrote *Discourses*.

Dorotheus of Sidon: A first-century AD Greek astrologer, probably based in Alexandria in Egypt, whose textbook in verse on horoscopes, *Carmen Astrologicum*, mainly survives via a ninth-century Arabic translation.

Epictetus: Greek (?) Stoic philosopher (AD 55–135). Born a slave, at some point he was freed and taught; he left no writings, but a student's notes record much of his observations and thinking.

Epigraphy: The study of writings on stone, bronze, or other durable material.

Epistles: Letters; the New Testament epistles used here include those of Paul (to Christians at Corinth, Rome, and Thessalonica, and to his friend Philemon), and of unknown authors fictively to others (Peter, Timothy, Titus).

Fable: A brief story that features animals or other nonhumans as characters and which teaches a lesson.

Gaius: Roman legal writer (*c.* AD 110–79) whose *Institutes* are a basic text of Roman law.

Galen: Roman doctor, medical writer, and philosopher (129 to the early third century AD). The most famous physician of his day; many of his works have survived and were central to medical knowledge into early modern times.

The Golden Ass: Apuleius' major work, also known as *The Metamorphoses*, a novel of transformation and salvation that contains many accurate details of the daily life of ordinary people.

graffiti: Writing or images scratched, painted, drawn, etc., on surfaces of property.

Greek Anthology: Greek poems, in large part epigrams, written over a thousand-year period beginning in the seventh century BC.

Greek Magical Papyri: A mass of papyri texts dealing with magic and religion and dating to the second to fifth centuries AD. Bought in Thebes, Egypt, about 1827 and dispersed to various private and public collections thereafter.

Heliodorus: Author (*c.* third century AD) from Syria who wrote the Greek romance *An Ethiopian Story*.

Herodian: Historian (c. AD 170–240) who wrote an account of Rome during the period AD 180–238.

Horace: Q. Horatius Flaccus (65–8 BC), famous Roman lyric poet whose father was a freedman and who was part of the literary circle of the emperor Augustus.

Juvenal: Roman satirist who wrote during the late first and early second centuries AD.

Lactantius: Christian writer (*c.* AD 240–320) who specialized in explaining and defending Christianity to polytheists.

Lucian: Rhetorician and satirist (*c.* AD 125–80) from Samosata (Syria). Born into a subelite family, his education and brilliance served elites but his writings often retain a sense for the experience of ordinary Romans.

Lucretius: Roman philosopher and poet (*c.* 99–55 BC) whose *On the Nature of Things* is an epic poem dealing with Epicurean philosophy.

Martial: A Spanish provincial who made it in Rome as a poet. His *Epigrams* are mostly sharp satires of the lives of those in his circle and of his elite patrons.

Material culture: Physical remains of society, usually discovered and identified through archaeology.

Mishnah: Early Jewish oral tradition about legal opinions and debates which was written down *c.* AD 220 and is a foundation of Rabbinic Judaism, as well as a fundamental element of the Talmud.

Musonius Rufus: Roman philosopher of Stoicism (*c.* AD 20/30–101) who, like his pupil Epictetus, apparently wrote nothing himself but whose students collected and published material based on his lectures.

New Testament: The name given to twenty-seven Christian (as opposed to Jewish) sacred texts accepted as the foundation of early Christianity: the four Gospels, the Acts of the Apostles, twenty-one letters, and Revelation. The corpus was generally accepted as complete by the late second century AD.

Papyrology: The reading and study of writings on papyri, rot-resistant paper produced from the papyrus plant of the Nile Delta and elsewhere.

Paul: A Jew of Tarsus (*c.* AD 5–67) who, though he had not been with Jesus of Nazareth while he was alive, was the main player in early Christian preaching and teaching and an energetic letter writer and missionary to many town populations of the Eastern Empire.

Petronius: Called 'Arbiter' (*c.* AD 27–66) because he was the 'arbiter of elegance' in the emperor Nero's court, and usually assumed to be the author of the *Satyricon* (see below).

Phaedrus: Roman fabulist (*c.* AD 15–50) whose collection Latinizes the Greek fables of 'Aesop'.

Philo: An elite Hellenized Jew of Alexandria, Egypt (AD 20–50).

Philostratus: A Greek sophist (*c.* AD 170–250) who wrote *The Life of Apollonius of Tyana*.

Plautus: Roman writer of comedies (*c.* 254–184 BC).

Pliny the Elder: Roman political and military figure and polymath (AD 23–79) who wrote the encyclopedic *Natural History*.

Pliny the Younger: Nephew of Pliny the Elder (AD 61– *c.* 112). A political and cultural figure who wrote letters and a panegyric of the emperor Trajan.

Plutarch: A member of the provincial elite from Boeotia (*c.* AD 46–120) whose voluminous *Parallel Lives* and *Customs* survived antiquity and remained popular.

Priapeia: An ancient, anonymous collection of ninety-five Latin poems centered around Priapus, the phallic god.

Publilius Syrus: Born a slave (first century BC), he was freed and became a successful actor of mimes, as well as the author of a collection of Roman proverbs.

Satyricon: A fragmentary tale of humorous, erotic, antiheroic adventures told in a mixture of prose and poetry. Petronius is usually accepted as the author. Many details reflect the reality of everyday life for ordinary Romans.

Seneca the Elder: Roman lawyer and rhetorician (*c.* 54 BC–AD 39) originally from Spain, whose *Controversiae* are exemplary treatments of themes used in training orators.

Seneca the Younger: Son of Seneca the Elder (*c.* 3 BC–AD 65) and a politically important literary figure and Stoic philosopher who wrote tragedies, essays, and philosophical treatises.

Strabo: Greek geographer (*c.* 63 BC–AD 24).

Suetonius: Roman polymath (*c.* AD 70–130) and biographer of the early emperors, most of whose works do not survive.

Tacitus: Roman historian (*c.* AD 56–117) of the early empire.

Talmud: A central Jewish text, this record of discussions regarding Jewish law and customs was compiled around AD 500 from earlier material.

Terence: Roman writer of comedies (*c.* 195/185–159 BC). Born a slave, his plays do not seem to contain much evidence of his life in that condition.

Tertullian: Christian intellectual (*c.* AD 160–220) and a polemicist who wrote against heresies (although he himself ended up in one) and the polytheistic world around him.

Ulpian: An important Roman legal authority (*c.* AD 170–223) whose work constitutes about a third of the *Digest* material.

Valerius Maximus: Roman rhetorician (first century AD) and writer whose *Memorable Deeds and Sayings* seems to be a compilation to provide grist for oratorical displays.

Varro: Roman politician and intellectual (116–27 BC) who wrote on many topics including Latin language and the management of agricultural estates. Most of his work is, however, lost.

Vegetius: Roman military writer (fifth century AD) whose *On Military Affairs* is the only surviving complete ancient manual on that topic.

Xenophon of Ephesus: Author of the Greek romance *An Ephesian Tale* (second to third centuries AD).

ABBREVIATIONS

AE	*L'Année épigraphique* (Paris: Presses universitaires de France, 1888–)
Anderson	G. Anderson (trans.), *An Ephesian Tale* by Xenophon of Ephesus, in *Collected Ancient Greek Novels*, ed. B. P. Reardon (Berkeley: University of California Press, 1989)
Betz	H. D. Betz, *The Greek Magical Papyri in Translation*, 2nd edn (Chicago: University of Chicago Press, 1992)
BGU	*Aegyptische Urkunden aus den Königlichen* (later *Staatlichen*) *Museen zu Berlin, Griechische Urkunden* (Berlin, 1895–)
Campbell	Brian Campbell, *The Roman Army 31 BC–AD 337: A Sourcebook* (London: Routledge, 1994)
Cary	E. Cary, *Dio's Roman History*, with an English translation (New York: Macmillan; London: William Heinemann, 1914), Loeb Classical Library
CIL	*Corpus Inscriptionum Latinarum* (Berlin, 1863–)
Cohoon	J. W. Cohoon, *Dio Chrysostom*, with an English translation (New York: G. P. Putnam's Sons; London: William Heinemann, 1932), Loeb Classical Library

Conybeare	F. C. Conybeare, *The Life of Apollonius of Tyana, the Epistles of Apollonius and the Treatise of Eusebius*, with an English translation (New York: Macmillan; London: William Heinemann, 1912), Loeb Classical Library
Daly	Lloyd W. Daly (trans.), *Aesop without Morals: The Famous Fables, and a Life of Aesop* (New York: Yoseloff, 1961), quoted in Hansen, *Ancient Greek Popular Literature*
Delacy and Einarson	Phillip H. Delacy and Benedict Einarson, *Plutarch's Moralia*, with an English translation (Cambridge, MA: Harvard University Press; London: William Heinemann, 1959), Loeb Classical Library
Gager	John G. Gager, *Curse Tablets and Binding Spells from the Ancient World* (Oxford: Oxford University Press, 1992)
Gallant	Thomas W. Gallant, *Risk and Survival in Ancient Greece: Reconstructing the Rural Domestic Economy* (Stanford: Stanford University Press, 1991)
Hansen	William Hansen (ed.), *Anthology of Ancient Greek Popular Literature* (Bloomington: Indiana University Press, 1998)
Harmon	A. M. Harmon, *Lucian*, with an English translation (New York: G. P. Putnam's Sons; London: William Heinemann, 1921), Loeb Classical Library
Horsley	G. H. R. Horsley, *New Documents Illustrating Early Christianity: A Review of the Greek Inscriptions and Papyri Published 1986–87* (North Ryde, N.S.W. : The Ancient History Documentary Research Centre, Macquarie University)
ILLRP	Attilio Degrassi, *Inscriptiones Latinae liberae rei publicae* (Firenze: La Nuova Italia, 1957–63)
ILS	Hermann Dessau, *Inscriptiones Latinae Selectae* (Berlin, 1892–1916)
ILTun	A. Merlin, *Inscriptions Latines de la Tunisie* (Paris: Presses Universitaires de France, 1944)
IPOstie	H. Thylander, *Inscriptions du port d'Ostie* (Lund: C. W. K. Gleerup, 1952)

Isaac	Benjamin Isaac, *The Limits of Empire: The Roman Army in the East* (Oxford: Oxford University Press, 2nd edn, 1992)
ISIS	A. Helttula, *Le iscrizioni sepulcrali latrine nell'Isola sacra* (Rome: Institutum Romanum Finlandiae, 2007)
Jones	H. L. Jones, *The Geography of Strabo*, with an English translation (Cambridge, MA: Harvard University Press; London: William Heinemann, 1944), Loeb Classical Library
Karasch	Mary C. Karasch, *Slave Life in Rio de Janeiro, 1808–1850* (Princeton: Princeton University Press, 1987)
Kilburn	K. Kilburn, *Lucian*, with an English translation (New York: Macmillan; London: William Heinemann, 1913), Loeb Classical Library
Long	George Long, *The Discourses of Epictetus* (London: George Bell & Sons, 1877)
Luck	Georg Luck, *Arcana Mundi: Magic and the Occult in the Greek and Roman Worlds: A Collection of Ancient Texts* 2nd edn (Baltimore: Johns Hopkins University Press, 2006)
MacLeod	M. D. MacLeod, *Lucian*, with an English translation (Cambridge, MA: Harvard University Press; London: William Heinemann, 1967), Loeb Classical Library
Malahide	Talbot de Malahide, 'On the Longevity of the Romans in North Africa,' *Journal of the Anthropological Institute of Great Britain and Ireland* 12 (1883), 441–8
M.Chr.	L. Mitteis and U. Wilcken, *Grundzüge und Chrestomathie der Papyruskunde, Juristischer Teil* (Leipzig and Berlin, 1912)
Morgan	J. R. Morgan (trans.), *An Ethiopian Story* by Heliodorus, in *Collected Ancient Greek Novels*, ed. B. P. Reardon (Berkeley: University of California Press, 1989)
Nelson	C. A. Nelson, 'Receipt for Tax on Prostitutes,' *Bulletin of the American Society of Papyrologists* 32 (1995), 23–33

Nutton	Vivian Nutton, *Galen, On Prognosis: Text, Translation, Commentary*, CMG V.8.1 (Berlin: Akademie Verlag, 1979)
O. Berl.	*Ostraka aus Brussel und Berlin*, ed. P. Viereck (Berlin and Leipzig, 1922)
P. Brem.	*Die Bremer Papyri*, ed. U. Wilcken (Berlin, 1936)
P. Mich.	*Michigan Papyri* (Ann Arbor, 1931–)
P. Münch.	*Die Papyri der Bayerischen Staatsbibliothek München* (Stuttgart, 1986)
P. Oxy.	*Papyrus Oxyrhynchus*, published by the Egypt Exploration Society in *Graeco-Roman Memoirs* (London, 1898–)
Paton	W. R. Paton, *The Greek Anthology*, with an English translation (New York: G. P. Putnam's Sons; London: William Heinemann, 1918), Loeb Classical Library
Perrin	B. Perrin, *Plutarch: Parallel Lives*, with an English translation (New York: G. P. Putnam's Sons; London: William Heinemann, 1916), Loeb Classical Library
PG	J. P. Migne, *Patrologia Graeca* (Paris 1857–66)
PGM	*Papyri Graecae Magicae*, 2 vols., ed. K. Preisendanz, revised by A. Heinrichs (Stuttgart, 1973–4)
PSI	*Papiri greci e latini*, Pubblicazioni della Società Italiana per la ricerca dei papiri greci e latini in Egitto (Florence, 1912–79)
Robert	L. Robert, *Les gladiateurs dans l'Orient grec* (Paris: Champion, 1940)
Rowlandson	Jane Rowlandson (ed.), *Women and Society in Greek and Roman Egypt: A Sourcebook* (Cambridge: Cambridge University Press, 1998)
SB	*Sammelbuch griechischer Urkunden aus Aegypten*, 1915–
Waddell	Helen Waddell, in Ross S. Kraemer, *Maenads, Martyrs, Matrons, Monastics: A Sourcebook on Women's Religions in the Greco-Roman World* (Philadelphia: Fortress Press, 1988)

White   H. White, *Appian's Roman History*, with an English translation (New York: Macmillan; London: William Heinemann, 1912–13), Loeb Classical Library

Whittaker   C. H. Whittaker, *Herodian: History of the Empire*, with an English translation (Cambridge, MA: Harvard University Press, 1969; London: William Heinemann, 1969), Loeb Classical Library

Wiedemann   T. E. J. Wiedemann (ed.), *Greek and Roman Slavery: A Sourcebook* (London and New York: Routledge, 1990)

Winkler   J. J. Winkler (trans.), *Leucippe and Clitophon* by Achilles Tatius, in *Collected Ancient Greek Novels*, ed. B. P. Reardon (Berkeley: University of California Press, 1989)

WO   U. Wilcken (ed.), *Griechische Ostraka aus Aegypten und Nubien* (Leipzig and Berlin, 1899)

Yonge   Charles Duke Yonge (trans.), *The Works of Philo Judaeus, the Contemporary of Josephus, by Philo, of Alexandria* (London: H. G. Bohn, 1854–5)

NOTE ON TRANSLATIONS

Material from a number of my main sources are given from others' excellent translations as follows, with the permission of the relevant publisher:

Curse tablets: John G. Gager, *Curse Tablets and Binding Spells from the Ancient World* (Oxford: Oxford University Press, 1992).

Dorotheus of Sidon: *Carmen Astrologicum*, trans. David Pingree (Abingdon, MD: Astrology Classics, 2005); original publication in *Carmen Astrologicum*, trans. David Pingree (Munich: K. G. Saur, 1976).

The New Testament: THE HOLY BIBLE, NEW INTERNATIONAL VERSION®, NIV® Copyright © 1973, 1978, 1984, 2010 by Biblica, Inc.™ Used by permission. All rights reserved worldwide.

Papyri: Roger S. Bagnall and Raffaella Cribiore, with contributions by Evie Ahtaridis, *Women's Letters from Ancient Egypt, 300 BC–AD 800* (Ann Arbor: University of Michigan Press, 2006); Jane Rowlandson (ed.), *Women and Society in Greek and Roman Egypt: A Sourcebook* (Cambridge, UK: Cambridge University Press, 1998).

Popular literature: William Hansen (ed.), *Anthology of Ancient Greek Popular Literature* (Bloomington, Indiana University Press, 1998).

All other translations are my own, except for those attributed to another scholar in this format: '/Luck.' These scholars can be found in the list of Abbreviations on pp. 342–6.

ACKNOWLEDGMENTS

Next to the satisfaction of seeing a completed book in your hands, the greatest pleasure comes from acknowledging the help others have offered along the way. And the way has been long, from the initial encouragement of Donald Lateiner through some bemused if not skeptical receptions to acceptance and, at last, final completion. My editor, John Davey, has been steady in his support, seeing promise and nurturing the book with just the right combination of nudging, praise, and discipline. Colleagues have helped in various ways, some with simple belief in the project, others by taking their valuable time to set me straight on details or to read chapters and offer insightful suggestions for improvements. I would particularly like to express my appreciation to Natalie B. Kampen, who not only had steadfast, inspiring enthusiasm for the project, but spent many long hours reading early versions of sections. Likewise Erich Gruen was supportive and patient with requests for help. Arthur Pomeroy generously shared his own work and ideas; Abigail Turner's labors on soldiers set me on the right path; Douglas Oakman helped with early Christian perspectives; and William Fitzgerald showed me how stimulating thinking a bit outside the norm could be – he, Carlos Galvao-Sobrhino, Lauren Petersen, and my Berkeley colleague Susanna Elm all helped greatly with the sections on slaves, freedmen, and ordinary men. Finally, Jeffrey Smith, who wanted to be mentioned, and most of all my wife, who has lived a quarter of her life with this project, supporting it always not only with the usual spousal encouragement, but with many insights and stimulating comparative suggestions derived from her own work on a different people and its empire, the British; I doubt that many family dinner tables have seen the stimulating conversations ours has on the wide range of topics treated in *Invisible Romans*. Finally, the book is dedicated to my mother, who always wanted me to write a book she could read. Although she is gone now, my filial duty is met at last. *Dis manibus matris amantissimae filius pius f.c.*

LIST OF FIGURES

LIST OF ILLUSTRATIONS

1. Street in Pompeii. Pompeii, Italy. Photo: Werner Forman/Art Resource, NY
2. Fresco mural of forum activity, Pompeii. Museo Archeologico Nazionale, Naples, Italy. Photo: Erich Lessing/Art Resource, NY
3. Relief of cutlery merchants, Pompeii. Vatican Museums, Vatican State, Italy. Photo: Scala/Art Resource, NY
4. Carpenters' procession. Fresco (1 CE) from the Bottega del Profumiere, Pompeii. Museo Archeologico Nazionale, Naples, Italy. Photo: Erich Lessing/Art Resource, NY
5. Sorceress. Mosaic from Pompeii, House of the Dioscuri. Museo Archeologico Nazionale, Naples, Italy. Photo: Scala/Art Resource, NY
6. Religious procession. Fresco on the wall of the Shop of the Procession to Cybele, Pompeii. Soprintendenza Archeologica di Pompei. Archivio Fotografico degli Scavi
7. The Big Game Hunt. Mosaic in the ambulatory of the Villa del Casale, Piazza Armerina, Sicily, Italy. (3–4 CE). Photo: Erich Lessing/Art Resource, NY
8. Prostitutes. Fresco on the wall of the Terme Suburbane, Pompeii, Italy. Photo: Fotografica Foglia, courtesy of Scala/Art Resource, NY

16. Tomb relief of a butcher, 2 CE, Roman. Marble, Inv. ZV44. Photo: Elke Estel. Skulpturensammlung, Staatliche Kunstsammlungen, Dresden, Germany. Photo courtesy of Bildarchiv Preussischer Kulturbesitz, Berlin/Staatliche Kunstsammlungen, Dresden/Elke Estel/Art Resource, NY

17. Danae and the fisherman. Fresco from the Exedra, casa V,I,18, Pompeii. Museo Archeologico Nazionale, Naples. Photo: Erich Lessing/Art Resource, NY

18. Beggar. Fresco of a market scene from the atrium of the House of Julia Felix, Pompeii. Museo Archeologico Nazionale, Naples, Inv. Num. 9059. Photo: A Maiuri, *Roman Painting* (Milan: Skira Publishing, 1953) plate 78, p. 140

19. A slave is struck. Relief from the Roman theatre, at the base of the stage, Sabrata (Sabratha), Tripolitania, Libya. Photo courtesy of Luca Bonacina

20. A slave is whipped. A portion of the Big Game Hunt, mosaic in the ambulatory of the Villa del Casale, Piazza Armerina, Sicily, Italy (3–4 CE). Villa del Casale, Piazza Armerina, Sicily, Italy. Photo: Erich Lessing/Art Resource, NY

21. Slave at work. Roman mosaic from Carthage. Inv. MA1796. Photo: Hervé Lewandowski. Louvre, Paris, France. Réunion des Musées Nationaux/Art Resource, NY

22. Slave collar. Iron collar with bronze plate. Imperial Rome, (4–6 CE). Museo Nazionale Romano nelle Terme di Diocleziano, Roma. Photo: Vanni/Art Resource, NY

23. A procuress. Fresco from Pompeii, 1 CE. Museo Archeologico Nazionale, Naples, Italy. Photo: Erich Lessing/Art Resource, NY

24. Interior of Pompeian brothel. Photo: Fotografica Foglia. House of the Lupanare, Pompeii, Italy. Scala/Art Resource, NY

25. High-class prostitutes at a dinner. Fresco painting from the House of the Chaste Lovers, Pompeii. Photo courtesy of Michael Larvey su concessione del Minstero per i Beni e le Attività Culturali – Soprintendenze Speciale per i Beni Archeologici di Napoli e Pompei

26. Aerial view of Coliseum, Rome. View into the structure. 72–80 CE. Coliseum, Rome, Italy. Photo: Alinari/Art Resource, NY

INDEX